EMERSON
ON THE
SCHOLAR

The Scholar as Lecturer
The "rainbow" portrait of Emerson, painted at Edinburgh in 1847 by David Scott (1806–1849). (By permission of the Concord Free Public Library.)

EMERSON
ON THE
SCHOLAR

❖

MERTON M. SEALTS, JR.

*A scholar is the favorite of Heaven and earth, the excellency of his country,
the happiest of men.*

—Emerson, "Literary Ethics" (1838)

University of Missouri Press
Columbia and London

Library of Congress Cataloging-in-Publication Data

Sealts, Merton M.
    Emerson on the scholar / Merton M. Sealts, Jr.
        p.   cm.
    Includes bibliographical references and index.
    ISBN 0–8262–0831–2 (alk. paper)
        1. Emerson, Ralph Waldo, 1805–1882. American scholar.
    2. Emerson, Ralph Waldo, 1805–1882—Knowledge and learning.
    3. United States—Intellectual life—19th century. 4. Learning and
    scholarship in literature. I. Title.
    PS1615.A84S43   1992
    001.2—dc20   92–197
                                                                        CIP

Designer: Rhonda Miller
Typesetter: Connell-Zeko Type & Graphics
Printer and Binder: Thomson-Shore, Inc.
Typeface: Weiss

For Bill Coolidge

The first to know
that I could be a scholar

CONTENTS

V. THE SAGE OF CONCORD

EPILOGUE

ILLUSTRATIONS

ABBREVIATIONS

❖

The following abbreviations appear parenthetically throughout this book to identify primary texts that are cited repeatedly:

CEC *The Correspondence of Emerson and Carlyle.* Edited by Joseph Slater. New York and London: Columbia University Press, 1964.

CW *The Collected Works of Ralph Waldo Emerson.* Edited by Alfred R. Ferguson et al. 5 vols. to date. Cambridge: The Belknap Press of Harvard University Press, 1971–.

EL *The Early Lectures of Ralph Waldo Emerson.* Edited by Stephen E. Whicher, Robert E. Spiller, and Wallace E. Williams. 3 vols. Cambridge: Harvard University Press, 1959; The Belknap Press of Harvard University Press, 1964, 1972.

J *Journals of Ralph Waldo Emerson.* Edited by Edward Waldo Emerson and Waldo Emerson Forbes. 10 vols. Boston and New York: Houghton Mifflin Company, 1909–1914.

JMN *The Journals and Miscellaneous Notebooks of Ralph Waldo Emerson.* Edited by William H. Gilman, Ralph H. Orth, et al. 16 vols. Cambridge: The Belknap Press of Harvard University Press, 1960–1982.

L *The Letters of Ralph Waldo Emerson.* Edited by Ralph L. Rusk. 6 vols. New York: Columbia University Press, 1939.

PN *The Poetry Notebooks of Ralph Waldo Emerson.* Edited by Ralph H. Orth, Albert J. von Frank, Linda Allardt, and David W. Hill. Columbia: University of Missouri Press, 1986.

TN *The Topical Notebooks of Ralph Waldo Emerson.* Edited by Ralph H. Orth et al. 1 vol. to date. Columbia and London: University of Missouri Press, 1990–.

W   *The Complete Works of Ralph Waldo Emerson.* Edited by Edward Waldo Emerson. 12 vols. Boston and New York: Houghton Mifflin Company, 1903–1904.

YES   *Young Emerson Speaks: Unpublished Discourses on Many Subjects.* Edited by Arthur Cushman McGiffert, Jr. Boston: Houghton Mifflin Company, 1938.

Bibliographical data for those books and articles cited in appended notes will be found below, in Works Cited.

Two new editions of primary materials were not yet available for use when relevant portions of this book were being written. The University of Missouri Press is publishing *The Complete Sermons of Ralph Waldo Emerson,* edited by Albert J. von Frank et al., in 4 volumes (3 volumes to date, 1989–); *L* 7–10, edited by Eleanor M. Tilton (New York: Columbia University Press, 1990–), is to contain all the known letters, including those previously published, except for those in *L,* volumes 1–6 and *CEC.*

Cancellations in passages that are quoted from manuscript materials are indicated here, as in *JMN,* by angle brackets: < . . . > ; insertions are indicated by paired arrows: ↑ . . . ↓.

PREFACE

That statement only is fit to be made public which you have come at in attempting to satisfy your own curiosity.

—"Spiritual Laws" (*CW* 2:89)

To borrow a familiar phrase from Emerson, this book has had a long foreground. My interest in the man and his writings began in Stanley Williams' graduate seminar at Yale in 1939; since then, teaching Emerson on three other campuses and working with Emerson manuscripts at Harvard's Houghton Library—two reciprocally beneficial activities—have fostered and increased that interest. In 1961 I was invited to join in editing the Belknap Press edition of *The Journals and Miscellaneous Notebooks* (here *JMN*), and in 1962–1963, as a Guggenheim Fellow, I also began to study what I thought of then as "the experiential strain" in Emerson. These two scholarly projects led ultimately to the writing of *Emerson on the Scholar.*

The intermediate stages can be noted briefly. In 1969, in collaboration with Alfred Ferguson, a distinguished Emersonian editor (now no longer living) who had been my classmate at Wooster, I published the first edition of our *Emerson's 'Nature': Origin, Growth, Meaning;* this book made available to other students what we had learned as editors of *JMN* about the genesis of the book in Emerson's thinking and earlier writing. In the following year I brought out the first of a series of journal-centered articles on the gradual development of Emerson's self-image as a scholar, and in 1975, as a Senior Fellow of the National Endowment for the Humanities, I was able to enlarge the scope of my research and to draft a substantial portion of this study. Since then, as the remaining volumes of *JMN* and the initial volumes of the new *Collected Works* have become available for reference and citation, I have been working intermittently on Emerson's thinking during his later years while also pursuing my long-standing interest in Herman Melville.

In addition to the encouragement and tangible support provided by the John Simon Guggenheim Memorial Foundation and the National Endowment for the Humanities, I have also received assistance for my work on Emerson during my years as a faculty member at Lawrence University and later at the University of Wisconsin-Madison; the Research Committee of the Graduate School on the Madison campus has also supported my research on both Emerson and Melville. I acknowledge all of this assistance with gratitude.

The frontispiece of this book is reproduced by permission of the Concord,

Massachusetts, Free Public Library from David Scott's painting of Emerson viewed as he lectured in the British Isles in 1847; Cranch's drawing of the Scholar as "transparent eye-ball" is reproduced by permission of the Houghton Library. Emerson materials in the Houghton Library, including manuscript pages that are reproduced as illustrations, are used here by permission of the Ralph Waldo Emerson Memorial Association and of the Houghton Library; both have encouraged and facilitated my research from its beginning. I am grateful for these authorizations and also for access to the computerized concordance to selected entries from Emerson's writings prepared at the University of Colorado, Boulder, by the late Professor Eugene Irey and by his associate, Professor Michael Preston. I have had the great benefit of constructive criticism from David M. Robinson, who read the manuscript in various stages as the book progressed, and later from Leonard Neufeldt, who read it in its semifinal form and made valuable suggestions for improvement; they too have my sincere thanks.

It is pleasant to acknowledge also the opportunities, encouragement, challenge, and assistance given so generously by my mentors at Wooster and Yale, by my students at Wellesley, Lawrence, and Wisconsin, by my teaching and editorial colleagues, and by my several sponsors, not forgetting the indispensable help of library and publishing staffs. Special thanks go first of all to Ruth Mackenzie Sealts, whom my late colleague Harry Hayden Clark at once recognized as having a significant part in my long involvement with Emerson; to Carolyn Jakeman, William H. Bond, Rodney Dennis, Marte Shaw, Jennie Rathbun, and the late William A. Jackson of the Houghton Library; to Marcia E. Moss of the Concord Free Public Library; to John C. Broderick, Douglas M. Knight, Linck C. Johnson, Joel Myerson, Charles Read, Charles T. Scott, and Nathalia Wright; and to the late Harry Hayden Clark, Leon Howard, Howard F. Lowry, Willard Thorp, Arlin Turner, and Wallace E. Williams.

Portions of this book have been presented in other forms to my students and colleagues at Madison, to the Madison Literary Club, and in public lectures at The College of Wooster, Edgewood College, Oregon State and Washington State Universities, The University of North Carolina at Chapel Hill, The University of Tennessee, Washington University, and Texas A&M University. I am grateful to editors and publishers for authorization to draw upon material that I have contributed to *PMLA* (1970) and *Ariel* (1976), to *Literature and Ideas in America: Essays in Memory of Harry Hayden Clark* (1975), to the second edition of *Emerson's 'Nature': Origin, Growth, Meaning* (1979), to *Emerson Centenary Essays* (1982), and to *Studies in the American Renaissance* (1985).

—M.M.S.

EMERSON
ON THE
SCHOLAR

INTRODUCTION

The key to every man is his thought. Sturdy and defying though he look, he has a helm which he obeys, which is, the idea after which all his facts are classified. He can only be reformed by showing him a new idea which commands his own.

—"Circles" (*CW* 2:180)

THE SCHOLAR IDEALIZED

---❖---

I have reached the middle age of man; yet I believe I am not less glad or sanguine at the meeting of scholars, than when, a boy, I first saw the graduates of my own College assembled at their anniversary. Neither years nor books have yet failed to extirpate a prejudice then rooted in me, that a scholar is the favorite of Heaven and earth, the excellency of his country, the happiest of men.

—"Literary Ethics" (*CW* 1:99)

On 24 July 1838, speaking by invitation before the literary societies of Dartmouth College, Ralph Waldo Emerson delivered an oration on the scholar's place in society that he later published under the title "Literary Ethics." Should any of his student listeners have been thinking of themselves as called by God "to explore truth and beauty," the orator admonished them in his peroration to "be bold, be firm, be true" and to dare to choose the life of a scholar. "The hour of that choice is the crisis of your history," he declared; "see that you hold yourself fast by the intellect" (*CW* 1:115).

In his public addresses Emerson often drew freely yet guardedly on his own experience; for him, "the capital secret" of a writer and speaker is "to convert life into truth" (*CW* 1:86). When telling the Dartmouth students that the hour of vocational choice is "the crisis of your history" he was surely remembering his own decision, made shortly before he turned twenty-one, to enter the Unitarian ministry—a decision he came in time to regret. While still in his thirties, having already resigned his first pastorate at Boston after less than three years of service, he began a protracted search for a new calling. Between 1832 and 1838, the year of his appearance at Dartmouth, he was regularly speaking and writing, both as an occasional supply preacher and with increasing success as a secular lecturer and orator. Although he continued to regard the clergy as "always, more universally than any other class, the scholars of their day," as he said in 1837 (*CW* 1:59), he ultimately gave up preaching altogether in favor of lecturing and publishing, no longer using the title "Reverend." By 1837 he was thinking of himself simply as a scholar among scholars.

Central to Emerson's mature thought is a basic dichotomy between the actual and the ideal—or, in the Coleridgean terminology he used in the 1830s, between the mundane province of the Understanding and the ideal realm of the Reason. As early as December of 1834 he had applied this distinction to his conception of the

3

scholar: "there is a real object in Nature . . . [,] the intellectual man," he wrote in his Journal A, "& though the scholar is not that object, he is its representative, & is, with more or less symptoms of distrust, honored for that which he ought to be" (*JMN* 4:370). The scholar as seen in everyday life thus *represents* a perhaps unattainable ideal—a kind of Platonic idea of the scholar as "the intellectual man"—that can be envisioned only with what Emerson liked to call "the eye of Reason" (*CW* 1:30).

Because it is this ideal figure that is celebrated in "The American Scholar," it is not strictly accurate to say that Emerson "defined himself as the 'American Scholar,'" as Robert E. Spiller once remarked,[1] since Emerson's self-definition pertains to an ideal he had come to conceive rather than an actuality he ever in fact attained. In the language of "Circles" (1841), that ideal conception had become the helm which he as scholar sought to obey; it is "the idea after which all his facts are classified." But any ideal is not only subject to "the moral fact of the Unattainable, the flying Perfect, around which the hands of man can never meet"; it is also open to expansion and change: "the principle that seemed to explain nature, will itself be included as one example of a bolder generalization. . . . Every man is not so much a workman in the world, as he is a suggestion of that he should be" (*CW* 2:180, 179, 181).

The concept of the ideal scholar had gradually taken form in Emerson's private journal—his literary "Savings Bank" (*JMN* 4:250)—during the early 1830s, when the sometime minister who had preached a sermon entitled "Find Your Calling" was still wrestling with problems of vocation and identity. Though natural science, the lives of great men, and landmarks of English literature attracted him in turn when he began giving public lectures, the implications of these topics for moral and religious life were always in his mind. He thought of becoming a naturalist, a lay religious teacher, or perhaps a writer—a poet, in the sense of one who sees and loves "the harmonies that are in the soul & in matter" (*L* 1:435). All of these concerns were taken up in his image of himself as a scholar—ideally, as *the* scholar.

In August of 1835, with the new formulation well under way, Emerson began making notes in his journal for a future "chapter on Literary Ethics or the Duty & Discipline of a Scholar" (*JMN* 5:84); these entries look forward to both "The American Scholar" of 1837 and "Literary Ethics" of the next year. Since Emerson spoke at Dartmouth in 1838, many listeners and readers have taken note of his "frequent invocation of the 'scholar,'" as the junior Henry James did in reviewing James Elliot Cabot's *Memoir* of Emerson in 1887. James found "a friendly vagueness and convenience" in Emerson's use of the term, which he regarded as "charming yet ever so slightly droll." By *scholar*, James thought, Emerson meant "simply the cultivated man, the man who has had a liberal education," and it seemed incongruous to expect of such a person "all the heroic and uncomfortable things, the concentrations and relinquishments, that make up the noble life."[2] But the term had a much more complex meaning for Emerson than James surmised, as later critics have come to see—particularly as the full text of Emerson's journals has become available for study. There the word is almost ubiquitous, though Emerson used it less often in his lectures and in his published works other than "The American Scholar" and "Literary Ethics."

A turning point in interpretation came in 1939 with a penetrating essay on "Emerson's Problem of Vocation" by the late Henry Nash Smith. If Emerson "found no profession already formed for him" as he separated himself from the church, Smith wrote, "he must create one for himself, even if only as an ideal." Moreover, this ideal "must not only be defensible before the world, but also represent adequately all the forces of tradition, temperament, and literary contagion that were at work" in Emerson himself. Of the various figures that Emerson delineated as ideal self-images—and there were many—the most characteristic and certainly the best known, as Smith remarked, "is of course the Scholar." Indeed, "The Scholar is the hero of Emerson's unwritten *Prelude,* and belongs with all the Werthers and the Childe Harolds and the Teufelsdröckhs of the period."[3]

Smith's fine essay might well have grown into a full-length biography of Emerson had its author not turned his attention from New England to the American West and from Emerson to Mark Twain. Certainly all subsequent Emersonians—myself included—have had to take account of his provocative analysis, whether or not we accept all of Smith's hypotheses in other sections of his essay. He was surely right in saying, for instance, that one can understand "the strongly apologetic basis of Emerson's conception of the Scholar" only by envisaging the Scholar's polar opposite, whatever his label—"the Actor," as Smith called him, or "the Man of the World," as Emerson himself referred to the antitype Napoleon in *Representative Men* (1850). But my own investigations have led me to think that the terms *actor* and *action* had anything but fixed connotations for Emerson, so that once again their every occurrence also "presents a fresh problem" for the reader (to borrow a phrase from Smith). Smith's objection that "The American Scholar" in particular addresses "the issue of Action *versus* Contemplation" only in "a long and confused discussion" demands reconsideration, as I demonstrate in chapter 6 below, where I examine Emerson's special understanding of the word *action* as it is used there and in his previous writings.[4]

Since 1939 there have been illuminating studies of such talismanic Emersonian phrasing as *correspondence, freedom and fate, truth and nature, race and history, virtue, compensation,* and *the soul,* but neither *action* nor the word *scholar* itself has yet received the thorough examination they both deserve.[5] None of Emerson's several biographers have fully tested Smith's identification of the Scholar as protagonist of Emerson's "unwritten *Prelude,*" although the late Stephen Whicher's "Inner Life" of 1953 posited a change in Emerson's self-conception following his "second crisis" of 1838–1844, implicitly challenging Smith's assertion that "the ideal of the Scholar seems not to have undergone any significant evolution" in his thinking after 1842. In fact, Smith's detailed examination of the canon had stopped with "The Transcendentalist" (1841) without going on to trace the course of Emerson's thinking through the eventful decades of the 1840s and 1850s. Instead, he cited only two very late addresses, "The Man of Letters" (1863) and "The Scholar" (1876), which in Smith's words "are little more than repetitions of Emerson's earlier utterances."[6]

Smith's ground-breaking essay appeared before the publication of Emerson's *Letters* and *Early Lectures* and the new editions of his *Journals and Miscellaneous Notebooks* and *Collected Works*. There is more to be learned about the evolving concept of the Scholar from these new editions, the full text of the journals in particular. But though some of the critics making use of these primary sources have challenged Whicher's interpretation of the later Emerson, as Leonard Neufeldt explicitly did in *The House of Emerson* (1982), Smith's contention that Emerson's "ideal of the Scholar" remained essentially unchanged after 1842 has yet to be systematically reexamined.

The purpose of the present study is to trace Emerson's self-image as a scholar throughout his mature years, from its beginnings in the early 1830s until the very end of his life. Part One, "Toward 'The American Scholar,'" shows how the term gradually took on special meaning for him during the early 1830s. Dissatisfaction with his role as a Unitarian minister led him first to resign his pulpit and then to identify in turn with various personae, such as the Naturalist, the Teacher, the Poet, and the Thinker, as he sought both a new vocation and a new identity. Between 1835 and 1837, the year of "The American Scholar," the long-familiar image of the Scholar emerged as the ideal figure of greatest significance. As "Man Thinking," the idealized American Scholar of the oration ultimately subsumed *all* of these converging roles.

Part Two, "The Scholar Engaged," deals with the period of challenge and testing that began with the storm over Emerson's Divinity School Address of 1838 and continued through more than two decades of personal and civic crises. His "angle of vision," as he called it, was consistently that of the scholar, though he seldom invoked the term explicitly unless he was addressing an academic audience. To understand his thinking about the scholar during these later years—and particularly about the scholar's duty as a member of society—requires consideration of the whole context of his speaking and writing.

Long before purely academic scholars in this country began fulminating over the supposed dichotomy of "publish or perish," Emerson consistently affirmed that "the true scholar"—a favorite phrase—must be both a *see*-er and a *say*-er; for him there could be no real severance between the pursuit of learning and its dissemination. The scholar and the teacher, he believed, were essentially one, as my Epilogue attests. A much more troublesome problem for him, as Smith long ago pointed out, was the proper role of the scholar-teacher in the world of public affairs: should the see-er be a *do*-er as well as a say-er, a man of action as well as a man of thought and speech?

Emerson in fact believed that the scholar has the duty and the responsibility to "act upon the Public," as he said as early as 1834 (*JMN* 4:368). But does *action* mean participating directly in public affairs and taking a stand on every issue of the day? In particular, how deeply should Waldo Emerson involve himself in active opposition to slavery, an institution that he abhorred? From the years of his pastorate in Boston, when he opened his pulpit to the reform agitator Samuel May, this was an increasingly acute question for Emerson; on the eve of the Civil War he surprised even some of his closest friends and deeply offended his more conservative contemporaries by his public support of John Brown, both before and after the events of 1859 at Harpers Ferry. On the pressing issue of slavery, it seems clear, his thinking underwent a gradual evolution, and as later chapters of this book will show, that evolution is reflected too in his conception of the public duty of scholars as representatives of Intellect. To follow what he came to say and do in the 1840s and after is not only to grasp the full development of Emerson's own thought but also to encounter a perennial challenge: what part should any man or woman of ideas play in American society, then and now?

Throughout the writing of this book I have kept in mind that "fundamental law of criticism" that Emerson himself liked to cite from George Fox: works under examination, like the Scriptures themselves, must be interpreted "by the same spirit that gave them forth" (*JMN* 4:31; cf. *JMN* 4:94; *EL* 1:170, 210–11; *CW* 1:23). "The key to every man is his thought," Emerson wrote (*CW* 2:180), and since "life" for him consisted "in what a man is thinking of all day," as he said in the 1840s (*JMN* 10:146; *W* 12:10), the primary focus here is on the course of his own thinking over the years, not on his literary sources. Though Emerson read widely, his goal as a writer and speaker was original creation. "Books are for the scholar's idle times," he declared in a memorable passage of "The American Scholar," believing as he did that when the scholar "can read God directly, the hour is too precious to be wasted in other men's transcripts of their readings" (*CW* 1:57). Seeking to interpret Emerson's thinking about the Scholar by the spirit that gave it forth, I have honored these characteristic pronouncements.

PART ONE
TOWARD "THE AMERICAN SCHOLAR"
❖

The scholar is that man who must take up into himself all the ability of the time, all the contributions of the past, all the hopes of the future.

—"The American Scholar" (CW 1:69)

I

FIND YOUR CALLING

Every individual mind has its assigned province of action, a place which it was intended of God to fill, and to which always it is tending. It is that which the greatest cultivation of all his powers will enable him to do best. . . . It may be hidden from him for years. Unfavorable associations, bad advice, or his own perversity may fight against it but he will never be at ease, he will never act with efficiency, until he finds it. Whatever it be, it is his high calling. This is his mark and prize.

—Sermon 143, 1832 (*YES* 167)

1. EMERSON AND
THE CHURCH, 1824–1832
❖

No, he never loved his holy offices—and it is well he has left them.
    —Mary Moody Emerson to Charles Chauncy Emerson, 8 January 1833[1]

From his early years Ralph Waldo Emerson was known as a studious boy. His father had wished him to be "a bright scholar,"[2] and even before he entered college he was already "prejudiced" in favor of an intellectual life, as he was to acknowledge long afterward in "Literary Ethics." Yet neither his correspondence nor the journal he began keeping in 1820 made more than passing use of the term *scholar* until the early 1830s, during his uneasy tenure as minister of a Unitarian parish in Boston, when for Emerson the word began to take on more than its conventional meaning.

The word *scholar* had appeared occasionally in Emerson's previous writing as the equivalent of "studious man" (*JMN* 1:189), and to engage in private reading was thus "to affect the scholar," as he put it in 1825 (*L* 1:158–59). During his student days at Harvard, though aspiring to some form of scholarly endeavor that would win him "a place in the inclinations & sympathy of men," he had lamented his tendency to engage in "endless, thankless, reveries" instead of steadily applying himself to his books: "How immensely would a scholar enlarge his power could he abstract himself wholly, body & mind from the dinning throng of casual recollections that summon him away from his useful toil" (*JMN* 1:40–41). A year later, in opening an essay of 1821 "On the advantages of knowledge," he had declared further that "it is the office of the scholar to *write*" (*JMN* 1:189), and when he later decided to enter the ministry it was the opportunity to write and deliver sermons that especially attracted him.

As a practicing clergyman Emerson found himself drawn far more to his studies than to his required pastoral work, and the resulting struggle between inclination and duty, as his biographers have agreed, was one of several private conflicts that in time led him to resign his pulpit. In 1832 he faced the problem of finding a calling more suited to his talents and temperament than the ministry. What were his "powers" as an aspiring scholar, and what "assigned province of action" did God intend him ultimately to fill? These questions he had confronted before when he began the study of divinity; he inevitably confronted them again as he sought "new bearings" for a new career.

i. A Crisis of Conscience

Early in February of 1832 the young pastor of Boston's Second Church, Unitarian, addressed his congregation in a sermon about vocational choice entitled "Find Your Calling" in which he considered "how complex is the action and reaction of a man upon his profession and his profession upon the man." The various employments that persons follow, he declared, serve "not only to occupy their attention and keep them from the misery of idleness but to engage and invigorate their faculties, to form the virtues, in short, to educate the man" (*YES* 164). So at least it ought to be, for clergymen as well as for laymen. But Waldo Emerson, who only the year before had suffered the death of his wife after barely fourteen months of marriage, was becoming increasingly restive in his own work. Like his marriage, his pastoral experience was brief; what he had once called "the most august station which man can fill," the position of an ordained Christian minister (*YES* 27), had been his for less than three years. "In my study my faith is perfect. It breaks, scatters, becomes confounded in converse with men," he had recently written in his private journal (*JMN* 3:314). The journal also recorded other signs of his restlessness: boredom with the routine of his duties, such as his "poor Tuesday evening lectures" on the Scriptures, and the recurrence of "hideous dreams" that seemed to embody his own "evil affections" (*JMN* 3:315, 317).

The very topics of Emerson's more recent sermons indicate that the minister was undergoing a crisis of conscience related to his own vocation, as the first editor of the sermons—himself a preacher—remarked in 1938: "If ever a preacher preached to himself," in the words of Arthur Cushman McGiffert, "Emerson was doing so when he preached on, 'Do Thyself No Harm' (No. 141), 'Find Your Calling' (No. 143), 'Judging Right for Ourselves' (No. 145), and 'The Genuine Man' (No. 164)."[3] The theme of "Find Your Calling," Emerson's sermon of 5 February 1832, had been chosen more than two weeks before, when he imperfectly recalled a sentence from Philippians 3.14—"I press toward the mark for the prize of the high calling of God which is in Christ Jesus"—and began to work out a sermon on the Pauline text. "Every man has a mark, has a high calling," he declared, "to wit, his peculiar intellectual & moral constitution, what it points at, what it is becoming. Let it run, & have free course, & be glorified" (*JMN* 3:319–20). "Write on personal independance," he added two days later, asserting that a man who desires to improve his own circumstances cannot merely follow the fashions of the day but must rather "adhere in his acts to the decisions of his own judgment" (*JMN* 3:320).

In "Find Your Calling" Emerson developed these interrelated ideas of self-expression, self-fulfillment, and self-reliance in terms that foreshadow the argument of his later essays. "Every man is uneasy," the young preacher told his congregation, "until every power of his mind is in freedom and in action; whence arises a constant effort to take that attitude which will admit of this action" (*YES* 166). In a canceled passage evidently not read from the pulpit, he then explored

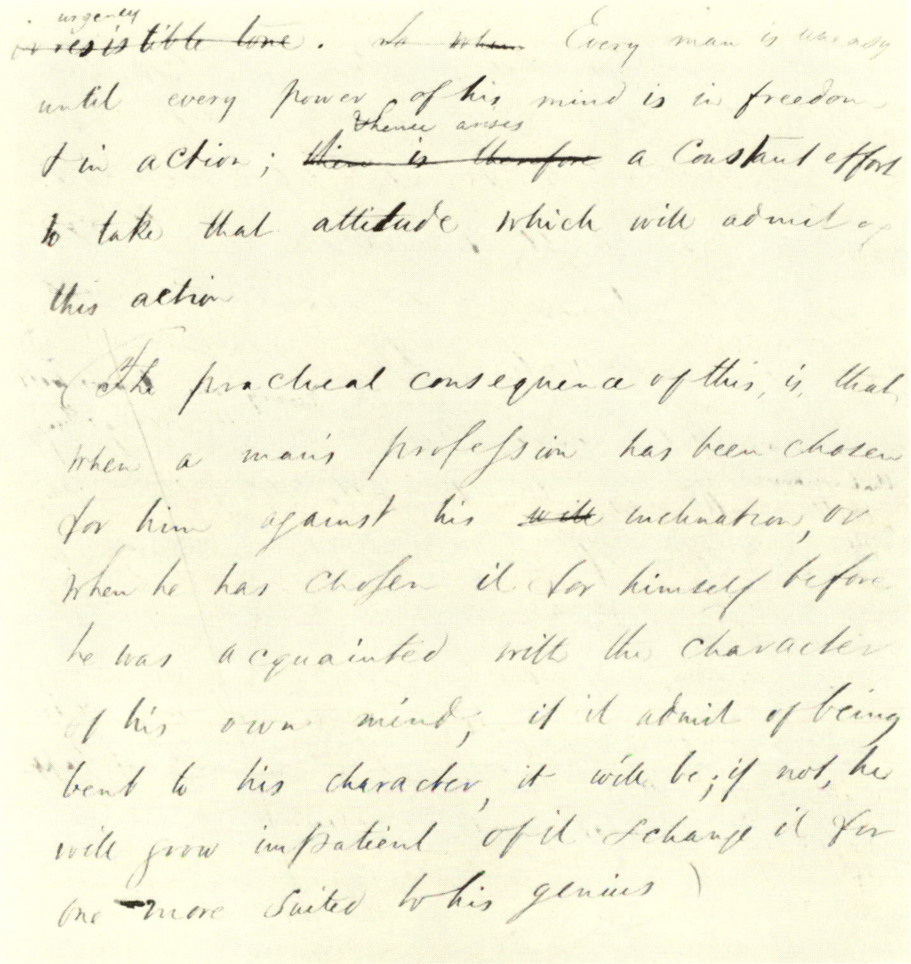

[handwritten manuscript facsimile]

"A man's profession"

Canceled passage from Sermon 143, "Find Your Calling," first preached on 5 February 1832; see *YES* 166 and 251 n. 1.

the "practical consequence" of the position he was outlining: "that when a man's profession has been chosen for him against his inclination, or when he has chosen it for himself before he was acquainted with the character of his own mind, if it admit of being bent to his character, it will be; if not, he will grow impatient of it and change it" (*YES* 251 n. 1). Deciding to keep these sentiments to himself, he went on to say publicly:

Let a man have that profession for which God formed him that he may be useful to mankind to the whole extent of his powers, that he may find delight in the exercise of his powers, and do what he does with the full consent of his own mind. Every one knows well what difference there is in the doing things that we have with all one's heart and the doing them against one's will. (*YES* 166)

A corollary of Emerson's position concerning the full exercise of one's talents is his further declaration that persons unsuited to their callings lack the wholeness, the integrity, that he himself longed for: they are "but half themselves" (*YES* 167). In a journal entry made a month earlier he had been even more pointed with regard to his own profession: "It is the best part of the man, I sometimes think, that revolts most against his being the minister." What he especially disliked, as the passage explains, was the "official goodness" expected of a clergyman. The pressure to conform, to accommodate himself to external standards rather than whole-heartedly following his own bent, meant an inevitable sense of diminution, a loss "of so much integrity & of course of so much power" (*JMN* 3:318–19). The concepts of personal integrity and self-reliant independence and power were already becoming familiar to those who heard Emerson's sermons, just as they are now to every reader of his later essays; what those who listened to his preaching probably did not realize was the immediate relevance of their pastor's words to his own situation and to his future course of action.

On the evidence of "Find Your Calling" it seems clear that by 1832 Emerson had come to think that his own decision to enter the ministry had been taken before he knew his own character or understood the special conditions under which a clergyman was obliged to live and work. Either the profession or the man, it now appeared to him, must be "bent" to the other's nature; if both should prove inflexible, then the man who reverences "his peculiar intellectual & moral constitution" will have to reexamine his vocational choice, at whatever cost. On this point the sermon is explicit and blunt:

Be content then, humbly and wisely to converse with yourself; to learn what you can do, and what you cannot; to be deterred from attempting nothing out of respect to the judgment of others, if it be not confirmed by your own judgment. . . . Nor ever consider that your ties in life, your obligations to your family, or to your benefactors or to your creditors or to your country shut you out of your true field of action, by forbidding you to correct the errors of choice of pursuit into which you have fallen. (*YES* 168)

The reference here to "ties" and "obligations" may suggest the external influences that had affected though not determined Emerson's decision to enter the ministry, a course which he had chosen some eight years before when he was not yet twenty-one. Born into a clergyman's family and educated for a professional career virtually as a matter of course, he was the second of five brothers, four of whom graduated from Harvard College under the handicaps of grinding poverty and recurrent illness. The three eldest—William, Ralph Waldo, and Edward—all took their turns in what Ralph L. Rusk called "the family purgatory of schoolteaching" in order to help one another with their educational expenses while also supporting their widowed mother and their handicapped brother Bulkeley.[4] The Emersons formed a closely knit family group, united by habitual piety that withstood the ravages of physical debility and the challenge of spiritual doubts.

During their college years both Edward and Charles Emerson achieved local reputations as orators. Charles, as Waldo said of him to William, "was born with a tongue you & I with a pen"; his written pages, Waldo came later to think, "do him no justice" (*L* 1:333; *JMN* 5:151). The two orators gravitated immediately toward the law, which also attracted William when he returned in 1825 from a period of theological study in Göttingen. William had grown fearful that if he became a minister he would be forced to accommodate his newly liberalized religious views to the prevailing winds of doctrine at home; "every candid theologian," he told Waldo in a letter from Germany, will "after careful study" find himself diverging from "the traditionary opinions of the bulk of his parishioners. Have you yet settled the question, whether he shall sacrifice his influence or his conscience?"[5]

The analogy between William Emerson's dilemma of 1825 and his brother's crisis of seven years later is obvious; it was fortunate for William that he reached his decision to renounce the ministry before assuming a pastorate. William's change of vocation, determined during a storm at sea on his way home from Europe, was made just as Waldo was beginning his own formal study of theology—not at Göttingen, as William had once urged, but at the Theological School in Cambridge, newly established under Unitarian auspices. The occurrence of severe eye trouble, which interrupted Waldo's studies for several months in 1825, may well suggest that he had moved toward a ministerial career in spite of unconscious reservations. Rusk, the first biographer to raise the possibility that the illness was psychosomatic, also held that family records of the time are too scanty to settle the question; both Gay Wilson Allen and John McAleer reject a psychosomatic explanation. Evelyn Barish, who has closely considered Emerson's "crisis of health" between 1825 and 1827, attributes his physical difficulties to "a chronic mild case of tuberculosis" but she also traces his mingled physical and emotional suffering to "religious, vocational, and personal conflicts," including "the high but contradictory nature of his professional self-image and ambition."[6]

ii. "My starting point"

The most powerful external influences urging Waldo to enter the ministry were the examples of his father and other relatives and the active promptings of his eccentric but strong-minded aunt, Mary Moody Emerson, who saw in him a future prince of the pulpit. At Harvard, where he graduated in 1821 as Class Poet, he did not equal the scholastic records made by his brothers but was known rather for "general literary ability, classical culture, and eloquence," as Moncure Conway wrote of him. In his own eyes Waldo was more a writer than a speaker, as he told

William, but his immediate ambition when he graduated, or so he informed Conway in later years, was "to be a professor of rhetoric and elocution."[7] For the time being, however, he was doomed to earn money for himself and his family by teaching in the school that William had set up before going to Germany—a far cry from a college professorship. Although several of Emerson's students were to look back with gratitude on their experience in his classroom, Waldo Emerson himself "never expected success" as a schoolmaster, according to his own testimony. "My scholars are carefully instructed, my money is faithfully earned, but the instructor is little wiser"; more significantly, "the duties were never congenial with my disposition" (JMN 2:241).

These comments occur in a long passage of self-analysis that Emerson entered in his journal shortly before his twenty-first birthday, when the possibility of escaping the schoolroom renewed the question of a permanent vocational choice. There is no mention in the entry of a professorship or a career in literature; by this time Aunt Mary—the "Tnamurya" of the early journals—was pushing him toward the church, and the profession of clergyman at least seemed more attractive than either law or medicine, whatever doubts he may have had about the ministry itself or his suitability for it. Law, which had already attracted Edward Emerson, seemed in Waldo's judgment to demand "a good deal of personal address, an impregnable confidence in one's own powers . . . , & a logical mode of thinking & speaking— which I do not possess, & may not reasonably hope to attain"; medicine "also makes large demands on the practitioner for a seducing Mannerism" (JMN 2:239). Though confessing that his aspirations exceeded his abilities, the unwilling schoolmaster had decided to undertake whatever "professional studies" would qualify him for the pulpit. "In a month I shall be *legally* a man," he wrote. "And I deliberately dedicate my time, my talents, & my hopes to the Church" (JMN 2:237).

That a young Harvard graduate known for his literary interests should thus "choose theology" as his vocation might well seem strange, as Emerson himself recognized at the time. His principal attributes, he thought, were "a strong imagination," "a keen relish for the beauties of poetry," and an "inordinate fondness for writing"; conversely, he considered his "reasoning faculty" to be "proportionately weak." But in 1824 it had seemed to him that men of "moral imagination" among his contemporaries were really better equipped for "the highest species of reasoning upon divine subjects" than were the rationalist thinkers he had been obliged to study at Harvard: "the 'Reasoning Machines' such as Locke & Clarke & David Hume." Moreover, the preaching then in vogue "depends chiefly on imagination," he went on to say, "and asks those accomplishments which I believe are most within my grasp" (JMN 2:238). As his model he named the Dudleian lectures of William Ellery Channing, leader of the liberal wing among American Unitarians, who, as the young man's pastor in Boston, had done much to form Waldo Emerson's conception of the ideal minister.

For a clergyman's pastoral duties outside the pulpit, however, Emerson regarded himself as less well prepared. Owing to what he called "a signal defect of character," he confessed to feeling "a sore uneasiness in the company of most men & women" and exhibiting a coldness and formality in manner and speech that he attributed to his family heritage. But from the same source, he supposed, came also his "passionate love for the strains of eloquence" and an endowment with "those powers which command the reason & passions of the multitude" (*JMN* 2:238–39). On balance, he concluded, he could successfully fulfill the duties of the ministerial office, to which he looked forward both as an opportunity for altruistic service to mankind and as a means of self-development. "In Divinity I hope to thrive," he wrote, trusting "that my profession shall be my regeneration of mind, manners, inward & outward estate; or rather my starting point, for I have hoped to put on eloquence as a robe, and by goodness and zeal and the awfulness of virtue to press & prevail over the false judgments, the rebel passions & corrupt habits of men" (*JMN* 2:239, 242).

Such was Emerson's acknowledged vocational "starting point" in 1824. This long passage of self-analysis tells us much about the young man's conception of himself and of the role he was planning to fill. Though he had chosen what he called "Theology" for his study, his real interest was obviously more in eloquent preaching than in doctrinal disputation or in the pastoral work expected of a minister by his parishioners. As for matters of doctrine, he inclined toward the liberal side of current religious issues like his father before him, although the immediate example of Channing was a more powerful model than memories of the senior William Emerson, who had died when Waldo was only eight. But there was also the close relationship maintained by the Emerson brothers with their more conservative Aunt Mary. She was a constant reminder of the personal piety of orthodox forebears among the Emersons and Moodys in the days before Congregational Unitarians broke away from Congregational Trinitarians and in turn separated into conservatives and liberals. "The key to her life," Emerson once remarked, was in "the conflict of the new & the old ideas in New England" (*JMN* 7:446).

Although Emerson characteristically abjured those forms and beliefs that were merely traditional, the persistent habit of self-examination that came to New England with the Puritans seems reflected in the candid analysis of his own strengths and weaknesses he had offered as he dedicated himself to the church. His self-assessment was to prove remarkably accurate. The young man who had denigrated his own "reasoning faculty" would have little to say in his future sermons about fine points of doctrine; "the great object of my life," he was to tell his Boston congregation, was simply "to explore the nature of God" (*YES* 72). His ambitions as a speaker and writer, reflected here in his emphasis on "moral imagination" and eloquence in the pulpit rather than on the pastoral ministry, were to prove a source of future difficulty during his tenure at the Second Church. As Emerson came to feel constrained by the conventional duties of his position and the expectations of his parishioners, so they in turn complained that he was devoting too much time to his studies at the expense of visitations among his flock. With respect to this latter charge, temperament was more a factor than personal ambition. Shy as he was, Emerson would always be less comfortable on purely social occasions than when separated from "the company of most men & women" by retirement to his study or ascent to the pulpit or platform, first as a preacher and later as a lecturer.

Emerson's actual preparation for the ministerial office was somewhat informal, even by the standards of his own day. Once having decided that the church should be his "regeneration," he kept up for a time both his schoolteaching and his private study of divinity until the end of 1824, when he closed his school and continued to "affect the scholar" at home until the beginning of a new term at the Theological School in February of 1825 (L 1:158–59). There he was admitted as a member of the middle rather than the entering class, in recognition of his age and background if not of the private reading he had been doing. But his regular studies were frequently interrupted over the next few years by poor health and several intervals of renewed schoolteaching under financial pressures. When William Emerson gave up his ministerial studies in 1825 the response of Mary Moody Emerson was to urge Waldo to begin preaching as soon as he could obtain authorization from the church. Looking forward to his approbation in 1826, Waldo assured her that he found no objections in himself to this step, though he was admittedly somewhat perplexed by the vocational prospect opening before him: "'Tis a queer life," he wrote, "and the only humour proper to it seems quiet astonishment. Others laugh, weep, sell, or proselyte. I admire" (L 1:170).

In the next year, 1827, Emerson took a master's degree at Harvard while filling a number of Unitarian pulpits and beginning to accumulate a supply of original sermons that could be drawn upon as he moved to new engagements. By the time of his ordination in 1829 he had preached nearly two hundred times, establishing a growing reputation as a young man on the rise, and had the offer of several permanent appointments. Even so, there are hints scattered through his letters and journals that the preacher himself was not altogether easy in the role he had elected, which already seemed not comprehensive enough to engage all his talents. "It occurs to me lately that we have a great many capacities which we lack time & occasion to improve," he wrote to his aunt in May of 1827, going on to illustrate the possibilities he had in mind. Reading Walter Scott's *Bride of Lammermoor*, he told her, aroused "a thousand imperfect suggestions" which, could he give heed to them, would make him a novelist; lighting upon "a verse or two of genuine poetry" awakened through "forcible sympathy" a "fine tiny rabble" of little goblins within the soul that would make him a poet "if I had leisure to attend." In his daydreams he thought too of painting, "besides all the spasmodic attachments I indulge to each of the Sciences & each province of letters. They all in turn play the coquette with my imagination & it may be I shall die at the last a forlorn bachelor jilted of them all" (L 1:198).

iii. Ordination and Marriage

It was Waldo Emerson's apprenticeship preaching that led the shy young man into the one rapturous emotional relationship of his long life, terminating his literal bachelorhood. In December of 1827 he was asked to preach before a new Unitarian congregation in Concord, New Hampshire, where on Christmas Day he first saw Ellen Tucker. She was then a girl of seventeen; Emerson himself was twenty-four. Their acquaintance developed over the next year during his further preaching engagements in Concord. Ellen too had aspirations as a writer, regretting that her poor health interfered with the development of her poetic powers; like the Emersons themselves, the Tucker family was afflicted with tuberculosis, the scourge of nineteenth-century New England. Along with her literary gifts she possessed both beauty and spirit. As Waldo described her to his brother William in January of 1829, shortly after the couple's formal engagement to marry, "She is perfectly simple though very elegant in her manners; then she has common sense; then she has imagination & knows the difference between good poetry & bad; then she makes fine verses herself, then she is good,—& has character enough to be religious. then she is beautiful, & finally I love her. If my story is short, it is true" (L 1:259).

Even as Emerson wrote, however, he was obliged to tell his brother also that Ellen "has made me very sorry by being very ill," and that because of her condition he had delayed his acceptance of a call to become junior pastor at the Second Church, where for some months of 1828 he had been supplying the pulpit. Nevertheless, with encouraging word from her doctors he ultimately determined to accept the call, with the expectation of being ordained in March of 1829 and of eventually succeeding to the pastorate itself whenever Henry Ware, Jr., should resign it to accept a faculty post at the Cambridge Theological School. In his letter of acceptance he confessed that he would have preferred to postpone his entrance into "this solemn office," citing lack of "any sanguine confidence in my abilities, or in my prospects." But though modest about his qualifications he was able to "speak firmly" of his resolve to perform his duties faithfully "as far as in me lies" (L 1:261). On 11 March 1829 he was ordained as junior pastor in a simple ceremony, with the Emerson and Tucker families in attendance.

At first the young minister seemed nearly overwhelmed by the round of professional duties he confronted, which left him little time for books or correspondence. As he explained to William, most of his weekday mornings were spent in writing and his afternoons in parish visiting; the visits, he told his brother, "cannot be numbered or ended" (L 1:270, 268–69). After a busy Sunday devoted to preaching, performing a marriage, and assisting in the administration of the Lord's Supper, he confessed to his stepgrandfather, the venerable pastor Ezra Ripley, that he now feared none of his ministerial tasks "except the preparation of sermons. The prospect of one each week, for an indefinite time to come is almost terrifick" (L 1:267). But in point of fact it was writing and preaching his sermons that most engaged Emerson, not his interminable visiting. What he had to say as a preacher gained steadily in eloquence and depth, for the young minister was finding his authentic way of speaking. "Every man has his own voice, manner, eloquence, and, just as much, his own sort of love, and grief, and imagination, and action," he declared in a characteristic sermon first preached in 1830.

> He has some power over other men that arises to him from his peculiar education and the cast of his circumstances and the complexion of his mind; and it were the extreme of folly if he forbears to use it, because he has never seen it used by any body else. Let him scorn to *imitate* any being. Let him scorn to be a secondary man. Let him fully trust his own share of God's goodness, that if used to the uttermost, it will lead him on to a perfection which has no type yet in the universe, save only in the Divine Mind. (*YES* 108)

As he might have anticipated, the originality Emerson both cherished and cultivated did not please all his listeners in the Second Church. From his senior colleague, Henry Ware, Jr., he received a series of warnings about the character of his preaching that had begun while he was still serving as supply pastor. Cautioned against using secular rather than biblical illustrations in his sermons, Emerson acknowledged that in one instance he had been "rather bolder than the usage of our preaching warrants" but had spoken "on the principle that our religion is nothing limited or partial, but of universal application, & is interested in all that interests man." He agreed to add "the authority of scripture quotation," as Ware had evidently urged him to do, "when I shall have the occasion to repeat that sermon" (*L* 1:257). After he became Ware's junior colleague he received further criticisms and suggestions, some of them turning on his handling of the Bible. In response, he promised to guard against the possible impression that he lacked due respect for the Scriptures—a charge which "would give me great uneasiness if it is well-founded," he assured his mentor. Although Ware's letters indicate his continued anxiety about possible heretical tendencies in his younger colleague, as Rusk remarked, Emerson's reply also shows that he "still had a long way to go before he could write *Nature*" in 1836 or could shock Ware with his Divinity School Address in 1838. The Bible, Emerson affirmed in the summer of 1829, is a book "of divine authority" which establishes "almost all we wanted to know" concerning "the Immortality of the Soul" and "the being & character of God" (*L* 1:273 and n. 50).

Meanwhile, as Emerson was settling into his ministerial duties, there was continued anxiety among the Tuckers and the Emersons over Ellen's recurrent illness. In August and September of 1829 he arranged to go to New Hampshire and take Ellen and her mother touring for the sake of his fiancée's health. Open-air traveling seemed to benefit her, and on the last day of September they were married at her home. Although Ellen's condition during their engagement had been a constant threat to their happiness, it did not prevent the young pair from writing seemingly lighthearted verse journals while on their travels or from exchanging affectionate letters and poetry when they were separated. Throughout their courtship Emerson displayed an openness, a warmth, and even a sense of gaiety and humor that must have surprised those who thought of him only as shy, reserved, and wholly serious. At last the young couple settled near his church in Boston, where the new minister began to receive notice in religious circles beyond his parish and to take on community obligations as well. Shortly after his ordination he had been named chaplain of the Massachusetts Senate, and in December of 1829 he was elected to the Boston School Committee, a post that required much hard work and brought him into public controversy over various school policies.

Apart from the ever-present problem of Ellen's health the marriage was altogether happy, though Emerson privately confessed uneasiness on one score. Ellen's late father had been well-to-do, and thanks to her inheritance the young couple were enjoying amenities to which Waldo in his poverty had been wholly unaccustomed. He was not only somewhat uncomfortable in his new prosperity but he even felt "soreness" in the presence of others still more prosperous than he. His characteristic response, as he was well aware, was to seek "unfrequented woods & pastures" so as to forestall possible encounters with any such persons. Why should this be? His explanation, which appears in a journal entry of September 1830, was that a still-unconquered "desire of worldly good" causes "the scholar" to imagine in others a superiority they do not really possess because the scholar himself "is not scholar enough in his heart" (*JMN* 3:196). This entry is the first of many instances in which Emerson identifies himself as "the scholar." Here, moreover, *scholar* also serves as a normative term in this passage: the young minister is indeed a scholar, but "not scholar enough" to overcome his feelings of inferiority.

It is clear from the dedication of his talents to the church in 1824 that the scholarly aspects of clerical life were uppermost in Emerson's mind from the outset. Though he had mentioned then his "inordinate fondness for writing," he came to quail after his ordination at the prospect of having to turn out a sermon a week for the indefinite future. Conversely, as an active minister he soon began to chafe at the pastoral duties which took him away from his private study and placed him in direct contact with the men and women of his parish, making demands on both his time and his unsocial temperament. These conflicting requirements of his calling were set forth in a sermon of 1830, "The Ministry: A Year's Retrospect," that marked the first anniversary of his Boston pastorate. As always, he was candid about his shortcomings as the year had revealed them: the scholar-minister was not wholly satisfied with the sermons he had given, his parishioners wanted him to do more pastoral calling, and both found his activities as preacher and pastor "in some measure incompatible" (*YES* 70). Like his journal entry of the same year on the scholar and society, this sermon on his ministry addressed the recurrent Emersonian theme of society and solitude. To his congregation he explained that the minister, possessing "no better spiritual light than his brethren," needs time for study and writing if he is to discharge the scholarly side of his office. Meditation is essential, since "for the most part the thoughts which are greatest and truest, do not flash upon the soul in a moment in all their fulness," though complete isolation would be self-defeating: "sometimes silence and solitude; sometimes conversation; sometimes action; sometimes books"—all these "are necessary to repair the flagging powers of the soul, and enable it to carry on its inquiry" (*YES* 70).

Emerson's early recognition of these alternating psychological needs anticipates a passage of "The American Scholar," written seven years later, which enunciates "that great principle of Undulation," or "Polarity," that he saw operating in human life as well as in the world of nature (*CW* 1:61). But in 1830 he was still struggling with the competing claims he was facing as a busy clergyman, for as he went on to say in the sermon, "the laws of thought" as pursued by the scholar "are not accommodated to the divisions of time" that constrain the preacher and pastor.

> The services of the church are periodical, but the development of truth within the mind is not. Obviously then the minister who makes it an important aim to convey instruction must often stay at home in the search of it when his parishioners may think he would be more usefully employed in cultivating an acquaintance with them. You will therefore have the charity to think when you do not see your pastor as often or at the times when you could wish it and desire it, that he may be employed with earnest endeavours to speak to you usefully in this place. (*YES* 70–71)

Emerson had once told his Aunt Mary that preaching did not seem to engage all his talents; now he was saying that the ministry was demanding more of him, or at least more of his time, than he found possible to give. What he did not mention, except for an initial reference to his "recent absence" from the pulpit (*YES* 67), was his ever-present concern over Ellen's uncertain health, which in March of 1830 had taken both of them to Philadelphia for a change of climate. Without the strain of his wife's illness the young minister might more readily have worked out solutions to the difficulties he acknowledged in the sermon; it is tempting to speculate about the future course of his career with Ellen remaining at his side to keep up his spirits and perhaps to draw him out as a social being. But travel brought her only temporary relief, and by the end of the year her condition was obviously precarious. Death came to her as a release on 8 February 1831, but Ellen's passing left her husband in what he called a "miserable debility" (*JMN* 3:226).

Emerson was long in escaping his physical and psychological reaction to Ellen's death; in later years, even after his second marriage in 1835, he continued to think longingly of her. "She had stirred him more than anybody else had ever done or could do," as Rusk has written. The possible connection between Emerson's loss of Ellen and his growing discontent with his profession over the year that followed is a question that has long engaged his biographers. In the judgment of Henry F. Pommer, the chronicler of Emerson's courtship and marriage, "Pervasive ennui, child of his grief, almost surely hastened a decision for which intellectual doubts and unfitness of temperament were the chief motives."[8]

iv. New Bearings

Emerson's depression persisted through the summer of 1831, when he was invited to write a poem for the annual meeting of the Harvard chapter of Phi Beta Kappa, a society to which he had been elected an honorary member in 1828, seven years after his college graduation. The invitation, he replied, would have been welcome a few months since, "but I have not at present any spirit for a work of that kind, which must not be a dirge" (L 1:326). The meeting itself, which he attended in August, did little to lighten his mood. Reporting on it in a letter to Edward, he also wrote of his lingering despair and confessed that he had lost his spiritual and ethical bearings—an unhappy predicament for a minister above all other men. "I am trying to learn to find my own latitude," he told Edward, adding that if he were richer he would literally "have an observatory" in which to study the heavens (L 1:330). His desire to take up science was increased when he read a discourse on the physical sciences by the astronomer William Herschel; in a letter to his brother William he termed Herschel's work noble enough "to tempt a man to leave all duties to find out natural science." Though he was still not prepared to renounce the ministry, he was sufficiently interested in science to want "a laboratory & a battery" as well as "an observatory & a telescope" (L 1:343).

Emerson's new interest in science was no mere enthusiasm of the moment. During the crucial year of 1832, perhaps as a way of finding his bearings once again, he read widely in scientific books and articles. His layman's familiarity with current scientific thinking not only provided metaphors for his writing but also reinforced his liberal handling of religious questions while he was still serving the Second Church; in later years he found in science a subject for popular lectures. A number of his sermons, like the early "Summer," express pleasure in the sheer beauty of the physical world, anticipating passages of *Nature* (1836) and the opening of the Divinity School Address (1838). Other sermons reflect his admiration for the wonders of the heavens. "Astronomy," first given in 1832, develops a proposition laid down in the journal: that although astronomy "proves theism" it nevertheless "irresistibly modifies all theology" (*JMN* 4:26).[9] Astronomical imagery recurs in later writings as Emerson continued to think of himself as a kind of moral astronomer, a "Watcher" (*JMN* 4:370), studying "in his private observatory" not the outer heavens but the inward sky, and "cataloguing obscure and nebulous stars of the human mind," as he was ultimately to put it in "The American Scholar" (*CW* 1:62).

As an amateur scientist especially fascinated by astronomy and familiar with the work of men such as Herschel and Newton, Emerson tended to conceive the universe in terms of Newtonian celestial mechanics and to write of eternal and immutable laws that operate in the realm of ethics as well as in the realms of astronomy and physics. "The laws of moral nature answer to those of matter as face to face in a glass," he would declare in lectures of 1833 and 1834 and reaffirm in *Nature*; further, "the axioms of physics translate the laws of ethics" (*CW* 1:21; cf.

EL 1:24–25, 290). On the other hand, when he turned from astronomy to the findings of biologists and geologists he saw the world in terms of life and growth and change. Influenced too by his reading of Wordsworth and Coleridge and his discovery later in 1832 of Carlyle and the German Romantics, he inclined toward a natural philosophy and theology of dynamic organicism. What Emerson had to say about nature in the 1830s was therefore not entirely consistent, since it reflected both older and newer literary, scientific, and theological thinking. At times, like most American Unitarian theologians of the day, he wrote of a transcendent Creator who occasionally intervened miraculously in the world below by suspending the laws of His creation. More characteristically, however, Emerson came to think of an immanent Spirit immediately present both in nature and in mankind, and to speak of all life, all being, as a perpetual miracle.[10]

The idea of an immanent God, so central to Emerson's later thinking and so important to his conception of the scholar as divinely inspired, was the major intellectual development of his years as a minister. As Wesley Mott observes, *God within us* is "the definitive theme" of his sermons.[11] Thus in 1832 Emerson could speak of "the immortal life" dwelling at the bottom of every heart and of "this supreme universal reason in your mind which is not yours or mine or any man's, but is the Spirit of God in us all" (*YES* 183, 186). "Blessed is the day when the youth discovers that Within and Above are synonyms," he was to write in 1834 (*JMN* 4:365). Belief in this divine presence within is the foundation of Emersonian self-reliance, which in his own formulation is essentially a religious conception; it is what he meant in 1840 when he affirmed his "one doctrine, namely, the infinitude of the private man" (*JMN* 7:342), and in 1854 when he spoke of "self-reliance, the height and perfection of man," as "reliance on God" (*W* 11:236). It is the basis too of Emerson's idea of democracy, as he was to declare it at the conclusion of "The American Scholar" in 1837, where he envisions "a nation of men" as existing "because each believes himself inspired by the Divine Soul which also inspires all men" (*CW* 1:70). Then and later, moreover, he regarded each citizen as at least a potential scholar.

But there are other corollaries of this same belief that could have negative implications for social action, as Emerson himself was well aware throughout his career. Insofar as the Emersonian man looks inward rather than outward, he is likely to be not only introspective but otherworldly. "It is really of trifling importance what events await America," the young Emerson had gone so far as to declare in an early sermon of 1827; "for we are citizens of another country" (*YES* xxxi). After a year at the Second Church he asserted in 1830 his conviction that a minister proclaiming or insinuating from the pulpit his views on public men and public issues would be violating "the plainest decorum" (*YES* 76). On the same occasion he granted that there is indeed a connection between a person's private life and his public duties, but for Emerson the one best recipe for making society better was first to transform the individual man and woman. "This is the true way to reform states," he told his congregation. "You compel people to be better by being better yourself" (*YES* 81). Even so, he worked actively for the public good as a member of the Boston School Committee, though he was relieved when he failed of reelection after a year in office.

Meanwhile, Emerson's private concern with the issue of slavery was growing. Although he did not preach on that subject himself, he did permit Samuel May—well known as an Anti-Slavery crusader—to speak from his pulpit in the spring of 1831 on "Slavery in the United States." May's address was "fully reported" by the Boston press, as Rusk noted, and in the public mind "the pastor was thus linked with the reformer."[12] What his congregation may have thought about this seeming break with "decorum" as their minister defined it is not recorded, although the fact that the Society for the Abolition of Slavery held its annual meeting at the Second Church late in 1832 (*YES* 256) may suggest that both the membership and the former minister (Emerson had by then resigned his post) regarded slavery as a special case.

Emerson in the 1830s was himself no abolitionist, however, and as for his pronouncements on purely religious topics, there is nothing in the written record other than Ware's early criticisms to suggest that his increasingly liberal theology was alienating his parishioners or provoking hostile reaction. Perhaps his listeners were not fully aware of the direction their minister's thought was taking or of the undercurrents in his more recent sermons about vocational choice. Matters came to a head, however, in the spring of 1832, when Emerson himself formally apprised the Second Church of a new development in his thinking. His decision to take this step probably came late in May during what he described in the journal as "a week of moral excitement" (*JMN* 4:27). The problem immediately on his mind did not involve the content of his sermons or his shortcomings as a pastoral visitant, but another topic about which neither he nor his congregation had previously differed: the ordinance of the Lord's Supper. The minister had changed his opinions about this observance, he now acknowledged, and wished to recommend altering the mode of its administration (*L* 1:351).

In all that Emerson had to say about the Lord's Supper, both in the spring of 1832 and later in the year, he was undoubtedly sincere, but the real basis of his memorandum to the Second Church was broader than his attitude toward this one particular sacrament. During the previous winter he had privately complained of his inability to "bend" his profession to fit his own temperament, although other ministers he knew had managed in one way or another to make their individual accommodations. "Thus Finney can preach, & so his prayers are short," Emerson had written at the time. "Parkman can pray, & so his prayers are long. Lowell can visit & so his church service is less. But what shall poor I do who can neither visit nor pray nor preach to my mind?" (*JMN* 3:324). There was no mention of the observance, however, when he complained in January about the difficulty of conforming a man's "external condition" to his "inward constitution," nor in February when he had spoken from his pulpit about the other alternative to accommodation, that of finding a new calling. Now he had at last determined to settle matters once and for all—less, one suspects, because of his altered opinions about the Lord's Supper than in response to the more inclusive thought confided to his journal on 2 June: that "in order to be a good minister it was necessary to leave the ministry. The profession is antiquated. In an altered age, we worship in the dead forms of our forefathers" (*JMN* 4:27). Taking the ordinance as a case in point, he now posed the issue, first to himself and then to the Second Church: either the church must agree to alter the form or the pastor must sever the ministerial tie.

As Emerson may well have anticipated, the issue as he himself had formulated it could have only one resolution. The committee appointed to consider his statement brought in a recommendation against changing the administration of the ordinance, and on 21 June 1832 the church itself concurred. The minister, in ill health that was to last for the remaining months of this critical year, had withdrawn to the White Mountains to await the response to his letter, and there he drafted a sermon explaining his position. What he did not say, at least in its printed version (see *W* 11:1–25), was that he could no longer bring himself to go "with indifference & dislike" to an institution deemed "holiest" by his congregation; he meant, of course, the Lord's Supper, though he could easily have widened the application of his words. Admittedly, he might have been overly conscientious in his scruples about the ordinance, as he granted to himself in his journal; "without accommodation," he recognized, "society is impracticable" (*JMN* 4:30). But Waldo Emerson was no Finney or Parkman or Lowell, and like his brother William before him he was making his choice not for accommodation but for conscience.

On 9 September 1832 Emerson delivered his sermon, and two days later, keeping his promise from the pulpit, he formally resigned his pastoral office. In the letter of resignation he described himself as "pained at the situation" as it had developed (*L* 1:356). So undoubtedly he was, and many if not most of the congregation were genuinely sorry to see him go. But when he looked back later on this "severing of our strained cord," he called the separation "a mutual relief." In a letter to William in November he wrote that "It is sorrowful to me & to them in a measure, for we were both suited & hoped to be mutually useful. But though it will occasion me perhaps some, (possibly, much) temporary embarrassment yet I walk firmly toward a peace & freedom which I plainly see before me albeit afar" (*L* 1:357–58).

2. PULPIT AND PLATFORM, 1833–1834

❖

I like my book about nature & wish I knew where & how I ought to live. God will show me.

—Entry of 6 September 1833 in Journal Sea 1833, written on shipboard off the coast of Ireland. (*JMN* 4:237)

When the proprietors of the Second Church met on 28 October 1832 to act on their minister's resignation, they not only granted Emerson's request for release from his pastoral charge but also voted to continue his salary until the end of the year if he would arrange for supplying the pulpit at his own expense. He himself was in no condition at that time, physically or psychologically, either to continue preaching or to settle on an alternative vocational choice. The search for a new calling was to be his primary concern for some time to come.

What Emerson knew best was writing—writing and speaking. During the previous winter he had listed possible chapter headings for a projected book, but the book was still unwritten.[1] He toyed with another idea that would involve him in original literary work: establishing a magazine on which to place his own unmistakable stamp. Most periodicals, he thought, "depend on many contributors who all speak an average sense & no one of them utters his own individuality. Yet that the soul of a man should speak out, & not the soul general of the town or town pump." On the other hand, as he well realized, there are "the limits of human strength" that argue against "a paper conducted by one man." A "Goethe or Schiller" might succeed, but he must have "a constitution that does not belong to every lean lily-livered aspirant of these undigesting days" (*L* 1:358).

In December of 1832, with his health still no better, Emerson determined on the usual family remedy, a sea voyage—not to the Caribbean to join Edward as he had first intended, but rather to the Mediterranean and Europe. Once embarked, he continued to think of himself as a scholar, one now traveling abroad for instruction and improvement. In Europe, besides visiting museums and scientific collections, he would seek out teachers from whose writings he had already learned: Walter Savage Landor, William Wordsworth, Samuel Taylor Coleridge, and Thomas Carlyle. Once he returned with health renewed and confidence in his own powers restored, he might even become a teacher himself.

i. A Scholar Abroad

The Atlantic crossing that winter was stormy, confining ships' passengers to their staterooms. Emerson took comfort more than once by recalling "nearly the whole of Lycidas, clause by clause" (*JMN* 4:103, 111), though on other occasions he complained of his faulty memory. When the weather cleared he studied navigation with the friendly captain, but he had to confess himself "a dull scholar as ever in real figures."

> Seldom I suppose was a more inapt learner of arithmetic, astronomy, geography, political economy than I am as I daily find to my cost. It were to brag much if I should there end the catalogue of my defects. My memory of history—put me to the pinch of a precise question[—]is as bad; my comprehension of a question in technical meta-physics very slow, & in all arts practick, in driving a bargain, or hiding emotion, or carrying myself in company as a man for an hour, I have no skill. What under the sun canst thou do, pale face! Truly not much, but I can hope. (*JMN* 4:110)

The stout Captain Ellis, by contrast, was a resourceful and versatile "man of action" who at sea was clearly "worth a thousand philosophers." Though his skill— his "brain"—lay primarily in his hand, as Emerson put it, he was knowledgeable enough in Scripture to confound the "scholar's brain" of his passenger by posing detailed questions about the Bible that the sometime minister was quite unable to answer (*JMN* 4:115, 111). As his recorded comments indicate, Emerson was con-tinuing to think of himself habitually as a scholar and also to compare himself unfavorably with men of action.

The warmer climate of the Mediterranean proved as beneficial as Emerson had hoped, and after some weeks in Italy he described himself in April of 1833 as "in better health than I remember to have enjoyed since I was in college" (*L* 1:375). While in Europe he regarded himself as once again a student, learning as he traveled and keeping his customary journal; in June he moved northward to Paris and in July he was in London, but his extensive student's notes about the persons and places he was seeing never managed to crowd out his familiar introspective musing. To him it seemed "sound philosophy" to reflect that wherever men go and whatever they do, "self is the sole subject we study & learn" (*JMN* 4:67–68). Except for two lectures on Italy given in 1834, after his return to Boston, Emerson would make little use of his more descriptive journal entries until after he had again visited Europe: in composing *English Traits* (1856) he compared the impressions left by his first and second visits to England.

The tone of the two lectures on Italy was less than enthusiastic toward the fruits of travel. The most profitable lessons to be learned abroad, he declared, "are only confirmation in unexpected quarters of our simplest sentiments at home," and any "truly diligent and well regulated mind will attain to the same thoughts and feelings in Sicily, in Rome, in New England" (*EL* 1:90). These remarks of 1834 anticipate the dismissal of traveling in "Self-Reliance" (1841) as mere "superstition" and "a fool's paradise." First journeys, Emerson says there, "discover to us the indifference of places"—an idea he explored throughout the 1830s. The particular example given in "Self-Reliance" is in fact a visit to Italy, where "beside me is the stern Fact, the sad self, unrelenting, identical, that I fled from." Travel, in short, may well be restorative, but it is never an escape: "My giant goes with me wherever I go" (*CW* 2:46).[2]

Emerson's immediate response to Italy had in reality been much happier than these later remarks imply. "I strive to possess my soul in patience," he assured his Aunt Mary in a letter describing his reactions to Rome and Florence, and, "escaping both giddiness & pedantry, to feel truly & think wisely." Although he was finding Italy impressive, he told her, the people he had been meeting interested him even more than "Art or magnificence." But, idealist though he was, he felt continually thwarted in his perpetual search for the figure that forever eluded him: "the wise man—the true friend—the finished character." Even the most congenial companions "always awaken expectations in me which they always disappoint," he told his aunt; they give no genuine instruction, and "I want instructers. God's greatest gift is a Teacher" (*L* 1:375–76). The scholar's search for instruction and especially for some great Teacher persisted as he moved across Europe and sought out various celebrities, much as his brother William had sought out Goethe eight years before.

This quest for a Teacher is the subject of a profoundly felt comment that the scholar-traveler entered in his journal on the eve of his departure for home. Written in September of 1833 as Emerson waited in Liverpool for his ship to sail, the passage takes the form of a prayer of thanks to "the great God who has led me through this European scene[,] this last schoolroom in which he has pleased to instruct me," who has "shown me the men I wished to see." Emerson singles out four of them, all writers whose works he had admired before his trip began: Landor, whom he met in Florence; Wordsworth and Coleridge, interviewed in England; and Carlyle, visited at his home in Scotland. Even with Carlyle, whom he found "so amiable that I love him," it had been the old pattern once again, for he too had not quite lived up to Emerson's high expectations; indeed, none of the four men seemed to possess "a mind of the very first class." In his judgment their insight had proved "deficient" in the one area that he regarded as his own special province: moral and religious truth. In his words, "They have no idea of that species of moral truth which I call the first philosophy" (*JMN* 4:78–79).

Listening to such eminent persons and hearing them talk frankly and without pretense of the things that were puzzling them was in one way disappointing to Emerson, but it was at the same time a positive experience, for he had thus been "comforted & confirmed" in his own deepest convictions. For this great benefit he returned thanks to God. Hereafter, he knew, he would "judge more justly, less timidly, of wise men forevermore" (*JMN* 4:78). His persistent search for a Teacher, culminating in the realization that the "wise men" of the world really knew no more of the truth than he had learned for himself, was another demonstration of a principle at the heart of his own thinking. This principle is epitomized in the maxim from Persius that became the motto for "Self-Reliance": Ne[c] te quæsiveris extra—or, as he translated it in 1834, "Thou art sufficient unto thyself" (CW 2:25; JMN 4:318). During his homeward voyage he had time to reflect, in his new spirit of confidence in himself and his own powers, on his situation and future prospects. While on his way to Europe nine months before he had deprecated himself as "a dull scholar" lacking the practical skills needed for the world's work; now, newly instructed by his experience in the European schoolroom, he was beginning to think of assuming the Teacher's role himself.

ii. A Would-be Teacher

Remembering his previous observation that "the great men of England are singularly ignorant of religion" (JMN 4:80), Emerson composed on shipboard an extended analysis of "the errors of religionists" generally, a statement that grew into an affirmation of what he had called "the first philosophy." The chief problem of contemporary religion he identified as the sectarian narrowness and shallowness that limits any faith, Christian or pagan, when it is taught by "incapable teachers." In their own ignorance such men simply "do not know the extent or the harmony or the depth of their moral nature, that they are clinging to little, positive, verbal, formal versions of the moral law & very imperfect versions too, while the infinite laws, the laws of the Law, the great circling truths whose only adequate symbol is the material laws, the astronomy, &c, are all unobserved, & sneered at when spoken of, as frigid & insufficient" (JMN 4:83). Here he may have been looking back to his own sermon of 1832 on "Astronomy," perhaps recalling also the earlier objections of Henry Ware, Jr., to the secular images in his preaching. The great need in religion, he went on to say, is for "a true Teacher," one in whose hands sectarian falsehoods are abandoned and "the sublimity & the depth of the Original is penetrated & exhibited to men" (JMN 4:83). By "the Original" Emerson of course meant "the God Within," for him the spiritual basis of man's moral constitution. As he had once told his former congregation, his own "great object" was "to explore the nature of God."

That Emerson was drawing on his own experience as a minister is obvious throughout this passage. Even before going to Europe he had lamented that because of fear of shocking the formalists there was "nobody" in the ministry teaching what he called "the heart of Christianity": the doctrine of "man's moral nature." The constraints a clergyman feels will inevitably cripple his teaching by requiring him to justify this "essential truth" in terms of conventional religious precepts when it is actually "selfevident." "Instead of making Christianity a vehicle of truth," he had written, "you make truth only a horse for Christianity" (JMN 4:45). Now, freed of his restrictive pastoral charge, Emerson was beginning to envision some new pulpit, inside or more likely outside the institutionalized church, where as student-turned-teacher he could set forth religious truth as he saw it without being hemmed in by the traditional sanctions.

The kind of teaching Emerson had in mind was something both very new and very old, being the same revelation that had come to men of every faith—Socrates, à Kempis, Fénelon, Butler, Penn, Swedenborg, and Channing are the names he mentions. All of them "think & say the same thing": that by virtue of "the moral law," human nature has certain remarkable properties.

A man contains all that is needful to his government within himself. He is made a law unto himself. All real good or evil that can befal him must be from himself. He only can do himself any good or any harm. Nothing can be given to him or taken from him but always there is a compensation. There is a correspondence between the human soul & everything that exists in the world,—more properly, everything that is known to man. Instead of studying things without the principles of them[,] all may be penetrated unto within him. Every act puts the agent in a new condition. The purpose of life seems to be to acquaint a man with himself. He is not to live to the future as described to him but to live to the real future by living to the real present. The highest revelation is that God is in every man. (*JMN* 4:84)

This is Emerson's "first philosophy" as he summed it up in September of 1833, a reaffirmation of the principles he had been formulating before he resigned his pulpit, privately in his journal and even publicly in his more recent sermons to the Second Church. Several of the component ideas had already been listed as potential subjects for treatment in the book he had thought of writing—for example, his faith in what he had earlier called "a perfect system of compensations, that exact justice is done" (*JMN* 3:316, 317). Now, seventeen months after Ellen's death and a year after he had resigned his pastorate, he rephrased the principle to read: "Nothing can be given to him or taken from him but always there is a compensation." Time and change had confirmed in Emerson's own experience what he had long held in theory; for even "when very young," he was later to write in the essay called "Compensation" (1841), it had seemed to him that "on this subject, Life was ahead of theology, and the people knew more than the preachers taught" (*CW* 2:55). Like "Self-Reliance," "Compensation" had a very long foreground in Emerson's earlier life and thought.

But the would-be teacher of 1833 was not yet ready to write such essays, however firmly their themes were already grounded in his mind. He was confronting immediate problems, one of them being to find or create an audience for the kind of teaching he had in mind. Before his return to Boston in October his brothers were speculating that he might revive the project of establishing a magazine, but he apparently took no action to do so, perhaps realizing that he lacked both editorial experience and the requisite financial backing. Meanwhile, whether in search of an audience or simply for the sake of a regular income, he began filling engagements as a supply preacher in Boston and especially in New Bedford, where he could probably have taken a regular pastorate had he been willing to entertain a call. Among his various engagements were two appearances in his old pulpit at the Second Church. His October sermon there, newly written for the occasion, particularly reflected his recent thinking on both religious and vocational matters. Preliminary notes in the journal indicate his intention to deal with some of the ideas about religion and religious instruction that had engaged him during the voyage home from Liverpool. The "true Teacher" of religion, he had affirmed, would drop the formalities of creed and sect in order to exhibit the sublimity of the moral law; here he made the further point that "the teacher of the coming age" should not merely busy himself with interpreting Scripture. The objective of such a teacher—and of course of Emerson himself—must be far more comprehensive: "the study & explanation of the moral constitution of man" (*JMN* 4:83, 93–94).[3]

In the sermon itself, after beginning with a warm greeting to his former congregation, Emerson addressed the general subject of religious instruction, saying that even before leaving his pulpit he had "anxiously desired" to speak to them about "that change which seems to be taking place under our eyes in the opinions of men on religious questions; of that Teaching which all men are waiting for, and of that Teacher who has been predicted and hath not yet come" (*YES* 192). Although he did not presume to identify himself as the longed-for messianic Teacher promised by Jesus, "the Spirit of Truth" (*YES* 194), he did repeat ideas and phrasing about teaching and learning that had appeared in his correspondence and journal during the European trip. "The greatest gift of God," he declared once again in the sermon, "is a Teacher and teaching is the perpetual end and office of all things. Teaching, instruction, is the main design that shines through the sky and the earth" (*YES* 192). In setting down what he meant by "the moral law of human nature" he had previously remarked that "to acquaint a man with himself" seems to be the very purpose of life itself; in the sermon he equates living with the continuously active process of learning.

> The end of living is to know; and, if you say, the end of knowledge is action,—why, yes, but the end of that action again, is knowledge. . . . The sun grudges his light, and the air his breath to him who stands with his hands folded in this great school of God, and does not perceive that all are students, all are learning the art of life, the discipline of virtue, how to act, how to suffer, how to be useful, and what their Maker designed them for. (*YES* 192–93)

"The Spirit of Truth," Emerson held, is forever speaking to men "by a thousand thousand lips"—which is to say by "the simple occurrences of every day," through which Providence "is always instructing those who are in the attitude of scholars." But "the essential condition of teaching is a ripe pupil. The wisest Teacher can impart no more than his disciple can receive. . . . No teacher can teach without the hearty cooperation of the scholar," and even Jesus himself needed to accommodate his discourses to the capacity of his listeners (*YES* 194, 197).[4] The time has come, said Emerson, for modern teachers of religion to respond to that "revolution of religious opinion taking effect around us" which has "separated the individual from the whole world and made him demand a faith satisfactory to his own proper nature, whose full extent he now for the first time contemplates." And what was his answer to this demand? It was the same "amazing revelation" that had come to Emerson in his own time of separation: to the individual soul in search of faith a voice replies, saying "that God is within him, that *there* is the celestial host" (*YES* 199–200).

For all Emerson's chafing over the constraints that he felt to be restricting the ministers of his day, there is no evidence that preaching his "first philosophy" in 1833, either to his former congregation or to other audiences, aroused any immediate objections. Despite his reservations about institutional religion, he continued to supply a variety of Unitarian pulpits, preaching nearly every Sunday from the fall of 1833 until the spring of 1838, when the furor he provoked by the tenor of his address to the graduating class of the Divinity School at Cambridge served to interrupt his customary practice; his final sermon was preached at Concord, Massachusetts, on 20 January 1839. By acting as supply preacher during the mid–1830s he was able to enjoy a regular source of income without having to carry out the pastoral duties he had found so uncongenial during his regular ministry. Only half a dozen of his discourses were new; for most of his engagements, as his Preaching Record indicates, he repeated or combined earlier sermons, so that he was able to command a fairly steady return from the accumulated capital of his previous writing. For nearly five years, in other words, Emerson remained a preacher but not a pastor while he sought a still-wider audience for his teaching than the congregation of a full-time parish minister could provide.

At the very beginning of this period, as a way of accumulating further literary resources in a more orderly manner, Emerson modified his system of journal keeping. For the first time he began buying commercially bound copybooks, lettering them in alphabetical sequence and indexing each one after he had filled it. The new manuscript volumes are a tangible sign of his still-unfulfilled aspirations as a writer and speaker. "This Book is my Savings Bank," he wrote as he opened the new Journal A in early December of 1833. "I grow richer because I have somewhere to deposit my earnings; and fractions are worth more to me because corresponding fractions are waiting here that shall be made integers by their addition" (*JMN* 4:250–51). The imagery appropriately mirrors Emerson's method of literary composition; it suggests as well his desire for that personal integration and fulfillment he came to call "self-union" (*JMN* 5:34, 208). Persons unsuited to their callings "are but half themselves," he had written in a sermon of 1832 (*YES* 167); what they require, he was to explain later in writing on the poet, is full and unconstrained self-expression (*EL* 3:348–49; *CW* 3:4). In such a declaration Emerson was drawing once again on his own experience.

iii. The Scholar as Naturalist and Poet

Writing in 1931 on "Emerson and Science," Harry Hayden Clark raised the hypothetical question "whether the greatest impact on Emerson's mind in Europe was not caused by his observations in museums of natural history, listening to scientists, and by his contemplation of religious problems in the light of science" (234).[5] It is certainly true that while Emerson was abroad his continuing interest in scientific matters had taken him to lectures and museums in Italy, France, and England, and that there are significant relations between these visits and his thinking and writing about nature and natural law. His single most notable experience of this kind was a visit to the Jardin des Plantes at Paris, an episode that both confirmed and enriched his earlier thought.

The garden itself he found "admirably arranged. They have attempted to classify all the plants *in the ground*, to put together, that is, as nearly as may be the conspicuous plants in each class on Jussieu's system," and to represent almost all the animals "that Adam named or Noah preserved" (*JMN* 4:200). Within doors he inspected the cabinets of Natural History and Comparative Anatomy, marveling at the beauty of the birds in the ornithological chambers and "the inexhaustible riches of nature" displayed in the other rooms. These exhibits affected him powerfully. "The Universe," he declared in the journal,

> is a more amazing puzzle than ever as you glance along this bewildering series of animated forms,—the hazy butterflies, the carved shells, the birds, beasts, fishes, insects, snakes,—& the upheaving principle of life everywhere incipient in the very rock aping organized forms. Not a form so grotesque, so savage, nor so beautiful but is an expression of some property inherent in man the observer,—an occult relation between the very scorpions and man. I feel the centipede in me—cayman, carp, eagle, & fox. I am moved by strange sympathies, I say continually "I will be a naturalist." (*JMN* 4:199–200; cf. *EL* 1:10)[6]

Emerson visited the Jardin des Plantes in July of 1833; by the time he sailed for home in September he was thinking of writing a book specifically "about nature" (*JMN* 4:237), and at Boston between November and the following May he delivered four nontechnical lectures on various scientific topics. Of course he had neither the aptitude nor the training to become a professional scientist, but his amateur's interest was genuine. Natural history and scientific discovery generally were attracting a great deal of popular attention in the 1830s, in America as well as in Europe, and for a scholarly mind such as his, which was quick to see an analogy, there appeared to be fascinating teleological implications in what he had beheld at the Jardin des Plantes. The arrangement of exhibits by species and class, the striking similarities in bodily structure that he observed among various animal families, fostered interpretation of natural history in terms of unfolding design according to some overarching cosmic purpose. Even man himself, he was to declare in one of the lectures, "On the Relation of Man to the Globe," "is no upstart in the creation, but has been prophesied in nature for a thousand thousand ages before he appeared," and "from times incalculably remote there has been a progressive preparation for him" (*EL* 1:29). The world is man's residence; it was given him to possess; man is "accurately adjusted" by a purposing creator to the globe he inhabits. Emerson was not only "impressed by solitary works of designing wisdom" in the world of nature; he was "thrilled with delight by the choral harmony of the whole. Design! It is all design. It is all beauty. It is all astonishment" (*EL* 1:48–49).

The invitation to deliver the first of his lectures on science came to Emerson from the Natural History Society of Boston within a day or two of his return from Europe—an invitation prompted by his brother Charles and his cousin George Emerson. He accepted at once, taking as his subject "The Uses of Natural History" and making notes in his journal immediately following material intended for his October sermon to the Second Church. For the Natural History Society, a laymen's group rather than a professional association, he was expected to speak informatively but not with technical expertise. In preparing for his appearance on 4 November 1833 he made exploratory journal entries that begin by citing "the amazing discoveries that the Naturalists of this day have made," then introduce the universal analogy that Emerson perceived between the life of nature and the life of man, and conclude with the seminal idea that was to reappear three years later in a key chapter of *Nature:* that nature is a kind of language. "I wish to learn the language," Emerson wrote in the journal, "not that I may know a new set of nouns & verbs but that I may read the great book which is written in that tongue" (*JMN* 4:94–95; cf. *EL* 1:26).

In the lecture itself, where Emerson developed these same points, he used his recent visit to the Jardin des Plantes to illustrate the progress of science and to convey his own sense of the larger implications of scientific studies. After first considering their immediately practical values, he argued that the "greatest office" of science is more than utilitarian: it is "to explain man to himself." Science for Emerson was clearly instrumental; his ultimate concern was with what he had called "the moral constitution of man." Scientific knowledge, the lecturer affirmed, will help to "give man his true place in the system of being," though not without a special kind of perception. The key to interpretation is the Emersonian vision that "the whole of Nature is a metaphor or image of the human Mind. The laws of moral nature answer to those of matter as face to face in a glass" (*EL* 1:23–24, 290; cf. *CW* 1:21).

With this renewed assertion of a reciprocal relation between natural law and moral law Emerson was already committing to paper the very ideas and phrases he would soon be employing in *Nature*, which was even to repeat the topical progression he had followed both in the preliminary journal entry and in the lecture of 1833. Nothing he had previously written can match in eloquence the passages of the lecture which pair matter and mind, natural law and moral law. It is this "correspondence of the outward world to the inward world of thoughts and emotions" that endows nature with its "power of *expression*," he declared, and thereby opens to man as thinker, writer, and speaker the rich resources of metaphorical language (*EL* 1:24). This same doctrine of correspondence, reflecting Emerson's familiarity with the Platonic tradition of treating matter as a shadow of spirit and deriving more immediately from his reading of Emanuel Swedenborg, was to become the basis for the fourth chapter of *Nature,* "Language." The doctrine of correspondence was also to provide the theoretical underpinnings for his comments in *Nature* and elsewhere on poetic imagination as the source of both written and spoken eloquence.

There were further implications as well for Emerson's aspirations as a moral teacher. In the process of separating himself from his pastorate he had by no means lost his religious faith, but that faith had significantly changed. Now he was looking to science rather than institutional religion for new "bearings" that would guide his future course. Man and nature he had come to think of as animated by one common spirit, outwardly expressing itself in material forms and operating in accordance with discoverable laws; the moral law, he had written, is symbolized in material laws just as nature itself is "a metaphor or image of the human Mind." The study of nature and natural laws can therefore be a way of apprehending spiritual laws. In his lectures on science he had a timely opportunity to explore the implications of these ideas without the constraints he might still sense while speaking from a pulpit.

"The Uses of Natural History," Emerson's first lecture on science, was both well attended and well received, according to contemporary reports. "The young & the old opened their eyes & their ears," said Charles Emerson, who told his brother William in New York that he was "glad to have some of the stump lecturers see what was what & bow to the rising sun" (*L* 1:397 n. 118). An occasional lecturer himself, Charles may have discerned a new career opening outside the church for Waldo, who soon received and accepted two additional invitations for lectures to be given in January. Waldo himself had reason to be pleased with the "felicity" of his life as the old year closed. "The call of our calling is the loudest call," he wrote in his new Journal A on 11 December 1833; a few days later he remarked that his situation "seems to me singularly free & it invites me to every virtue & to great improvement" (*JMN* 4:252–53). But while he welcomed his secular speaking engagements, he was not yet ready to make a career of "this new drudgery of Lecturing," as he called it in a letter to William written shortly after his second January appearance (*L* 1:404).

Emerson's first platform engagement of 1834 was to deliver one of the Franklin Lectures in Boston, his subject being "On the Relation of Man to the Globe"; his second, before the Boston Mechanics' Association, was on the more prosaic topic of "Water." In getting up his various lectures on science he read "as much geology chemistry & physics as I could find," he told William, while his "ethics & theologics" lay "in abeyance," but he had been persuaded to return to New Bedford in February for a month of supply preaching (*L* 1:404–5). Both the lecturing and the preaching were evidently temporary expedients until some permanent vocation should present itself. Meanwhile, he was to face periods of discouragement because of his seeming indecision and inaction with respect to a new calling.

What Emerson was later to call his "philosophy of *Waiting*" (*JMN* 4:368) was in the ascendant with him during much of 1834, an outwardly uneventful year that was nevertheless as significant for his inward development as any he had yet experienced. On his way home from Europe, thinking of his possible "book about nature," he had wished that he knew "where & how I ought to live," adding confidently, "God will show me" (*JMN* 4:237); in October he had told the Second Church that if the scholar is receptive he will be continually instructed by Providence through every day's experience (*YES* 194). But a passage in his letter to William in January of 1834 seems more defensive, though it reasserts his faith in providential dispensations and justifies his inactive "waiting" with a quotation from Milton. "If nobody wants us in the world," the letter continues, "are we not excused from action & may we not blameless use the philosophy which teaches that by all events the individual is made wise & that this may be an ultimate object in the benevolence of the creator. He does not want hands. 'Thousands at his bidding speed They also serve who only stand & wait'" (*L* 1:405).

As for the immediate matter of where to live, Waldo on his return from Europe had at first roomed in Boston near Charles, who was establishing himself as a lawyer. He later went with his mother to Newton and spent several months there,[7] moving with her in October to the manse of Reverend Ezra Ripley, his step-grandfather, at Concord, Massachusetts. "Hail to the quiet fields of my fathers!" he wrote at Concord in mid-November. "Not wholly unattended by supernatural friendship & favor let me come hither. Bless my purposes as they are simple & virtuous" (*JMN* 4:335). As the late Carl Strauch has admirably shown in "The Year of Emerson's Poetic Maturity," "the fully mature poet emerged in Emerson" during this year of waiting while he was living quietly in Newton and later at Concord.[8] The poetic impulse was directly related to the close observation of his natural surroundings that was reflected in the journal during 1834, extending even to passages of technical botanizing after the fashion of the day.[9] "I will be a naturalist," Emerson had promised himself; his firsthand study of nature was complemented by his further reading, which now ranged from botanical manuals to White's *Natural History of Selborne*, and it was guided even more by the sharp eyes of his brother Charles, who joined him for long walks in the countryside. "His senses were those of a Greek," Waldo was to write of Charles after his brother's death in 1836. "I owe to them a thousand observations. . . . I had no leave to see things till he pointed them out, & afterwards I never ceased to see them" (*JMN* 5:152).

From Waldo Emerson's more imaginative notations of what he had learned to see in nature grew the best poems he had yet written: "The Rhodora," "Each and All," and "The Snow-Storm," poems which also integrated cardinal philosophical ideas that Professor Strauch traced to Emerson's intensive reading in Coleridge, Swedenborg, Gérando, Cudworth, and Goethe—writers repeatedly named in the journal. Both his direct observations and his concurrent reading were also combining to influence Emerson's prose writing, in journal entries and in the lecture manuscripts of 1834 and 1835, where his first book continued to take tangible form. The "bare common" and the inviting fields that appear in the first chapter of

Nature (*CW* 1:10) were no mere abstractions but immediate daily presences. "I do not cross the common," he wrote at Concord in December of 1834, "without a wild poetic delight notwithstanding the prose of my demeanour" (*JMN* 4:355).

"Perhaps it is the province of poetry rather than of prose," Emerson later remarked, "to describe the effect upon the mind and heart" of those "nameless influences" we derive from the works of nature (*EL* 1:72–73). So he affirmed in the fourth of his lectures on science, "The Naturalist," given at Boston in May of 1834 before the annual meeting of the Natural History Society. In this lecture he was considering the place of natural history in education and weighing its value to laymen of cultivation. As in "Each and All," written during this same year, he celebrated "the effect of Composition" in nature, "the contrast between the simplicity of the means and the gorgeousness of the result" (*EL* 1:73), but he also enumerated definite intellectual advances deriving from scientific studies: they restrain imitation, "the vice of overcivilized communities," and sharpen the student's power of discrimination, teaching "the difficult art of distinguishing between the similar and the same" (*EL* 1:74–75). The danger is that the devotee of natural history will come to value immediate means above ultimate ends, forgetting "the Love and Faith from which these should flow. This passion, the enthusiasm for nature, the love of the Whole, has burned in the breasts of the Fathers of Science," whose aim as Emerson saw it was to proceed "in an ever narrowing circle" toward "the elemental law, the *causa causans,* the supernatural force" (*EL* 1:80).

At its best, Emerson's own poetic prose of these years unites observation with imagination and reverence, joining poetry and religion to science as he knew it, or, in the Coleridgean terminology he was using in the 1830s, reading the language of nature with the Reason as well as with the Understanding. In the same month as his delivery of "The Naturalist" he defined *Reason* as "the highest faculty of the soul— what we mean often by the soul itself; it never *reasons,* never proves, it simply perceives; it is vision." In contrast, "The Understanding toils all the time, compares, contrives, adds, argues, near sighted but strong-sighted, dwelling in the present the expedient the customary" (*L* 1:412–13). Insofar as Emerson was routinely reading and observing throughout 1834, he would have said, he was cultivating the Understanding, but in his original thinking and writing he was responding to the promptings of Reason; the year of relative inactivity afforded him the opportunity to do both.

During May of 1834, as Emerson told his brother Edward, the Tucker family estate, which had been in the hands of lawyers, was "so far settled that I am made sure of an income of about $1200. wherewith the Reason of Mother & you and I might defy the Understanding upon his own ground" (*L* 1:413–14). As Ellen Tucker Emerson's sole heir, Waldo Emerson had by this time received cash and securities with a total value of about $11,600; in July of 1837 he would come into the remainder of his inheritance, a slightly larger figure. The practical effect of this infusion of capital was to provide the financial security he needed to settle permanently in Concord, where he was to buy his own residence in 1835. With supplementary income from preaching, lecturing, and later from publishing, he could maintain his freedom and independence. Providence indeed appeared to be showing him where and how to live, and in a wholly unforeseen way to be compensating him in some measure for the loss of Ellen three years before. At the moment, however, the Emersons seemed "pretty nearly as poor as ever," Charles wrote in May of 1834, "only Waldo does without a Profession" (*L* 1:413–14 n. 34).

iv. "The Philosophy of *Waiting*"

Once settled with Dr. Ripley at Concord, Emerson began in November of 1834 to compose his first regularly scheduled series of lectures, entitled "Biography," that was to begin at Boston in January. At this time he resolved that in his future writing he would never "utter any speech, poem, or book that is not entirely & peculiarly my work." He had no desire to repeat the "drudgery" that had gone into his earlier lectures on science or the derivative versifying of the Phi Beta Kappa poem he had delivered at Harvard in August.[10] "I will say at Public Lectures & the like, those things which I have meditated for their own sake," he promised himself, "& not for the first time with a view to that occasion." Any other practice, he felt, meant only "lost time to you & lost time to your hearer. It is a parenthesis in your genuine life" (*JMN* 4:335). Every mind, he was persuaded, "is given one word to say," and a man "should sacredly strive to utter that word & not another man's word; his own, without addition or abatement" (*JMN* 4:348–49). From this time on, therefore, he would present as a public speaker not what his audience would expect to hear but "what is fit for me to say" (*JMN* 4:372).

These affirmations demonstrate Emerson's conviction that he was ready to speak from the platform on his own terms; they do not signify that by the end of 1834 he was thinking of lecturing as his primary vocation. One consideration was the matter of finances. Sponsored courses like his projected series on biography, which was given under the auspices of the Society for the Diffusion of Useful Knowledge, yielded the speaker only twenty dollars per lecture, as he was to explain in a letter to Carlyle written after the series was completed. If a man wished to conduct his own course, renting and arranging for the necessary advertising and ticket-selling, he might do better financially, but he could also fail to recover his expenses should the series draw poorly (*CEC* 122–24).

As for his own plans, Emerson had already acknowledged to Carlyle that since returning from abroad he had been "left very much at leisure," without yet entering upon a new vocation. "It were long to tell all my speculations upon my profession & my doings thereon," he wrote in November of 1834; "but, possessing my liberty, I am determined to keep it at the risk of uselessness, (which risk God can very well abide,) until such duties offer themselves as I can with integrity discharge. One thing I believe,—that, Utterance is place enough: & should I attain through any inward revelation to a more clear perception of my assigned task, I shall embrace it with joy & praise" (*CEC* 109–110).

What Emerson told Carlyle about his profession was elaborated in an extended journal entry made a month later that summed up his continuing search for some still-undisclosed calling. At the beginning of the year he had quoted Milton's tribute to those who but "stand and wait"; in December he observed that "The philosophy of *Waiting* needs sometimes to be unfolded." Obviously pondering his seeming inaction and isolation at Concord, perhaps as he appeared in the eyes of his village neighbors or of Dr. Ripley, he began on a defensive note: "Thus he who ⟨acts⟩ is qualified to act upon the Public,if he does not act on many, may yet act intensely on a few; if he does not act much upon any[,] but from insulated condition & unfit companions seem[s] quite withdrawn into himself, still if he know & feel his obligations, he may be (unknown & unconsciously) hiving knowledge & concentrating powers to act well hereafter & a very remote hereafter" (*JMN* 4:368). But as Emerson was later to remark in "The Transcendentalist" (1841) following a brief passage of dialogue between persons who *wait* and others who *act*—to those who wait "it seems a very easy matter to answer the objections of the man of the world, but not so easy to dispose of the doubts and objections that occur to themselves" (*CW* 1:212–13). Very likely he was once again looking back on his own situation, as of 1834.

In the journal entry on *Waiting* Emerson continued by acknowledging the services rendered to others by such persons as his late brother Edward, who had died in Puerto Rico in early October, and their Aunt Mary, the mentor of their youth and still a vital presence for Waldo. Two pages later, evidently inscribed as part of this same long entry, is a closely related passage making the typically Emersonian distinction between what a man is, what he appears to be in the sight of others, and what he ought to be ideally. "I suppose the graduate underestimates the grocer," Emerson remarked, "whilst the grocer far overestimates the graduate, & so the strong hand is kept in submission to what should be the ⟨strong⟩ ↑wise↓ head. The reason why Mr Graduate's secret is kept & never any accident . . . discovers his bankruptcy & produces a permanent revolution, is, that there is a real object in Nature to which the grocer's reverence instinctively turns." That "real object" is "the intellectual man"—what Emerson was later to call "the Thinker" (*EL* 1:226) and, in "The American Scholar," "*Man Thinking*" (*CW* 1:53). The "scholar" of actual life, though he is "not that object" and may not perfectly exemplify so high an ideal, is nevertheless "its representative, & is, with more or less symptoms of distrust, honored for that which he ought to be" (*JMN* 4:370).

In this long journal entry Emerson was formulating his first extended characterization of the scholar, at once an idealization of his own aspirations as "the intellectual man" and a recognition of the disparity between the ideal and the actual. The discussion continues on a more positive note as Emerson warms to the subject, setting down the "claims" to the scholar's office in a further extended passage that he would later quarry for the thought and phrasing of "The American Scholar." In 1831 he had coveted for himself a literal "observatory & a telescope"; in 1834 he was seeing the scholar much as he would be visualized in the later oration,

The Scholar as "intellectual man"

". . . though the scholar is not that object, he is its representative." Entry of 21 [22?] December 1834, Journal A, p. 137; see *JMN* 4:370.

figuratively "cataloguing obscure and nebulous stars of the human mind" (*CW* 1:62). The scholar of 1834 is already a moral astronomer: a "Watcher" set on a tower "to observe & report of every new ray of light in what quarter soever of heaven it should appear." Society should receive his findings "eagerly & reverently."

But though the Watcher's office is "open to all men," the passage continues, and

The Scholar as Watcher

"His office is to cheer our labor as with a song by highest hopes." Entry of 21 [22?]
December 1834, Journal A, p. 140; see *JMN* 4:372.

though all men "see their interest in it," very few are inclined "to adopt it as their
vocation," for most men are called to other forms of the world's work (*JMN*
4:370–72)—or, as Emerson was to say in the oration of 1837, men in the social state
function not only as scholars but as farmers, professors, engineers, priests, states-
men, producers, and soldiers (*CW* 1:53). "A small number of men," however,

> have a contemplative turn & voluntarily seek solitude & converse with themselves ↑a
> work↓ which to ⟨many⟩ most persons has a ⟨sta[l]e prison savor⟩ ↑jail-smell↓. This
> needs a ⟨rare &⟩ peculiar constitution, a dormancy of some qualities & a harmonious
> action in all, that is rare. It has its own immunities and also its own painful taxes like
> the rest of human works. But where it is possessed, let it work free & honoured, in
> God's name. It is our interest as much in the economical way as that the pin or the
> chaise maker should be free[,] & in a moral & intellectual view far far oh infinitely
> more. Every discovery he makes[,] every conclusion he announces is tidings to each
> of us from our own home. His office is to cheer our labor as with a song by highest
> hopes. (*JMN* 4:372; cf. *CW* 1:62–63)

This analysis of the Watcher and his function made in December of 1834 not
only anticipates "The American Scholar"; it is also reminiscent of another journal

passage written ten years earlier, when as a would-be minister Emerson was weighing his strengths and weaknesses in talent and personality against the qualities expected of a preacher and pastor. Although his initial emphasis in the entry of 1834 was on contemplation and solitude rather than public service, his emerging definition of the scholar's role moved toward a recognition of certain reciprocal obligations between himself and society. The Watcher is both "to observe & report," to see and to say; the public is to receive his findings "eagerly & reverently." The Watcher's withdrawal into solitude, like Emerson's own fruitful rustication in Newton and Concord, is in preparation for some unspecified form of future action "upon the Public." While "hiving knowledge & concentrating powers" in the present, the scholar as Watcher is thus girding himself "to act well hereafter," however remote the time for action may ultimately be. Thus he exemplifies, like Emerson himself in 1834, the "philosophy of *Waiting.*" Being representative to society of "the intellectual man," the Emersonian scholar must be left free to make his own discoveries as an observer or see-er of spiritual truth, and in his own good time to report to the rest of mankind his conclusions as a thinker and would-be actor.

3. BIOGRAPHY AND LITERATURE, 1835

---❖---

We wish to hold these fellow minds as mirrors before ourselves to learn the deepest secret of our capacity.
—Emerson's lecture on George Fox, delivered on 26 February 1835 (*EL* 1:165)

Emerson's concern with the scholar as both observer and actor is reflected in his six lectures on biography, a series delivered in Boston early in 1835 before the Society for the Diffusion of Useful Knowledge. As the editors of the *Early Lectures* observe, he had known Plutarch's *Lives* from childhood and had for some time been thinking of a "modern Plutarch" (*JMN* 4:35). Moreover, "the idea of history as the lives of great men and of the great man as an example of good action were basic to his early thinking" (*EL* 1:94).

In the introductory lecture of the course,[1] which struck the keynote of the series, Emerson offered a number of touchstones for testing the true worth of any man (no women were discussed). What are his aims? Is he earnest, unselfish, good-humored? Is he free of local prejudices? Can he move the minds of others? Does he believe in supernatural influence? Judged by such standards, some supposedly great men would clearly fall short of true greatness, despite their worldly achievements and historical eminence. Such a man was Napoleon (*EL* 1:424), a figure otherwise excluded from these early lectures who would turn up again a decade later as Emerson's representative man of action and power. Throughout the intervening years, just at the time when Emerson was developing his self-image as a scholar, he would devote many pages of his journal to the contrasting figures of Napoleon and Goethe. Goethe, designated as "the Writer" in *Representative Men* (1850), he was later to call "the one efficient source of influence" in the 1830s;[2] during these same years Napoleon haunted his imagination as a repellent yet persistently attractive type that he was finally to characterize as "the Man of the World." In *Representative Men* he placed Napoleon and Goethe as the complementary "halves" of nineteenth-century life (*CW* 4:156).

The early lectures on biography, which are not as schematized as *Representative Men*, do not systematically juxtapose contemplative or intellectual figures with men of action and power; instead, they study contrasting tendencies within single individuals who combined contemplation with action. During the 1830s Emerson hoped to achieve just such a combination in his own life. In 1834 he had written of his "Watcher" as having an inherent obligation "to act upon the Public"; the five persons examined in his lectures of early 1835 are all great men of thought who in their several ways also fulfilled the Emersonian ideal of public action. One of them, Martin Luther, is specially named as "a scholar or spiritual man." Both the lectures on biography and the subsequent series on English literature mark significant stages in Emerson's developing conception of the Scholar, who now appears variously as a poet, philosopher, or historian who views the material world metaphorically, as symbolizing the spiritual world, and as a Thinker who both thinks and speaks for Universal Man. These ideas would figure prominently during the next two years in both *Nature* and the oration of 1837 on "The American Scholar"; in the oration he would refer to "action" as one of the primary "resources" of the Scholar.

i. The Scholar as "student of Man"

Although it is not certain whether Emerson himself chose the general topic for the series on biography or was following a suggestion of the sponsoring organization, the five subjects of the individual lectures were clearly of his own selection. In a journal entry of 29 October 1834 he listed four of them: Michel Angelo Buonaroti, John Milton, Martin Luther, and George Fox (*JMN* 4:328)—an artist, a poet, and two religious leaders, all known at least in part for their writing. During his visit to Italy Emerson had admired Michelangelo's work as a painter, sculptor, and architect, and more recently he had been studying his life, poetry, and philosophy as well. Milton and Luther, both Protestant rebels, had been much in his mind when he was beginning to think of leaving the ministry, and at the time of his decision in 1832 he was reading a history of the Quakers and taking notes on the life of George Fox. The Quakers' rejection of what Emerson called "the use of the outward ceremony" of the Lord's Supper (*EL* 1:181–82) prefigured his own break with his congregation over that same issue. The fifth figure, Edmund Burke, whom Emerson respected both for his eloquence and for his high principles as a statesman and man of affairs, was not among the original nominees for discussion. Burke seems to have been added by late December of 1834 (see *JMN* 4:376), just at the time when the lecturer was privately recognizing "action upon the Public" as an essential obligation of a scholar. In the lives of these five men, all self-reliant and courageous in defense of their ideals and convictions, Emerson obviously saw personal analogues. As a lecturer, however, he proposed to speak not subjectively, or even as the biographer of particular men, but generically, as "the student of Man" (*EL* 1:165, 176). The conception of Universal Man was to play an increasingly important part in Emerson's later thinking.

Despite his continuing interest in science, Emerson did not choose a scientist as the subject of even one of these new lectures. Much as he revered such men as Newton, Linnaeus, Davy, and Cuvier, whom he had recently praised collectively as "the Fathers of Science" in his lectures on natural history (*EL* 1:80), his concern now was with minds of a different stamp. Though a man such as Luther lacked "fitness to receive scientific truths," his learning being admittedly antiquated, he qualified for treatment in the new series as "a scholar or spiritual man"—a noteworthy Emersonian apposition (*EL* 1:131, 127). The 1835 lecture depicts Luther as a scholar-leader who "achieved a spiritual revolution by spiritual arms alone" (*EL* 1:127). In so acting upon society Luther illustrates Emerson's conviction that "the true scholar" deals with intangibles rather than material facts; his "treasures," according to the journal, are "poetry, religion, philosophy" (*JMN* 4:297).

Ideally, even the naturalist "in his severest analysis" ought to be a poet, Emerson had argued in his lectures on science—or rather, ought to "make the Naturalist subordinate to the Man" (*EL* 1:81). But the science of the day, preoccupied as it was with recording facts (*EL* 1:225) or with mere description and classification, failed in his judgment to perform the very task he had identified as its "greatest office": "to explain man to himself" and show him "his true place in the system of being" (*EL* 1:23). To study science "humanly," as Emerson himself wished to do (*JMN* 5:169), meant effecting a marriage between natural history and human history (*JMN* 4:311); it required turning from observation of particular natural facts to perception of general scientific laws, in the manner of Newton (*EL* 1:80); finally, in his view, it meant going on to show that natural laws "express also an ethical sense" (*JMN* 4:254). Properly speaking, this meant leaving the province of the naturalist for that of the moral philosopher, as Emerson himself would be doing after 1834, when his own thinking concerned itself more and more with universal principles rather than individual instances.

Emerson appears to have written concurrently on Luther and Michelangelo, finishing his lecture on Luther first but preferring to read it only after speaking of the expressive artist (*L* 1:435). The life of Michelangelo, he told his audience, corresponded with his fame; in the four fine arts of painting, sculpture, architecture, and poetry Michelangelo "strove to express the Idea of Beauty. This was his nature and vocation" (*EL* 1:100). Luther, another idealist, was also "a Poet but not in the literary sense," Emerson declared (*EL* 1:132). Milton, the subject of the fourth lecture, is of course the preeminent writer of the group, and it is Milton who stands out in the series as the figure closest to Emerson's evolving archetype of the Scholar—the writer, the moralist, the spiritual man who is more than a secluded and inactive student. Milton in his love of moral perfection had long been a man for Emerson to emulate, as he acknowledged in his journal during the voyage to Italy; here in this lecture Milton receives Emerson's praise for exemplifying as well as delineating a "heroic image of man" (*EL* 1:150).

Like Luther, Milton played the double role Emerson coveted for himself: that of "an accomplished scholar" who was also a noteworthy public figure, a man able to act upon others "by an influence purely spiritual" (*EL* 1:146, 149). Milton appeared to him not only as a great poet but as a dedicated truth-seeker, an idealist whose opinions were "formed for man as he ought to be," and what the lecturer called "a consistent spiritualist, or believer in the omnipotence of spiritual laws" (*EL* 1:159, 160); *spiritualism* and *spiritual laws* were both to become key terms in Emerson's thinking. Moreover, Milton was not only a writer; he was a teacher, as Emerson himself wished to be. "Better than any other," the lecturer affirmed, he "discharged the office of every great man, namely, to raise the idea of Man in the minds of his contemporaries and of posterity,—to draw after nature a life of man, exhibiting such a composition of grace, of strength, and of virtue, as poet had not described nor hero lived. Human nature in these ages is indebted to him for its best portrait" (*EL* 1:149). "The idea of Man" would be central to Emerson's own delineation of the American Scholar.

The late Stephen Whicher saw "an early sketch" of the Scholar in the lecture on George Fox, which seemed to him "the most personal" of the series.[3] But Emerson did not present Fox as a scholar, it must be noted, though he applied the term to both Luther and Milton. Unlike any of the other four figures treated in these lectures, Fox possessed no personal or social advantages; his great strength and source of power Emerson traced to "the Religious sentiment," which for Fox "was in the place of all, was father, mother, friends, house, and land" (*L* 1:165–66). Sensing that vitality had gone out of the religion of his day, Fox countered the formalists and stirred common men and women like himself by preaching that universal creed Emerson called "the first philosophy." Its essence, according to the lecture, is "the doctrine of the infinitude of Man as seen in the conviction that his soul is a temple in which the Divine Being resides"—or, more simply, the faith that "God is within us" (*EL* 1:180–81). There is a close affinity between Emerson's own religious thought and the Quaker sense of an Inner Light; "the infinitude of the private man," he was to say in later years, is the "one doctrine" of all his lectures (*JMN* 7:342). The tribute to Fox specifically recalls the central idea of his sermon to the Second Church in 1833 after his return from Europe: that a faith in the God Within would prove the answer to persons seeking a new basis for belief at a time of revolution in religious opinion.

After Emerson had lectured on Fox in February of 1835, he had one more figure left to treat, Edmund Burke. In writing on Burke, however, he was much less impassioned. Burke did not appear to him as a spiritual man in the same sense as Fox or Luther or as an artist like Milton or Michelangelo; in Emerson's view Burke could "never compare" with Francis Bacon either in literary merit or as "an observer and legislator for the human intellect" (*EL* 1:188). But Burke qualifies as a philosopher, or more accurately as "the *philosophical politician*," a man who "brought principles to bear upon the public business of England" (*EL* 1:189). Among men devoted merely to political expediency Burke was clearly exceptional; among orators, though he could not be classed as naturally eloquent, given his harsh voice, he again stood out as "the founder and head" of the modern school of "philosophic eloquence" (*EL* 1:200)—and on this last score alone he no doubt won Emerson's sincere admiration.

Although none of Emerson's five subjects was either a scientist like Newton or a man of action and power in the Napoleonic manner, he held that all of them possessed great force of character and brought notable benefits to humanity in their own day and since. Each in his individual way was an idealist, and in that sense all were spiritual men, believing in the reality of intangible things and acting upon others through nonmaterial means. Michelangelo, though he dealt with tangible substances, served the idea of Beauty; Burke, a working politician, was nevertheless a man of principle who brought philosophic ideas to bear on the legislative process. Of the five, Emerson at this time probably felt the closest kinship with George Fox and John Milton: Fox for his faith in the Inner Light and Milton for acting out his own heroic image of Man. Both were teachers, one of religion and the other of moral excellence, as Emerson also wished to be.

The admiring tribute to Milton looks forward in subject and theme to Emerson's next series of lectures, the course on English literature that he began in Boston in November of 1835. Besides confirming him in his belief that there was an audience for lectures on topics that he himself wanted to discuss, the course on biography helped him to move from the realm of natural history into the even more congenial world of books and reading, where he had long been at ease and at home. There would be other series to follow, all centering on topics of his own choosing.

ii. "My nature & vocation"

In January of 1835, just as Emerson was completing the first of his lectures on biography, he became engaged to marry Lydia Jackson of Plymouth. Their acquaintance had been relatively short, and after their engagement they had much to learn about one another and many decisions to make about their future life together. One major issue was the question of where to live. Emerson insisted that they settle not in a city but in some country town such as Concord, and certainly not in Plymouth. "Plymouth is streets," he declared in a letter to his fiancée at the beginning of February; "I live in the wide champaign." Why the country? Because, as Emerson explained, he was a writer, and as a writer he needed the inspiration that only direct contact with nature could provide. For the first time since his resignation from his pastorate in Boston, the former minister had now openly professed a new calling. Echoing the phrasing of his lecture on Michelangelo, whose "nature and vocation" was "to express the Idea of Beauty," he continued: "I am born a poet, of a low class without doubt yet a poet. That is my nature & vocation" (L 1:435).

For Emerson to specify his calling as that of a poet may at first seem to contradict his earlier statements about vocational choice, or at least to restrict his literary aspirations to writing in verse. But he was using the term *poet* in a broader sense, as when he had declared that naturalists should be poets and that Luther as an idealist was indeed a poet. What he meant, both in his earlier statements and in 1835, is explained in this same letter:

My singing voice be sure is very 'husky,' & is for the most part in prose. Still am I a poet in the sense of a perceiver & dear lover of the harmonies that are in the soul & in matter, & specially of the correspondences between these & those. A sunset, a forest, a snow storm, a certain river-view, are more to me than many friends & do ordinarily divide my day with my books. Wherever I go therefore I guard & study my rambling propensities with a care that is ridiculous to people, but to me is the care of my high calling. (L 1:435)

The Emersonian poet may indeed write "for the most part in prose." Elsewhere in Emerson's writings of 1835 the poet appears to be equivalent to such other ideal figures as "the philosopher,"[4] "the orator," and even more generally "the man of genius." As Henry Nash Smith rightly observed, such terms "are to some extent interchangeable." When contemplating "the harmonies that are in the soul & in matter" the poet must evidently be a studious Naturalist and also a Teacher and a Watcher as well—to recall those other roles Emerson had been assuming in 1833 and 1834. Most comprehensively, of course, he will be a Scholar. Later in 1835, as Emerson began drafting his winter lectures on "English Literature," he would use the terms *scholar* and *writer* as virtual synonyms.

In this same eventful year of 1835, when Emerson for a second time became engaged to marry, declared himself a writer, and ultimately persuaded Lydia Jackson that they should settle permanently in Concord, he also expressed his continuing intention of publishing a book—not by printing his recent lectures or poems but by writing the volume that had been taking form in his mind for at least three years: as a study of "the first philosophy," a "book about nature," or perhaps as both. In January of 1835 he thought of writing and printing "a discourse upon Spiritual and Traditional Religion" (L 1:431); in May it was to be "a book on spiritual things"—"Essays" that would "mend Montaigne," "take the hint of nature," and address "the young American" (JMN 5:40–41).[5] Such essays would inevitably embody Emerson's "primal philosophy," that "fragmentary highest teaching" he had recently thought of treating in a public lecture (JMN 4:354–55).

In June, very likely with the projected book in mind, Emerson undertook another partial restatement of his philosophical principles. For this purpose he brought together in Journal RO Mind (JMN 5:269–76) relevant journal entries from as early as August 1832 and as recent as the early months of 1835. By "the First Philosophy," Emerson explained here, he meant "the original laws of the mind."

↑It is the Science of what *is*, in distinction from what *appears*.↓ It is one mark of them that their enunciation awakens the feeling of the Moral sublime, and *great men* are they who believe in them. They resemble great circles in astronomy, each of which, in what direction soever it be drawn, contains the whole sphere. So each of these . . . implies all truth.

These laws are Ideas of the Reason, and so are obeyed easier than expressed. They astonish the Understanding and seem to it gleams of a world in which we do not live. (JMN 5:270)

Later paragraphs in this sequence of entries treat the human mind in its relation to divinity, emphasizing the distinction between Reason and Understanding that so impressed Emerson in the 1830s and taking account once again of the mind's alternating states of action and inaction.[6] Although this material, like his earlier statements of "the First Philosophy," never coalesced into a single finished essay, he did develop these same topics during the next few years: first in *Nature* and his lectures of 1836–1837 on "The Philosophy of History," then in "The American Scholar" in 1837 and the Divinity School Address in 1838. By late June of 1835, in a letter to his friend Frederic Henry Hedge, Emerson further described his projected volume as "a book of Essays chiefly upon Natural Ethics," planned "with the aim of bringing a pebble or two to the edification of the new temple whilst so many wise hands are demolishing the old" (*L* 1:447). It was probably for this book on "Natural Ethics" that a few weeks later, in a journal entry of 6 August, he proposed "one of these days to write a chapter on Literary Ethics or the Duty & Discipline of a Scholar" (*JMN* 5:84)—a subject he was to address both in "The American Scholar" and more directly in the oration of 1838 specifically entitled "Literary Ethics."

In going on to say, with reference to the projected "chapter," that one of the scholar's emblems should be "the camel & his four stomachs," Emerson was applying a remark about reading and digesting lawbooks that had come from his brother Charles: "what law he reads in the morning he puts into the first stomach till evening; then it slides into the second" (*JMN* 5:84; cf. 4:381). Throughout the summer of 1835, as his impending marriage in September approached, the scholar-poet was likewise reading and digesting varied materials for a diverse schedule of public addresses and lectures. "Sometime in August," he told Hedge, "I am to read a discourse . . . on the means of inspiring a taste for English Literature—or some kindred topic. Then in September I am to read an Historical Discourse on the 200th anniversary of the settlement of Concord. And in the winter I must give 8 or 10 lectures"—his new course in English literature (*L* 1:446–47). Meanwhile he was actively gathering ideas for what he would refer to in 1836 as the "Sermon to Literary Men which I propose to make," "the Sermon to scholars," and "the scholar's Ethics" (*JMN* 5:164, 167, 187).

iii. The Scholar as Man of Letters

As Emerson read and prepared during the summer of 1835 for his more immediate speaking engagements he also entered preparatory notes and extracts in a copybook that he labeled *L*, writing in two sequences—front to back and back to front. The first sequence, "L Concord," assembles material for his projected "Historical Discourse"; the second, "L Literature," looks forward to the winter lecture series. At the beginning of the latter sequence, on a page headed "Materials for Lectures, Nov. 1835." and facing another page of cross references to relevant passages in his journal, Emerson introduced "The character of the scholar" as a

"The character of the Scholar"
Undated entries prior to November 1835, Notebook L Literature, p. 3; see *JMN* 12:35–36.

topic to be considered for the winter course, which was to begin at Boston in early November (*JMN* 12:35–36). The latest journal entry cited on these facing pages is dated 2 August 1835;[7] the pages themselves may well have been inscribed either just before or just after Emerson's journal entry of 6 August proposing a chapter on "the Duty & Discipline of a Scholar." Certainly the idea of the Scholar was much in his mind during that month; his address "On the Best Mode of Inspiring a

Correct Taste in English Literature," given at the annual meeting of the American Institute of Instruction at Boston on the 20th, is really a discourse about scholars and their education.

In the opening paragraph of this August address Emerson develops the proposition that no "mechanical means" will suffice to promote any such "spiritual end" as the development of literary taste: physicians cannot manufacture one drop of blood, nor can "colleges make one scholar nor the best library a reader." Division of labor within human society—another topic to which Emerson would return in 1836 and 1837—is ordained by the Providence that "appoints sailors and soldiers as well as poets from the cradle and makes strong hands separate from strong heads." Thus Emerson accepts the general conviction that "we cannot make scholars. They must be born" (*EL* 1:210)—just as he had affirmed a few months before that he himself had been "born a poet."

The address then offers the familiar Emersonian separation of the real from the apparent in distinguishing "natural scholars" from a "much larger class" guided to literature only by "the custom of the day." Men who would become soldiers if born during a military age become speculators in a community given to trade; in "a reading community" they may even become "men of letters," though never real scholars: "Sciolists are never nearer scholars than hypocrites are to saints" (*EL* 1:210–11). "The main action of every lover of letters," Emerson continues, "will of course be spent" on the class of natural scholars and not dilettantes or pedants. To develop such true scholars, he now holds, is to serve society, because these men are meant for leadership: "In bringing a scholar into acquaintance with himself and his proper objects we render all men such a service as he does to an army who nominates Washington or Napoleon to the Command in chief" (*EL* 1:211). This affirmation is in consonance with Emerson's belief that life's purpose is "to acquaint a man with himself"; the new emphasis on the scholar as an active leader of mankind, like the five men celebrated in his earlier lectures on biography, is a measure of the movement of Emerson's thought since he had formulated his "philosophy of *Waiting*" late in 1834.

Emerson's preoccupation with the character of scholars continued in the later months of 1835 following his discourse in Boston, his "Historical Discourse" in Concord on 12 September, and his marriage to Lydia Jackson two days later. His first notes in Notebook L Literature for the November lectures had introduced the Scholar both as he appeared ideally in the January lectures—"working with invisible tools to invisible ends"—and as he is seen in actuality through less sympathetic eyes: by other men he is "supposed an idler, or worse, brainsick: defenceless to idle masons & clerks, that have done nothing all the day, pounce on him fresh for wasting [time] at night." And on the same page appears this seminal passage:

> Set Men upon thinking & you have been to them a god. The whole of History is poetry; the globe of facts whereon they tread, is bullion to the scientific eye: the

meanest life is a thread of empyrean light. You have to convert for them the dishonored facts ⟨on⟩ which they know, into trees of life, their life into a garden of God by
suggesting the Principle which classifies them. (*JMN* 12:36)

In making this latter entry Emerson was being both retrospective and prospective. Two years before, in "The Uses of Natural History," he had explained to his
audience how scientific knowledge "will make the face of the earth significant to
us: it will make the stones speak and clothe with grace the meanest weed," for
"there is not an object in nature so mean or loathsome . . . but a knowledge of its
habits would lessen our disgust, and convert it into an object of some worth;
perhaps of admiration. Nothing is indifferent to the wise" (*EL* 1:16–17). The key
words in this earlier passage are *knowledge*, a noun, and *convert*, an active verb that
held a special meaning for Emerson. Now the would-be scholar ("You") must apply
in this same spirit what he has come to know so as to "convert . . . dishonored facts
. . . into trees of life." In January of 1836 Emerson was to incorporate the entire
paragraph into an extended journal entry on the scholar in which the personal
pronoun disappears and "You have to convert" becomes "Scholar converts" (*JMN*
5:117).

How was this essential conversion to be effected? As Emerson had recently
written in the journal, "Every day's doubt is whether to seek for Ideas or to collect
facts. For all successful study is the marriage of thoughts & things. A continual
reaction of the thought classifying the facts & of facts suggesting the thought"
(*JMN* 5:72). This characteristic observation recalls his earlier remarks about contemporary science: lesser men are content with merely assembling facts, but true
scientists such as Newton ascend through classification from factual knowledge to
apprehension of "the elemental law" (*EL* 1:80). What enables great thinkers to do
this is their power of imagination: "The Imagination is Vision, regards the world as
symbolical & pierces the emblem for the real sense," Emerson had written (*JMN*
5:76). As the imaginative see-er, or poet, who reads languages—including the
language of nature—symbolically, the scholar will behold "the whole of History"
as poetry; his "scientific eye" will recognize as precious the natural facts on which
all men tread but whose value few men recognize. To the heightened perception
of an Emerson (or a Whitman), "the meanest life" in the grass underfoot will thus
reveal "a thread of empyrean light."

The ability to marry thoughts with things and so present vision in terms that
other men and women can readily apprehend is necessary to the scholar: the see-
er as say-er must "convert *for them* the dishonored facts which they know, into trees
of life, their life into a garden of God by suggesting the Principle which classifies
them." This idea of an imaginative transformation or conversion of life into truth,
of experience into art, is central to Emerson's conception of how the scholar
creates. He would develop the idea more fully, first in his lectures on literature and
later in the "Philosophy of History" series of 1836–1837 and in "The American
Scholar."

The more immediate objective, Emerson's winter lectures of 1835–1836, is the focus of his further notes in Notebook L Literature. An undated entry "On the Nature of literature" reflects his thinking about both science and art since his visit to Europe. Literature, he writes, is "founded . . . in the belief of occult but universal relations between man & nature: in the belief that man exists to noble ends: in the belief of God." It is of interest not merely to the few; as "the public Depository of the Thoughts of the human race" it is "every man's interest." Why then do makers of literature sometimes arouse antagonism? Only because they are confused in the popular mind with those "sciolists" Emerson had previously distinguished from true scholars. "The blacksmith & the truckman have an interest in keeping the poet free from common cares↑, and would too↓. It is only ignorant or interested men who tax learning." All men are indebted, however indirectly, to some "divine thinker" for originating "the truths & sentiments in common circulation among us" (*JMN* 12:49–50; cf. *EL* 1:230).

A subsequent notebook entry on "The Character of the Man of letters" (*JMN* 12:50–51) brings together a series of extracts that Emerson quarried from his earlier journals and lectures on a variety of figures, including himself—both in his own person and in his idealized role as Scholar.[8] Here, it is the scholar as writer or man of letters who represents for him "the intellectual man"; in this entry and in the subsequent lectures he also equates the scholar with "the Bard—an omniscient teacher" and "the Thinker"; in "The American Scholar" he would ultimately see the Scholar in his "right state" as "*Man Thinking*" (*CW* 1:53). The concept of Universal Man, as previously noted, was already in his mind by this time; as recently as 7 November 1835 he had written that "the fact of the identity of human nature" is an advantage to "the Spiritual man" (*JMN* 5:107), and here he affirms that the man of letters "knows all by one" (*JMN* 12:51). Perhaps this principle of "identity"—"the many in one or Multitude in Unity" (*EL* 1:101)—applies also to the seeming interchangeability of terms used by Emerson as he explored his Protean "nature & vocation."

Between 1833 and 1835, as the preacher in the pulpit became also a secular lecturer and public orator, the Emersonian student had metamorphosed into a teacher, the would-be naturalist had turned into a professing poet who also wrote in prose on religion and philosophy, and "the true scholar"—appearing first as a reader—had soon aspired to be a maker of literature himself. Early in 1835, when after his year of "*Waiting*" Emerson declared himself a poet, he was simply saying openly that he had determined on a literary vocation, broadly and freely interpreted. Through the remaining months of that year, seeing at last where and how he was to live, he rechristened his new wife "Lidian," settled with her in their own house in Concord, and began establishing himself not only as a lecturer and orator but as a practicing author. The notes on literature and the man of letters look forward both to the new lecture series and beyond it: to the book on "Natural Ethics" that he would publish in 1836 as *Nature* and to his growing conception of the Scholar as Representative Man.

iv. The Scholar as Thinker

In addressing basic questions about the nature of literature and the character of the man of letters Emerson came to another inevitable issue, the matter of language. His earlier lectures on science had considered nature as itself a language and as a source of vocabulary for communicating spiritual truth; the most original of the ten lectures in his course on English literature carry his thinking about language and communication considerably further.

The new lecture series opened on 5 November 1835 and continued—with one exception in early December—until 14 January 1836. Despite Emerson's earlier resolution to do only original writing and speaking, several of the lectures draw heavily on secondary materials for necessary historical background; this is especially true of the second and third of the series, "Permanent Traits of the English National Genius" and "The Age of Fable." Three authors are treated individually in the succeeding lectures: Chaucer, Shakespeare (in two lectures), and Bacon; others are discussed in groups. Approached in the light of the speaker's own commitment to a literary vocation, the most rewarding segments of the course are the introductory discussion, which provides a theoretical framework for everything that follows, and the generous treatment of Shakespeare, Emerson's preeminent poet.

In the opening lecture, drawing not only on preliminary entries in Notebook L Literature but more broadly on ideas already developed in his lectures on science, Emerson attempts some necessary definitions. Literature itself, he declares, may appropriately be thought of as "the books that are written. It is the recorded thinking of man" (EL 1:218; cf. JMN 12:51–52). The medium of man's thinking is his language, defined functionally as "a naming of invisible and spiritual things from visible things. The use of natural history is to give us aid in supernatural history. The use of the outer creation is to give us language for the beings and changes of the inward creation" (EL 1:220; cf. CW 1:18). Emerson had said as much in 1833; now, in a key passage, he goes considerably further. In its infancy, he holds, language "is all poetry; or, all spiritual facts are represented by natural symbols."

Although recognizing that this statement no longer holds good for the language of most men and women in modern society, Emerson nevertheless affirms that the true masters of language—the "poets, orators, and philosophers"—are those who "most sharply see and most happily present emblems, parables, and figures" (EL 1:221). They do so through imaginative conversion of things into thoughts.

> Especially is it the office of the poet to perceive and use these analogies. He converts the solid globe, the land, the sea, the sun, the animals into symbols of thought: he makes the outward creation subordinate and merely a convenient alphabet to express thoughts and emotions. This act or vision of the mind is called Imagination. It is that active state of the mind in which it forces things to obey the laws of thought; takes up

all present objects in a despotic manner into its own image and likeness and makes the thought which occupies it the center of the world. Lear thinks no evil can come to any man but through daughters. The intensity of thought gives the speaker the right to take hold of every high and vast thing as in common moods he uses familiar and trivial objects to explain his meaning. (EL 1:224)

In adapting this passage for use in his first lecture on Shakespeare and later in *Nature* (CW 1:19–20),[9] Emerson added his characteristic distinction between an imaginative and an unimaginative mind: "one conforms things to its thoughts and the other conforms its thoughts to things."[10] The imaginative mind "views all nature as fluid and impresses its own character thereon"; the unimaginative mind "views nature as rooted and fast" (EL 1:291; cf. CW 1:31); for the lecturer himself, nature appears unmistakably dynamic. It was in the very spirit of these quoted words that Emerson had declared himself by nature and vocation to be a poet— which is to say, a man of imagination who sees nature as flowing and uses the language of analogy and symbol, drawn from nature, in his speaking and writing.

As Emerson's earlier address to the American Institute of Instruction distinguishes true scholars from ordinary readers,[11] so the initial lecture of the new course on literature sets forth his conviction that there are two orders of writers. The genuine scholar, he had already observed, shows himself a philosopher in his plan of study, as Schiller had said, and not merely a "trader in science & literature" or a hired "workman for the booksellers" (JMN 6:107; 5:93);[12] instead, he will display that "meek self reliance" Emerson believed to be "the law & constitution of good writing." By contrast, the mere journeyman writer, thinking only "to sing to the tune of the times, . . . to be the decorous sayer of smooth things, to lull the ear of society," must "lay aside all hope to wield or so much as to touch the bright thunderbolts of truth which it is given to the true scholar to launch & whose lights flashes through ages without diminution" (JMN 5:92–93).

In the journal this now-familiar characterization of "the true scholar" had embodied Emerson's own growing aspirations as a writer, but in the lecture he preferred to speak in terms of still another related idealization: those "august geniuses" who "make up the body of English literature." To these worthies he applies the very phrases from the journal he had used with reference to the scholar, with his "bright thunderbolts of truth." As the natural scholar ranks above mere readers, so the true scholar-as-writer stands forth here in the company of men of genius as a modern Milton: a truth-teller, a Teacher, a leader pointing to the future, since "the office of a great genius" is "to guide the future, not follow the past" (EL 1:231–32).

In so beginning his new lectures Emerson was entering another phase of his search for a calling and his exploration of the role of American Scholar. During the closing months of 1835, with increasing confidence in his natural endowments, he clearly felt himself destined to be enrolled in that order of writers which guides and inspires mankind. His consideration of the scholar in his function as poet and "maker of literature" embraces his earlier conception of the true or ideal scholar as the "intellectual" and "spiritual" man. The writer's aim, he now declares, is "nothing less than to *give voice to the whole of spiritual nature* as events and ages unfold it, to record in words the whole life of the world." Emerson then poses a series of questions in which the maker of literature is specifically equated with still another idealized figure: "the Thinker." "What interest have men" in literature? "Is it made for a few? Is it made only for the Makers? Who are the Makers? and for whom do they work? What service is rendered us by the Thinker, or man of letters, and in what manner?" (*EL* 1:226). Emerson's answer to these questions, though cast in terms of the writer as poet, philosopher, and historian rather than specifically as a scholar, directly anticipates his later definition of the Scholar himself in his "right state" as "*Man Thinking.*"

The answer begins, moreover, with a significant restatement of a basic Emersonian conception—that of one generic Man comprising all particular or individual men—that would soon be adapted for a key passage of *Nature:*

> It is in the nature not of any particular man but of universal man *to think;* though the action of reflexion is very rare. The relation between thought and the world, of which I have spoken, is not fancied by some poet, but stands in the will of God, and so is free to be known by all men. It appears to men, or it does not appear. But there it is. He who perceives it, and every man, whilst he perceives it, is a poet, is a philosopher. To perceive it, is to take one's stand in the absolute, and consider the passage of things and events purely as a spectacle and not as action in which we partake. This the poet, this the philosopher, this the historian does. The habit of men is to rest in the objects immediately around them, to go along with the tide, and take their impulse from external things. The Thinker takes them aside and makes them see what they did as *in dumb show.* (*EL* 1:226; cf. *Nature, CW* 1:22)

Emerson's "Thinker" is thus a see-er, or, in his earlier figure, a "Watcher," but he is more than a detached observer. By perceiving, by reflecting, and by causing other men to see, he acts not merely for himself or for men like himself, but in the service of all mankind: in the words of the lecture, "the great Thinker thinks for all; and all have a property in his wisdom" (*EL* 1:229). In "The American Scholar" of 1837 and again in "The Poet" of 1844 Emerson would enlarge on this very theme: a scholar, an orator, a poet is *representative;* he thinks and speaks for all men—for *Man.* Let him then remain for a time the quiet Watcher and practice "the philosophy of *Waiting.*" Or, in the consonant words of "The American Scholar," let him maintain his silence and steadiness, adding "observation to observation, patient of neglect, patient of reproach," biding his own time until he can satisfy "himself alone" that "he has seen something truly." When at last he is prompted by "instinct" to "tell his brother what he thinks"—to *say* as well as to *see*—he will be acting upon the public. What is more, by following the principle that the Scholar ideally "knows all by one" he will learn a new lesson reassuring to himself: "in going down into the secrets of his own mind, he has descended into the secrets of all minds," for—as their representative—"he is the complement of his hearers" (*CW* 1:63).

II

LIFE INTO TRUTH

Every man's condition is a solution in hieroglyphic to those inquiries he would put. He acts it as life, before he apprehends it as truth.

—Introduction to *Nature* (*CW* 1:7)

The scholar of the first age received into him the world around; brooded thereon; gave it the new arrangement of his own mind, and uttered it again. It came into him—life; it went out from him—truth.

—"The American Scholar" (*CW* 1:55)

4. *NATURE,* 1836

◆

> The first in time and the first in importance of the influences upon the mind is that of nature. . . . The scholar must needs stand wistful and admiring before this great spectacle. He must settle its value in his mind. What is nature to him?
>
> —"The American Scholar" (*CW* 1:54)

Early in 1836, scarcely more than a week after Emerson's lecture series on English literature had closed in Boston, he was actively planning a new composition that would involve his developing conceptions of the ideal Scholar and of the practicing scholar's day-to-day functioning in society. It was probably on 22 January, in his current Journal B, that he began to assemble a collection of extracts from his earlier writings concerning scholars (*JMN* 5:116–17). The initial observation in this journal about the Scholar as working "with invisible tools to invisible ends" had previously been set down in slightly different words among his preliminary notes for the lectures on English literature. Most of the other items had been collected in Notebook L Literature during the autumn of 1835, and several of the extracts had been used in later pages of the notebook or in the lectures themselves to characterize the scholars in their alternative role as men of letters. Here, however, the figure under discussion is not "the writer" or "the Thinker" but simply "the Scholar."

Holding that literature is the concern not merely of a few persons but of mankind in general, Emerson had said in 1835 that in setting other men "to think" the scholar as writer must "convert for them the dishonored facts which they know, into trees of life, their life into a garden of God by suggesting the principle which classifies them." Now, after recalling these same words, he adds a rhetorical question which a scholar is evidently to answer with affirmative demonstrations: "We ⟨stand⟩ ↑build↓ the sepulchers of our fathers: can we never behold the Universe as new and ↑feel↓ that we have a stake as much as our predecessors[?]" In this challenging question of 1836, which echoes a famous remark by Daniel Webster,[1] is the germ of that notable paragraph standing at the very beginning of Emerson's first book, calling for a new and direct vision of God and nature and "an original relation to the universe":

> Our age is retrospective. It builds the sepulchres of the fathers. It writes biographies, histories, and criticism. The foregoing generations beheld God and nature face

128

The Scholar works with invisible tools to invisible ends. So passes for an idler or worse; brain sick; despised to idle carpenters, masons, & merchants, that having done nothing most laboriously all day pronounce on him fresh for spoil at night. [p. 60. 47] Character founded on natural gifts as specific & as rare as military genius; the power to stand beside his thought, or, to hold off his thought at arm's length & give them perspective; to form in him well 'imo; he studies the art of solitude (scrabble p. 60) he is gravelled in every discourse with common people (J 1833 p 119) He shows thought to be infinite wh. you had thought exhausted (see above p. 60) There is a real object in nature to wh. ye grocer turns, ye intellectual man (J 1833 p 137)

praestantia novat
Plurima, mentis opes amplas, subjectore fervans
Omnia vestigans sapientum docta reperta.
Empedoc. de Pythag. Cudworth II. 271

So Bacons globe of crystal & globe of matter
The Thinker like Glauber keeps what others throw away
He is aware of Gods way of hiding things in light,
Also he knows all by one (See above p 17)
Set men upon thinking & you have been to them a god. All history is poetry; the globe of facts whereon they trample is bullion to ye scientific eye. Meanest life a thread of empyrean light Scholar converts for them ye dishonored facts which they know, into trees of life; their daily routine into a garden of God by suggesting ye principle which classifies ye facts. We build the sepulchers of our fathers: Can we never behold the Universe as new and that we have a stake as much as our predecessors

The Scholar's "invisible tools"
Undated entry of January 1836, Journal B, p. 128; see JMN 5:116–17.

to face; we, through their eyes. Why should not we also enjoy an original relation to the universe? Why should not we have a poetry and philosophy of insight and not of tradition, and a religion by revelation to us, and not the history of theirs? Embosomed for a season in nature, whose floods of life stream around and through us, and invite us by the powers they supply, to action proportioned to nature, why should we grope among the dry bones of the past, or put the living generation into masquerade out of its faded wardrobe? The sun shines to-day also. There is more wool and flax in the fields. There are new lands, new men, new thoughts. Let us demand our own works and laws and worship. (*CW* 1:7)

i. "A true theory of nature & man"

Since the years of his Boston pastorate, when Emerson had complained in his journal that "we worship in the dead forms of our forefathers" (*JMN* 4:27), he had been preaching "a religion by revelation," emphasizing not institutions, creeds, and past miracles but the perpetual miracle of man's being itself, inspired in the living present by the God Within. This notion of man's "infinitude" is the essential teaching of his "First Philosophy." In 1833 and 1834 he had lectured on nature as "a metaphor or image of the human Mind" (*EL* 1:24) and had written verse about nature that deserves to be called "a poetry of insight," as in his projected book he intended to offer "a philosophy of insight." The new work would be his most comprehensive report to date of what as "Watcher" he had learned to see in nature since his decision that in order to be a good minister he had to leave the ministry.

Throughout the 1830s, moreover, Emerson had continually turned away from institutions and works of the past in favor of new creation in the present with an eye to the future. "The office of a great genius," he declared in opening his lectures on English literature in November of 1835, is "to guide the future, not follow the past" (*EL* 1:232). A "true theory of nature & man," he wrote in 1836, first in his journal and again in *Nature*, must have in it something "progressive" (*JMN* 5:182; *CW* 1:36), something that looks to the future; so in an early sermon he had declared it to be "the blessed law of heaven" that "our nature should be progressive" (*YES* 54). This same theme was to persist. "The American Scholar" (1837) characterizes the "active soul" of the true scholar as "progressive"; it is not content to "stop with some past utterance of genius" but exemplifies originality and creativity in the present (*CW* 1:56–57). The Divinity School Address (1838) declares that in religion "a true teacher" will likewise "show us that God is, not was; that He speaketh, not spake" (*CW* 1:89). The most radical expression of this aspect of Emerson's thought was to come in 1841: as "an endless seeker with no Past at my back," he would declare in "Circles," "I unsettle all things." That essay gives fair warning to the timid: "Beware when the great God lets loose a thinker on this planet. Then all things are at risk" (*CW* 2:188, 183).

A scholar, as Emerson had repeatedly said by 1836, is not only a thinker himself but the cause of thinking in others. In his social function he is able to "set men upon thinking" by converting or transforming "dishonored facts," and he does this "by suggesting the principle which classifies" them. Emerson amplifies the idea in his journal, returning again and again to the idea of *classifying* facts through the application of *principles*. "Every man must live upon a principle," he wrote in 1835. "I have seen the adoption of a principle transform a proser into an orator. Every transgression that it makes of routine makes man's being something worth. . . . Every principle is an eye to see with" (*JMN* 5:70–71). When Emerson sought to "behold the Universe as new" instead of building "the sepulchers of our fathers" (JMN 5:117) he was advocating new principles of living and thinking that would shift men's "angles of vision" (cf. JMN 10:76, 133, 173; W 12:10), enabling them to see their world with what he liked to call the eye of Reason.[2] He was once more making the Coleridgean distinction between the Reason and the Understanding. "Every fact studied by the Understanding is not only solitary but desart. But if the iron lids of Reason's eye can be once raised, the fact is classified immediately & seen to be related to our ⟨school⟩ nursery reading & our profoundest Science" (JMN 5:85).

Although ready-made systems of classification are offered to us under various titles, such as history, science, religion, economy, and taste, Emerson held that "in every man the facts under these topics are only so far efficient as they are arranged after the law of *his* being" (JMN 5:89). "Instead of studying things without the principles of them," he had written in 1833, "all may be penetrated unto within him" (JMN 4:84). Within every individual, within the sphere of one's own experience, lies the existential answer to his or her questions about the self and the world. Emerson developed this idea in his Introduction to *Nature*, following a conversation of 5 March 1836 with his brother Charles, who "instructed" him that "every man has certain questions which always he proposes to the Eternal, and that his life & fortune, his ascetic, are so moulded as to constitute the answers, if only he will read his consciousness aright" (JMN 5:135). In Emerson's own phrasing, "Every man's condition is a solution in hieroglyphic to those inquiries he would put. He acts it as life, before he apprehends it as truth. In like manner, nature is already, in its forms and tendencies, describing its own design" (CW 1:7).

A scholar's basic task, then, is to understand his own experience in nature by learning to see it with the eye of Reason. He can then classify it, arrange it, and ultimately convert it into living thought and art for the benefit of others. "The scholar of the first age," Emerson was to say in 1837, "received into him the world around; brooded thereon, gave it the new arrangement of his own mind, and uttered it again. . . . It was—dead fact; now, it is quick thought" (CW 1:55). Given "an eye to see with," the scholar of any age will follow the same procedure.

Although Emerson apparently began in January of 1836 to write a book about the Scholar, as the journal entry on that subject suggests, the volume that finally took form in 1836 as *Nature* includes no specific "chapter" about a scholar's "Duty & Discipline"; in fact, even the word *scholar* occurs only once within its pages, in an incidental reference to "a scholar's garret" (CW 1:45). Why Emerson's intention seems to have shifted is unclear; perhaps he was thinking of a separate composition that would deal specifically with a scholar's duties. The focus of the argument in *Nature* is rather on "what thought, what Revelation," a scholar as "Watcher" *sees* (JMN 5:135)—or rather on *how* he sees, and how others through his teaching and example may learn to see as well. In this sense the book is very much a part of Emerson's thinking about the scholars and ultimately *the* Scholar.

Emerson's *Nature* is indeed a book about vision, the process of vision, the uses of vision. Metaphors of sight and seeing both open and close his discussion, which begins with the charge that in a "retrospective" age we behold God and nature only through the eyes of our forefathers but which ends, in a forward-looking chapter called "Prospects," by invoking the "wonder" that "the blind man feels who is gradually restored to perfect sight" (CW 1:45). The component chapters—even subdivisions of chapters—are arranged so as to appeal in turn to the senses of the reader (particularly his visual sense), then to his Understanding, and ultimately to his Reason. In this way the book fosters that movement from sight to insight which Emerson took as the sign of a man's spiritual growth and self-fulfillment. "A man is a method, a progressive arrangement," he liked to say with Coleridge (CW 1:84);[3] in both its form and its function a book setting forth a new vision of the universe, "a true theory of nature & man," must also be progressively arranged.

ii. Transparence and Opacity

"Our American literature and spiritual history," Emerson once declared, are "in the optative mood" (CW 1:207), and his own Introduction to *Nature* is an illustration. "Undoubtedly we have no questions to ask which are unanswerable," according to this sanguine declaration of faith. "We must trust . . . that whatever curiosity the order of things has awakened in our minds, the order of things can satisfy." Recognizing in 1836 that men are still "so far from the road to truth, that religious teachers dispute and hate each other," as he had long been noting with regret, and that "speculative men"—presumably in the Latin sense of Watchers on a tower, as Emerson saw himself—"are esteemed unsound and frivolous," as the scholar had been said to pass "for an idler or worse," he is nevertheless confident that "the most abstract truth is the most practical." "The truth of truth," he had written earlier, is "that it is selfevident[,] selfsubsistent" (JMN 4:45); in the Introduction he declares that "a true theory," including that theory of nature which is the aim of all science, "will be its own evidence," and once it is discovered it "will explain all phenomena" (CW 1:7–8).

The customary distinction between subject and object made by philosophers becomes in Emerson's phrasing the difference between ourselves and "all that is separate from us, all which Philosophy distinguishes as the NOT ME, that is, both nature and art, all other men and my own body." He minimizes the popular differentiation between nature and man's art, arguing that all of mankind's operations on external nature taken together "are so insignificant . . . that in an impression so grand as that of the world on the human mind, they do not vary the result." This deliberate passing over of human artifice means that Emerson intends to concentrate in *Nature* on "essences unchanged by man; space, the air, the river, the leaf" (CW 1:8). But although he does not explicitly say so in the Introduction, his real concern is less with external nature in itself than with nature in relation to man—that "original relation" he was seeking to foster—and the "impression" it makes on the human observer. "The scholar," as he would put it in 1837, must settle the *value* of nature *"in his mind*. What is nature *to him?"* (*CW* 1:54; emphasis added). The orientation of *Nature* is unabashedly subjective. "Montaigne said, himself was all he knew," Emerson had remarked while in Italy. "Myself is much more than I know, & yet I know nothing else" (*JMN* 4:68). To study nature, he would argue in "The American Scholar," is to understand human nature, so that "the ancient precept, 'Know thyself,' and the modern precept, 'Study nature,' become at last one maxim" (*CW* 1:55).

The basic difficulty is that most men and women do not— perhaps can not— really *see* the world around them, even with their natural eyes, let alone with the spiritual insight that Emerson wished to demonstrate and encourage. "To speak truly, few adult persons can see nature," he writes in chapter 1 of *Nature*. "Most persons do not see the sun. At least they have a very superficial seeing. The sun illuminates only the eye of the man, but shines into the eye and heart of the child." This passage repeats a point Emerson had been making since his lecturing on science: both the senses and the affections must be brought into play if one would deal adequately with nature. "The *lover* of nature is he whose inward and outward senses are still truly adjusted to each other; who has retained the spirit of infancy even into the era of manhood. His intercourse with heaven and earth, becomes part of his daily food" (*CW* 1:9; emphasis added). Emerson is not merely echoing the commonplaces of Romantic theory about nature and childhood that he could have picked up in reading Wordsworth and Coleridge (cf. *JMN* 5:363); he is speaking out of his own experience, just as he does again and again throughout *Nature*.

Being both naturalist and poet, "in the sense of a perceiver & dear lover of the harmonies that are in the soul & in matter" (*L* 1:435), Emerson drew sustenance from living in a country town, where so prosaic an experience as crossing the Concord common on a December day had brought him "a wild poetic delight" (*JMN* 4:355). He recalled the occasion in *Nature* in order to show that men and women of his generation in New England villages could also "enjoy an original relation to the universe" without merely existing on the accumulated spiritual capital of their forefathers: "Crossing a bare common, in snow puddles, at twilight, under a clouded sky, without having in my thoughts any occurrence of special good fortune, I have enjoyed a perfect exhilaration" (*CW* 1:10).

As Jonathan Bishop has remarked, the episode as described in *Nature* comprises "a concrete image" of a time when "New England weather is at its ugliest, the villages at their meanest," while the voice of the speaker "obliges you to take another look at the potential beauty of mean situations."[4] This is finely said; Bishop exactly captures both Emerson's intention and his rhetorical strategy. But "the 'bare common' sentence," as Bishop calls it, is only part of what Emerson is driving at. Moving his discourse out of the village into the nearby woods, he goes on to say in the same paragraph that there, beyond the streets and houses, is "perpetual youth," and within these unsettled "plantations of God" an adult, whatever his age, "casts off his years, as the snake his slough," and returns "to reason and faith" (*CW* 1:10).

This is to affirm that nature effects a transformation in the adult, restoring that true adjustment of the "inward and outward senses" which Emerson had associated with childhood, and thereby bringing about a recovery of religious faith as well as renewed psychological wholeness. It is in this context that he makes a celebrated declaration:

> There I feel that nothing can befal me in life,—no disgrace, no calamity, (leaving me my eyes,) which nature cannot repair. Standing on the bare ground,—my head bathed by the blithe air, and uplifted into infinite space,—all mean egotism vanishes. I become a transparent eye-ball. I am nothing. I see all. The currents of the Universal Being circulate through me; I am part or particle of God. The name of the nearest friend sounds then foreign and accidental. To be brothers, to be acquaintances,— master or servant, is then a trifle and a disturbance. I am the lover of uncontained and immortal beauty. In the wilderness, I find something more dear and connate than in streets or villages. In the tranquil landscape, and especially in the distant line of the horizon, man beholds somewhat as beautiful as his own nature. (*CW* 1:10)

Within this latter portion of the paragraph is "the notorious eyeball sentence," as Bishop calls it, which is "perhaps the best known sentence of Emerson's among readers who wish to make fun of him." Among Emerson's own contemporaries, Christopher Pearse Cranch "unerringly picked this image out to caricature"; Cranch's drawing, Bishop writes, "shows the one concrete picture these words irresistibly muster up, a preacherly eyeball staring into the heavens.[5] The *doctrine* about the Soul's relation to Nature, so far as it is paraphrasable, is the same as that of the 'bare common' sentence. But the speaker, the I, is innocently absurd at best; the rhythm is a coarse parody of the watchful casualness of the other sentence; and the language is vapid."[6]

Bishop is right in saying that readers have had difficulties with Emerson's "transparent eye-ball"—especially unsympathetic readers; any classroom teacher of *Nature* has encountered his share of them. But Bishop surely errs in arguing that in the latter part of this paragraph Emerson is merely repeating what he had already said about the implications of the preceding experience on the common. *There,* on the bare common, his speaker is still in the village; *here,* when he is made to leave the village for the woods, the level of discourse significantly shifts along with the setting, and the ensuing episode takes place on what Emerson would later call another "platform" of experience.

With these developments, moreover, the speaker himself is in fact transformed. He is now "uplifted into infinite space"; he transcends what he has previously been as consciousness of personal identity gives way to a new sense of identification: the perceiver becomes one with what he sees; there are no longer the usual impediments between the "I" and "the Universal Being"; in short, he declares himself "part or particle of God."[7] The "eye-ball" may well be an unfortunate image for what

"Standing on the bare ground, — my head bathed by the blithe air, & uplifted into infinite space, — all mean egotism vanishes. I become a transparent Eyeball."

Nature, p. 13.

The Scholar as "transparent eye-ball"
Drawing by Christopher Pearse Cranch, made at Cincinnati, 12 January 1839.

Emerson seeks to convey here. But this part of the paragraph clearly involves more than "exhilaration." The clue to that further transformation Emerson wishes to suggest is the single word *transparent*—a word that plays a significant role in other passages of *Nature* that also treat moments of supreme vision.[8] The paragraph is artfully arranged to build upward to an epiphany, or what Emerson himself liked to call—in the manner of Xenophanes, Cudworth, and Goethe—"an $\epsilon\nu$ $\kappa\alpha\iota$ $\pi\alpha\nu$."[9]

Emerson repeatedly uses images drawn from sense experience as analogies for psychological processes that transcend the operations of the senses themselves. There is another apposite example in a journal passage of June 1836 characterizing his new friend Bronson Alcott, whose inflexible self-centeredness Emerson contrasted unfavorably with his own openness and receptivity. Alcott, he wrote, was constitutionally unable to interest himself in the ideas of others, spoken or written, and therefore could not "delight in Shakspear" as Emerson himself did. "I go to Shakspear, Goethe, Swift, even to Tennyson, submit myself to them, *become merely an organ of hearing,* & yield to the law of their being. I am paid *for thus being nothing* by ⟨a new⟩ an entire new mind & thus a Proteus I enjoy the Universe through the powers & organs of a hundred different men" (*JMN* 5:178; emphasis added). The speaker in *Nature* has an analogous experience, except that he becomes "merely an organ of *seeing*"—the "eye-ball"; he too is "nothing" himself as "all mean egotism vanishes," and for the time he also "yields" himself to "powers & organs" not his own. What Emerson means in the journal passage is that he could be stimulated and invigorated by surrendering himself to the thinking of other minds—though inspiring books, as he was to say in "The American Scholar," are "for the scholar's idle times" (*CW* 1:57). "Hearing" the words of Shakespeare requires receptivity; speaking for oneself demands active creation. For his scholar, Emerson wanted both: "The alternations of speaking & hearing," he believed, "make our education" (*JMN* 5:98).

When Emerson employed sight imagery he carried the same ideas still further. Essential truth, self-evident truth, "is light," he had written in 1832—and "You don't get a candle to see the sun rise" (*JMN* 4:45). *Light* is his characteristic sign of the divine presence: "God is, not was," is what he means by writing in the Introduction to *Nature* that "The sun shines to-day also" and in chapter 1 that "every night" the stars "light the universe" (*CW* 1:89, 7, 9). "One might think the atmosphere was made *transparent* with this design," he writes, "to give man, in the heavenly bodies, the perpetual presence of the sublime" (*CW* 1:8; emphasis added). As for man himself, Emerson had remarked in a sermon of 1832 that "the genuine man" assumes no veil and needs none: "He is *transparent*" (*YES* 185). According to a relevant journal entry of 1835, a man of true perception is endowed with a mind that operates like "a lens formed to concentrate the rays of the Divine laws to a focus which shall be the personality of God," and this focus "falls so far into the infinite that the form or person of God is not within the ken of the mind" (*JMN* 5:83–84).

That same perceiving lens reappears in *Nature* as the "transparent eye-ball," which is also directed toward the infinite: there the see-er is figuratively "uplifted into infinite space" to become "part or particle of God." When the outward senses are dominant, as a later chapter of *Nature* has it, the universe seems "not transparent but opake" (*CW* 1:43). But when the inward eye of Reason is opened, then both perceiver and perceived become entirely transparent, "and the light of higher laws . . . shines through." This transformation from opacity to transparence takes place whenever the eye is "instructed" (*CW* 1:22; cf. *JMN* 4:96)—that is, when the perceiver has learned to grasp the true "relation between the mind and matter," as Emerson writes in the chapter on "Language"; in an earlier version of the same sentence he had said "between thought and the world" (*EL* 1:226). To the perceiving eye, according to the journal, "All things" are transparent; they "show God through every part & angle" (*JMN* 5:176). Thus "transparency" applies equally to what is seen and to the individual who sees, his perception of their essential oneness betokening the operation of the divine spirit that animates them both.

The idea of transparence is further elaborated in a key passage of chapter 6, "Idealism," which delineates the role of Reason in the process of learning to see man and nature as they exist beyond the realm of the senses:

> To the senses and the unrenewed understanding, belongs a sort of instinctive belief in the absolute existence of nature. In their view, man and nature are indissolubly joined. Things are ultimates, and they never look beyond their sphere. The presence of Reason mars this faith. The first effect of thought tends to relax this despotism of the senses, which binds us to nature as if we were a part of it, and shows us nature aloof, and as it were, afloat. Until this higher agency intervened, the animal eye sees, with wonderful accuracy, sharp outlines and colored surfaces. When the eye of Reason opens, to outline and surface are at once added, grace and expression. These proceed from imagination and affection, and abate somewhat of the angular distinctness of objects. If the Reason be stimulated to more earnest vision, outlines and surfaces become transparent, and are no longer seen; causes and spirits are seen through them. The best, the happiest moments of life, are these delicious awakenings of the higher powers, and the reverential withdrawing of nature before its God. (*CW* 1:30)

"Grace and expression," Emerson says here, "proceed from imagination and affection." As early as his lecture on "The Uses of Natural History" in 1833 he had spoken of the "power of *expression*" in external nature that makes it a resource for metaphorical language (*EL* 1:24); in 1834 he had insisted in "The Naturalist" that nature will reveal its ultimate laws only to the man who approaches her with "Love and Faith," not with an indiscriminate appetite for undigested facts (*EL* 1:80). In 1835, beginning with his lectures on English literature, he had explained that the poet, by "converting" natural objects into "symbols of thought," makes the outward creation "merely a convenient alphabet to express thoughts and emotions. This act or vision of the mind is called Imagination" (*EL* 1:224). Now in "Idealism" he defines imagination as "the use which the Reason makes of the material world"

(*CW* 1:31)[10] and in "Prospects" he goes on to assert once again that nature demands affection as well as perception from those who would see her truly.

In "Prospects," it will be noted, Emerson writes in terms of restoration and recovery, both of natural vision and of spiritual wholeness:

> The problem of restoring to the world original and eternal beauty, is solved by the redemption of the soul. The ruin or the blank, that we see when we look at nature, is in our own eye. The axis of vision is not coincident with the axis of things, and so they appear not transparent but opake. The reason why the world lacks unity, and lies broken and in heaps, is, because man is disunited with himself. He cannot be a naturalist, until he satisfies all the demands of the spirit. Love is as much its demand, as perception. Indeed, neither can be perfect without the other. In the uttermost meaning of the words, thought is devout, and devotion is thought. Deep calls unto deep.

"But in actual life," Emerson continues, "the marriage is not celebrated."

> There are innocent men who worship God after the tradition of their fathers, but their sense of duty has not yet extended to the use of all their faculties. And there are patient naturalists, but they freeze their subject under the wintry light of the understanding. Is not prayer also a study of truth,—a sally of the soul into the unfound infinite? No man ever prayed heartily, without learning something. But when a faithful thinker, resolute to detach every object from personal relations, and see it in the light of thought, shall, at the same time, kindle science with the fire of the holiest affections, then will God go forth anew into the creation. (*CW* 1:43–44)

iii. Discipline

"To write a very little takes a great deal of time," Emerson remarked to his friend Hedge in a letter of 14 March 1836. Although he had been doing more writing than reading during the winter months, he had "little to show for his solid days," he confessed, chiefly because in the book under his hand he had been unable to satisfy his desire for "the beautiful in composition" (*L* 2:7). By this date he had drafted many isolated passages that would later be transferred from his journal to the manuscript of *Nature*, but he still needed a basis for organizing its component chapters and arranging them in a functional sequence.[11] A scholar, he had said in January, employs "the principle which classifies the facts," but it was late in March before he hit upon a classifying principle that would enable him to *compose* the existing materials for chapters 2 though 5: "Commodity," "Beauty," "Language," and "Discipline."[12] He found his principle by applying to nature itself his conception of a progressive ascent of spirit by way of successive levels, or platforms, of significance, writing as follows in the journal.

> Thus through Nature is there a striving 〈for〉 upward. Commodity points to a greater good. Beauty is nought until the spiritual element. Language refers to that which is to be said. . . .

> Finally; Nature is a discipline, & points to the pupil & exists for the pupil. Her ⟨nature⟩ being is subordinate; his is superior. Man underlies Ideas. Nature receives them as her god. (*JMN* 5:146, 147)

In other words, the order of chapters in his manuscript should reflect that principle of "progressive arrangement" that Emerson saw operating in nature as in human nature. "Man," he wrote in this same entry, "is an analogist," and the delight he finds in classification is "the first index of his Destiny," which is "to put Nature under his feet" by knowing her laws, or "to apprehend Nature in Ideas[.] The moment an idea is introduced among facts the God takes possession. Until then, facts conquer us. The Beast rules Man" (*JMN* 5:146).

As we know, Emerson had already worked out much of chapter 6, the long discussion of "Language," in his earlier lectures, developing the thesis advanced here: that "in a simple, double, and three-fold degree," external nature serves man as "the vehicle of thought":

1. Words are signs of natural facts.
2. Particular natural facts are symbols of particular spiritual facts.
3. Nature is the symbol of spirit. (*CW* 1:17)

Although he no doubt found it necessary to reshape some of the already existing material of "Language" to its new context, it is probable that most of his work on *Nature* during 1836 went into other parts of the book. By early April, as his journal entries indicate, he was beginning to address the issues to be covered in later chapters, particularly "Idealism" and "Spirit," which deal with nature in its ultimate relation to Deity. At the same time he was reflecting not only on the general topic of "Discipline," the subject of chapter 5, but also on "the Ascetic of the man of letters" (*JMN* 5:149)—in effect his old project of a chapter on the particular "Duty & Discipline of a Scholar."[13] When read in the light of later events his brief comments on discipline in the journal seem portentous. "A persistent & somewhat rigorous temperance," Emerson wrote on 2 April, cannot well be avoided by a man of letters—the scholar. "Saved from so many hurts & griefs, he must impose a discipline on himself. He must out of sympathetic humanity wound his own bosom, bear some part of the load of wo, and ⟨so to⟩ the most convenient & graceful to him is a quiet but unrelaxing self-command. If he accept this & manfully stablish it, it shall stablish him." But Emerson did not go on to complete the entry, being more immediately concerned with the larger design of his book about nature.

In the book, opening his planned sequence of chapters 2 through 5 with a short discussion of "Commodity" (chapter 2), Emerson began on the lowest of his successive "platforms" by considering "those advantages which our senses owe to nature." How he intended to proceed in the chapters that were to follow is suggested in "Commodity" by his assurance to the reader that this "benefit" of nature "is temporary and mediate, not ultimate, like its service to the soul" (*CW* 1:11).

According to the next chapter in the sequence, "Beauty" (chapter 3), the sight of natural forms is itself a delight, but the beauty to be seen in virtuous actions of men introduces a higher "spiritual" element, and finally, on a still higher level, perception of the beauty of the world as "an object of the intellect" is a necessary prerequisite to artistic creation (*CW* 1:13, 15, 16).

This threefold analysis is of course designed to prepare the reader for the following chapter on "Language" (chapter 4), already in partial draft. That chapter is designed to illustrate, in terms of Emerson's doctrine of correspondence between spirit and matter, what it means to see nature as poets and sages do: as an object of the intellect rather than of the senses, a transparent manifestation of higher laws made visible to the eye of Reason. But the actual composition of chapter 3 in accordance with these "three aspects of Natural Beauty," as they are distinguished in the journal, was delayed until some time after 30 May 1836, the date on which this tripartite division of his topic had first occurred to Emerson during a walk "in the wood" (*JMN* 5:166). It was not until mid-June that he drafted key passages of the fifth chapter, "Discipline," to follow his treatment of "Language." For approximately six weeks of April and May he was obliged to suspend work on the book under the pressure of unexpected events.

Since January of 1836, when he gave the last lecture of his course on English literature, Emerson had been repeating selected lectures by invitation at Salem, Massachusetts, and also at Concord and Cambridge. On 18 April he had gone to Salem for what was to be a two-week course of lectures on biography and literature, drawn from his two Boston series of the previous year. But word from Concord of Charles Emerson's sudden illness obliged him to interrupt his lecturing on 22 April in order to accompany his brother as far as New York on a projected trip southward to a warmer climate. Leaving Charles in New York with their brother William and their mother, Waldo returned to lecture in Salem on 2 May, only to learn that Charles, after seeming to improve, had taken a turn for the worse. He again set out for New York a few days later, this time escorting Charles's fiancée, Elizabeth Hoar of Concord, but his brother died suddenly on 9 May, before their arrival—another victim of tuberculosis, like Ellen and Edward.

Waldo Emerson was deeply affected by this new loss, as various friends attested after seeing him at the funeral and in ensuing weeks at home. He and Charles had been particularly close, especially during their residence in Concord, and Waldo was remodeling his new house to provide quarters for Charles and Elizabeth after their marriage. Writing to his wife from New York, Waldo declared that Charles had been a soul "so costly & so rare that few persons were capable of knowing its price. . . . I determined to live in Concord, as you know, because he was there, and now that the immense promise of his maturity is destroyed, I feel not only unfastened there and adrift but a sort of shame at living at all." The best of his own strength, he said, had come from Charles. "How much I saw through his eyes. I feel as if my own were very dim" (*L* 2:20).

Returning to Concord with his mother and Elizabeth Hoar, Emerson slowly found himself again, as he wrote in the journal, remembering "states of mind that perhaps I had long lost before this grief" (*JMN* 5:160). He set about collecting his reminiscences of Charles and attempting to assess just what their close companionship had meant to him, acknowledging once more that Charles had sharpened his own vision: "The eye is closed that was to see Nature for me, & give me leave to see," he wrote on 16 May (*JMN* 5:152). Ideas discussed by the two brothers often found their way into Waldo Emerson's writing, which "borrowed color & sometimes form" from Charles, Waldo felt, to the degree that "it would not be possible for either of us to say, This is my thought, That is yours" (*JMN* 5:151). Now with Charles gone he had to take what consolation he could from balancing his gains and losses according to his stoical doctrine of compensation (*JMN* 5:171).

Elizabeth Hoar came to stay for a time with the Emersons, and in attempting to insulate one another against their grief she and Waldo agreed in conversing that "we are no longer permitted to think that the presence or absence of friends is material to our highest states of mind." Emerson's characteristic comment on their talk is close to what he said in the "transparent eye-ball" passage of *Nature* about one's necessary detachment from even the name of his dearest friend and brother. "In those few moments which are the life of our life when we were in the state of clear vision, we were taught that God is here no respecter of persons[,] that into that communion with him which is absolute life . . . our dearest friends are strangers. There is no personëity in it" (*JMN* 5:170). This observation anticipates what he would say in his later writings about the impersonality of the Deity and the fugacity of human relationships.[14] But meanwhile there was work to be done. It is the scholar's duty to apply his philosophy to his own condition, and as a writer, to convert facts and events into truth. So Emerson had held; now it was his task once again to draw what wisdom he could from knowing and losing a loved one, as in that other dark period following the loss of Ellen five years before.

The turning point came for Emerson on 14 June 1836 as he walked in "the oracular woods" near Concord and formulated once again a familiar lesson now seemingly taught by nature itself: that man can and must "conform to his character" not only "particular events but classes of events & so harmonize all the outward occurrences with the states of mind" (*JMN* 5:174). Obviously he was searching for some spiritual principle that would show him the meaning of events—not just the death of Charles but the untimely passing of Ellen and Edward as well—and so enable him to transform even the fact of their loss into some tree of life, as he had said the scholar must do for the good of other men and women. This same idea of "conforming" whole classes of events so as to harmonize them with one's own mind is carried over into the fifth chapter of *Nature*, the discussion of "Discipline" he had projected in April before the death of Charles, and there his thesis is both echoed and expanded (*CW* 1:25).

The beginning of chapter 5 reaffirms what Emerson had said after returning from Europe in 1833: Providence, through "the simple occurrences of every day," is "always instructing those who are in the attitude of scholars" (*YES* 194, 197); thus the conditions of earthly life, according to *Nature*, "give us sincerest lessons, day by day," that "educate both the Understanding and the Reason" (*CW* 1:23). The chapter as a whole comprises Emerson's considered response to even the harsher facts of life as he had come to know them, from the remembered poverty of his childhood to the recent death of Charles. For its conclusion (*CW* 1:28–29), he drew upon a long paragraph of "pleasing sober melancholy truth" that he had entered in the journal following his meditations in the woods on 14 June. Then he had both posed and answered the renewed question of what it means to have—and inevitably to lose—a beloved friend, a "real person" sent by God "to outgo your ideal." Once "enamoured" of that person and inspired by him to "a new measure of excellence" and "a confidence in the resources of God,"

> you will readily see when you are separated, as you shortly will be[,] the bud, flower, & fruit of the whole fact. As soon as your friend has become to you an object of thought, has revealed to you with great prominence a new nature, & has become a measure wherof you are fully possessed to guage & test more, ⟨then expect⟩ as ⟨t⟩his character become[s] solid & sweet wisdom it is already a sign to you that his office to you is closing[;] expect thenceforward the hour in which he shall be withdrawn from your sight. (*JMN* 5:174)

In "Discipline" and again in other chapters of *Nature* are a number of revised journal passages originating in recollected hardship or grief. All were rewritten, as this one was, in the impersonal terms that Emerson used in his published writings to mark a conversion from particular facts of an individual life into general truths pertaining to all men and women.[15] "It were a wise inquiry for the closet," runs a sentence in the chapter called "Prospects," "to compare, point by point, especially at remarkable crises in life, our daily history, with the rise and progress of ideas in the mind" (*CW* 1:44). This sentence too was originally drafted on 14 June 1836 (*JMN* 5:175), when Emerson returned from the woods to practice a scholar's duty and discipline by resuming his work on *Nature*.

iv. Spirit

Late in June of 1836, in a letter to his brother William, Emerson was able to announce that his "little book" was at last "nearly done" although still not ready for publication. "Its title is 'Nature.'" The contents being brief, as he explained, his intention was "to follow it by & by with another essay, 'Spirit'; and the two shall make a decent volume" (*L* 2:26). Since mid-June, besides finishing the chapter on "Discipline," he had also composed the concluding chapter, "Prospects," which expresses the fundamental Emersonian conviction that empirical science alone "is apt to cloud the sight, and, by the very knowledge of functions and processes, to bereave the student of the manly contemplation of the whole" (*CW* 1:39).

Again elaborating on themes first explored in his earlier lectures on science,

Emerson goes on to argue in "Prospects" that man learns of his relation to the world not "by any addition or subtraction or other comparison of known quantities, but . . . by untaught sallies of the spirit, by a continual self-recovery, and by entire humility." Physiologists and naturalists, in their preoccupation with means rather than ends, are too often content with facts rather than principles, Emerson charges. He himself "cannot greatly honor minuteness in details, so long as there is no hint to explain the relation between things and thoughts; no ray upon the *metaphysics* of conchology, of botany, of the arts"; no effort, that is, to show the relation of natural and artistic forms to the mind and to "build science upon ideas." The "half-sight of science" must therefore be supplemented by the insight of poetry, and "a wise writer" possessing both sight and insight will seek to answer "the ends of study and composition . . . by announcing undiscovered regions of thought, and so communicating, through hope, new activity to the torpid spirit" (CW 1:39, 40, 41).

The opening paragraphs of "Prospects," which epitomize Emerson's reasons for identifying himself as a poet rather than the naturalist he had once thought of becoming, serve to introduce a longer section of the chapter ascribed chiefly to an unnamed "Orphic poet" who had written in praise of spirit and its "remedial force" (CW 1:41–42, 44–45). This material had first taken form in the journal between 22 and 24 June 1836 immediately following a visit from Bronson Alcott, who returned again to Concord for three days on the 15th. Some readers have identified Alcott as the "Orphic poet" of these pages,[16] which were obviously composed while Emerson was under his immediate stimulus, as even their phrasing suggests. For example, a journal entry for 22 June refers to Alcott as "a world-builder" who studies not "particular" facts but "the Whole" (JMN 5:178), and in "Prospects" Emerson himself not only calls for "contemplation of the whole" but also admonishes his reader to "Build, therefore, your own world" (CW 1:39, 45). But Emerson regarded Alcott's mind as essentially narrower and less flexible than his own, as we have seen, and was later to refer to him as "onetoned" (JMN 5:457). Although the visit of his friend certainly influenced Emerson to write in the Orphic vein, there is nothing in "Prospects" out of harmony with his own thought and style. Indeed, the exaltation of spirit in this concluding chapter is in keeping with the book's central idea—that nature is the symbol of spirit—and its theme of vision lost and recovered is poignantly close to his own recent experience following the death of Charles Emerson, already reflected more solemnly in "Discipline."

It was on 28 June 1836, just after Alcott left Concord, that Emerson wrote of his book as virtually complete, and in another letter to William early in the next month he reported that from Boston booksellers he had received an estimate of "a little more than a hundred dollars to make a handsome little book" (L 2:28). He made relatively few entries in his journal during July, when he must have been busy putting the finishing touches on his manuscript. He was probably adding more recent extracts from the journal at strategic points, as he had done in chapter 1, and supplying new transitional material, in his usual manner, wherever it seemed to be needed. By 20 July, immediately before Margaret Fuller was to arrive for her first visit with the Emersons, he informed his friend Hedge that he now "had a Chapter which I call 'Nature' in solid prose." To Hedge as to William he expressed his intention of also writing "another chapter called 'Spirit'" but only after first printing *Nature* as it then stood (*L* 2:30).

Emerson did not release the manuscript to the printer, however, until mid-August. "There is, as always, one crack in it not easily to be soldered or welded," he had written to William on 8 August, hoping that "if this week I should be left alone . . . I may finish it" (*L* 2:32). Alcott had recently made another visit, Miss Fuller was not to leave the Emersons until the 12th, Lidian Emerson was expecting their first child in October, and Waldo himself was occupied as executor of Charles Emerson's estate, which was then being probated. The "crack" he complained of was soon mended by unspecified revision of whatever stood in the manuscript between "Discipline" and "Prospects" so as to form one or both of the chapters now entitled "Idealism" and "Spirit" (chapters 6 and 7 in the published text); Emerson did not write the separate essay under the latter title that he had projected earlier. With this last problem in continuity solved, he dispatched his manuscript to the printer in time to receive the first proofsheets on 27 August (*JMN* 5:190).

Why Emerson was dissatisfied with *Nature* as it stood in early August and exactly what he did to the manuscript by way of remedy have been topics for speculation. James Elliot Cabot conjectured in 1887 that "Idealism" was the last chapter to be written, but "Spirit" may very well have an equal claim; Rusk apparently inferred that Emerson incorporated into his manuscript the material he had previously intended for a separate essay on "Spirit."[17] Both "Idealism" and "Spirit" are in fact mosaics of old and new writing. In "Idealism" the material that can be dated ranges from journal passages first written as early as 1834 and already used in lectures of 1835 to other journal material as recent as June of 1836; in "Spirit," there are slightly later journal passages, from July and even early August of 1836. But this evidence is not conclusive, since a large portion of both chapters is independent of any specific source or parallel in the journal or lectures, and there is no way to date the component material even approximately.

It is possible that during August, feeling pressed for time, Emerson simply divided an existing chapter into two, adding enough new material to sharpen his distinction between traditional philosophical idealism and what he and his friends liked to call "Spiritualism" and titling the resulting chapters accordingly. He had been formulating ideas about idealists and spiritualists in scattered journal entries at least as early as the previous February (*JMN* 5:124), and in June he had asked himself "Whether the Ideal Theory is not merely introductory to Spiritual views. It diminishes & degrades matter in order to receive a new view of it, namely this, that the world is the new fruit of Spirit evermore" (*JMN* 5:183). This question anticipates passages in what is now chapter 6, "Idealism," concerning the "degrading" of material nature and asserting its "dependence on spirit" (*CW* 1:34, 35). A related entry of 30 July similarly looks forward to the key paragraph of "Spirit":

"Man," according to the journal, "is the point where matter & spirit meet & marry. The Idealist says, God paints the world around your soul. The spiritualist saith, Yea, but lo! God is within you. The self of self creates the world through you, & organizations like you. The Universal Central Soul comes to the surface in my body" (*JMN* 5:187; cf. *CW* 1:38, quoted below).

Within *Nature* itself, taking up his familiar theme of "the senses and the unrenewed understanding" giving way to the higher perceptions of Reason, Emerson holds in "Idealism" that by "the effects of culture" the reflective individual will gradually incline toward philosophical idealism as he considers the relation between man and nature. Even mechanical shifts in his literal point of view will suggest differences between man the observer, who remains stable, and the world of nature, which appears to him as a moving and changing spectacle. The poet's imagination makes use of this spectacle to communicate his thoughts and feelings, as Emerson had repeatedly said in his lectures and again in "Language." The philosopher and the theoretical scientist work in a realm of abstraction, the world of ideas, preferring intellectual analysis to empirical observation, and so they "transfer nature into the mind" (*CW* 1:34); so too an exaltation of spirit over matter is characteristic of the teachings of religion and ethics. Hence that "noble doubt" which perpetually arises in the mind, "whether nature outwardly exists" (*CW* 1:29).

The idealist's hypothesis that "matter is a phenomenon, not a substance," is adequate "to account for nature by other principles than those of carpentry and chemistry," Emerson goes on to say in his companion chapter, "Spirit." But such a theory is nevertheless incapable of dealing with first and final causes: "Whence is matter? and Whereto?" If idealism "only deny the existence of matter, it does not satisfy the demands of the spirit," for "It leaves God out of me," thus providing no grounding in religion for ethical self-reliance. Idealism makes the solipsistic perceiver a lone wanderer in "the splendid labyrinth" of his perceptions, balking his affections by "denying substantive being to men and women" and making nature "foreign" to him without accounting for "that consanguinity which we acknowledge to it" (*CW* 1:37–38). In what he called "Spiritualism" Emerson found his answer to these objections against the "useful introductory hypothesis" of idealism. Out of "the recesses of consciousness," according to a climactic paragraph of "Spirit," the student may learn

> that the highest is present to the soul of man, that the dread universal essence, which is not wisdom, or love, or beauty, or power, but all in one, and each entirely, is that for which all things exist, and that by which they are; that spirit creates; that behind nature, throughout nature, spirit is present; that spirit is one and not compound; that spirit does not act upon us from without, that is, in space and time, but spiritually, or through ourselves. (*CW* 1:38)

This view of "spirit, that is, the Supreme Being, . . . admonishes me where the sources of wisdom and power lie": that is, *within,* as Emerson had long been saying.

Man, he declares, "has access to the entire mind of the Creator, is himself the creator in the finite." Such a confident belief, in keeping with the optative mood of the Introduction to *Nature*, "carries upon its face the highest certificate of truth." Not only does it constitute a progressive "theory of nature & man" but it also provides a basis for the ethical conduct of life—that individual world-building Emerson calls for in "Prospects": "It animates me to create my own world through the purification of my soul" (*CW* 1:38).

5. HUMAN NATURE, 1836–1837

❖

> The next great influence into the spirit of the scholar, is, the mind of the Past,—in whatever form, whether of literature, of art, of institutions, that mind is inscribed.
>
> —"The American Scholar" (*CW* 1:55)

Nature was published anonymously on or about 9 September 1836, the date on which it was first advertised for sale in Boston. Some six weeks later Emerson reported with satisfaction to his brother William that the "little book" was being received "with quite as much attention as I could have anticipated. 500 copies were gone when I inquired a fortnight since; which for a book purely literary or philosophical is a good deliverance" (*L* 2:42). Although he thought enough of *Nature* to distribute presentation copies generously among his friends and relatives, he clearly did not regard it either as a perfect work in itself or as the fulfillment of his literary ambitions. In his journal he made notes for possible "correction or enlargement" of the chapters on "Beauty" and "Language," observing that he should have stated more distinctly that "life is our inexhaustible treasure of language for thought" (*JMN* 5:257–58, 325–26). There was no immediate call for a new printing, however, and his further ideas about life and language went instead into other writings, notably "The American Scholar," the Divinity School Address, and "Literary Ethics."

At the time of the first appearance of *Nature* Emerson assured several friends that he had intended to write "something better." So he told Elizabeth Peabody, who had expressed what he called "overkind opinions" of the book but who thought it "wanted connexion"; Emerson replied dryly that in his own view "it resembled the multiplication table" (*L* 2:46). When sending a copy to Thomas Carlyle he was again depreciatory, describing the book as "an entering wedge, I hope, for something more worthy and significant. This is only a naming of topics on which I would gladly speak and gladlier hear" (*CEC* 149). Carlyle had read it with "true satisfaction," as he told Emerson, and lent his copy to others "till it is nearly thumbed to pieces." Rather than looking upon his friend's book as merely "the first chapter of something greater," Carlyle preferred to call it "the Foundation and Ground-plan on which you may build whatsoever of great and true has been given you to build" (*CEC* 157, 195). What other friends may have said about *Nature* is not known, though Alcott wrote of it in his journal as "a beautiful work" of "a high intellectual character" and "a gem throughout."[1]

i. *Nature* and the Reviewers

Nature received limited contemporary notice in both American and British periodicals, especially the organs of Unitarians and Swedenborgians. The reviewers were divided in their verdicts. Since it had been published anonymously, few of them attributed its authorship to Emerson; what they had to say about the book was closely related to their opinions concerning other writers of the day—Wordsworth and Coleridge, Carlyle and "the Transcendentalists"—with whom they associated it. A brief survey of their comments will suggest various attitudes of the day that were to affect the reception of Emerson's writings during the later 1840s and after.

In America, Orestes Brownson published a glowing review of this "singular book" in his *Boston Reformer*, noting that it "subordinates nature to spirit, the understanding to the reason, and mere hand-actions to ideas," and welcomed it as "an index to the spirit which is silently at work among us." Samuel Osgood, a young Divinity School graduate, contributed a generally favorable notice to the *Western Messenger*, a Unitarian journal edited in Cincinnati and Louisville, finding in the book "a poetry of Nature" reminiscent of Coleridge and Wordsworth. Osgood singled out the earlier chapters for special praise, but he had minor reservations about the speculative treatment of "Idealism" and some of the Orphic sentences in "Prospects."

Francis Bowen, a member of the Cambridge Divinity School faculty, was much less generous in his review for the Unitarian *Christian Examiner* of Boston. Although he was willing to grant that *Nature* was "a *suggestive* book" that offered its readers "beautiful writing" and even "sound philosophy," he clearly felt that on balance the work was fatally marred by the same vagueness, mysticism, and obscurity that he associated with Transcendentalists generally; he found these qualities especially prominent in "Spirit" and "Prospects." Bowen's opinions were very likely representative of the views of the New England Unitarian establishment—if indeed its members read *Nature* at all. His charge of obscurity was countered, however, by an unnamed writer for the *Democratic Review* of New York who recognized Emerson's authorship of *Nature*: to him it appeared as a poem composed in prose that was by no means obscure if carefully read. Although the New York writer liked the book, he also pointed to several gaps in its philosophical argument that in his judgment must disappoint even its "best lovers"—specifically, the author's treatment of the relation between matter and mind and the brevity of his chapter on "Spirit."

Among early British reviewers the reception of *Nature* was generally favorable. John A. Heraud supposed from its style that Alcott had written it; another London critic, Jonathan Bayley, took it instead to be the work of some American Swedenborgian. The Reverend David Goyder of Glasgow, a minister of the Swedenborgian Church of the New Jerusalem, also found Swedenborgian elements in the book but he nevertheless assigned its authorship to an unnamed "American Unitarian." Goyder thought *Nature* valuable enough to include the entire text in his *Biblical Assistant* (1841); his unauthorized reprinting was the first of several piracies of the book by various British publishers during the 1840s. Another New Churchman, John Westall, responded to Goyder in the *New Jerusalem Magazine* of Boston by demanding that he recall and repudiate that portion of the *Assistant* which included *Nature*—not because its printing was unauthorized but on the ground that disseminating such a work of Unitarian thinking among Swedenborgians was a "grievous error" surely "calculated to produce evil" within the New Church. (The book "is commonly understood to be the production of Mr. Ralph Waldo Emerson," Westall noted incidentally.)

The fullest treatment of *Nature* in British periodicals was written for the *Westminster Review* of London in 1840 by Carlyle's friend Richard Monckton Milnes; by this time Emerson's authorship of the book had become well known. Milnes's article, entitled "American Philosophy—Emerson's Works," emphasized the continuity of Emerson's thought as seen both in *Nature* and in his later published addresses of 1837 and 1838 that had since been sent to England in pamphlet form. Milnes too associated Emerson with "the Transcendental Philosophy" expounded by Coleridge and Carlyle but added that his distinctive form of "Idealistic Pantheism"—Milnes's term—was particularly well adapted to American popular democracy. Although Milnes could not have known Emerson's unpublished lectures on "The Philosophy of History," which were written and delivered in the fall and winter immediately following the appearance of *Nature*, there is one sentence of his review that epitomizes a central idea of both the lecture series and the later address on "The American Scholar." "The 'vox populi vox Dei,'" according to Milnes, "assumes a very special import when the 'vox populi' does not merely mean an historical utterance, but an expression of the universal Spirit, which is at once the Thought of God and the Instinct of Man." As in *Nature* Emerson had celebrated the omnipresence of spirit, so in his later lectures and addresses he affirmed its pervasive working in the mind of Man, in "The American Scholar" he would conclude that a truly democratic nation "will for the first time exist" when each of its citizens "believes himself inspired by the Divine Soul which also inspires all men" (*CW* 1:70).

ii. Spiritualism

What Brownson meant by "the spirit which is silently at work among us," and what less receptive contemporaries had in mind when they spoke of "the Transcendentalists," deserves some comment by way of introduction to Emerson's lectures on "The Philosophy of History." On 8 September 1836, immediately before the publication of *Nature*, Emerson had gone to Cambridge to attend the Harvard commencement exercises and Bicentennial Celebration. Following the ceremonies he kept an appointment with three other graduates, all active Unitarian ministers. One of these men, his friend Frederic Hedge, had invited him to meet with George Putnam of Roxbury and Emerson's cousin George Ripley of Boston. Their purpose, in Hedge's words, was to consider the "very unsatisfactory" state of opinion in contemporary theology and philosophy and to discuss what might be done by like-minded men "in the way of protest and introduction of deeper and broader views." Specifically, they wished to organize an informal "symposium." As Hedge in later years explained their thinking, its founding members objected to "the reigning sensuous philosophy, dating from Locke, on which our Unitarian theology was based," and they sought to give a wider circulation to the contrasting "spiritual" philosophy of Coleridge and Carlyle, which in Hedge's words had "created a ferment" in their minds.[2]

By the term *Spiritualism* these friends did not mean communicating with spirits on the other side of the grave, which is all that the word has come to signify in some quarters today. For them, Spiritualism expressed their conviction that the essence of reality is neither matter nor thought but *spirit.* In the words of Emerson's earlier lecture on Milton, it also represented their belief in "the omnipotence of spiritual laws" (*EL* 1: 160).[3] This conviction involved ethical corollaries as well. In a sermon of 1833 Emerson had described Christ's teaching as upholding "man's spiritual nature against the sensualism, the forms, and the crimes of the age in which he appeared," and again as "a defence of spiritualism against sensualism" (*YES* 195, 198–99); in 1834 he thanked Carlyle for "the brave stand you have made for Spiritualism" in *Sartor Resartus* (*CEC* 98).

Emerson himself distinguished the basic principles of Spiritualism from those of materialism on the one hand and from traditional philosophical idealism on the other. By *materialism* he meant both the doctrine that matter is the only reality and, in a less technical sense, the tendency to be more concerned with material success than with spiritual goals and values—the attitude he was to characterize in the familiar lines of a later poem:

> Things are in the saddle,
> And ride mankind.
>   (*W* 9:78)

By *idealism* he meant the converse of materialism, both in the popular sense of concern with ideal values and also in the more technical sense of the belief that the world as we know it is the product of human perception and abstraction rather than constituting some presumed material existence. This latter conception is what in chapter 6 of *Nature* he had called "the Ideal theory" (*CW* 1:29). He regarded philosophical idealism as unsatisfactory, chapter 7 had gone on to say, because it "does not satisfy the demands of the spirit," "Spirit" being the title of that chapter. Spiritualism rescues man from solipsism and links him with both nature and God because it sees God as spiritually present throughout His creation, which includes man and nature alike.

Emerson's habitual emphasis on God's spiritual presence, summed up in his repeated affirmation that "God is within you," suggests that his spiritualist thinking directly reflected his theological training and his experience as a Unitarian minister, being essentially religious in character rather than rigorously philosophical. There is irony in the fact that what he called "Hedge's Club" and "The Symposium" became known to the public as "the Transcendental Club," for their cardinal principle was the belief that God is *not* "transcendent," which is to say above or beyond nature, but immanent—within nature and within man. As any classroom teacher of Emerson can testify, the words "Transcendental" and "Transcendentalism" may easily confuse a student who comes to Emerson with the expectation that his writings will carry the traditional philosophical and theological implications of those terms—especially as they are used with reference to Kant and his school in Germany.

By 1836, as we know from various chapters of *Nature*, Emerson was thinking of spirit not as a mere inactive presence but as dynamic energy or force, "an instantaneous in-streaming causing power" (*JMN* 5:180; *CW* 1:43) that demands fulfillment in outward expression. "There seems to be a necessity in spirit to manifest itself in material forms," according to the key chapter on "Language" (*CW* 1:22). "Spirit, that is, the Supreme Being," is "the Creator," he declares elsewhere, and in nature it is spirit that "alters, moulds, makes" matter. "The immobility or bruteness of nature, is the absence of spirit; to pure spirit, it is fluid, it is volatile, it is obedient" (*CW* 1:38, 19, 44). In man, by analogy, spirit is likewise present as "a universal soul within or behind his individual life, wherein, as in a firmament, the natures of Justice, Truth, Love, Freedom, arise and shine. This universal soul [man] calls Reason: it is not mine or thine or his, but we are its; we are its property and men" (*CW* 1:18).

"As a plant upon the earth, so a man rests upon the bosom of God," Emerson writes in another revealing passage of *Nature*; "he is nourished by unfailing fountains, and draws, at his need, inexhaustible power. Who can set bounds to the possibilities of man? Once inhale the upper air, being admitted to behold the absolute natures of justice and truth, and we learn that man has access to the entire mind of the Creator, is himself the creator in the finite." It is not mere coincidence that Emerson wrote these words while he and his wife were expecting the birth of their first child. In the passage just quoted he also remarks that spirit acts not from without but "through ourselves, . . . as the life of the tree puts forth new branches and leaves through the pores of the old" (*CW* 1:38). In all likelihood the impending birth of young Waldo Emerson had stimulated his father's thinking—about human procreation and also about creativity in general, which is a major theme of his writing of 1836 and 1837.

Such passages as those just cited from *Nature*—the examples could easily be multiplied—constitute the immediate background of Emerson's twelve lectures on "The Philosophy of History" during the winter following publication of the book and the birth of Waldo. The first six lectures deal with various human activities and institutions deriving from the past (history, science, art, literature, politics, religion, and society); the second six turn to the contemporary scene, treating society, the trades and professions, manners, ethics, the present age, and the individual. He himself arranged for the hall, the advertising, and the sale of tickets, knowing that any resulting profit or loss would be his alone.

The course as a whole both amplified and extended the basic ideas of *Nature* in a more popular form, adapting them for oral presentation to a miscellaneous audience. Some of the component material came from journal entries drafted while he was still at work on the book. Most of the planning and writing, however, was done in October, November, and December of 1837, as we know from his further journal entries, from his working Notebook F No. 1 (printed in *JMN* 12:75–177), and from his correspondence. He chose "The Philosophy of History" as his title only after considering and rejecting several alternatives, including "Intellectual Culture" and "Omnipresence of Spirit"; still another possibility was "One Mind," a phrase that echoes as a recurrent leitmotiv throughout the course and again in "The American Scholar." All the lectures in the series are variations on a major theme of the spiritual philosophy: the apparent "necessity in spirit to manifest itself in material forms," for each of the human activities he examines is an outward expression of the spirit of man, that creator in the finite, just as external nature is a manifestation of the Supreme Being.

Among mankind, Emerson declares, "the gift of Reason" is the sign of what he called both "the Universal Central Soul" (*JMN* 5:187) and "the Universal Mind" that is antecedent to the material creation, all individuals have access through Reason to that Mind. This conception of a common spiritual bond existing not only between man and nature but also among all men, regardless of place, station, or time, underlies both Emerson's conception of history and his interpretation of the various other human creations, activities, and institutions that are examined in the lectures of 1836–1837. "There can be no true history written," he believed, "until a just estimate of human nature is holden by the historian" (*EL* 2:10).

Emerson's own philosophy of history embodies a conception of human nature that had been taking form for some time, reaching its fullest expression to date in the opening lecture of the new series. There he begins his exposition by asserting a need "to separate the idea of Man from any particular men," continuing with this extended statement:

> We early arrive at the great discovery that there is one Mind common to all individual men; that what is individual is less than what is universal; that those properties by which you are man are more radical than those by which you are Adam or John; than the individual, nothing is less; than the universal, nothing is greater; that error, vice, and disease have their seat in the superficial or individual nature; that the common nature is whole. . . .

In accordance with this "great discovery," moreover, the aim of education should be "to sink what is individual or personal in us, to stimulate what is torpid of the human nature, and so to swell the individual to the outline of this Universal Man and bring out his original and majestic proportions" (EL 2:11–12; cf. JMN 5:187).

Emerson's distinction here between what is purely individual in human nature and what is impersonal and universal is associated with his long-standing conception of man's "infinitude"—that is, the presence of God within each man as the essential spiritual basis for his self-reliance and self-realization. "This image of God in human nature," he had said as early as a sermon of 1830, "has placed a standard of character in every human breast, which is above the highest copy of living excellence. Every man has an idea of greatness that was never realized" (YES 110). Through our very conversation with one another we learn that because "our minds are made after one model," we all possess "a certain *standard idea of man*" (YES 64). Emerson's ideal of potential human greatness as reflected in this "standard idea of man" had underlain his lectures of 1835 on biography. There, as noted in chapter 3 above, he singled out John Milton for both delineating and exemplifying an image of human heroism and so raising "the idea of Man in the minds of his contemporaries and of posterity" (EL 1:150, 149). Such a conception of human nature has special implications for a scholar. To *think* "is in the nature not of any particular man but of universal man," Emerson had declared in another lecture of 1835 (EL 1:226). When the Emersonian scholar "thinks for all men," therefore, he becomes the surrogate for Man—or, in the words of "The American Scholar" (1837), the very image of *"Man Thinking"* (CW 1:53).

iii. Utterance

Religion, science, poetry, music, and philosophy are all "elements" of the One Mind, Emerson's introductory lecture of 1837 explains, and History itself is its record, its unfolding. "Religion is its self-respect; science, its insight of matter; poetry its language; music its voice; philosophy the announcement of its laws." To this One Mind "all men are born," and of it "each individual man is one more incarnation," Emerson declares, though only in a few persons is it manifestly *active* (EL 2:13, 12, 15). Each of the lectures which follow in "The Philosophy of History" series may be read as a study of man's creativity, since Emerson regarded all human enterprises as outward expressions of an inward and essentially spiritual condition. The third and fourth of the series, "Art" and "Literature," apply specifically to the arts those "common principles" he was endeavoring to demonstrate in all the lectures.[4]

"Art" in particular illustrates at least the first three of eight propositions Emerson had set down in his journal during October of 1836 as the "foundations" of his entire course. In their revised form they read as follows:

1. There is one mind common to all individual men.
2. There is a relation between man and nature so that whatever is in matter is in mind.
3. It is a necessity of the human nature that it should express itself outwardly and embody its thought. *As all creatures are allured to reproduce themselves*, so must the thought

be imparted in speech. The more profound the thought, the more burdensome. What is in will out. Action is as great a pleasure and cannot be foreborne. (*EL* 2:4; emphasis added)[5]

Thus "Art" (*EL* 2:42–54) begins with an introduction that might have opened any or all of the other lectures as well: "Every department of life" proceeds from a common source, the lecturer affirms. The human mind is in touch with this source, "with absolute truth, through thought and instinct"; at the same time it is moved to "the publication and embodiment" of thought, for "the man not only thinks but speaks and acts." The polarity between thought and speech, reflection and action, is significant here and throughout the lectures; so is Emerson's double orientation to both the absolute and the universal on the one hand and the relative and particular on the other. Those same dualities were to become even stronger in his later thinking.

Art for Emerson is a form of what he repeatedly calls "utterance." Although utterance, or outward expression of inward energy, may be either conscious or unconscious, he defines art at the beginning of the lecture as "The *conscious* utterance of thought, by speech or action, to any end" (emphasis added). "Art, universally, is the spirit creative," he continues; it will produce both "the Useful and the Fine Arts" in accordance with its immediate aims, whether "at use or at beauty." In either case, however, the personal contribution of the individual artist is necessarily subordinate: in the useful arts, to the power of nature, represented by the very materials with which he must work; in the fine arts, which aim at "beauty as an end," to "Ideal Nature."

Why is this so? Because what the artist contributes "is the least part of his work," in the words of the lecture, for the true creator of both the useful and the beautiful is spirit itself, or "the universal soul," which finds expression through the artist as its agent. Therefore the artist must "disindividualize himself, and be a man . . . through whom the soul of *all* men circulates" (emphasis added), and "an organ through which the universal mind acts." Such a conception of the relation between an artist and his art obviously differs from the idea of "depersonalized" art that would be advanced in a later century by such writers as Joyce and Eliot. In Emerson's view, we take pleasure in the several arts and observe the analogies among them because we recognize in artistic creation the operation of the very "mind that formed Nature" itself. All tangible products of the true human artist are "possible forms of the Divine mind" that the artist has "discovered and executed" rather than "arbitrarily composed," Emerson declares. It follows that for him "every genuine work of art"—note the qualifying adjective—is rooted "in the constitution of things" and has "as much reason for being as the earth and man."

Much of what Emerson had to say in "Art" is epitomized in one of his later poems, "The Problem," written in 1839 and first published in the following year. According to the poem, such architectural monuments as St. Peter's cathedral, the

Parthenon, the Pyramids, and England's Gothic abbeys were formed organically, like veritable works of nature:

> out of Thought's interior sphere
> These wonders rose to upper air;
> And Nature gladly gave them place,
> Adopted them into her race,
> And granted them an equal date
> With Andes and with Ararat.
>
> *These temples grew as grows the grass;*
> Art might obey, but not surpass.
> *The passive Master lent his hand*
> *To the vast soul that o'er him planned;*
> *And the same power that reared the shrine*
> *Bestrode the tribes that knelt within.*
>   (*W* 9:7–8; emphasis added)

Here Emerson is once again affirming that art, like mankind and like Nature itself, has its ultimate source in spirit, which employs the master artist's hand as its passive instrument; the "power" he refers to in the poem is what he would discuss in the *Essays* of 1841 as "the Over-Soul." As lecture and poem attest, his views as a spiritualist had engendered a remarkably austere conception both of art and of the individual artist.[6]

iv. Conversion

Emerson's lecture on "Literature" (*EL* 2:55–68), delivered a week later than "Art," shifts emphasis from what he regarded as the spiritual basis of artistic creativity to its psychological and sociological implications. In "Art," where many of his illustrations are taken from architecture and sculpture,[7] he had spoken more as an observer of art objects than as a creator, but in "Literature" he was able to draw on his own experience as a writer and speaker—or, as he had come to think of himself by the mid–1830s, a *scholar*. Although he regarded literary expression, including both oratory and preaching, as one of the forms of *art*—a term which he defines again at the beginning of the new lecture as "conscious utterance of thought by speech or action, to some end"—he is also aware of "a contrast of effects" in comparing literature with other artistic pursuits. Art, he says, "delights in carrying a thought into action," but literature is "the conversion of action into thought." His significant distinction between *acting* and *thinking* leads into the central section of the lecture, which is characteristically Emersonian in tone and far more original in its ideas than the lecture on "Art."

As we have already seen, the process of transformation, transmutation, or metamorphosis that Emerson commonly referred to as "conversion," as when he called literature "the conversion of action into thought," had by this time become central both to his theory of literary creation and to his conception of the ideal Scholar. The idea of such a process had been gradually taking form in his mind for some time, developing along with his ideas about scholars and their role in society. The term *conversion* itself, as pointed out in previous chapters, had emerged as early as 1833, in Emerson's lecture on "The Uses of Natural History." But when it appeared again, as in the notes he made in the autumn of 1835 for the lecture series on English literature, and in January of 1836, when he brought together in his journal a number of earlier entries on the scholar, it had clearly taken on further connotations.

In *Nature*, for example, in observing the dependence of language upon the natural world, Emerson had called language itself a form of conversion—"conversion of an outward phenomenon into a type," a symbol, of thought and feeling (*CW* 1:20). Scholars, he had repeatedly declared, serve other men by setting them "upon thinking," for a true scholar can reveal to them what they have not seen for themselves: the poetry in history and the treasure in everyday facts. Thus he "*converts* for them the dishonored facts which they know, into trees of life; their daily routine into a garden of God[,] by suggesting the principle which classifies the facts" (*JMN* 12:36; 5:117; emphasis added). This declaration of a scholar's social function looks directly forward to Emerson's announced intention in his "Philosophy of History" lectures: to demonstrate those "common principles" and "general causes" that he saw operating in all departments of human life.

In the 1837 lecture on literature, where the principle of conversion occupies a conspicuous place, Emerson illustrates the process of converting action into thought with reference to his earlier distinction between *acting* and *thinking*. "The way to touch all the springs of wonder" in another person, he remarks, is "to set before his eyes as Thought that which he is feeling and doing."

> Observe the distinction. The things we do, we think not. What I am, I cannot describe any more than I can see my eyes. The moment another describes to me that man I am, pictures to me in words that which I was feeling and doing, I am struck with surprise,—I am sensible of a keen delight. I be, and I see my being, at the same time. The soul glances from itself to the picture with lively pleasure. Behold what was in me, out of me! Behold the subjective, now objective. Behold the Spirit embodied. (*EL* 2:56–57)

"This act of delineating a thought" affects us both as pleasure and as power, the lecturer explains in succeeding paragraphs, where the argument follows directly from what Emerson had written in his journal a year earlier concerning scholars;[8] passages also anticipate what he would soon be saying to a Harvard audience about the American Scholar's function as "*Man Thinking.*" Here he observes how strongly we are attracted to anyone who, by employing the process of conversion, can make a truth or a fact appear to us as "an object of consciousness"; such a person has "a part of me; and I follow him that I may acquire myself."

Emerson's illustrations come from his experience—or his aims—as a professional speaker: the orator and the preacher should objectify through their words what listeners will recognize either as parts of themselves "which they were not yet ready to say" or "principles" which the speaker has detached for them from "the general instinct of life." In "The American Scholar" and other later writings the examples would be similar: a scholar as orator and as poet fulfills for other persons "their own nature" (CW 1:63); in clerical garb he utters from the pulpit "the speech of man to men" (CW 1:92); he is "representative," as Emerson would write of the poet, "stand[ing] among partial men for the complete man" (CW 3:4). Others look up to such a figure because he satisfies the universal need for utterance: "The man is only half himself," runs a famous sentence in "The Poet," for "the other half is his expression" (CW 3:4).

v. "The capital secret"

In the early months of 1837, a year of hard times for many and of financial worries, poor health, and low spirits for Emerson, there seemed cause for discouragement when he surveyed the world about him. Speaking in February on "The Present Age," the penultimate lecture in "The Philosophy of History" series, he granted that while the modern period of history had brought a wider diffusion of knowledge, it had come at considerable social cost: for the populace, "what is gained in surface is lost in depth," while the shortcomings of "formal and pedantic scholarship" have discredited the reverence in which earlier ages held the scholar and his learning (EL 2:164, 165).

Current literature, politics, and religion display only a "great hollowness," Emerson charged in a subsequent Address on Education, delivered in Providence, Rhode Island, on 10 June 1837. Their deficiencies are all the more glaring, he declared, in view of the "immense vital energy" at work in contemporary England and America. "A desperate conservatism clings with both hands to every dead form in the schools, in the state, in the church," he continued, and the world of actuality lies sick of a disease, its symptoms "the degradation of Man" through inaction of his "higher faculties" and "the usurpation by the senses of the entire practical energy of individuals, and the consequent prevalence of low and unworthy views of the manly character" (EL 2:197, 196). A Diogenes with his lantern searching for "individuals who satisfy the idea of Man" will come upon "here a strong arm, and there, cunning fingers; he will find a stout soldier; a ready writer; a shrewd banker,—he will find parts and beginnings, but no whole" (EL 2:196).

The Address on Education was written hastily in early June for the dedication of Hiram Fuller's new Greene Street School in Providence. Emerson went to the ceremony but half willingly, since he was feeling unwell and had found it difficult to prepare a manuscript, but he wished to lend his support to the kind of innovative teaching that Fuller and their mutual friend Bronson Alcott were offering in their experimental schools. Alcott was originally to be the speaker at Providence, but he had withdrawn because of the mounting controversy over his own Temple School in Boston, where he had even been threatened with mob violence. Late in March Emerson had written the editors of two Boston newspapers defending Alcott and the school against criticism arising from the recent publication of Alcott's *Conversations with Children on the Gospels,* which had alienated both ministers of the city and public school teachers (*L* 2:60–61, 62–63).[9] "I never regretted more than in this case my own helplessness in all practical contingencies," Emerson told Alcott himself. "But I was created a seeing eye, and not a useful hand."[10] He feared no "loss of faith" on the part of Alcott, whom he called a man "deeply grounded in God" and "a God-made priest" (*L* 2:62, 29), but there was good reason to be alarmed by the threat to his school, which Alcott was eventually forced to close as its enrollment steadily dwindled in the face of persistent criticism and increasingly hard times.

Alcott's unhappy situation was certainly in Emerson's mind as he prepared his address, which seems noticeably sharper in both diagnosing and prescribing for society's current ills than the final lectures of his winter series had been; his words reflect his own illness and the mood of increasing alarm he shared with Alcott and with the country at large as the current financial panic grew steadily worse. In "The Individual," the closing lecture of "The Philosophy of History," he had told his audience that the age in its sickness needs the scholar's illuminating power of Reason and habit of reflection "to emancipate the spirit from the bondage of fear" and "to neutralize all injurious influences" (*EL* 2:182, 184). At Providence his immediate targets were materialism and overspecialization; in "The American Scholar," written later in 1837, he would soon be saying that a scholar must be more than another specialist—more even than society's "delegated intellect" (*CW* 1:53). Education should not aim at making "accountants, attornies, engineers," he said at Providence, when it ought to be developing "heroes and saints" (*EL* 2:199). To such a nobler end, society has established its colleges, schools, and churches, appointing to them its learned men as a "priesthood" to foster "the superior nature of man." This class, the scholars of a nation, comprise "the clergy, the literary men, the colleges, the teachers of youth"; without their transforming vision a people will perish (*EL* 2:202).

Of all possible failures, the author of *Nature* declares characteristically, "the most deplorable" occurs "when the eye itself has become blind"—when a nation's teachers, "whether in the pulpit or in the Academy, lose sight of the capital secret of their profession, namely, to convert life into truth, or to show the meaning of events." As a cautionary example he then describes "a man formally dedicated to the task of public instruction," one who has "dwelt and acted with other men" and shared the experiences of common life, but who nevertheless falls short of his duty as scholar and teacher. How is this so? Because all his experience remains "aloof from his intellect," not yet "converted into wisdom," Emerson explains, "and instead, he entertains the people with words. Herein he utterly fails in his office" (*EL* 2:202).

As we know, Emerson had already observed in *Nature* that every individual must first act as life what he later apprehends as truth (*CW* 1:7). The special function of the scholar as teacher, he had repeatedly insisted, is to see the symbolic character of nature and history, to convert mundane facts into spiritual principles, and so to reveal to other individuals the truth of their own existence. Early in May of 1837, before his address for the Greene Street School had yet been written, he remarked in the journal "how strangely experience becomes thought or life, truth. The conversion is hourly going on" (*JMN* 5:320). His subsequent criticism of the would-be scholar who fails to make this essential conversion derives from a related journal passage written two days later, on 7 May 1837, after he and his wife had taken little Waldo to Sunday service in Concord for baptism by Dr. Ripley. The infant was then six months old; it was almost a year to the day since the death of Charles Emerson, and the boy was wearing "the selfsame robe" in which Charles had been baptized twenty-seven years before. The parents were mindful of "a group of departed Spirits . . . who hovered around the patriarch & the babe," as Emerson noted afterwards (*JMN* 5:324), but he himself was intensely dissatisfied with the ensuing sermon delivered by the Reverend Barzillai Frost, Dr. Ripley's junior colleague.

Emerson had been present at Frost's ordination three months before, but the Sunday of the christening was his first opportunity to hear Frost preach at Concord because he himself had been regularly supplying the Unitarian pulpit at East Lexington. The young minister, he complained at length in the journal, had not yet learned

> the capital secret of his profession namely to convert life into truth. Not one single fact in all his experience has he yet imported into his doctrine. & there he stands pitiable & magisterial, & without nausea reads page after page of mouthfilling words & seems to himself to be doing a deed. This man has ploughed & rode & talked & bought & sold[.] He has read books, & eaten & drunk; his cow calves; his bull genders; he smiles & suffers & loves. ↑All this has my man done yet was there not a surmise[,] a hint in all the discourse that he had ever lived at all. Not one line did he draw out of real history.↓ Yet, all this experience is still aloof from his intellect; he has not converted one jot of it all into wisdom. I thought we might well propose that as the end of education[,] to teach the pupil the symbolical character of life. Let him know that a people can well afford to settle large incomes on a man that he may marry, buy, & sell and administer his own goods if the practical lesson that he thus learns he can translate into general terms & yield them its poetry from week to week. Truly they will find their account in it. It would elevate their life also which is contemporary & homogeneous & that is what the priest is for. (*JMN* 5:324–25; cf. *EL* 2:202 and *CW* 1:86)

Above this indignant paragraph, which eloquently reveals Emerson himself effecting just the kind of "conversion" from experience into wisdom that Frost had failed to make, he inserted an apt sentence from the book of Proverbs: "Where there is no vision, the people perish." A month later, having committed himself to speak at Providence, he incorporated both the biblical phrasing and the illustrative example in his hastily written address. Although he was careful not to name the man he had specifically in mind, the unfortunate Concord minister was clearly his example—then and on later occasions as well[11]—of an incompetent preacher, a failed scholar, and, in the stinging words of the journal, "that large class, *sincere persons based on shams; sincere persons who are bred & do live in shams*" (JMN 5:463). Two orations of 1838, Emerson's Divinity School Address and "Literary Ethics," also draw on his private characterizations of Frost, who symbolized for him the very antithesis of his own ideal of the true scholar when observed in the particular role of preacher.

It should be noted that Emerson had no personal animus against his fellow townsman, with whom he shared membership on the local School Committee. By all accounts, Frost was an upright and conscientious citizen who soon made a place for himself in Concord. Respected by his neighbors and professional colleagues and active in contemporary reform movements, he was especially influential in the day-to-day work of a parish minister, involving the very pastoral duties that Emerson himself had found so uncongenial during his own ministry in Boston. But what repeatedly irritated Emerson was Frost's uninspired and uninspiring performance in the pulpit. The man was never an accomplished speaker; the staple of his preaching was the same orthodox Unitarian doctrine—especially the argument from miracles—that Emerson had also learned at the Divinity School but had long since discarded.[12] Moreover, while Emerson and other liberal Unitarians, such as his friends in Hedge's symposium of Spiritualists, had come to think of the preacher as a man who combines the functions of poet and priest, Frost "knew exactly the point where any subject shaded off into poetry, or sentiment, or mysticism," as a friend and fellow minister said of him, "and at that point he dropped it."[13]

Thus Frost cut himself off from the very practices that Emerson regarded as essential to the effective preacher, to the speaker and writer of power, to the true scholar as teacher. The pages of the journal over the years are filled with references to men who possessed that "capital secret" which Frost never learned but which Emerson had long coveted for himself: the ability to convert life into truth. Emerson's favorite examples among his own contemporaries of this transforming power were men of eloquence like Edward Taylor, pastor of the Seamen's Bethel in Boston and master of an astonishing play of metaphorical language, and Daniel Webster, always for Emerson the supreme orator, a man whom he had admiringly "followed about, all my young days," as he once told Carlyle, "from court house to senate chamber, from caucus to street," listening to his compelling voice (CEC 245). Among writers of the day he named as possessors of the secret were both Carlyle himself and Walter Scott, one of the few novelists he was able to read with pleasure (JMN 5:465).

The true scholar for Emerson must be such a man as these four: a see-er with the soul of a poet and an eloquent say-er who will teach his contemporaries not the inherited doctrines of a particular sect but the symbolical character of life itself.

To do his proper work he must begin, just as Emerson had gradually learned to do, with the facts of his own experience; the very words of such a man will accordingly be "rammed with life." But his experience must be transformed, or converted into truth and wisdom, so that though "he deals them out his life," as Emerson held, it will be "life metamorphosed," or "life passed through the fire of thought" (*JMN* 5:464–65; *CW* 1:86). Without the scholar's gift of life and his transforming vision, Emerson was saying early in 1837, the idea of Man will be lost to the sight of a people, and without vision that people will perish.

6. MAN THINKING:
"THE AMERICAN SCHOLAR," 1837

❖

In the *divided* or social state, . . . the scholar is the delegated intellect. In the right state, he is, *Man Thinking*.

. . . his duties . . . are such as become Man Thinking. They may all be comprised in self-trust. The office of the scholar is to cheer, to raise, and to guide men by showing them facts amidst appearances.
—"The American Scholar" (*CW* 1:53, 62)

The persistent illness that was troubling Emerson when he spoke at Providence had begun early in June of 1837 and lasted until mid-July. He described it as an "inflammation on the lungs" that kept him away from his journal for week after week and led him to think seriously of making "a long journey or a voyage" to restore his health (*L* 2:81, 83; *JMN* 5:339). His continuing weakness and lack of energy left him able to do a little reading but kept him altogether from writing, and whatever ideas he had entertained of turning his winter lectures into a second book seemed doomed. "Many trees bear only in alternate years," he told himself philosophically when he was once again adding to the journal. "Why should you write a book every year[?]" (*JMN* 5:347). Much as he enjoyed his current browsing in Boswell and Johnson, and in Byron and the older poets such as Donne, Cowley, and Marvell whose works had been the companions of his illness, he complained repeatedly that reading was no substitute for the original creation that was uppermost in his mind, for he had agreed to deliver the annual Phi Beta Kappa oration at the time of the Harvard commencement exercises in August.[1]

The unexpected invitation from Phi Beta Kappa came to Emerson late in June with the explanation that another speaker previously engaged, the Reverend Dr. Jonathan Wainright, had withdrawn his acceptance. Despite this rather unflattering circumstance and the relatively short notice, Emerson consented for the second time in 1837 to appear as a replacement speaker, though at the moment he was still not well enough to begin active work on an address. The family was absent from Concord over the Fourth of July, when Emerson's "Concord Hymn" was sung at the dedication of the new battle monument near Dr. Ripley's manse; they had gone to Plymouth for a week with Lidian's relatives. The change was beneficial to the invalid, and Emerson was at last able to resume writing in his journal on 17 July. He was already casting about for a subject suitable to Phi Beta Kappa, but inspiration for his August address seemed slow to come and his current reading offered him little prompting. Though books may "provoke thoughts," a journal entry rather grudgingly admits, reading is a "wholly subordinate" office: "I get thereby a vocabulary for my ideas. I get no ideas" (*JMN* 5:343–44).

i. "The Scholar's office"

In what he described as a vain effort "to awake in me the muse," Emerson went into Boston and turned through more books and journals at the Athenaeum, only to reproach himself for seeking inspiration from an outside source: "am I yet to learn that the God dwells within? that books are but crutches, the resorts of the feeble & lame, which if used by the strong, weaken the muscular power, & become necessary aids?" (*JMN* 5:345). In this very failure to find help on the printed page lay the solution to his problem of a theme for the unwritten oration, though he was slow in realizing that he was once more acting in life what he would later apprehend and declare as truth. That he had finally found both an appropriate topic and a central theme is first evident in a journal entry made four days after his excursion to Boston. "If the Allwise would give me light," he told himself on 29 July, "I should write for the Cambridge men a theory of the Scholar's office"—the very subject of that still-unwritten "chapter" he had projected nearly two years before, in August of 1835. Now, however, he would handle the old subject with a new emphasis, one already indicated in the two paragraphs of this same entry that immediately follow it: a succession of highly charged comments on the scholar as reader and writer that are based directly on his own recent experience.

"It is not all books" that the scholar must know, Emerson wrote in the journal, nor must he become a "bookworshipper"; the truth that the scholar is seeking is by no means confined to printed volumes. Indeed, "Books are for the scholar's idle times." How can this be? Emerson explains: "When he can read God directly, the hour is too precious to be wasted on other men's transcripts of their readings." Indeed, such transcripts become venerated for their own sake and not for the original vision that had inspired them.

> The poet, the prophet is caught up into the mount of vision, & thereafter is constrained to declare what he has seen. As the hour of vision is short & rare among heavy days & months so is its record perchance the least part of his volume. But the reverence which attaches to the record spreads itself soon over all his books especially for the bulk of mankind. Hence the book learned class who value books as such not related to Nature & the human constitution but as making themselves a Third Estate. (*JMN* 5:347; cf. *CW* 1:57, 56)

The true scholar, by contrast, is no such book-worshipper or pedant, no member of a self-constituted class standing apart from society at large. So Emerson was to

100

Many trees bear only in alternate years. Why should you write a book every year?

29 July. If the all-wise would give me light, I should write for the Cambridge men a theory of the Scholar's office. It is not all books which it behoves him to know, last of all to be a book-worshipper, but he must be able to read in all books that which alone gives value to books — in all to read one, the one incorruptible text of truth. That alone of their style is intelligible acceptable to him. ~~in~~ ~~Shakspear~~ ~~or Plato~~ ~~all else he rejects~~ were it never so many — ~~times the text of Plato~~

Books are for the scholar's idle times. When he can read God directly, the hour is too precious to be wasted on other men's transcripts of their readings. ~~It is~~ The poet, the prophet is caught up into the mount of vision, & thereafter is constrained to declare what he has seen. As the hour of vision is short & rare among heavy days & months so is its record perchance the least part of his volume. But the reverence which attaches to the record spreads itself soon over all his books especially for the bulk of mankind. Hence the book-learned class who value books as such not as related to nature & the human constitution but as making themselves a Third Estate. But the discerning man reads in his Shakspear or Plato only that least part, only the authentic utterances of the oracle, and all the rest he rejects were it never so many times Shakspear's & Plato's.

"A theory of the Scholar's office"
Entry of 29 July 1837, Journal C, p. 100; see JMN 5:347 and CW 1:57, 56.

say in pursuing this same line of thought in "The American Scholar" itself: the Scholar as ideally conceived stands forth as the spokesman for Man.

The long journal entry of 29 July is the immediate seed from which the entire oration developed during the month remaining before its delivery in Cambridge at the end of August. The paragraphs in the journal on books and reading reappear, with some rearrangement and amplification, as the vital center of "The American Scholar": that section of the address dealing with the creative process, the alchemy by which the scholar converts life into truth. As we have seen, creativity and its workings had been increasingly and almost obsessively on Emerson's mind in recent months. Of the truth which the scholar utters he had much to say. "Precisely in proportion to the depth of mind from which it issued, so high does it soar, so long does it sing," he first observes, introducing images that reappear later in the oration. Truth is something alive and not static, he goes on to explain; it cannot be captured once and for all by any creator in the finite, nor will any mere mortal "entirely exclude the conventional, the local, the perishable" from his work, for all his devotion to the universal and eternal (CW 1:55). Therefore the books of an earlier age will not serve the needs of humanity in a later period, and each generation must write its truth anew.

A few older books still speak universally across the centuries, however, as Emerson acknowledges; thus Chaucer and Marvell and Dryden—the very poets he had recently been reading—remain a joy to modern readers and persuade us "that one nature wrote and the same reads." They thereby illustrate the familiar Emersonian doctrine of "the identity of all minds," as the orator calls it here (CW 1:57–58). Good books, old and new, he declares, can be "the best of things, well used; abused, among the worst." Even when rightly read they are "for nothing but to inspire," but at worst that "sacredness which attaches to the act of creation,—the act of thought,—is instantly transferred to the record," and the book rather than the spirit which inspired it comes to be mistakenly exalted by readers and slavishly imitated by lesser writers (CW 1:56).

Taken negatively, Emerson's spirited words in this section of the address make a powerful case against books, and by extension the whole heritage of the past. Here speaks that "endless seeker with no Past at [his] back" who in Nature had turned away from "the sepulchres of the fathers" and called for "an original relation to the universe." To write against books and all external influences, to mount a blistering attack on books and bookworms, was actually his initial impulse in the summer of 1837 as he began the journal entry out of which these paragraphs developed. But in truth there have been few greater book-lovers than Emerson, and his ultimate intention, even in the journal and certainly in "The American Scholar" itself, was to make a positive statement about the essential originality and timeliness of truly creative scholarship. The unifying theme of the journal entry became the central message of the oration: original creation is the true function of the scholar.

"Creation," according to the journal, "is always the style & act" of men of genius; indeed, "To create, to create" is ultimately "the proof of a Divine presence."

Emerson's formulation in the journal makes clear once again, as in his recent lectures on "Art" and "Literature," the powerful religious element in his view of the creative process. *"Whoever creates is God,"* he writes, "and whatever talents are, ⟨exhibited⟩ if the man create not, the pure efflux of Deity is not his" (*JMN* 5:341; emphasis added). Here speaks Emerson the Spiritualist. What he means in saying that "Whoever creates is God"—a striking declaration that does not appear in the finished oration—is suggested by other related passages in his writings. "We see plainly that all spiritual being is in man," he had recently affirmed in "Religion," the tenth lecture in "The Philosophy of History" series; "as there is no screen or ceiling between our heads and the infinite heavens, so is there no bar or wall in the Soul, where man the effect ceases, and God the cause begins" (*EL* 2:85). So in "The Over-Soul," written for the *Essays* of 1841, he would term "ineffable" the "union of man and God in every act of the soul. The simplest person, who in his integrity worships God, becomes God" (*CW* 2:172–73). Thus for Emerson the soul that creates is expressing nothing less than its oneness with the God Within.

Although the corresponding passage of "The American Scholar" is not quite so daring as the antecedent journal entry, it nevertheless constitutes the finest statement Emerson had yet offered of his basic faith in man's creative potential. After declaring that he "had better never see a book than to be warped by its attraction clean out of my own orbit, and made a satellite instead of a system," the orator identifies "the active soul" as "the one thing in the world of value." This, "free, sovereign, active,"

> every man is entitled to; this every man contains within him, although in almost all men, obstructed, and as yet unborn. The soul active sees absolute truth; and utters truth, or creates. In this action, it is genius; not the privilege of here and there a favorite, but the sound estate of every man. In its essence, it is progressive. The book, the college, the school of art, the institution of any kind, stop with some past utterance of genius. . . . They look backward and not forward. But genius always looks forward. The eyes of man are set in his forehead, not in his hindhead. Man hopes. Genius creates. To create,—to create,—is the proof of a divine presence. Whatever talents may be, if the man create not, the pure efflux of the Deity is not his:—cinders and smoke, there may be, but not yet flame. (*CW* 1:56–57)[2]

These eloquent words epitomize all Emerson had been seeking to do as a writer and teacher: to utter only what he could offer as the poetry and philosophy of his insight and not of tradition, the sign of his own original relation to the universe. His characteristic drive to create, inspired by what he called the God Within, animates the oration and gives it distinctive substance and form. It is this same creative impulse that unmistakably identifies Emerson's "true scholar"—at once an idealized persona and, as "Man Thinking," his fully developed image for that "idea of Man" he was seeking to raise, like Milton before him, "in the minds of his contemporaries and of posterity."

ii. "The Scholar's function"

Given Emerson's central idea of man as "the creator in the finite," to borrow the language of *Nature*, there is little reason to suppose that he experienced any great difficulty in rounding out his oration in time for its delivery in Cambridge on 31 August 1837. Despite his remark in a letter to William Emerson on 7 August that "we cannot get any word from Olympus[,] any Periclean word" for Phi Beta Kappa (*L* 2:94), he had not hesitated to invite the embattled Alcott, who was recovering from an illness, to visit the Emersons in Concord;[3] Alcott came in mid-August with Hedge for "four or five days full of discourse," leaving on the morning of the 17th (*JMN* 5:362). On the following day, with less than two weeks remaining to complete the address, Emerson resumed his interrupted writing in the journal with his oration in mind. Had the chosen subject not been so congenial to his own thinking he could scarcely have composed both so rapidly and so well.

Encouragement of "philosophy, morality, and literature," as Emerson knew, is a stated objective of Phi Beta Kappa. "The hope to arouse young men at Cambridge to a worthier view of their literary duties" prompted him, he now wrote, "to offer the theory of the Scholar's function." What is his office in society? "To arouse the intellect; to keep it erect & sound; to keep admiration in the hearts of the people; to keep the eye open upon its spiritual aims" (*JMN* 5:364–65). For the initial paragraph of the oration itself Emerson later refashioned these words to express both a hope and a challenge. Observing that the anniversary meeting of the Harvard chapter was "simply a friendly sign of the survival of the love of letters amongst a people too busy to give to letters any more," he suggested that "the time is already come . . . when the sluggard intellect of this continent will look from under its iron lids and fill the postponed expectation of the world with something better than the exertions of mechanical skill" (*CW* 1:52). As these words suggest, he was casting himself in the scholar's role from the very beginning of the address as he set out "to arouse the intellect" of his listeners and to open among young Americans what he liked to call the iron lids of Reason.

It is in the light of his hope for American letters, Emerson goes on to say, that he accepts "the topic which not only usage, but the nature of our association, seem to prescribe to this day,—the AMERICAN SCHOLAR." The scholar's office was by no means a new topic in 1837, for many an American orator and essayist, holding forth at college commencement exercises, had already examined the state of scholarship and literature in the new country—often in a spirit of flamboyant cultural nationalism. Emerson himself had touched on this very subject as early as his lecture "The Naturalist," read in May of 1834, though with little satisfaction in what he saw in contemporary American life. "Imitation," he had charged, is "the vice of overcivilized communities" and "the vice eminently of our times, of our literature, of our manners and social action. All American manners, language, and writing are derivative. We do not write from facts, but we wish to state facts after the English manner" (*EL* 1:74–75). Again in January of 1836, concluding his course of lectures on English literature, he had acknowledged that "the American scholar" must feel a "degree of humiliation" in reckoning how little his countrymen had "added to the stock of truth for mankind" in comparison with the bards, the scholars, the philosophers of England (*EL* 1:381). Such passages unmistakably anticipate the challenge to his countrymen presented in the closing paragraph of "The American Scholar": American freemen have "listened too long to the courtly muses of Europe" (*CW* 1:69).

But the oration of 1837 is more than an exercise in fashionable literary nationalism, though it has too often been described and taught as such, and it is also more than a conventional commencement speech like any number of earlier addresses to Harvard graduates. Its roots lie too deep within Emerson's troubled thinking about his own problem of vocation to justify fitting it so easily into any standard pattern; indeed, what he said in Cambridge was addressed as much to himself as to his Phi Beta Kappa audience, setting forth to both the orator and his listeners the fundamental issues of originality and creativity that he had already posed in *Nature* and "The Philosophy of History." According to his own prescription, his topics for discussion must not be determined by mere assignment, since in his view "the Scholar who takes his subject from dictation & not from his heart . . . has lost as much as he seems to have gained" (*JMN* 5:46; cf. *EL* 1:381–82, and *CW* 2:89). As Phi Beta Kappa orator, however, he found no difficulty in addressing a seemingly conventional topic, since it coincided exactly with a subject he had long been meditating, both for its own sake and for his own, in public lectures as well as in the journal.

For Emerson in the mid–1830s, defining his self-appointed role as scholar meant working out both in actual practice and in public speech the questions that had faced him ever since he relinquished his pastoral charge in 1832. Who is the scholar, and what does he do and say? For whom and to whom does he speak? Such a one might well serve in the pulpit or on the platform, as Emerson had done; he might also be an editor, a teacher, a naturalist, a poet, a biographer, a literary historian, a philosopher, an orator. Emerson had now contemplated all these roles without committing himself exclusively to any one of them, though among poets and orators he felt most at home. His public account of the scholar must not confine him to any narrow vocational duties; society, as he had said earlier at Providence, was already paying the price of overspecialization. His strategy in "The American Scholar" meets the problem of narrow vocationalism by introducing the scholar in the inclusive terms of his own now-familiar concept of Universal Man.

According to an "old fable," the orator declares, the gods once divided "Man into men, that he might be more helpful to himself; just as the hand was divided into fingers."[4] This fable "covers a doctrine ever new and sublime: that there is One Man; . . . and that you must take the whole society to find the whole man." Man is not any one component, "not a farmer, or a professor, or an engineer, but he is all." In that "*divided* or social state" in which men live and perform their daily work, the planter, for instance, "sinks into the farmer, instead of Man on the farm," and most other workers, ridden by the routine of their chosen crafts, become metamorphosed into mere things: "The priest becomes a form; the attorney, a statute-book; the mechanic, a machine; the sailor, a rope of a ship" (CW 1:53). Of course Emerson had said all this before, in his lectures on "The Philosophy of History" and more pointedly in his Address on Education, but never quite so tellingly. Over against his cautionary examples he places next his idealized figure of the Scholar: not as "the delegated intellect," which is how men commonly distinguish him in the social state, but *as he ought to be.* Thus Emerson's ideal Scholar is no "mere thinker, or, still worse, the parrot of other men's thinking";[5] as *"Man Thinking,"* he is properly the representative of all mankind.

In such an exalted view of the American Scholar, the orator now observes,

> the whole theory of his office is contained. Him nature solicits, with all her placid, all her monitory pictures. Him the past instructs. Him the future invites. Is not, indeed, every man a student, and do not all things exist for the student's behoof? And, finally, is not the true scholar the only true master? But, as the old oracle said, "All things have two handles. Beware of the wrong one." In life, too often, the scholar errs with mankind and forfeits his privilege. (CW 1:53–54)

iii. The Scholar's Training

With these cautionary words as prelude, Emerson was ready to take his audience into the main body of his address. "The American Scholar" is organized on the plan of a classical oration with three principal divisions: the introduction, or *exordium;* an ensuing discussion, or *exhibition,* with several component sections and subsections; and a concluding *peroration.* The actual composition, as distinguished from preliminary drafting of individual passages in the journal (such as those examined above), evidently occupied him during the last ten days in August; during that time his journal entries first tapered off and then stopped altogether until early September, after delivery of the oration.[6] On 18 August he had noted that the scholar "must have a training by himself—the training of another age will not fit him" (JMN 5:365); in the finished address he enlarged on this idea by considering his scholar "in reference to the main influences he receives": *nature, the mind of the past,* and *action* all contribute to his education, and each influence receives analysis in its turn.

The ordering here is of course deliberate. First in time and importance Emerson placed the influence of nature (CW 1:54–55), whose values the scholar must settle in his mind as he himself had endeavored to do between 1832 and 1836. The speaker was benefiting, of course, from all that he had previously set down concerning nature in his early lectures on science, in his nature poems of 1834, and in his first book. With this work behind him he could now deal with the subject in only two paragraphs, stressing once more the importance of proper classification—as he had done in *Nature* and in his lecture of 1836 on "Humanity of Science"—and positing a correspondence between nature and the human mind in terms of a common spiritual source. Next, Emerson turned to the mind of the past (*CW* 1:55–58), just as he himself had moved from *Nature* to "The Philosophy of History." Here, taking books as "the best type of the influence of the past," he incorporated the thoughts on reading and creativity which had come to him in July as he cast about for the subject of his oration. This section of the address constitutes a sharp warning to "the book-learned class" not to value the products of creative activity above the process of creation itself, lest the would-be scholar descend into pedantry instead of ascending to his rightful place as Man Thinking. Finally, Emerson goes on to say, under the somewhat misleading heading of "action" (*CW* 1:59–62), that "Action is with the scholar subordinate, but it is essential" (59). This section of the address, which grew out of his earlier lectures on "Art" and "Literature," demands special examination, for it has proved a stumbling block for present-day readers.

Given Emerson's consistent application of spiritualist principles to his theory of creativity, with his further emphasis in "The Philosophy of History" on the essential passivity of the artist and thinker in the presence of the God Within, it may seem strange to find him specifying "action" as the third major influence upon the scholar. By *action*, as distinguished from *nature* and the *past*, Emerson means primarily the firsthand experience of day-to-day living among one's contemporaries. Without such experience the man of thought remains "a recluse, a valetudinarian"—exactly what "the so-called 'practical men'" suppose him to be. The "practical men" Emerson refers to are presumably those "idle carpenters, masons, & merchants" he had named in 1835 and 1836 as "pouncing" on the "defenceless" scholar and branding him "unsound and frivolous" (*JMN* 5:116; cf. *JMN* 12:35–36; *CW* 1:8). Any scholar lacking direct experience in society "is not yet man," the orator now acknowledges; without experience, his thought "can never ripen into truth," for action in this sense is the necessary "preamble to thought." A man *knows* only so much as he has *lived*, as we can tell from his very vocabulary: "Instantly we know whose words are loaded with life, and whose not."

Here, of course, Emerson was saying once more what he had said earlier in the Address on Education, prompted by such contrasting examples as Edward Taylor and Barzillai Frost. "So much only of life as I know by experience, so much of the wilderness have I vanquished and planted," the orator goes on to declare, "or so far have I extended my being, my dominion." Even "drudgery, calamity, exasperation, want are instructers in eloquence and wisdom," Emerson says here, much as he had written earlier of "Discipline" in a chapter of *Nature*. The opportunity of action—which is to say, of the day-to-day experience of living—is thus a source of power to the creative mind, being "the raw material out of which the intellect moulds her splendid products."

The process of converting experience into thought is indeed "strange," as Emerson had remarked in the journal early in May, when he was formulating his idea of the scholar's "capital secret" (*JMN* 5:320). For one thing, we do not regard our most recent experience as we do the long-past actions and events of our youth, he now observes, because it has not yet been converted into thought. "In its grub state" the new deed "is yet a part of life"; once the metamorphosis from life into truth takes place, he continues, picking up an earlier figure, it too "must soar and sing." In this way the scholar's experience, or "action," provides a subordinate but essential third element of his continuing education—or better, it is a "resource," since by alternating with reflection it serves to refresh his mind: "The mind now thinks; now acts; and each fit reproduces the other." Or as Emerson had written in *Nature,* "The intellectual and the active powers seem to succeed each other in man, and the exclusive activity of the one, generates the exclusive activity of the other" (*CW* 1:16). Thus "the scholar loses no hour which the man lives."

Though Emerson's treatment of action in "The American Scholar" has troubled even some distinguished Emersonians,[7] it now appears that he knew well enough what he was driving at, and that we can understand his intended meaning by going back to his earlier distinction, in the lecture on "Literature," between *acting* and *thinking.* There he was setting forth his familiar contrast between the uninterpreted experience of daily existence—what Socrates called "the unexamined life"—and that same experience transformed, or converted into thought; in "The American Scholar" he equates thinking with creation itself (*CW* 1:56). As a still-further development, thought is then made objective when uttered through the thinker's words as he writes or speaks. Emerson thus envisions a threefold sequence of *action, intellection,* and finally *utterance.* "The more profound the thought, the more burdensome," he had written in 1836. "What is in will out" (*EL* 2:4).

This same threefold progression is reviewed once again in "The American Scholar" when Emerson offers what he calls his "theory of books"—in essence his analysis of the creative process as it actually operates.

> The scholar of the first age received into him the world around; brooded thereon; gave it the new arrangement of his own mind, and uttered it again. It came into him— life; it went out from him—truth. It came to him—short-lived actions; it went out from him—immortal thoughts. It came to him—business; it went from him—poetry. It was—dead fact; now, it is quick thought. It can stand, and it can go. It now endures, it now flies, it now inspires. (*CW* 1:55)

Emerson's "theory," an outgrowth of his recent thinking about conversion, or what he speaks of in the next paragraph as "the process . . . of transmuting life into truth," throws light on his meaning when he terms action simply a "preamble of thought," the progression from acting to thinking being "the transition through which it passes from the unconscious to the conscious" (*CW* 1:59). A man's actions, Emerson thought, might be unpremeditated, but for him, as we know, all art was necessarily "*conscious* utterance."

Now it should be clear why Emerson's "true scholar" should take "every opportunity of action past by, as a loss of power," for action in the sense of experience, of life itself, "is the raw material out of which the intellect moulds her splendid products. A strange process too, this, by which *experience is converted into thought, as a mulberry leaf is converted into satin.* The manufacture goes forward at all hours" (*CW* 1:59; emphasis added; cf. *JMN* 4:371; 5:320). As a resource, "the resource *to live,*" action benefits the scholar as no book ever can; moreover, a scholar's thought and his action are in fact reciprocal. "Thinking is the function. Living is the functionary" (*CW* 1:61). As writer and speaker, the scholar exemplifies the third or *public* stage of progression from reception to intellection to utterance; he is also carrying out his responsibility to the society for whom and to whom he thinks and speaks.

iv. The Scholar's Duties

Having completed his survey of influences upon the scholar with his discussion of action, the orator turned next to the scholar's obligations as *Man Thinking* (*CW* 1:62–66). His duties, Emerson declares at the outset, "may all be comprised in self-trust." Though the scholar has a significant public function, being "one who raises himself from private considerations, and breathes and lives on public and illustrious thoughts," he must first of all be a private observer: he must *see* before he can *say.* But even as he tells his thoughts to others he will learn that "in going down into the secrets of his own mind, he has descended into the secrets of all minds," for each individual partakes of one common identity: "the Divine Soul which also inspires all men" (*CW* 1:62, 63, 70). Like the poet and the orator, the scholar is "the complement of his hearers" and "fulfils for them their own nature" (*CW* 1:63). "All men live by truth and stand in need of expression," according to Emerson's later essay on "The Poet" (1844), and truth and expression are what poets and scholars can provide for them.

Here again Emerson was on ground that he had already begun to explore in "The Philosophy of History." But in this same section of the oration, besides depicting the true scholar as one who should be thinking and speaking for Man, he also takes realistic account of "the state of virtual hostility" between a less than ideal society—especially "educated society"—and its practicing scholars. The troubles besetting Bronson Alcott may very well have been in his mind, but in referring to "the long period" of the scholar's "preparation" and "the self-accusation, the faint heart, the frequent uncertainty and loss of time which are the nettles and tangling vines in the way of the self-relying and the self-directed" he was surely looking back as well on his own experience of a few years before.

As elsewhere in "The American Scholar," Emerson was obviously making good use of his "Savings Bank," the journals of earlier years, as an aid in converting his own life into truth. The same extensive journal entry of 21 December 1834 that had outlined his professed "philosophy of *Waiting*" includes both the image of the scholar as astronomer—a lone "Watcher" scanning the heavens for light—and a pronouncement that the scholar's "office" is "to cheer our labor as with a song by highest hopes" (*JMN* 4:368, 370–71, 372). So in the oration, by way of an intermediate draft of 9 August 1837 (*JMN* 5:359), he writes: "The office of the scholar is to cheer, to raise, and to guide men by showing them facts amidst appearances. He plies the slow, unhonored, and unpaid task of observation . . . in his private observatory, cataloguing . . . stars of the human mind" (*CW* 1:62). Again in the entry of 1834, and in close juxtaposition with the figure of the "Watcher," is this proverb: "Time & patience change a mulberry leaf into satin" (*JMN* 4:371); this too turns up in the oration as part of the earlier treatment of the scholar's need for experience and action: "experience is converted into thought, as a mulberry leaf is converted into satin." In Emerson's writing, as one sees repeatedly, the journals contributed to this necessary metamorphosis both by storing for later use the raw material yielded by experience and by helping him to refine and finish the products moulded out of this material through intellection.

The concluding section of Emerson's discussion, where he turns his attention "to the time and to this country" (*CW* 1:66–70), virtually recapitulates the analysis of the contemporary world he had advanced a few months before in "The Philosophy of History"—particularly in the final lectures on "The Present Age" and "The Individual"; there are close verbal parallels to both lectures that suggest a recent rereading of the manuscripts on his part. Now, however, his tone is noticeably more confident. "This time, like all times, is a very good one," he declares, "if we but know what to do with it." Successive ages are said to have predominant modes, such as the classic, the romantic, and now the reflective; indeed, every individual, as Emerson liked to say, goes through the same cycle. The current reflective age, he believed, had elevated the low and the commonplace and given the individual a new importance because Reason—the sure sign of the One Mind, the One Soul— is present within every man. Aware of this presence, the source of creative power, the self-reliant scholar—the true American Scholar—will look only to the world he has internalized and given form rather than to external models, European or otherwise; his help "must come from the bosom alone":

> The scholar is that man who must take up into himself all the ability of the time, all the contributions of the past, all the hopes of the future. He must be an university of knowledges. If there be one lesson more than another which should pierce his ear, it is, The world is nothing, the man is all; in yourself is the law of all nature, and you know not yet how a globule of sap ascends; in yourself slumbers the whole of Reason; it is for you to know all, it is for you to dare all. Mr. President and Gentlemen, this confidence in the unsearched might of man, belongs by all motives, by all prophecy, by all preparation, to the American Scholar. (*CW* 1:69)

When the scholars of the nation fulfill their proper office, Emerson affirms in his peroration, the study of letters in America will cease to be "a name for pity, for doubt, and for sensual indulgence." And since it is given the scholar to act upon the public, as Emerson had long been saying, a democratic commonwealth of sovereign individuals "will for the first time exist" when the active scholar arouses his fellow citizens to awareness of "the whole of Reason"—the One Mind, the Divine Soul—that slumbers within every man.

v. At Cambridge and Concord

So Emerson told his audience on the appointed day, when a procession of 215 celebrants marched to the music of a band from Harvard Yard to the nearby meetinghouse of the First Church of Cambridge. The new building was crowded for the occasion. Among the dignitaries present were Governor Edward Everett, President Josiah Quincy of Harvard, Fellows of the Harvard Corporation, and members of both the Board of Overseers and the faculty. There were Harvard alumni like Dr. Oliver Wendell Holmes, Class of 1829; new graduates of the preceding day (among them David Henry Thoreau of Concord); and undergraduates such as James Russell Lowell. Bronson Alcott, though not the product of any college, was also in the audience. Lowell, writing in later years, recalled the mingled "enthusiasm of approval" and "grim silence of foregone dissent" that Emerson's address provoked. Among the dissenters was the venerable John Pierce, D.D., of Brookline, an inveterate spectator at such Harvard ceremonies, who wrote of the oration as being "in the misty, dreamy, unintelligible style of Swedenborg, Coleridge, and Carlyle." Its professed method escaped Pierce altogether, though he praised Emerson's delivery: "It was well spoken, and all seemed to attend," he acknowledged, "but how many were in my own predicament of making little of it I have no means of ascertaining." Holmes, who was sure that no listener, whatever his immediate reaction, ever forgot Emerson's address, contrasted the reservations expressed at the time by "grave professors and sedate clergymen" with the clear approval of "the young men," who had responded to Emerson "as if a prophet had been proclaiming to them 'Thus saith the Lord.'"[8]

As for Emerson himself, there was good reason to be satisfied with his performance, though neither his journal nor his letters take much notice of the oration or its immediate reception. "The American Scholar" is at once the best written and the most succinct presentation of his central ideas that he had so far produced, not excluding *Nature;* even as he spoke he must have felt that his own day of dependence and long apprenticeship, like that of the nation itself, was drawing to a close (*CW* 1:52). At a ceremonial dinner following the address Governor Everett spoke highly of his oratory, but what Emerson particularly liked was a witty toast proposed by Charles Warren of Plymouth: "*The Spirit of Concord. It makes us all of One Mind*"; Warren, he wrote, gave "the happiest turn to my old thrum" (*JMN* 5:376).

All the following day the members of Hedge's Club celebrated with conversation and feasting at Emerson's home in Concord, where Lidian delighted in serving good roast beef "for the Spiritualists."[9] In succeeding weeks, when the oration was published in pamphlet form, the first five hundred copies quickly sold out and a second printing was soon on order. It was the interest that "young men" were taking in his new views that especially pleased Emerson, as he told Carlyle, whose own response to the address must have been heartwarming: "The American Scholar" is "a clear utterance, clearly recognisable as a *man*'s voice," Carlyle wrote to him in December of 1837, "and I *have* a kinsman and brother." Jane Carlyle had remarked that there had been nothing like it "since Schiller went silent," so her husband continued, and Harriet Martineau reported that in America "some say it is inspired, some say it is mad." Carlyle himself was sure that Emerson had yet "a *fearful* work to do." His advice to his friend was to proceed with it slowly: "Be steady, be quiet, be in *no* haste; and God speed you well!" (*CEC* 177, 173–74).

Many of Emerson's later readers have responded more readily to "The American Scholar" than to *Nature,* partly because its author, as Rusk rightly noted, "was determined to keep this discourse intelligible to both his immediate audience and a much larger one beyond the walls of the meetinghouse." His theme of self-trust and self-realization, Rusk wrote, is "completely understandable to the most untranscendental minds," though there is "a sufficient hint to the imaginative" in the orator's occasional references to the spiritual grounding of the self-reliant man in that "one soul which animates all men."[10] Some commentators, including professional historians of literature, have followed the lead of Dr. Holmes, who called the address "our intellectual Declaration of Independence," by treating "The American Scholar" primarily as a document of cultural nationalism. But such a reading concentrates unduly on what is said in its opening and closing paragraphs, giving insufficient attention to Emerson's levies upon personal experience and his continuing focus on the ideal figure of the Scholar. As *Man Thinking,* the Scholar is representative not merely of Man in America, as some would have it, but of Universal Man in *all* times and places, even as he also epitomizes Emerson's own vocational pursuit and sense of mission.

PART TWO
THE SCHOLAR ENGAGED
❖

He who has put forth his total strength in fit actions, has the richest return of wisdom. . . . A great soul will be strong to live, as well as strong to think. . . . [T]he scholar loses no hour in which the man lives.

—"The American Scholar" (*CW* 1:60–61)

III

"THE NEW PHILOSOPHY"

The new statement will comprise the skepticisms, as well as the faiths of society, and out of unbeliefs a new creed shall be formed. For, skepticisms are not gratuitous or lawless, but are limitations of the affirmative statement, and the new philosophy must take them in, and make affirmations outside of them, just as much as it must include the oldest beliefs.

—"Experience" (*CW* 3:43)

7. "A SAD SELF-KNOWLEDGE," 1838–1839

❖

In all my lectures I have taught one doctrine, namely, the infinitude of the private man.

—Journal E, April 1840 (*JMN* 7:342)

Writing in May of 1838 to Thomas Carlyle, whose possible visit to Concord he was warmly urging, Emerson took stock of his own situation in the village. "My house," he said, "is now a very good one for comfort, & abounding in room." At home, he declared, "I am a rich man. . . . I have food, warmth, leisure, books, friends. Go away from home,—I am rich no longer." His yearly income he reckoned at roughly $2,100, coming mostly from the yield of his Tucker inheritance plus the profit from his winter lectures, "which was last year 800 dollars" (*CEC* 184). In his journal he also remarked that his habits of living were not dependent upon this "accidental freedom by means of a permanent income"; "my tastes, my direction of thought is so strong that I should do the same things,—should contrive to spend the best of my time in the same way as now, rich or poor" (*JMN* 7:71).

Emerson's prospects in the early months of 1838 were clearly much brighter than they had seemed a year earlier. 1837 was a time of national financial crisis and he himself was troubled by poor health and low spirits as the year began. Since then, however, his health had improved, the Tucker estate had at last been settled, and he had enjoyed the success not only of his Phi Beta Kappa address on "The American Scholar" but also of his most recent winter lecture series, "Human Culture," read in Boston between December of 1837 and February of 1838. Desiring through his teaching to awaken his listeners to the full potential within each individual, he had long shared the Unitarian devotion to self-cultivation, as David Robinson has demonstrated in *Apostle of Culture*; Emerson's choice of subject for this series is a further illustration. Although he still had a projected book of essays in mind, he remained dependent upon lecturing as a necessary source of income. With the close of the latest lecture series he terminated his service as supply preacher in East Lexington, Massachusetts—his sole remaining tie with his original calling. As he told Carlyle, he felt much more free on the lecture platform than in the pulpit. "But I preach in the Lecture-Room," he acknowledged, "and then it tells, for there is no prescription. You may laugh, weep, reason, sing, sneer, or pray, according to your genius. It is the new pulpit, and very much in vogue with my northern countrymen" (*CEC* 171).

Emerson continued to expound his "First Philosophy" in "Human Culture," building on the foundations he had laid down in *Nature* and "The Philosophy of History" and continuing to envision himself and his listeners as potential American Scholars; there were few overt references to scholars or scholarship, however, in any of the component lectures. In "The Head" he remarked incidentally that "a self-denial no less austere than the Christian's is demanded of the scholar," who, he said, "has not the temper of the man of the world" (*EL* 2:256, 258; cf. *CW* 2:202). Illustrative of what he would later call "the scholar's courage" (*JMN* 10:28) was a striking reference in "Heroism" to Elijah Lovejoy, an American clergyman who had recently been killed in Alton, Illinois, for repeatedly seeking to publish an antislavery newspaper. Emerson himself was no abolitionist in 1838, but he was very strongly affected by the murder and what it signified. "The brave Lovejoy," he declared, "gave his breast to the bullets of a mob, for the rights of free speech and opinion, and died when it was better not to live" (*EL* 2:338; cf. *JMN* 5:437 and *CW* 2:155). Emerson's friend George P. Bradford, who was present at the lecture, long remembered the "cold shudder" that ran through the audience at the speaker's "calm braving of public opinion twenty years before its ripening in the great cause of freedom" (*W* 2:426).

Emerson was to revise both "Heroism" and the paired lecture on "Prudence" for his *Essays* of 1841, which also included passages drawn from "The Head" and other components of "Human Culture." But his immediate concern in the spring and early summer of 1838 was not the book but composition of his Divinity School Address, given at Cambridge on 15 July, and "Literary Ethics," an oration delivered at Dartmouth College on 24 July. Both were written in the spirit of the Introduction to *Nature*, where Emerson had called for "a poetry and philosophy of insight and not of tradition, and a religion by revelation to us" rather than a history of past revelation to others (*CW* 1:7). The address in Cambridge, like his reference in the earlier lecture to Lovejoy and his fate, was certain to shock many of its listeners, as he must surely have known, for it constituted a frontal assault on key tenets of Unitarian orthodoxy being taught by the Divinity School faculty. But after his success with the Phi Beta Kappa oration in 1837 he was primed for another major challenge to his contemporaries. In his journal he expressed full confidence in the outcome: "when I have as clear a sense as now that I am speaking simple truth without any bias, any foreign interest in the matter,—all railing, all unwillingness to hear, all ⟨fear of⟩ danger of injury to the conscience, dwindles & disappears." So Emerson wrote on 8 July, a week before the event, adding: "I refer to the discourse now growing under my eye to the Divinity School" (*JMN* 7:41–42).

i. The Scholar as "true preacher"

Following the success of "The American Scholar" in 1837, Emerson had been visited by a number of divinity students who were unhappy with the instruction they were receiving at Cambridge, and on 21 March 1838 he was invited by a committee from the senior class to speak at their graduation ceremony in July (L 2:126, 129, 146–49 n. 169). The invitation gave him an opportunity to say what he had long been meditating about the decline of institutional religion in America; some of his ideas on that subject had already been voiced in "The Philosophy of History," particularly in the lecture on "Religion." On 18 March, immediately after enduring a lifeless sermon by Barzillai Frost, whose conventional preaching he had previously deplored, he told himself that he ought "to sit & think & then write a discourse to the American clergy showing them the ugliness & unprofitableness of theology & churches at this day & the glory and sweetness of the Moral Nature out of whose pale they are almost wholly shut" (JMN 5:464). The invitation to address the graduating divinity students, received only a few days later, offered him the occasion for just such a discourse.

Emerson's journal, his notes for the Address (JMN 12:8–13), and the published text itself (CW 1: 76–93) all show that what he referred to as "the intuition of the moral sentiment" (77) was his governing theme from the outset. In contrast to "the poverty stricken pulpit" he would set "the good ideal, the noble Ethics of Nature," he wrote in the journal (JMN 5:464). Such an ideal, the concept of morality as lying at the heart of both external nature and human nature, had long been central in his thinking as the very basis of his religious faith;[1] in the Address he called it "the essence of religion" (77). As early as 1832 he had complained that the doctrine of "man's moral nature" was not "fairly preached" in any of the churches. "The whole world holds on to formal Christianity," he wrote, "& nobody teaches the essential truth, the heart of Christianity, for fear of shocking &c" (JMN 4:45). "The laws of moral nature," he went on to declare in Nature, "answer to those of matter as face to face in a glass," and both derive from a common spiritual source. "The moral law lies at the centre of nature, and radiates to the circumference" (CW 1:21, 26). Now in 1838 he would tell his listeners that instead of teaching historical Christianity, their preaching should express "the moral sentiment in application to the duties of life" (85).

The Address opens with Emerson's exposition of this basic sentiment (CW 1:76–80), which he terms "an insight of the perfection of the laws of the soul"— laws which are apprehended intuitively and cannot be exactly stated. As the beauties of nature appeal to the senses and the laws of nature to the mind, so "the sentiment of virtue" appeals to the mind and heart and in turn awakens "the religious sentiment," just as it had done in his own thinking. The world, he says, is the product "of one will, of one mind," that is "everywhere active"; the individual, being "an inlet into the deeps of Reason" itself, is therefore "illimitable," and the moral sentiment that he finds within himself also "lies at the foundation of society."

Such an intuitive faith, being the product of direct inspiration, cannot be received at second hand. If that faith is lost, one is left with only "what addresses the senses."

The consequences of such a loss of faith are visible in the history of religion, Emerson declares in the central section of the Address (CW 1:80–89). The history of the Christian church in particular exhibits two principal "errors." First, instead of teaching "the doctrine of the soul"—which is to say the Emersonian belief that God is to be found within every man—the church has emphasized only Jesus as a person uniquely divine. Second, it has failed to explore what Emerson repeatedly calls the Moral Nature. He had once told his Boston congregation that his own "great object" was "to explore the nature of God" (YES 72), meaning the God Within. "Say, as Christ did, God is in me, I am God," he writes in his preliminary notes for the Address (JMN 12:9; cf. CW 1:81). "That which shows God in me, fortifies me," he declares in the Address itself. "That which shows God out of me, makes me a wart and a wen." To teach otherwise—for example, by pointing to biblical miracles as the primary evidences of Christianity, as Unitarian divinity students were then being taught to do—is to destroy the power of preaching "by withdrawing it from the exploration of the moral nature of man"; it is "a profanation of the soul."

As a cautionary example for his listeners Emerson describes here a "formalist" in the pulpit who has failed to learn "the capital secret of his profession, namely, to convert life into truth." Once again he is recalling a typical sermon by Barzillai Frost, though once again the man himself remains unnamed. On 18 March, in projecting his discourse to the clergy immediately after listening to Frost's preaching, he had written:

> Tell them that a true preacher can always be known by this, that he deals them out his life, life metamorphosed. . . . But of the bad preacher, it could not be told from his sermon, what age of the world he fell in, whether he had a father or a child, whether he was a freeholder or a pauper, whether he was a citizen or a countryman, or any other fact of his biography. But a man's sermon should be rammed with life. (JMN 5:464)

Emerson's "true preacher," it will be noted, is at one with his "true scholar"; indeed, the true preacher is simply a true scholar who has been called to the ministry. This entire passage, distinguishing good preaching "rammed with life" from a lifeless performance by such a man as Frost, is carried over into the Address (CW 1:85–86). There Emerson declares that merely formalist sermons leave the worshipper "defrauded and disconsolate." What in fact "characterizes the preaching of this country," with a few notable exceptions, is "tradition": a traditional sermon, he charges, "comes out of the memory, and not out of the soul"; it "aims at what is usual, and not at what is necessary and eternal."

The alternative path offered in the third section of the Address (CW 1:89–93) does not lie within the church as an institution but constitutes that "religion by revelation" Emerson had called for in *Nature*. The remedy is "first, soul, and second, soul, and evermore, soul."

> We have contrasted the Church with the Soul. In the soul, then, let the redemption be sought. . . . The stationariness of religion; the assumption that the age of inspiration is past, that the Bible is closed; the fear of degrading the character of Jesus by representing him as a man; indicate with sufficient clearness the falsehood of our theology. It is the office of a true teacher to show us that God is, not was; that He speaketh, not spake. (*CW* 1: 89)

"The true Christianity" is for Emerson "a faith like Christ's in the infinitude of man." His scholar as true religious teacher and preacher will "go alone," abjuring all models, and dare "to love God without mediator or veil." Once having gone himself, he will endeavor thereafter to bring other men to acquaintance "at first hand with the Deity." Ideally, "the new Teacher . . . shall see the world to be the mirror of the soul; shall see the identity of the law of gravitation with purity of heart; and shall show that the Ought, that Duty, is one thing with Science, with Beauty, and with Joy" (*CW* 1:93). So spoke the author of *Nature* and "The American Scholar" to the graduating students—and to some in the audience who were far from receptive to such unorthodox teaching.

ii. The Scholar's "Duty & Discipline"

"I think I may undertake one of these days to write a chapter on Literary Ethics or the Duty & Discipline of a Scholar." So reads an entry in Emerson's journal made in August of 1835 (*JMN* 5:84). He may have thought of including such a "chapter" in his projected book on "Natural Ethics" that ultimately developed into *Nature*. As we know, his preliminary notes for *Nature*, set down in January of 1836, refer to the scholar as an interpreter of the natural world, but the book as it subsequently took form does not deal explicitly with the scholar's role. After he had published *Nature* Emerson again considered writing on "Literary Ethics," this time as a possible subject for one of the lectures in his "Philosophy of History" series (*JMN* 12:174), but the chapter remained unwritten until the spring and summer of 1838. He had accepted "with great delight" the invitation to address the literary societies of Dartmouth College (*JMN* 5:479), but for a time he was uncertain about his topic. In mid-May he began drafting materials in his current Journals C and D, collecting possible references in Notebook L Literature (*JMN* 12:14–19), as he was currently doing as well with the Divinity School Address, and finally settling upon his old theme of the scholar's "Duty & Discipline." The resulting oration was subsequently printed in pamphlet form; the now-familiar title "Literary Ethics" was not given it, however, until 1849, when the text was reprinted in Emerson's *Nature, Addresses, and Lectures* (see *CW* 1:99–116).

The essentially religious character of what Emerson wished to say at Dartmouth is evident from a journal entry of 30 April 1838 that served as nucleus for the oration. Again his cautionary example is poor Barzillai Frost:

> Could not the natural history of the Reason or Universal Sentiment be written? One trait would be that all that is alive and genial in thought must come out of that. Here is friend B. F. grinds & grinds in the mill of a truism & nothing comes out but what was put in. But the moment he or I desert the tradition & speak a spontaneous thought, instantly poetry, wit, hope, virtue, learning, anecdote, all flock to our aid. This topic were no bad one for the Dartmouth College boys whom I am to address in July. (*JMN* 5:481; the entry is cited in *JMN* 12:14)

In drafting the oration itself Emerson went on to affirm that the scholar must honor Reason rather than tradition, just as at Cambridge he was to tell the divinity students to preach the Soul rather than historical Christianity. Frost is present in an adaptation of this same passage, where "B. F." and "he" are generalized, in typical Emersonian fashion, into "Men" and "they" (*CW* 1:105).

As Emerson continued his preliminary sketch of the Dartmouth oration he maintained his clerical focus, reminding himself not to overlook the inhibiting factors confronting even the scholar moved by indwelling Reason. If that "defining lockjaw" which afflicts all sectarians "shuts down his fetters" upon a scholar, he too will "dogmatise & rail" at others. "The great common sense (using the word in its higher sense) is the umpire that holds the balance" between two kingdoms. Against the one kingdom, that of Universal Reason, stands the contending kingdom that Emerson habitually sought to subordinate or transcend: the world of the immediate, the personal, the finite, illustrated in the journal by sectarians with their insistence on definition and dogma (*JMN* 5:481). Though he had acknowledged in the journal entry that even "antagonism" has a positive value, he was more conciliatory than contentious in the oration itself. There he stood somewhat apart from both opposing "kingdoms," speaking as a kind of surrogate for that "great common sense" that holds them safely in balance. To achieve equilibrium between the two while doing justice to both is Emerson's evident objective, not only in "Literary Ethics" but in major writings of his later years.

The published oration considers in turn "the resources, the subject, and the discipline of the scholar." The pattern of contrasting opposites that runs throughout is established in its opening paragraphs, which first show the scholar as he should appear—"the favorite of Heaven and earth, the excellency of his country, the happiest of men"—and then describe the scholar as he is actually regarded in the America of 1838. Antagonism to "the culture of the intellect," Emerson charges, is responsible for his young country's failure to fulfill in its arts "what seemed the reasonable expectation of mankind." To strike the desired balance in this portion of his account, he carefully distinguishes genuine "service of thought" from mere pedantry, much as he had done in "The American Scholar," affirming now that the scholar's work is realistic as well as sane and reasonable. In contrast is that "despotism of the senses" that leads some men to pursue only "ease or profit."

The ensuing discussion of the scholar's resources and subject matter (*CW* 1:101–5, 105–9) develops characteristic Emersonian ideas. As in *Nature*, "The American Scholar," and the Divinity School Address, Emerson calls again for an original and primary, not a secondary or derived relation to the universe, seeking to turn his listeners away from "the inscrutable, obliterated past" of tradition in order to celebrate "the enveloping Now" of the present. Growth of the intellect, which he holds to be "strictly analogous in all individuals," he identifies here with a "larger reception" of that "universal spirit" which "gladly utters itself" through each private man. He notes both the "infinitude and impersonality of the intellectual power": what hinders a person from attaining ideal justice and goodness is "the momentary predominance of the finite and individual over the general truth." Originality and creativity are again the keynotes when Emerson examines the many subjects open to scholarly exploration, whatever the field—history, religion, politics, philosophy, letters, or art. He flatly rejects the discouraging assumption that "all thought is already long ago adequately set down," not even by "mighty Homer or Milton," for "by virtue of the Deity, thought renews itself inexhaustibly every day."

The oration to this point is essentially an eloquent restatement of familiar Emersonian ideas; its remaining paragraphs, some of which are more prescriptive than inspiring, have been variously interpreted. The implicit premise of the long section on the scholar's discipline (*CW* 1:109–14) is that the great powers and great opportunities available to the true scholar make equally great demands upon him. Anyone dedicated to greatness dares not rest content with secondhand talk "of muse and prophet, of art and creation"; he must be creative himself. Emerson had said as much in "The American Scholar"; now the Puritan in him prescribes for the truly devoted scholar "a more rigorous scholastic rule," even an "asceticism," in order that he may "become acquainted with his thoughts" at their deepest level: "Silence, seclusion, austerity, may pierce deep into the grandeur and secret of our being, and so diving, bring up out of secular darkness the sublimities of the moral constitution." In this way the scholar will discover the source of his greatness, for a finite human "is great only by being passive to the superincumbent spirit." In so emphasizing receptivity rather than action Emerson is echoing what he had said earlier in "The Philosophy of History" concerning the essential passivity of the creative process; in 1839 he would carry the latter idea still further in his poem "The Problem," with its idea of the artist as a "passive Master."

This recurrent aspect of Emerson's thinking may seem to belie both his insistence on the significance of everyday experience and his early conviction that the scholar should "act upon the Public." Some critics then and now, beginning with Orestes Brownson in 1839, have assumed that in "Literary Ethics" Emerson was advocating only a regimen of withdrawal and passivity, though in the oration itself he disclaimed any such "superstition." Instead, he again calls for a sensible balance: "Let the youth study the uses of solitude and of society. Let him use both, not serve either."[2] The scholar, he acknowledges, cannot afford to be ignorant of the world about him—particularly if he is a literary man "dealing with the organ of language." As Emerson had observed in 1837, "life is our inexhaustible treasure of language for thought": this point, he wrote, "ought to have been more distinctly stated" in *Nature* (*JMN* 5:325–26). In "The American Scholar," emphasizing action as a major "resource" for the scholar, he noted once again that living in the world provides "a language by which to illustrate and embody our perceptions" (*CW* 1:61), and in the Divinity School Address he had said that "a man's sermon should be rammed with life." In "Literary Ethics," while still recognizing inspiring Reason as the scholar's primary resource, he holds that in the experience of life itself the scholar will find "the richest material for his creations." Since the laws of one's life are "concealed under the details of daily action," the scholar can apprehend those laws in only one way: by taking some active part in the world of human society and bearing "his share of the common load."

"Literary Ethics" thus advocates less a specific program for the scholar than simply a "mutual reaction of thought and life" that will "make thought solid, and life wise." In this respect it is consonant with the notion of polarity advanced in "The American Scholar": that the mind "now thinks; now acts; and each fit reproduces the other" (*CW* 1:61); in a journal entry of 12 June 1838 which Emerson drew upon for the address at Dartmouth he had written that "Solitude is naught & society is naught. Alternate them & the good of each is seen. . . . Undulation, Alternation, is the condition of progress, of life" (*JMN* 7:14). Even so, as the oration also recognizes pragmatically, the day-to-day tasks that a scholar must face in his solitude are unavoidably laborious. Having access to superincumbent Reason by no means justifies any scholar who refuses the yoke of study. He must "know, if he can, the utmost secret of toil and endurance," since a healthy scholarship must be informed as well as inspired. It requires a certain amount of hard and routine work—Emerson's word for it is "drill," though in "The American Scholar" he had praised not drill but creativity (*CW* 1:58). He might well have cited his own scholarly labors in writing and indexing his journals and notebooks before addressing the public; instead, he offers an instructive example in an altogether different individual: Napoleon. Whatever his "defects or vices," Bonaparte was no believer in mere luck, but, "faithful to facts" and "by the calculations of genius," he planned how best to apply "means to ends." So the scholar must not neglect "the work to be done," by way of thorough preparation and steady application, if "the secret of the world is to be learned, and the skill truly to unfold it is acquired."

Emerson experienced some difficulties in completing "Literary Ethics," which remained unfinished until after his arrival in Hanover. His best thoughts about the scholar had already gone into his Phi Beta Kappa oration of 1837; in 1838 his prior engagement at the Divinity School obviously called forth more of his passion and eloquence than did his appearance at Dartmouth. The disproportionately long third section of "Literary Ethics," with its emphasis on discipline and drill, seems addressed as much to his own divided mind as to his prospective listeners. In attempting to sum up his conception of a dual allegiance, to both the world of men and the world of Reason, Emerson sought to make his scholar "not a fragment" but a person both healthy and whole. A "twofold goodness—the drill and the inspiration"—will inform his work just as it "characterizes ever the productions of great masters." For a climactic passage in his peroration he turned back to a journal entry of 1836 that he had already used in "The Philosophy of History":

> The man of genius should occupy the entire space between God or pure mind, and the multitude of uneducated men. He must draw from the infinite Reason, on one side; and he must penetrate into the heart and sense of the crowd, on the other. From one, he must draw his strength; to the other, he must owe his aim. The one yokes him to the real; the other, to the apparent. At one pole, is Reason; at the other, Common Sense. (CW 1:113; cf. JMN 5:249–50, EL 2:61–62)

If the scholar settles for only one alternative in each pair without embracing the other also, as the speaker himself well knew, "his philosophy will seem low or utilitarian; or it will appear too vague for the uses of life."

In concluding, Emerson directly warns his young listeners against disobedience to the heavenly vision in the event that God has inspired any of them "to explore truth and beauty." "Be bold, be firm, be true," he urges. For if one renounces such inspiration, "then once more perish the buds of art, and poetry, and science, as they have died already in a thousand thousand men. The hour of that choice is the crisis of your history; and see that you hold yourself fast by the intellect" (CW 1:115).

iii. "The storm in our washbowl"

Before delivering his oration at Dartmouth, Emerson confessed some uncertainty about its suitability for a college audience, but it apparently caused no problems for his listeners. The earlier Divinity School Address at Cambridge was a different matter altogether, however, despite his sanguine expectations. Although some liberal Unitarians approved, it immediately provoked a strong reaction from the more orthodox, and their anger increased after the Address appeared as a pamphlet. Emerson's letters and journals of the period reflect his obviously agitated response. "Steady, steady," he told himself in a representative entry, made after he had attended the Phi Beta Kappa anniversary in Cambridge at the end of August—a year after his success there with "The American Scholar."

> I am convinced that if a man will be a true scholar, he shall have perfect freedom. The young people & the mature hint at odium, & aversion of faces to be presently encountered in society. I say no: I fear it not. No scholar need fear it. For if it be true that he is merely an observer, a dispassionate reporter, no partisan, a singer merely for the love of music, his is a position of perfect immunity. . . . (JMN 7:60)

Then, shifting to the first person, he affirmed that "Society has no bribe for me, neither in politics, nor church, nor college, nor city. My resources are far from

86

28 August. It is very grateful to my feelings to go into a Roman Cathedral, yet I look as my countrymen do at the Roman priesthood. It is very grateful to me to go into the English Church & hear the liturgy read. Yet nothing would induce me to be the English priest. I find an unpleasant dilemma in this, nearer home. I dislike to be a clergyman & refuse to be one. Yet how rich a music would be to me a holy Clergyman in my town. It seems to me he cannot be a man, quite & whole; Yet how plain is the need of one, & how high yes highest is the function. Here is Division of labor that I like not. A man must sacrifice his manhood for the social good. Something is wrong, I see not what.

31 August. Yesterday at Φ.Β.Κ. anniversary. Steady, steady. I am convinced that if a man will be a true scholar, he shall have perfect freedom. The young people & the mature hint at odium, & aversion of faces to be presently encountered in society. I say no; I fear it not. No scholar need fear it. For if it be true that he is merely an observer, a dispassionate reporter, no partisan, a singer merely for the love of music, his is a position of perfect immunity; to him no disgusts can attach; he is invulnerable. The vulgar think he would found a sect & would be installed & made much of. He knows better & much prefers his melons & his woods. Society has no bribe for me, neither in politics, nor church, nor college, nor city. My resources are far from exhausted

"If a man will be a true scholar. . . ."
Entry of 31 August 1838, Journal D, p. 86; see *JMN* 7:60.

exhausted. If they will not hear me lecture, I shall have leisure for my book which wants me."

Even so, Emerson was clearly shaken by the rancor of his critics, especially Professor Andrews Norton, formerly of Harvard, a noted biblical scholar and author of *The Evidences of the Genuineness of the Gospels* (1837, 1844). Norton, writing in the Boston *Daily Advertiser*, bitterly castigated Emerson's animadversions on historical Christianity and its emphasis on miracles. But Emerson refused to be drawn into controversy, with Norton or with anyone else. Replying on 8 October to a letter from Henry Ware, Jr., with whom he had served at the beginning of his ministry in Boston, he declined Ware's request for "arguments" in support of what he had said at Cambridge. "No scholar," he told Ware, was "less willing or less able" than himself "to be a polemic" (*L* 2:167). Still, as he wrote in his journal four days later, "It seems not unfit that the Scholar should deal plainly with society & tell them that he saw well enough before he spoke the consequence of his speaking" and "fore-heard this Babel of outcries." Instead of explaining or justifying himself he would continue to speak his mind, "for I have a great deal more to say that will shock you out of all patience. Every day I am struck with new particulars of the antagonism between your habits of thought & action & the divine law of your being & as fast as these become clear to me you may depend on my proclaiming them" (*JMN* 7:105).

To Carlyle, who had been sent copies of the Address, Emerson wrote on 17 October that its publication

> has been the occasion of an outcry in all our leading local newspapers against my "infidelity," "pantheism," & "atheism." The writers warn all & sundry against me, & against whatever is supposed to be related to my connexion of opinion, &c; against Transcendentalism, Goethe & *Carlyle*. I am heartily sorry to see this last aspect of the storm in our washbowl. . . . You were getting to be a great favorite with us all here, . . . but just now, *in Boston*, where I am known as your editor, I fear you lose by the association. (*CEC* 196–97)

Carlyle's reaction was much to his friend's liking: "let the washbowl storm itself out," he advised. "Be *silent*, do not speak" (*CEC* 200), and in fact Emerson continued to hold himself aloof from public controversy. Had the beleaguered author any desire to engage in a pamphlet war, his most obvious opponent would have been the redoubtable Norton, "the Unitarian Pope," who returned to the attack in 1839 with *A Discourse on the Latest Form of Infidelity*. But Emerson held his fire.[3]

Despite his fears that another series of lectures might fail if potential listeners were put off by the Divinity School controversy, Emerson's ten discourses on "Human Life," given in Boston between December and February as a kind of sequel to "Human Culture," were well received, though they were not as financially rewarding as the earlier series. By April of 1839, as he indicated in a letter to Alcott, he was at work on his projected book (*L* 2:194), but he was soon obliged to put it aside under the pressure of events. His continuing efforts to promote

American editions of Carlyle's writings had required much time and effort on his part ever since 1836, when he wrote a preface for a Boston edition of *Sartor Resartus*. In 1837 and after he arranged for successive publication of *The French Revolution, Critical and Miscellaneous Essays,* and *Heroes and Hero-Worship,* sending the profits to Carlyle; in 1840 he was obliged to go into debt in order to meet current bills for printing.

There were also increased responsibilities at home: Lidian Emerson had given birth to their second child on 24 February 1839, naming her Ellen after her husband's first wife. And in that same year Emerson and a circle of like-minded friends were making plans for a new journal; by late October Margaret Fuller agreed to serve as editor with Emerson's assistance. The first number of *The Dial: A Magazine for Literature, Philosophy, and Religion* appeared in July of 1840 with an introductory note by Emerson. In preparing this issue and its successors there was much for him to do, for in effect he was both coeditor and occasional contributor; in 1842 he was to become editor in fact.

In October of 1839 Emerson decided once more to make what he called "my annual inventory of the world" in another course of winter lectures, to be called "The Present Age" (*JMN* 7:270, 283). He gave the lectures in Boston to what he reckoned afterward as an average audience "of about 400 persons," and at Providence in March he then repeated the earlier series on "Human Life." The Boston lectures gave him "little pleasure," however, as he confessed in his journal, for "I have not done what I hoped when I said, I will try it once more" (*JMN* 7:338). In April, looking back over his recent appearances on the platform, he remarked that his listeners accept "readily enough, & even with loud commendation," his "one doctrine, namely, the infinitude of the private man," provided only that his announced topic must be a secular one. It could thus be "Art; or Politics; or Literature; or the Household; but the moment I call it Religion,—they are shocked, though it be only the application of the same truth which they receive everywhere else, to a new class of facts" (*JMN* 7:342). As for the Divinity School controversy in particular, all that he would ever say publicly is expressed indirectly, as in passages of his essay on "Self-Reliance" (1841), or in ironic verse: the young protagonist of his poem "Uriel" (1846), whose unorthodox pronouncements have disturbed "the stern old war-gods," withdraws quietly "into his cloud," having derived "a sad self-knowledge" from the encounter (*W* 9:14–15; cf. *JMN* 9:170–71). By 1845, remembering the charges that had been leveled against him, he was able to generalize, observing that "Great believers are always reckoned infidels" (*CW* 4:102).

8. TRANSITION, 1839–1842

---❖---

Valor consists in the power of self-recovery, so that a man cannot have his flank turned, cannot be outgeneralled, but put him where you will, he stands. This can only be by his preferring truth to his past apprehension of truth; and his alert acceptance of it from whatever quarter.

—"Circles" (*CW* 2:183)

When Emerson began assembling materials for his second book in the spring of 1839, his objective was to have the manuscript ready by the end of that year, but it was January of 1841 before he could send it to the printer. At the outset he spoke of "writing a little and arranging old papers more" (*L* 2:194); his characteristic method of composition, as in earlier years, was to select appropriate passages from his previous journals and lectures, to organize his citations in sequence by topic and subtopic in various notebooks, and then to copy them out, together with newly composed connective matter, to make a finished lecture or chapter.[1] But to the scholar who repeatedly exalted original creation over what he called "drill" the process came to seem more laborious than creative. By October of 1840 he complained of the book in progress much as he had complained of his recent lectures:

> I have been writing with some pains Essays on various matters as a sort of apology to my country for my apparent idleness. But the poor work has looked poorer daily as I strove to end it. My genius seemed to quit me in such a mechanical work, a seeming wise,—a cold exhibition of dead thoughts. When I write a letter to any one whom I love, I have no lack of words or thoughts: I am wiser then myself & read my paper with the pleasure of one who receives a letter, but what I write to fill up the gaps of a chapter is hard & cold, is grammar & logic, there is no magic in it; I do not wish to see it again. (*JMN* 7:404–5)

As these negative comments on both his lectures and his essays suggest, Emerson in 1840 was obviously troubled by the gap between his idealistic hopes for the future and his actual performance in the present, which too often seemed merely retrospective rather than prospective—out of keeping with the progressive spirit of *Nature*, "The American Scholar," the Divinity School Address, and "Literary Ethics." In later years, though he continued to draw on his more recent journals, his practice was to write lectures that could go into print with relatively little revision.

i. Living from Within

Although Emerson incorporated much of his earlier thinking and writing in the *Essays* of 1841, the book as a whole did not seem flat or stale to persons other than its author when it finally appeared, nor does it seem so now. For the present-day student it serves as a veritable Emersonian chrestomathy, useful in tracing successive stages of a scholar's developing thought. Thus "Compensation," the third essay, opens with the statement that "Ever since I was a boy, I have wished to write a discourse on Compensation" (*CW* 2:55); the concept appears and reappears in his writings of the earlier 1830s.[2] Among some modern commentators the idea has not fared well: Stephen Whicher, for example, declared in 1953 that the notion "is without question the most unacceptable of Emerson's truths."[3] But with renewed interest in Emerson and his thinking, recent interpreters have treated compensation more sympathetically, seeing in the idea a Stoic insulation against the early loss of his father, his own subsequent poverty and recurrent illnesses, and the later deaths of his beloved first wife and brothers Edward and Charles. As noted earlier, he took literally Bacon's advice to conform "the shows of things to the desires of the mind" (see chapter 3 above, n. 10). By internalizing each deprivation confronting him, he sought to identify some purely spiritual gain to himself.

A similar internalizing is evident in "Self-Reliance," a virtual anthology of Emersonian passages on that recurrent theme. The essay is in part a scholar's apologia for speaking the truth as he sees it, regardless of popular reaction. "For nonconformity," as Emerson well knew from the response to his Divinity School Address, "the world whips you with its displeasure. And therefore a man must know how to estimate a sour face. The bystanders look askance on him in the public street or in the friend's parlor" (*CW* 2:32–33). But "What I must do, is all that concerns me," he now declares, "not what the people think. This rule [is] equally arduous in actual and in intellectual life." Then, in a sentence that recalls his effort in "Literary Ethics" to balance the opposing claims of society and solitude, he adds the further comment that "it is easy in the world to live after the world's opinion; it is easy in solitude to live after our own; but the great man is he who in the midst of the crowd keeps with perfect sweetness the independence of solitude" (*CW* 2:31).

As a motto for "Self-Reliance" Emerson chose a maxim from Persius that he had translated in 1834 as reading "Thou art sufficient unto thyself" (*JMN* 4:318). The scholar's duties, he had declared in 1837, "are such as become Man Thinking. They may all be comprised in self-trust" (*CW* 1:62), and self-trust is likewise an essential attribute of the Emersonian hero (*EL* 2:331; *CW* 2:148). Emerson believed in self-sufficiency and self-trust because he believed in the infinitude of the private man. In relying on himself, the individual in his infinitude draws strength from a sustaining "fountain of action and of thought," "the aboriginal Self" within him (*CW* 2:37); thus, Emersonian self-reliance—small *s*—is ultimately Self-reliance—capital *S*—meaning God-reliance, for "there is a great responsible Thinker and Actor working wherever a man works" (*CW* 2:35).

To borrow a figure from the essay on "Circles" (*CW* 2:180), this intuitive faith is the helm that Emerson's thinking had long obeyed.[4] His fundamental belief that "Within and Above are synoymns" (*JMN* 4:365) has of course been attacked, both in his own day and since. In "Self-Reliance" he dramatizes an earlier challenge: "On my saying, What have I to do with the sacredness of traditions, if I live wholly from within?" a "valued advisor" had once warned him that "'these impulses may be from below, not from above.' I replied, 'They do not seem to me to be such; but if I am the Devil's child, I will live then from the Devil'" (*CW* 2:30; cf. *JMN* 5:48–49). This defiant credo (which in the classroom I have called "the Emersonian wager") has predictably offended traditionalists who mistrust the intuitive basis of Emerson's faith; for them, "Within and *Below*"—not Above—may well be the real synonyms. Some modern readers have taken his "one mind" within all men to be neither the Devil's nor God's but an altogether human collective unconscious; still others, either flatly rejecting or—more often—merely ignoring the religious dimensions of his teaching, translate "Self-Reliance" into a purely secular argument for competitive American individualism.[5]

ii. Spiritualism

As we have seen, the belief that God is a pervasive, impersonal spirit, present and creatively active not only in man but in nature as well, had become the basis of Emerson's thinking by the mid–1830s, when he thought of himself and the so-called "Transcendentalists" as "spiritualists." Material from this period and after appears in such essays of 1841 as "Spiritual Laws" and "Intellect" along with "History" and "The Over-Soul." Like the "Philosophy of History" lectures of 1836–1837 and especially the Divinity School Address of 1838, which had drawn charges of "'infidelity,' 'pantheism,' & 'atheism'" against Emerson, certain passages of these compositions present fundamental religious and philosophical issues. Believing as he did in an impersonal deity, Emerson was neither an atheist nor a conventional theist, but his more transcendental utterances do indeed seem close to pantheism.[6] "Ineffable is the union of man and God in every act of the soul," he wrote in "The Over-Soul." "The simplest person, who in his integrity worships God, becomes God" (*CW* 2:172–73; cf. "Religion," *EL* 2:85).

A corollary problem is the old question of human freedom and responsibility: is an individual then to be either credited or blamed for his own actions? First in "The Philosophy of History," then in "Literary Ethics," and again in his poem "The Problem" Emerson had written of the inspired artist, writer, and scholar as less active than "passive to the superincumbent spirit" (*CW* 1:113; cf. *EL* 2:94). Even in "The American Scholar," with its celebration of "the active soul," he took human creativity to be "proof of a divine presence" working within and through the individual (*CW* 1:57). By advancing his old notion of polarity Emerson had sought to make passivity and action complementary, alternating as they apparently did within his own experience, but the dichotomy continued to trouble him. David Robinson, examining the *Essays* of 1841 "in theological perspective," has characterized these opposing elements as "quietist acceptance" versus "moral effort," or in theological terms, "grace" versus "works," seeing in Emerson and his book a tension between them "not new to the student of New England thought."[7]

As Emerson himself surely realized, a further question of responsibility is involved as well. Melville's Ahab, in an altogether different context, demands to know, "is it I, God, or who, that lifts this arm?"[8] If Emerson's God Within prompts all human actions, can man then be free? And if God is in truth responsible for all that He has created, then what can we say of evil and weakness? Emerson advanced one answer to the latter question in his Divinity School Address: "Good is positive. Evil is merely privative, not absolute. It is like cold, which is the privation of heat. All evil is so much death or nonentity" (*CW* 1:78). But he could not rest in that monistic assumption, for some evils are not merely negative, an absence of good, but actively oppressive, as he well knew; slavery in the United States, as he came increasingly to recognize, was one of them.

Hardly a systematic philosopher, Emerson the scholar was no monist, or not a consistent one; what he had said in "Self-Reliance" about consistency, he later thought, "would be better written thus; Damn Consistency" (*JMN* 7:524; cf. *CW* 2:33). As Whicher aptly remarked, "His is a baffling monistic dualism, or dualistic monism."[9] A journal entry of 1837 expresses Emerson's own uncertainty: "I behold with awe & delight many illustrations of the One Universal Mind," he wrote. "As a plant in the earth so I grow in God. I am only a form of him. He is the soul of Me. I can even with a mountainous aspiring say, *I am God.*" Still, though "A believer in Unity, a seer of Unity, I yet behold two." "Ah wicked Manichee!" he exclaims. "[I]n certain moments I have known that I existed directly from God, and am, as it were, his organ. And in my ultimate consciousness Am He. Then . . . the ⟨se⟩ contradictory fact is familiar, that I am a surprised spectator & learner of all my life" (*JMN* 5:336–37).

Emerson the "surprised spectator & learner"—"merely an observer, a dispassionate reporter," as he had described himself after the Divinity School Address—is scarcely the actively inspired scholar of the Phi Beta Kappa oration. But "let me record day by day my honest thought without prospect or retrospect," he wrote in "Self-Reliance," and in time "it will be found symmetrical, though I mean it not, and see it not" (*CW* 2:34).

iii. Solitude and Society

Other strands of thinking in the *Essays* that are clearly less philosophical than personal had first become prominent in the three lecture series that Emerson gave between 1838 and 1840–1841. As noted above, the complementary essays on "Prudence" and "Heroism" are revised versions of lectures with those same titles in

"Human Culture"; the essay on "Love" is a reworking of a lecture in the series on "Human Life"; from both series and from "The Present Age" came individual passages used in various other essays. As in the lectures, Emerson had little to say of the scholar except incidentally; he had of course already published both "The American Scholar" and "Literary Ethics." But "Love" and the companion essay on "Friendship" are new commentaries on the claims of solitude and society that he had confronted in the latter address and also in "Self-Reliance." After "transcribing" the original lecture on "Love" he wrote of its "inadequateness," going on to characterize his own temperamental inwardness in a revealing self-appraisal:

> I ⟨am⟩ cold because I ↑am↓ hot,—cold at the surface only as a sort of guard & compensation for the fluid tenderness of the core,—have much more experience than I have written there, more than I will, more than I can write. In silence we must wrap much of our life, because it is too fine for speech, because also we cannot explain it to others, and because somewhat we cannot yet understand. (*JMN* 7:368)

As Emerson acknowledged in the essay "Love," it was charged "that in some public discourses of mine my reverence for the intellect has made me unjustly cold to the personal relations" (*CW* 2:101). The complaint had been voiced during the summer of 1840 by Margaret Fuller and a circle of her young friends—Caroline Sturgis, Anna Barker, and Samuel Gray Ward—who had sought a greater intimacy with their admired Emerson than he could comfortably admit. Passages in his correspondence and journal at the time show how deeply the situation troubled him;[10] in the new essay on "Friendship," which he circulated in manuscript before its publication, he wrote of his own divided feelings: "The instinct of affection revives the hope of union with our mates, and the returning sense of insulation recalls us from the chase" (*CW* 2:117). His genuine regard for friends was circumscribed not only by his temperamental reserve but also by his commitment to an inward spiritual life and his fealty to the God Within. "Why should I play with the young people this game of idolatry?" he asked himself. "Rich, noble, & great" they may be, "but truth is sad. O blessed spirit, whom I forsake for these, they are not Thee!" (*JMN* 7:369). Once more he had gained "a sad self-knowledge" through troubling personal experience.

iv. "New and larger circles"

One other component of the *Essays* remains to be considered: that antinomian, rebellious, even revolutionary element of Emerson's thinking that had set him against conventional society and motivated his gradual withdrawal from the Unitarian religious establishment, beginning with his resignation from his pastorate in 1832 and coming to a climax with his delivery of the Divinity School Address in 1838. In 1835 he had praised Martin Luther as "a scholar or spiritual man" who "achieved a spiritual revolution by spiritual arms alone" (*EL* 1:127). The scholar, he told himself after his Phi Beta Kappa oration of 1837, ought to be great in action as well as in speculation; he had been reading "with joy" of men such as Hampden, Pym, and Penn who were "conversant with governments & Revolutions" (*JMN* 5:394). But as Whicher rightly observed, "The kind of action Emerson understood best was that of the preacher,"[11] and it was with the hope of instigating a new spiritual revolution that he challenged the clergy with his Divinity School Address. "Whenever a man comes," he warned them, "there comes revolution" (*CW* 1:89).

In "Circles," the last essay of the 1841 volume to be written, Emerson recognizes that "The new statement is always hated by the old, and, to those dwelling in the old, comes like an abyss of skepticism" (*CW* 2:181); so it had been with the stern Unitarian war-gods, whom he had promised himself in 1838 to shock once again. "Beware when the great God lets loose a thinker on this planet," he wrote in 1840. "Then all things are at risk" (*CW* 2:183). And further: "I unsettle all things. No facts are to me sacred; none are profane; I simply experiment, an endless seeker with no Past at my back" (*CW* 2:188). By the time Emerson at last finished his book, weary with recasting old thoughts, he reaffirmed the truth of what he had written in "Self-Reliance": that power "resides in the moment of transition from a past to a new state" (*CW* 2:40). "The life of man," in the words of the new essay, is "a self-evolving circle, which, from a ring imperceptibly small, rushes on all sides outwards to new and larger circles, and that without end. The extent to which this generation of circles, wheel without wheel will go, depends on the force or truth of the individual soul" (*CW* 2:180). During the next decade and after, *transition*—or in later years, as he took an increasingly longer view, *metamorphosis*—would be Emerson's watchword,[12] and the "new and larger circles" in his own life would engage the scholar more and more with social and even political issues.

v. The Scholar and the Times

When Emerson decided in the fall of 1841 on another course of winter lectures, he envisioned a freer and simpler rhetoric for the platform that would differ both from the formal oration and also from his recently published essays, many of them recast with much labor from earlier writings. To both Carlyle and his brother William he wrote at the end of October of his hopes for a new form of eloquence, telling his brother that "these 'lectures'" might be "capable of a variety of style & matter which no other form of composition admits" (*L* 2:460; cf. *CEC* 308). Perhaps his next offerings, which he was then planning, could attain such eloquence. They could then be printed with but little revision in *The Dial*, the new quarterly edited, with Emerson's help, by Margaret Fuller, or collected in a volume of their own.

Between early December of 1841 and late January of 1842, Emerson delivered eight lectures on "The Times" in Boston, repeating most of them in Providence, Rhode Island, and later in New York. Of the eight, he did indeed choose three—

his "Introductory Lecture," "The Conservative," and "The Transcendentalist"—
for publication in *The Dial* in 1842 and 1843 and for later collection in *Nature,
Addresses, and Lectures* in 1849. Two others, "The Poet" and "Prospects," have since
been printed from surviving manuscripts (*EL* 3:347–82); the remaining three,
"Manners," "Character," and "The Relation of Man to Nature," which have apparently not survived, were presumably incorporated in later writings.

As the "Introductory Lecture" indicates, Emerson had begun working on his
new series with the specific intention of providing "a portrait gallery" of contemporary types: "a series of sketches which would report to the next ages the color
and quality of ours" (*CW* 1:170).[13] This idea had occurred to him in October 1841,
apparently after watching a "Daguerrotype professor" at work (cf. *JMN* 8:113–14,
115–16), but only three of the original lectures conform to this scheme: "The
Conservative," "The Transcendentalist," and "The Poet." He would employ a
somewhat similar plan in *Representative Men* (1850), where he treats six historical
figures as respective examples of "the Philosopher," "the Mystic," "the Skeptic,"
"the Poet," "the Man of the World," and "the Writer." As Henry Nash Smith long
ago suggested, all of these characters, like Emerson's idealized Scholar, were "in
some sense Emerson," constituting partial self-portraits. They struck Smith as "a
collection of embryos that might have developed eventually into characters of
fiction, save for the fact that Emerson did not have a truly dramatic imagination."[14]

The "Introductory Lecture" (*CW* 1:167–83) is organized around two familiar
Emersonian ideas: his conception of Polarity and his awareness of the discouraging
contrast between the ideal and the actual. Standing in polar opposition are "two
omnipresent parties of History," the party of the Past, represented by the Conservative, and the party of the Future, represented by the Reformer. In turning first
to the active reformers within what he calls "the movement party," Emerson builds
upon his previous writings. Each program of reform "is magnified by the natural
exaggeration of its advocates," as he had often charged, but all reform movements
are really "parts of one movement": one which involves "comparison of the idea
with the fact." Although every "effort at the Perfect" originates "in that mysterious
fountain of the moral sentiment in man," and though "the impulse and the theory"
are beautiful, "the practice is less beautiful." "The Reformers affirm the inward life,
but they do not trust it, but use outward and vulgar means. They do not rely on
precisely that strength which wins me to their cause; not on love, not on a principle, but on men, on multitudes, on circumstances, on money, on party; that is, on
fear, on wrath, and pride" (*CW* 1:176). In short, "the reforming movement . . . is in
its origin divine; in its management and details timid and profane."[15]

Next to be examined are those inactive members of the movement party, the
"students"—Emerson does not say "scholars," but he does employ the first person.
We suffer the "new disease" of our age, he declares in professedly speaking for the
students, "and our torment is Unbelief, the Uncertainty as to what we ought to do;
the distrust of the value of what we do, and the distrust that the Necessity (which
we all at last believe in) is fair and beneficent." Such men "pine to be employed, but

are paralyzed by the uncertainty what they should do." Still, he says of them, "Their unbelief arises out of a greater Belief; their inaction out of a scorn of inadequate action. By the side of these men, the hot agitators have a certain cheap and ridiculous air; they even look smaller than the others. Of the two, I own, I like the speculators best" (CW 1:180).

When the lecturer specifies the cause of the students' "uneasiness" as "the love of greatness, . . . the contrast of the dwarfish Actual with the exorbitant Idea," he is again on familiar Emersonian ground. The students are now identified, like Emerson himself in 1836, with the spiritualists, who believe in "the indwelling of the Creator in man" and wish to see "the spiritual principle" demonstrate itself "in all possible applications to the state of man, without the admission of anything unspiritual." What is charged as their fault—"that they have stopped at the intellectual perception; that their will is not yet inspired from the Fountain of Love"—is reminiscent of the complaint against himself that Emerson had publicly acknowledged in the Essays: that "reverence for the intellect" had made him "unjustly cold to the personal relations" (CW 2:101).

This first lecture concludes on a more positive note with a reaffirmation of faith in the eternal spirit which transcends the Times: "underneath all these appearances," Emerson declares, "lies that which is, that which lives, that which causes." And at this point his "true scholar" reappears: "To a true scholar the attraction of the aspects of nature, the departments of life, and the passages of his experience, is simply the information they yield him of this supreme nature which lurks within all. That reality, that causing force is moral. The Moral Sentiment is but its other name" (CW 1:182). Only so far as "that reality . . . shines through them, are these times or any times worth consideration." And "What is the scholar, what is the man for, but for hospitality to every new thought of his time . . . , every unproven opinion, every untried project, which proceeds out of good will and honest seeking." Inactive though he may be, the student as "true scholar" clearly looks to the future.

Emerson's second lecture in the new series (CW 1:184–200), which is less self-revealing than the first, grew out of his belief that "there are better things to be said for the conservative side than have yet been said" (JMN 8:25). The lecture itself argues that "of these two metaphysical antagonists," Conservatism and Reform, "each is a good half, but an impossible whole." So Emerson had previously written of such other polarities as thought and action, society and solitude, advocating a healthy alternation of the two. Conservatism, he holds, "stands on man's incontestable limitations; reform on his indisputable infinitude"—a duality that would increasingly preoccupy him in the years ahead. Conservatives make up the establishment party, which "never puts the foot forward; in the hour when it does that, it is not establishment, but reform."[16] The best thing about conservatism as a principle is its recognition of "the fact which men call Fate"—a fact which reformers ignore at their peril. The objection to a conservative party, however, is "that in its love of acts, it hates principles; it lives in the senses, not in truth; that it sacrifices to despair; it goes for availableness in its candidate, not for worth; and for expediency in its measures, and not for the right" (*CW* 1:196). But as "there is no pure reformer, so . . . there is no pure conservative," and "in a true society, in a true man, both must combine." Reform has to begin with fact, with things as they are, and even as hope for the future has been generated out of the past, so "amidst a planet peopled with conservatives, one Reformer may yet be born."

"The Conservative," with its recognition of "Necessity" and "Fate," anticipates a later, more realistic Emerson, the scholar who in 1851 would be lecturing on "Fate" as a part of his series on "The Conduct of Life." By contrast, "The Transcendentalist" (*CW* 1:201–16) is to some degree retrospective, as though the lecturer were looking back over a phase of his life that now lay behind him. Emerson clearly wished to dissociate himself from the Transcendentalists,[17] and in his public voice he speaks here of "I" and "them." Even so, "The Transcendentalist" constitutes another partial self-portrait.

vi. The Transcendentalist as Idealist

As Emerson had previously divided mankind into two groups, Conservatives and Reformers, in "The Transcendentalist," he distinguishes Materialists and Idealists, defining each in a more comprehensive and understanding way than he had done six years before in *Nature*. "Transcendentalism," he declares, "is Idealism; Idealism as it appears in 1842." The Materialist, by contrast, is much like the Conservative, insisting "on facts, on history, on the force of circumstances, and the animal wants of man"; but as an Idealist the Transcendentalist insists "on the power of Thought and of Will, on inspiration, on miracle, on individual culture." Both modes of thinking are "natural" enough, but the idealist contends that his way is "in higher nature."

Where the Materialist "takes his departure from the external world, and esteems a man as one product of that," the Idealist is inclined, on the basis of personal experience, "to behold the procession of facts you call the world, as flowing perpetually outward from an invisible, unsounded centre in himself, centre alike of him and of them, and necessitating him to regard all things as having a subjective or relative existence, relative to that aforesaid Unknown Centre of him" (*CW* 1:203). The Transcendentalist, moreover, "adopts the whole connexion of spiritual doctrine." (Here Emerson is restating the spiritualist creed, repeating phrases from his "Introductory Lecture.") He "believes in miracle, in the perpetual openness of the human mind to new influx of light and power; he believes in inspiration, and in ecstasy. He wishes that the spiritual principle should be suffered to demonstrate itself to the end, in all possible applications to the state of man, without the admission of anything unspiritual; that is, anything positive, dogmatic, personal" (*CW* 1:204; cf. 1:181).

Believing as he does, the spiritualist "resists all attempts to palm other rules and measures on the spirit than its own," and thus he "easily incurs the charge of antinomianism." He tends also to be an extremist: "If there is anything grand and daring in human thought or virtue, any reliance on the vast, the unknown; any presentiment; any extravagance of faith, the spiritualist adopts it." Such an attitude, Emerson notes, has produced "no such thing as a Transcendental *party*"; indeed, "there is no pure Transcendentalist," for all spiritualists, aiming at perfection, have necessarily "stopped short of their goal." As a "Saturnalia, or excess of faith," Transcendentalism is excessive only when man's "imperfect obedience hinders the satisfaction of his wish." Moreover, it is no recent development:

> This way of thinking, falling on Roman times, made Stoic philosophers; falling on despotic times, made patriot Catos and Brutuses; falling on superstitious times, made prophets and apostles; on popish times, made protestants and ascetic monks, preachers of Faith against the preachers of Works; on prelatical times, made Puritans and Quakers; and falling on Unitarian and commercial times, makes the peculiar shades of Idealism which we know. (*CW* 1:206)

Emerson turns next to the Transcendentalist tendency "to respect the intuitions," which has "deeply colored" the conversation, the poetry, and the religion of the day and led to a phenomenon peculiar to the times: "many intelligent and religious persons," he observes, have lately been moved to withdraw from society in favor of "a certain solitary and critical way of living." They "feel the disproportion between their faculties and the work offered them," yet—like the "students" of the "Introductory Lecture"—they are "crying out for somewhat worthy to do!" Their retirement is not a matter of mere whim; it is chosen "both from temperament and from principle; with some unwillingness, too, and as a choice of the less of two evils." They are lonely; they want love—but loneliness rather than love is likely to be their lot "because of the extravagant demand they make on human nature," for they are "the most exacting and extortionate critics." Inactive as they are, they "prolong their privilege of childhood" by "doing nothing"; "these children" are "not good citizens, not good members of society." "The philanthropists inquire whether Transcendentalism does not mean sloth. They had as lief hear that their friend was dead as that he was a Transcendentalist; for then is he paralyzed, and can never do anything for humanity."

Emerson himself, though ready to grant that "the good and wise must learn to act," is not unsympathetic to the charges against the times levied by the Transcendentalists. In their view, each popular "Cause" such as Abolition, Temperance, Calvinism, or Unitarianism "becomes speedily a little shop," retailing its particular specialty "in small quantities to suit purchasers." Within society as a whole they detect "a spirit of cowardly compromise and seeming, which intimates a frightful skepticism, a life without love, and an activity without an aim." Perhaps it is indeed better to "wait." So had Emerson himself thought in previous years: first during the early 1830s, in practicing his "Philosophy of *Waiting*" until he should find a new profession after resigning his pulpit, and more recently in maintaining "a wise

Emerson's own "philosophy of *waiting*"

" . . . he may be . . . hiving knowledge & concentrating powers to act well hereafter. . . . "
Entry of 21 [22?] December 1834, Journal A, p. 134; see *JMN* 4:368.

passiveness" until he could "see how to act with truth" in the cause of Reform (*EL* 3:266). Now, "to come a little closer to the secret of these persons," he finds it "not so easy to dispose of the doubts and objections that occur to themselves."

Here too there are autobiographical implications, though Emerson is careful to attribute what is being said to others and not to himself: "When I asked them concerning their private experience," they answered "somewhat" as he reports, the essence of their reply being that their faith is based on "a certain brief experience" which comes unexpectedly and is gone "in the space of an hour." Those that were questioned, he notes, would willingly "exchange this flash-of-lightning faith for continuous daylight, this fever-glow for a benign climate." Emerson's own comment on what he calls "these two states of thought" is revealing. From the standpoint of exalted "moments of illumination," he is constrained to say, our ordinary lives have but little meaning.

> Much of our reading, much of our labor, seems mere waiting: it was not that we were born for. Any other could do it as well, or better. So little skill enters into these works, so little do they mix with the divine life, that it really signifies little what we do, whether we turn a grindstone, or ride, or run, or make fortunes, or govern the state. The worst feature of this double consciousness is, that the two lives, of the understanding and of the soul, which we lead, really show very little relation to each other, never meet and measure each other: one prevails now, all buzz and din; and the other prevails then, all infinitude and paradise; and, with the progress of life, the two discover no greater disposition to reconcile themselves. (CW 1:213–14)

Emerson's counsel, here and later in "Experience," is "Patience, and still patience" (cf. CW 3:48–49). "When we pass, as presently we shall, into some new infinitude, out of this Iceland of negations, it will please us to reflect that . . . we bore with our indigence, nor once strove to repair it with hypocrisy or false heat of any kind." Meanwhile, there are more positive things to be said for these troublesome Transcendentalists. They are notably "lovers and worshippers of Beauty," he acknowledges. "In the eternal trinity of Truth, Goodness, and Beauty, each in its perfection including the three, they prefer to make Beauty the sign and head." So Emerson himself had declared in *Nature* that the world "exists to the soul to satisfy the desire of beauty. . . . God is the all-fair. Truth, and goodness, and beauty are but different faces of the same All" (CW 1:17).

Despite their shortcomings, the Transcendentalists, in surrendering themselves "to the heavenly guide," contribute to society: they "show the road in which man should travel, when the soul has greater health and prowess." Society in turn, Emerson concludes, has its duties to such persons, who, "amidst the downward tendency and proneness of things" in an age of materialism, speak to mankind for "thoughts and principles not marketable or perishable." So-called "improvements and mechanical inventions" will be superseded, but "the thoughts which these few hermits strove to proclaim by silence, as well as by speech, not only by what they did, but by what they forbore to do, shall abide in beauty and strength."

9. EXPRESSION, 1842–1844

❖

For all men live by truth, and stand in need of expression. In love, in art, in avarice, in politics, in labor, in games, we study to utter our painful secret. The man is only half himself, the other half is his expression.

—"The Poet" (*CW* 3:4)

In January of 1842 Emerson reported to his brother William that his lectures on "The Times" had yielded "about $320 or about $40. for each lecture. One year I received $57.00" (*L* 3:5). Needing additional money because one of his principal investments had failed to pay a scheduled dividend, he lectured again in Providence; when the audience there proved small and the reward "trivial," he arranged through William to speak for the first time in New York, at the New York Society Library. His lectures "had about the same reception there as elsewhere," he wrote: "very fine & poetical but a little puzzling" (*JMN* 8:203). From this time on he would continue to venture beyond New England as a professional lecturer, his reputation continually growing both from his appearances on the platform and from his published writings.

With the conclusion of his lectures on "The Times" Emerson completed a difficult year. Though neither his letters nor his journals of the period appraise the series in the light of his hopes for achieving a new form of eloquence, he certainly did not complain of the lectures as he had previously denigrated his *Essays* of 1841.[1] Having given much thought to the pressing question of reform and reformers, the scholar had now placed himself unequivocally within the more speculative wing of what he called the movement party, or the party of the Future. Opposing both the conservative "establishment," the party of the Past, and also the organized reformers within the movement party, for whom he had little use, he continued to believe, like William Ellery Channing before him, that reform is a matter of individual self-improvement. Even so, there was nothing in his more recent writing comparable to "The American Scholar" of 1837 or the Divinity School Address of 1838. Though he occasionally wrote of "the true scholar" and his role, his tone in the early 1840s had become less assertive than defensive, whether he was considering scholars in relation to social activism or to Transcendentalism.

i. The Scholar as Skeptic

Since Stephen Whicher's influential examination of Emerson's "inner life" in *Freedom and Fate* (1952), most students of Emerson have agreed that along with the controversy occasioned by the Divinity School Address an incipient skepticism was beginning to challenge his own previously confident faith in himself and even in man's infinitude. The evidence lies less in what Emerson was acknowledging openly than in his private writing, though there are occasional hints in passages of the 1841 *Essays* and the lectures and addresses that he gave later in that same year. In particular, he was troubled by the inevitably transient nature of intense religious experience and perplexed by second thoughts about man's "intuition of the moral sentiment" (*CW* 1:77).

Over the years Emerson had found much to say, both privately and publicly, about the old philosophical problem of the One and the Many, the universal and the particular. As a minister in Boston, we recall, he had told his congregation that his "great object" was "to explore the nature of God" (*YES* 72). In the "transparent eye-ball" passage of *Nature* in 1836 he had described an ecstatic moment in which "The currents of the Universal Being circulate through me; I am part or particle of God" (*CW* 1:10); in 1837, in a celebrated journal entry, he could write that "As a plant in the earth so I grow in God. I am only a form of him. He is the soul of Me"—and then go on to confess that though "A believer in Unity, a seer of Unity, I yet behold two," finding "little access to this Me of Me" (*JMN* 5:336–37). As the years went by the moments of ecstasy seem to have become fewer and more occasional.

It is evident that the subject was of particular concern for Emerson during the early 1840s. In the opening paragraph of "Man the Reformer" in 1841 he declared— with a half-concealed glance at the hostile response to his Divinity School Address—that "the community in which we live will hardly bear to be told that every man should be open to *ecstasy or a divine illumination,* and his daily walk elevated by intercourse with the spiritual world." But in concluding the same lecture he nevertheless pronounced it "better that joy should be spread over all the day in the form of strength, than that it should be *concentrated into ecstasies,* full of danger and followed by reactions," and in "The Transcendentalist" he wrote of those who "wish to exchange this flash-of-lightning faith for continuous daylight, this fever-glow for a benign climate" (*CW* 1:145, 160, 213; emphasis added).

As for "the moral sentiment," David Robinson has recently observed that Emerson's "most profoundly disturbing moments of thought" are "those in which the moral value of human actions is questioned—especially, as in 'Circles,' when his own premises lead him to suspect that there is 'an equivalence and indifference of all actions.' He labeled this form of skepticism 'Pyrrhonism' and struggled with it repeatedly in the 1840s."[2] The "progressive" element in "Circles" posits what Emerson calls there the "law of eternal procession"—a law that extinguishes each partial truth or virtue "in the light of a better" (*CW* 2:186) and so demands a never-ceasing movement toward an infinitely receding goal, "the Unattainable, the flying Perfect" (*CW* 2:179). The implication for the scholar, of course, is that there may be no resting-place along the way, no fixity amid the flux, and no final certainty with respect to either belief or action. Emerson's immediate response in "Circles" is a familiar one: "We learn that God IS; that he is in me," thus affording a "principle of fixture or stability in the soul"—just as amid "eternal generation" in external nature "the eternal generator abides" (*CW* 2:183, 188). And in a later oration at Waterville College in Maine (now Colby College) he affirmed specifically that a man is sustained by "the grace and presence of God" (*CW* 1:122).

As early as June of 1840 Emerson had planned "to write a new Chapter on Nature"—presumably as a sequel to his little book of 1836—for inclusion in his projected volume of essays (*JMN* 7:374, 498). He wished to conclude the book with "Nature" as a "balance" to the essay on "Art," but left it out "unwillingly" because of "some passages which I could not finish to my mind" (*L* 2:387). When he was invited to speak at Waterville College he chose "The Method of Nature" as an appropriate topic, but again the subject gave him trouble. Composition of the address advanced but slowly, and only in mid-July, during a recuperative visit to Nantasket Beach, could he say that "such materials as I have" would indeed "work into an oration, although I have not had any of those visitations of the high Muse which make a few moments of every life memorable" (*L* 2:427). Emerson delivered the oration in August 1841, printed it in a pamphlet, and subsequently collected it, along with "Man the Reformer," in *Nature, Addresses, and Lectures* (1849).

Like "Circles," "The Method of Nature" (*CW* 1:120–37) "stands on the edge between the earlier and later periods in [Emerson's] thought," as Whicher wrote of the related essay;[3] it expresses a scholar's troubled state of mind as Emerson was confronting the conflicting claims of his old faith and his newer skepticism. He opened the Waterville oration by taking note of the immediate occasion, striking a positive note reminiscent of his earlier remarks to similar academic audiences. "A literary anniversary is a celebration of the intellect," he declared to the literary society at Waterville, and "the scholars are the priests of that thought which establishes the foundations of the earth." They "stand for the spiritual interest of the world" and must not "neglect their post in a country where the material interest is so predominant as it is in America." Instead of falling into mere pedantic routine, "the scholar must be a bringer of hope, and must reinforce man against himself." In celebrating the intellect in this address to scholars Emerson proposed first to explore "the *method of nature*" and then "try how far it is transferable to the literary life"—very much a concern of his own in the summer of 1841.

"Intellect," Emerson holds in the oration, "is primary; nature, secondary." And nature, he had come increasingly to think since the mid–1830s, is in perpetual flux. In this new reading of nature he recognizes both a challenge and an opportunity. "We can point nowhere to anything final," he continues, much in the spirit of "Circles"; "but tendency appears on all hands: planet, system, constellation, total nature is growing like a field of maize in July; is becoming somewhat else; is in rapid metamorphosis." Both *metamorphosis* and *tendency* were becoming key terms in Emerson's writings of the 1840s and after, along with *ecstasy*; nature, he declared at Waterville, is indeed "a work of *ecstasy*" ever tending toward growth and change. It "does not exist to any one or to any number of particular ends, but to numberless and endless benefit, [and] there is in it no private will, no rebel leaf or limb, but the whole is oppressed by one superincumbent tendency, obeys that redundancy or excess of life which in conscious beings we call *ecstasy*" (CW 1:126–27).

So too in man. "His health and greatness consist in his being the channel through which heaven flows to earth, in short, in the fulness in which an ecstatical state takes place in him." Here again, that state "seems to direct a regard to the whole and not to the parts; to the cause and not to the ends; to the tendency, and not to the act. It respects genius and not talent; hope, and not possession; the anticipation of all things by the intellect, and not the history itself; art, and not works of art; poetry, and not experiment; virtue, and not duties" (CW 1:131). Every "office or function of man," Emerson continues, is "rightly discharged by this divine method" and must not be "detached from its universal relations."

With reference to "the literary life," Emerson was restating at Waterville the position he had worked out in the "Philosophy of History" lectures in 1836–1837: a writer is but the receptive agent of the superincumbent spirit that creates through him, and he ought therefore to will only the surrender of his own will to "the Universal Power." So runs the inspirational message of "The Method of Nature," which is entirely in keeping with Emerson's earlier thinking about the nature of the creative process. But the oration also carries other implications. "There is virtue, there is genius, there is success, or there is not," the speaker declares. "There is the incoming or the receding of God: that is all we can affirm; and we can show neither how nor why" (CW 1:127; cf. JMN 7:441–42). Should the scholar cease to experience the incoming of the superincumbent spirit and be forced to affirm only its receding—what then? In Robinson's words, Emerson had begun to realize that the necessity of an ecstatic experience "is no guarantee of its availability. Even when he celebrates this experience, his language betrays what was becoming the central problem of his spiritual and intellectual life." Moreover, his recognition of "the elusive nature of truth" might well have troubling implications for a man who had "forged a vocation of truth-seeking for himself, in the form of his conception of the 'scholar.'"[4]

To complicate Emerson's life further, there were important domestic changes during the early 1840s: the passing on 21 September 1841 of Dr. Ripley, "this oak of ninety years" (JMN 8:53); the birth on 22 November of a second daughter, Edith; and on 27 January 1842, the untimely death from scarlet fever of young Waldo Emerson, not yet six years of age. The Emersons were devastated by loss of their beloved Waldo. "Lidian, the poor Lidian, moans at home by day & by night," her husband told Carlyle in reporting the death of that "sweet & wonderful boy" (CEC 317). The stricken father's numerous letters and journal entries concerning the child are poignant indeed. He could find no adequate way to express his inward feelings in the face of an outward event that somehow seemed unreal: "Alas! I chiefly grieve that I cannot grieve," he wrote in early February to Caroline Sturgis, lamenting "that this fact takes no more deep hold than other facts, is as

dreamlike as they" (L 3:9). The mood persisted, driving him further into subjec-
tivism and fostering his already latent skepticism.[5]

In 1841, describing in "The Transcendentalist" what he called the "double consciousness," Emerson had observed regretfully that our "two lives, of the understanding and of the soul," never come together (CW 1:213). During the next few
years they seemed to diverge even more radically for him—especially after the
debilitating loss of Waldo. In January of 1844, on the second anniversary of the
boy's death, he confessed to Margaret Fuller that he was still not reconciled, either
to his "calamity" or to "the inarticulateness of the Supreme Power" (L 3:238–39).
Lidian Emerson's health remained poor and her spirit frighteningly low; a canceled journal entry of 1843 set down by her husband quotes her as wishing "she
had never been born. I do not see how God can compensate me for the sorrow of
existence" (JMN 8:365).

In a moving passage of "Experience," included in his Essays: Second Series of 1844,
Emerson himself was to write of that "innavigable sea" that "washes with silent
waves between us and the things we aim at and converse with."

> Grief too will make us idealists. In the death of my son, now more than two years ago, I
> seem to have lost a beautiful estate,—no more. I cannot get it nearer to me. . . .
> [S]omething which I fancied was a part of me, which could not be torn away without
> tearing me, nor enlarged without enriching me, falls off from me, and leaves no
> scar. . . . I grieve that grief can teach me nothing, nor carry me one step into real
> nature. . . . Nothing is left us now but death. We look to that with a grim satisfaction,
> saying, there at least is reality that will not dodge us. (CW 2:29; cf. JMN 8:200–201)

As his inner life grew darker Emerson had sought to occupy himself with external
activities: watching over his troubled wife and surviving children, spading his
garden, arranging for lectures, talking with Irish laborers on the new railroad
entering Concord, dealing with visitors, helping his friends. Meanwhile, he was
writing verse and working intermittently on his new volume of essays, where the
old Emersonian dualisms of the understanding and the soul, the particular and the
universal, are recurrent themes.

ii. *Essays: Second Series*

Emerson's grasping for some tangible objective "reality" after the death of Waldo
may account to some degree for his increasing preoccupation with outward affairs
during ensuing years. In March of 1842 he reluctantly agreed to take over full
editorship of *The Dial* "for a time" from Margaret Fuller, who felt unable to continue carrying the burden. The position was unpaid, since the magazine was
perennially in financial straits, and the only alternative seemed to be suspending
publication. "Perhaps I shall rue this day of accepting such an intruder on my
peace such a consumer of my time" as *The Dial,* Emerson wrote, hoping for a

"rotation in martyrdom" rather than a "partnership of oversight" (L 3:35). For two years he continued as sole editor, soliciting contributions from his friends, printing some of his own lectures, and even going into debt to keep the magazine alive despite a steadily decreasing readership, until finally ending its history with the number for April 1844.

In the early months of 1843 and again in 1844 Emerson spoke in various eastern cities and towns, including Baltimore, Philadelphia, and New York, usually offering some or all of a new series of five lectures on "New England" that has so far remained unpublished. During this period he took time from his own writing to arrange for publication in Boston of Carlyle's *Past and Present* (1843), which he reviewed in *The Dial,* and Margaret Fuller's *A Summer on the Lakes* (1844). On 10 July 1844 Lidian gave birth to a son, Edward. Meanwhile, though "poor enough to need to lecture," her husband had decided against preparing another complete lecture course in order to "make a new book, of which the materials collect themselves, day by day" (L 3:214).[6] Instead, he would either repeat old lectures or speak only on special occasions.

When Emerson determined the final order of the nine chapters that comprise his *Essays: Second Series* he arranged eight of them in pairs. Some, like "Character" and "Manners," are complementary while others are contrasting, like the major essays on "The Poet" and "Experience" that open the volume. As a would-be see-er of Unity who repeatedly saw two, he habitually thought in terms of paired entities of all kinds, as we know from the essay of 1841 on "Compensation" and the even earlier announcement in "The American Scholar" of his often-cited dualistic principle of Undulation or Polarity (CW 1:61). There is a key to the orientation of his new book in "Nominalist and Realist," the eighth essay of 1844, where he reasserts his old sense of doubleness-in-unity: "All the universe over, there is but one thing, this old Two-Face, creator-creature, mind-matter, right-wrong, of which any proposition may be affirmed or denied" (CW 3:144). Believing as he did, Emerson as a professional writer had come to think that no single sentence—or, for that matter, no single essay—"will hold the whole truth."

This conviction on Emerson's part has much to do with both the organization and the tone of *Essays: Second Series* and the works that followed it. Asserting that "everyman is a partialist," he could then add—with equal justification—that "every man is a universalist also." Indeed, we are all "amphibious creatures, weaponed for two elements, having two sets of faculties, the particular and the catholic"—or, in terms of "the famous dispute" among medieval philosophers, we are both Nominalists and Realists (CW 3:144, 135, 136). As a Realist and generalist, Emerson wrote "The Poet," his last essay in the idealistic line of "The American Scholar" and the Divinity School Address; as a Nominalist and particularist, he wrote "Experience." Within a single essay of 1844, "Politics," where he again acknowledges the universal "fact of two poles," he considers both the actual and the ideal aspects of political life. On the one hand he notes the tendency of social organizations, political movements included, to "degenerate into personalities." On the other, though distressed by the state of contemporary politics, he can still look optimistically toward the future because of his own generalist's faith in "the beneficent necessity which shines through all laws." Emerson subscribed to the familiar idea that "the less government we have, the better," because he believed in "the influence of private character, the growth of the Individual," and looked idealistically to "the appearance of the wise man, of whom the existing government, is, it must be owned, but a shabby imitation" (cf. *EL* 3:242).

Emerson's "wise man," a Realist's concept that had first emerged in the lecture on "Politics" of 1840, is envisioned in much the same spirit as his American Scholar of 1837. Both are ideal figures, not living individuals:

> To educate the wise man, the State exists; and with the appearance of the wise man, the State expires. The appearance of character makes the State unnecessary. The wise man is the State. He needs no army, fort, or navy,—he loves men too well. . . . He needs no library for he has not done thinking; no church, for he is a prophet; no statute book, for he has the lawgiver; no money, for he is value; no road, for he is at home where he is; no experience, for the life of the creator shoots through him, and looks from his eyes. (*CW* 3:126; cf. *EL* 3:243)

But in "Nominalist and Realist," writing as a Nominalist, Emerson grants that in actuality no living man can wholly realize the idea that he partially embodies (*CW* 3:134). This statement, obviously a qualification of his earlier idea of the Scholar as Universal Man, the Thinker who represents and thinks for all mankind, is clearly an anticipation of the lectures on "Representative Men" that he would deliver during the following winter.

Apart from the idealized scholar-like figure of the wise man, there is little explicit reference to scholars in *Essays: Second Series*, and in this respect it resembles both *Nature* and the *Essays* of 1841. In "New England Reformers," for example, Emerson points to a "destitution of faith" among scholars and other members of "the literary class," tracing it to the shortcomings of current educational practice in New England (*CW* 3:158–59). In "Experience" he notes that "among the farms" a scholar—meaning "the artist, the orator, the poet"—is commonly taken as exhibiting a single tendency apparently carried to excess: such persons are "nature's victims of expression," and those who see them "too near" pronounce them "failures,—not heroes, but quacks" and charge that their arts "are not for man, but are disease." Yet "Irresistible nature made men such," the essayist affirms in their defense, "and makes legions more of such, every day" (*CW* 3:38).[7]

iii. The Scholar as Poet

In pairing "The Poet" with his new essay on "Experience" Emerson apparently intended to contrast poetry with life, or the ideal with the actual, for in "The Poet" he was once more delineating an ideal figure while in the companion essay he was dealing with day-to-day living. The Divinity School Address of 1838 had envisioned the scholar in the specific role of "true preacher"; "The Poet" (*CW* 3:1–24) idealizes the true scholar-poet as "the man of Beauty." In other essays of 1844, as we have seen, Emerson grouped artists, orators, poets, and other writers as "scholars"; since the early 1830s he had in fact used such terms almost interchangeably.[8] Moreover, he employed the very word "poetry" to cover a wide range of writing, embracing imaginative prose as well as verse, and in the essay of 1844 he emphasized imaginative perception rather than technical proficiency as essential to the making of true poetry.

"The Poet" deals in turn with three principal topics: the essential qualities of poetry and the poet, the poetic function of imagery and symbol—a matter which had fascinated Emerson since the mid–1830s—and a new subject, the current state of poetry in America. At the outset the essay recurs to the concepts of expression and representation that Emerson had previously developed in the "Philosophy of History" lectures and "The American Scholar." As "Man Thinking," the Scholar of 1837 had represented the idea of Man to other men; "the poet," Emerson now declares, is likewise "representative," for he "stands among partial men for the complete man, and apprises us not of his wealth, but of the commonwealth." Thus "The young man reveres men of genius, because, to speak truly, they are more himself than he is. They receive of the soul as he also receives, but they more" (*CW* 3:4). The difference between "the young man" and the poet is a matter of degree, in their ability not only to "receive of the soul" but also to express in some form whatever truth may be lodged within them: "For all men live by truth and stand in need of expression. In love, in art, in avarice, in politics, in labor, in games, we study to utter our painful secret. The man is only half himself, the other half is his expression" (*CW* 3:4). Expression, it will be noted, is not simply a matter of speaking or writing: "Words and deeds are quite indifferent modes of the divine energy" that prompts all forms of utterance. "Words are also actions, and actions are a kind of words" (cf. *JMN* 8:252).

Given "this necessity to be published," it is unfortunate that among most men and women, "adequate expression is rare." The poet, by contrast, is "the man without impediment, who sees and handles what others dream of, traverses the whole scale of experience, and is representative of man, in virtue of being the largest power to receive and to impart." "The true poet" is a man of genius; lesser writers are only "men of talents who sing, and not the children of music." For a mere "lyrist," or versifier, the argument of his poem is purely secondary while "the finish of the verses is primary"; for the true poet, however, "it is not metres, but a metre-making argument, that makes a poem." The primary means and materials that the poet employs are images from nature, the "picture-language" that symbolizes "'Things more excellent than any image.'" Here Emerson's ideas are in keeping with his thinking during the early 1830s that had culminated in the "Language" chapter of *Nature*. Now he declares that the poet, by "an ulterior intellectual perception," gives material things "a power which makes their old use forgotten, and puts eyes, and a tongue, into every dumb and inanimate object."

The poet also understands and applies what Emerson in 1841 had described as "the *method of nature*," that dynamic force for change he repeatedly called "metamorphosis." Through his "better perception" the poet "sees the flowing or metamorphosis; perceives that thought is multiform; that within the form of every creature is a force impelling it to ascend into a higher form; and following with his eyes the life, uses the forms which express that life, and so his speech flows with the flowing of nature" (*CW* 3:12). In *Nature* Emerson had defined imagination as "the use which the Reason makes of the material world" (*CW* 1:31); now he writes that the poet's insight "expresses itself by what is called Imagination." Insight is "a very high sort of seeing, which does not come by study, but by the intellect being where and what it sees, by sharing the path, or circuit of things through forms, and so making them translucid to others" (*CW* 3:15). Moreover, the true poet draws on "a great public power . . . by unlocking, at all risks, his human doors, and suffering the ethereal tides to roll and circulate through him" (cf. *JMN* 8:378). His imaginative use of symbols may well prove intoxicating to both himself and his reader, for symbolism "has a certain power of emancipation and exhilaration for all men": "This is the effect on us of tropes, fables, oracles and all poetic forms. Poets are thus liberating gods. Men have really got a new sense, and found within their world, another world, or nest of worlds, for, the metamorphosis once seen, it does not stop" (*CW* 3:17).

As for the poet's subject matter, Emerson had long noted with approval that writers of the time had come to explore and poetize "the near, the low, the common" rather than "the sublime and beautiful." "I embrace the common," he had declared in a much-quoted passage of "The American Scholar," and therefore seek the meaning of such common things as "The meal in the firkin; the milk in the pan; the ballad in the street; the news of the boat; the glance of the eye; the form and the gait of the body."

> Show me the ultimate reason of these matters;—show me the sublime presence of the highest spiritual cause lurking, as always it does lurk, in these suburbs and extremities of nature; . . . and the shop, the plough, and the leger, referred to the like cause by which light undulates and poets sing;—and the world . . . has form and order; there is no trifle; there is no puzzle; but one design unites and animates the farthest pinnacle and the lowest trench. (*CW* 1:67–68)

Believing that "the experience of each age requires a new confession," as he writes in "The Poet," Emerson had remarked in his essay on "Art" in 1841 that "the artist must employ the symbols in use in his day and nation" (*CW* 2:210). With his dynamic conception of an inner life ever seeking to express itself outwardly in whatever form might readily serve, he drew no hard-and-fast line between the so-called fine arts and those regarded only as useful. And like Wordsworth before him, who had described man's inventions as nature's "lawful offspring," he found no essential difference between the bounty of nature and the artificial products of man's mind and hand. Thus he affirms in "The Poet" that "the factory-village, and the railway" are fit subjects for contemporary poetry, for the true poet "sees them fall within the great Order not less than the bee-hive, or the spider's geometrical web. . . . The chief value of the new fact, is to enhance the great and constant fact of Life, . . . to which the belt of wampum, and the commerce of America, are alike" (CW 3:11–12).

But in spite of this enlarged conception of poetry and the poet, Emerson was obliged to acknowledge regretfully in his concluding paragraphs of "The Poet" that "I look in vain for the poet whom I describe."

> We have yet had no genius in America, with tyrannous eye, which knew the value of our incomparable materials, and saw, in the barbarism and materialism of the times, another carnival of the same gods whose picture he so much admires in Homer; then in the middle age; then in Calvinism. Banks and tariffs, the newspaper and caucus, methodism and unitarianism, are flat and dull to dull people, but rest on the same foundations of wonder as the town of Troy and the temple of Delphi, and are as swiftly passing away. Our logrolling, our stumps and their politics, our fisheries, our Negroes, and Indians, our boasts, and our repudiations, the wrath of rogues, and the pusil-lanimity of honest men, the northern trade, the southern planting, the western clear-ing, Oregon, and Texas, are yet unsung. Yet America is a poem in our eyes; its ample geography dazzles the imagination, and it will not wait long for metres. (CW 3: 21–22)

In both "Art" and "The Poet," as Leo Marx has recently observed, Emerson was indeed propounding an idealist's program for coping with technological changes occurring in American life, and we know that there were writers and artists of nineteenth-century America who took his words to heart.[9] Marx writes percep-tively of Emerson's evident faith that artists, by resolving "conflicts of value and meaning in their work," could help others to resolve similar conflicts in society:

> To his injunction that artists employ symbols . . . in use in their own day and nation, Emerson therefore would add this: employ them in a manner calculated to overcome any destructive consequences they might have. . . . [He] calls upon artists to depict typical scenes of the era, such as the new factories, steamboats, or railroads in the landscape, but to depict them from an ideal viewpoint, affirmatively, as a farsighted, aspiring citizen of a young republic would want and expect them to look.[10]

iv. "The new philosophy"

Though Emerson's own verses of the 1840s scarcely match his sweeping vision of what the new American poetry should be and do, they have their own special values for both author and reader. For example, the slow process of reconciliation and healing that helped him come to terms with the loss of Waldo is reflected in his poem called "Threnody" (W 9:148–58), begun in the spring of 1842, within weeks of the boy's death in January, and published in the Poems of 1846. Its first 175 lines, incorporating phrases from the father's recent letters to friends, poignantly express Emerson's immediate sense of desolation. In the remaining lines, written in 1843 or perhaps even later, "the deep Heart" answers the bereaved poet's complaint, calling him once again to "ope thy heart to know / What rainbows teach, and sunsets show"—that *"What is excellent, / As God lives, is permanent,"* and though *"Hearts are dust, hearts' loves remain. . . ."* A similar thought appears in "Nominalist and Realist" (*CW* 3:131–45):

> It is the secret of the world that all things subsist, and do not die, but only retire a little from sight, and afterwards return again. Whatever does not concern us, is concealed from us. As soon as a person is no longer related to our present well-being, he is concealed, or *dies,* as we say. Really, all things and persons are related to us, but according to our nature, they act on us not at once, but in succession, and we are made aware of their presence one at a time. All persons, all things which we have known, are here present, and many more than we see; the world is full. (*CW* 3:142)

Emerson's emphasis here on "succession" is in keeping with what he had written of "the law of eternal procession" in "Circles" and "The Method of Nature"; it anticipates the influential concept of the "stream of consciousness" in the empirical philosophy of William James, who learned much from Emerson's writings. "Succession" occurs also as one of the "lords of life" in the essay on "Experience" (*CW* 3:25–49), to which "Nominalist and Realist" serves as a kind of gloss; both essays seek to express and somehow to reconcile life's seeming contradictions. Concerning "Experience," a study by David W. Hill of the textual evidence in Emerson's journals and notebooks demonstrates that his "ideas about the essay and its subject became more problematical the further he was in time from the death of his son," the event "to which many commentators attribute the uncertainty and darkness of tone in the essay."[11] Though Emerson incorporated passages written shortly after Waldo's death in 1842, he also went back to earlier journals for material. He drafted still other passages in the spring and summer of 1843 after making a tentative outline, but did not put the essay in final form until the summer of 1844, shortly before it went to the printer.

"Every man's condition," Emerson had written in *Nature,* "is a solution in hieroglyphic to those inquiries he would put. He acts it as life, before he apprehends it as truth" (*CW* 1:7). In 1837 he had remarked on the strange process of "conversion" by which "experience becomes thought or life, truth"; the scholar's special office as a teacher, he believed, is "to convert life into truth" and even to "deal out" to others his own life: "life metamorphosed" (*JMN* 5:320; *EL* 2:202; *JMN* 5:464). Having "set [his] heart on honesty" in composing "Experience" (which he had tentatively titled "Life"), Emerson studied to utter his own painful secrets, referring specifically to the death of Waldo and also giving open expression to the skeptical strain already discernible in his thinking since the late 1830s. Writing in the first person and using "I" as well as the more customary "we," he recognized that "I am not the novice I was fourteen, nor yet seven years ago"—that is, in 1830, when he was a young minister in Boston, or even in 1837, when he delivered "The American

The Scholar's "new philosophy"
Entry of 8 February 1843, Journal Z[A] (written from back to front), pp. 97–96; see *JMN*
8:335–36. Three of the paragraphs on these pages of the journal were used in "Experience."

Scholar." Though now more experienced, he still believed that "in going down
into the secrets of his own mind" he also "descended into the secrets of all minds,"
as he had written of the scholar (*CW* 1:63); in this spirit he would share with his
readers a "new statement," one which "will comprise the skepticisms, as well as the
faiths of society."

By *skepticisms,* Emerson explains, he means "limitations of the affirmative statement" which "the new philosophy" must incorporate along with "the oldest beliefs"
(*CW* 3:43; cf. *JMN* 8:337, 336). For a scholar who had long thought of himself as a
kind of moral astronomer, a "Watcher" on a tower "cataloguing obscure and nebulous stars of the human mind" (*JMN* 4:370–71; 5:135; *CW* 1:62), the challenge of
skepticism had come as a matter not of living but of *seeing*—that same long-trea-
sured faculty of sight and insight that Emerson had celebrated as early as *Nature*
(characterized in chapter 4 above as "a book about vision, the process of vision,
the uses of vision") and as recently as "The Poet." In their contrasting treatments of
perception, "Experience" and "The Poet" can profitably be read as the obverse and
reverse sides of the same coin.

The issue emerges in the initial paragraph of "Experience." "Where do we find
ourselves?" the essayist asks. His immediate answer—not his final one—is composed in the same key as his first sad reflections on the death of Waldo and his still-
earlier admission in "Circles" that "eternal procession" might well foster "a fine

pyrrhonism." Confused by our "illusions," we suppose ourselves to be somehow placed in an infinite *series*—

> a series, of which we do not know the extremes, and believe that it has none. We wake and find ourselves on a stair; there are stairs below us, which we seem to have ascended, there are stairs above us, many a one, which go upward and *out of sight*. . . . Sleep lingers all our lifetime *about our eyes*. . . . All things swim and glimmer. *Our life is not so much threatened as our perception*. Ghostlike we glide through nature, and should not know our place again. (*CW* 3:27; emphasis added)

The essay repeatedly offers similar qualifications or limitations of Emerson's affirmative statements in his previous writings. Instead of stressing the private man's "infinitude," that potential openness to what in *Nature* he had called "the currents of the Universal Being" and in "The Poet" "the ethereal tides," Emerson now speaks of spiritual aridity. We are "like millers on the lower levels of a stream," he laments, "when the factories above them have exhausted the water." As a symbol of spiritual life and power, water is ubiquitous in Emerson. A similar expression of regret for its absence occurs in "The Poet": "On the brink of *the waters of life and truth*, we are miserably dying" (*CW* 3:19; emphasis added).[12] In that essay Emerson affirms that the poet is empowered to emancipate us from this dread condition; in "Experience," where he applies in a prose composition his conception of poetic practice, the very structure and movement of the argument and especially the essayist's skillful use of a poet's "picture-language" effectively demonstrate his belief that the scholar-as-poet can serve mankind as a "liberating god."

The initial premise of "Experience" is that "we lack the affirmative principle": being literally without inspiration, we therefore "have no superfluity of spirit for new creation." Proceeding from this seemingly unpromising starting-point, the essay grapples in turn with the seven "lords of life" that in various ways affect one's ability to perceive and in turn to create: Illusion, Temperament, Succession, Surface, Surprise, Reality, and Subjectiveness. (The order of topics had shifted as the essay slowly took form.) In each instance, Emerson employs apt metaphorical language to establish the desired tone. Beginning with the striking images already noted in the opening discussion of Illusion, he moves next to Temperament, holding that our temperament "shuts us in a prison of glass"—a prison *"which we cannot see"* (emphasis added). The image of imprisonment within an invisible glass prison contrasts with the exuberant "transparent eye-ball" passage of *Nature*, where nature itself, Emerson had written, becomes transparent and her ecstatic beholder "see[s] all." "Life," the essayist now declares metaphorically, is "a train of moods like a string of beads, and as we pass through them, they prove to be many-colored *lenses* which paint the world their own hue, and each allows only what lies in its focus. . . . Temperament is the iron wire on which the beads are strung" (*CW* 3:30; emphasis added).

As recently as 1841, in "Circles," Emerson had declared that "The only sin is limitation. As soon as you once come up with a man's limitations, it is all over with him" (*CW* 2:182–83); now he acknowledges Temperament as "the veto or limitation-power" in one's constitution. Again in "Circles" and in "The Method of Nature," he had hailed the process of continuous change, or metamorphosis, operating both in nature and in human life. But now, in next considering "the succession of moods or objects" he writes: "Gladly we would anchor, but the anchorage is quicksand. This onward trick of nature is too strong for us."

With another shift in mood and tone the essayist next reacts against what is termed a purely "intellectual tasting of life" by offering, under the rubric of Surface, what he calls "practical wisdom."

> There are objections to every course of life and action, and the practical wisdom infers an indifferency, from the omnipresence of objection. The whole frame of things preaches indifferency. Do not craze yourself with thinking, but go about your business anywhere. Life is not intellectual or critical, but sturdy. Its chief good is for well-mixed people who can enjoy what they find, without question. . . . To fill the hour,—that is happiness; to fill the hour, and leave no crevice for a repentance or an approval. We live amid surfaces, and the true art of life is to skate well on them. (*CW* 3:35)

And when the essayist turns to the subject of writers and writing, he has similar advice for scholars—himself included:

> Expediency of literature, reason of literature, lawfulness of writing down a thought, is questioned; much is to say on both sides, and, while the fight waxes hot, thou, dearest scholar, stick to thy foolish task, add a line every hour, and between whiles add a line. . . . [S]tay there in thy closet and toil, until the rest are agreed what to do. . . . Thy sickness, they say, and thy puny habit, require that thou do this or avoid that, but know that thy life is a flitting state, a tent for a night, and do thou, sick or well, finish that stint. (*CW* 3:37–38)

So Emerson himself had stuck to his own scholar's task—foolish or otherwise—despite the doubts and despair he was experiencing during the early 1840s.

It is easy for the unwary reader of "Experience" to be beguiled by the persuasive tone of what the essay has to say about any one of the "lords of life"—especially Surface, which appears not only to counsel a dualist's acceptance of "the clangor and jangle of contrary tendencies" but to advocate a life of moderation and balance; at one time, in making a tentative outline for "Experience," Emerson in fact thought of heading a section of the projected essay "The golden mean" (*JMN* 8:412). "Human life is made up of the two elements, power and form," according to the completed essay, "and the proportion must be invariably kept, if we would have it sweet and sound. Each of these elements in excess makes a mischief as hurtful as its defect"—and it is at this climactic point in his treatment of Surface that Emerson ironically adduces "the scholars," among them "the artist, the orator, the poet," as "nature's victims of expression."

But here the overall movement of the essay takes a significant rhetorical turn as Surface gives way to Surprise in the pivotal fifth section, where concepts and images prominent in Emerson's earlier writings emerge once again. "How easily, if fate would suffer it, we might keep forever these beautiful limits, and adjust ourselves, once for all, to the perfect calculation of the kingdom of known cause and effect." So the new section begins. Here both content and metaphor shift dramatically as the essayist moves from surface to depth and from tangible form to intangible power. Power—in some respects the underlying subject of the entire essay, whether the concern is with its absence or its presence—"Power keeps quite another road than *the turnpikes of choice and will,* namely, *the subterranean and invisible tunnels and channels of life,*" and life itself is "a series of surprises, and would not be worth taking or keeping, if it were not. . . . Nature hates calculators; her methods are saltatory and impulsive. Man lives by pulses; our organic movements are such; and the chemical and ethereal agents are undulatory and alternate; and the mind goes antagonizing on, and never prospers but by fits" (*CW* 3:39; emphasis added).

"Power" as Emerson conceived it is that very "superfluity of spirit for new creation" which had seemed so utterly lacking at the opening of the essay. Here, writing in an altogether different mood, he defines in terms of his old faith the ultimate source of creative power: "The ardors of piety agree at last with the coldest skepticism,—that nothing is of us or our works,—that all is of God. Nature will not spare us the smallest leaf of laurel. All writing comes by the grace of God, and all doing and having. . . . I can see nothing at last, in success or failure, than more or less of vital force supplied from the Eternal" (*CW* 3:40; cf. *JMN* 8:148). Given that vital spiritual force, that divine power, one can accomplish great things; without it, little or nothing. "The individual," if unaided and alone, "is always mistaken."

Having drawn a larger circle that both recognizes and incorporates "limitations of the affirmative statement" while also reaffirming Emerson's "oldest beliefs," the essayist can move on from Surprise to Reality. Life, he tells us here, "has no memory."

> That which proceeds in succession might be remembered, but that which is coexistent, or ejaculated from a deeper cause, as yet far from being conscious, knows not its own tendency. So it is with us, now *skeptical, or without unity, because immersed in forms and effects all seeming to be of equal yet hostile value,* and now *religious, whilst in the reception of spiritual law. . . .* Underneath the inharmonious and trivial particulars, is a musical perfection, the Ideal journeying always with us, the heaven without rent or seam. (*CW* 3:40–41; emphasis added)

Here, we should note, "Experience" is at one with both "Self-Reliance" and "Circles" in exalting the One over the Many, the abiding Universal over the "trivial particulars." And if, as a Nominalist, Emerson had "described life as a flux of moods," Emerson as Realist "must now add, that there is that in us which changes not, and which ranks all sensations and states of mind" (*CW* 3:42; cf. *JMN* 7:429).

In his ensuing topic, Subjectiveness, the essayist engages the persistent question of perception, honestly acknowledging that "we have no means of correcting these colored and distorting lenses which we are, or of computing the amount of their errors. Perhaps these subject-lenses have a creative power; perhaps there are no objects." Such solipsistic thoughts breed loneliness, as Emerson well knew; they may even lead an egoist to permit to himself what he would term "sin" in others. "As I am, so I see," he realizes, for "use what language we will, we can never say anything but what we are." But the Emersonian correlative of all these difficulties and limitations is "the capital virtue of self-trust": "a main lesson of wisdom" is "to know your own from another's" and so to pursue, undistracted by pressures from without, your own aim.

In concluding "Experience" the essayist returns to the old charge against the scholar that he had alluded to in discussing Surprise: "People disparage knowing and the intellectual life, and urge doing. I am very content with knowing, if only I could know." While well aware that "the world I converse with in the city and in the farms, is not the world I *think*," Emerson would continue to observe and respect their difference. "One day," he conjectured, "I shall know the value and law of this discrepance. But I have not found that much was gained by manipular attempts to realize the world of thought"—a thrust, one suspects, at certain contemporary reformers. Meanwhile, he would practice his philosophy of *waiting*: "Patience and patience" is again the watchword (*CW* 3:48–49), as he had said previously in "The American Scholar" and "The Transcendentalist" (*CW* 1:69, 214), for—given his spiritualist's faith in the inevitable tendency of things toward betterment—"we shall win at the last." Meanwhile,

> in the solitude to which every man is always returning, he has a sanity and revelations, which in his passage into new worlds he will carry with him. Never mind the ridicule, never mind the defeat: up again, old heart!—it seems to say,—there is victory yet for all justice, and the true romance which the world exists to realize, will be the transformation of genius into practical power. (*CW* 3:49; cf. *JMN* 9:53)

10. REPRESENTATION, 1845–1846

I cannot often enough say, that a man is only a relative and representative nature. Each is a hint of the truth . . . which yet he quite newly and inevitably suggests to us. . . . All our poets, heroes, and saints, fail utterly in some one or in many parts to satisfy our idea . . . and so leave us without any hope of realization but in our own future. Our exaggeration of all fine characters arises from the fact, that we identify each in turn with the soul. But there are no such men as we fable.

— "Nominalist and Realist" (*CW* 3:133–34)

With the appearance of *Essays: Second Series* in October of 1844 Emerson resumed lecturing in various Massachusetts cities and towns, apparently making use during the fall and winter of existing manuscripts in the "New England" series. Then on 2 April 1845 he read in Concord a new lecture on "Bonaparte," an early draft of "Napoleon, or the Man of the World" in the series on "Representative Men" that he was to present in Boston during the following winter. In the summer of 1845 he delivered the first address devoted entirely to the scholar that he had given since "Literary Ethics" in 1838: on 22 July, in his words, he made "a literary speech to the students of Middlebury College," and on 6 August he repeated it, "now enlarged & retrenched," at Wesleyan University.

The New York *Daily Tribune* of 4 August carried a favorable notice of the oration as presented at Middlebury, calling it an "earnest and eloquent exposition of the 'natural functions of the scholar and educated man.'" Emerson himself reported to Lidian that it "passed very well" at Wesleyan, being "all the better for having had a rehearsal at Middlebury" (*L* 3:293, 294–95 and note). As late as 1 September he had some thought of printing the address, as he told his new friend James Elliot Cabot (*L* 3:299). Instead, he began to incorporate a number of its more eloquent paragraphs in the new lectures on "Representative Men" that he would later publish as a book in 1850—particularly in passages of "Montaigne, or the Skeptic" (*CW* 4:102–4) and "Goethe, or the Writer" (*CW* 4:152–55). Long afterward, in 1876, Cabot would adapt the remaining portions of the manuscript for Emerson to read at the University of Virginia under the title of "The Scholar" (*W* 10:259–89).[1]

i. The Scholar Once More

As shown in Emerson's "Middlebury Notes" (*JMN* 12:548–49; cf. 12:496–97), he had thought first of "Literature" as his subject for the address of 1845. As materials for the "Discourse at Middlebury College" took form in his notebook and journal, however, he began to focus specifically on his old ideal of the scholar, now characterizing him as "sane-man, connector, generalizer, spiritualist" (*JMN* 12:550)—in short, as a Realist. According to the manuscript of the "Discourse," Emerson found "a provision in the Constitution of the world for the class of scholars, for the theorist, the writer, for him who is to show identity & connexion where men see nothing but fragments, & to supply the axis on which the frame of things turns" (p. 5); in "Goethe" he expanded this sentence, identifying "the class of scholars or writers" as those individuals

> who see connexion, where the multitude see fragments, and who are impelled to exhibit the facts in ideal order, and so to supply the axis on which the frame of things turns. Nature has dearly at heart the formation of the speculative man, or scholar. It is an end never lost sight of, and is prepared in the original casting of things. He is no permissive or accidental appearance, but an organic agent in nature, one of the estates of the realm, provided and prepared from of old and from everlasting, in the knitting and contexture of things. (*CW* 4:153–54)

Emerson had accepted the invitation to speak at Middlebury only twenty days before he was due to appear there (*L* 3:291). As he set about composing his rather loosely structured address, apparently outlining as he went along,[2] he drew heavily upon undated entries in Journal W (used from March to September 1845), took a few other passages from earlier journals, and added much new material. Opening with remarks on the fellowship of "lettered men," he announced as his topic "the natural and permanent function of the Scholar" (*W* 10:261, 264). Then he offered an impressive argument for the scholar's value to a society of "practical" people—a segment used in part in "Goethe" (cf. *CW* 4:153–55), where he retained much of what he had once again written on the old subject of action. *In*action is preferable to *mis*action, he declared in the "Discourse" (*W* 10:268); in "Goethe" he warned that "A certain partiality, a headiness, and loss of balance, is the tax which all actions must pay. Act, if you like, but you do it at your peril. Men's actions are too strong for them. Show me a man who has acted, and who has not been the victim and slave of his action." What particularly troubled him was "actions that divorce the speculative from the practical faculty, and put a ban on reason and sentiment," for at bottom, as "the Hindoos write in their sacred books, . . . 'the speculative and the practical doctrines are one.' For great action must draw on the spiritual nature" (*CW* 4:154; cf. *JMN* 9:231, 254).

The true scholar, Emerson continued in the "Discourse," will exhibit both energy and courage. Indeed, "The speculative man, the scholar, is the right hero," and "the scholar or spiritual man" is "indispensable to the Republic or Commonwealth of Man. Nature could not leave herself without a seer and expounder" (*W* 10:274, 275). Being the "ripened" product of self-culture, the scholar will serve as that "mediator between the spiritual and the actual world" that Emerson had called for in "Man the Reformer" and earlier in "Literary Ethics"; he will both think and act, converting intellect into energy:

> It is excellent when the individual is ripened to that degree that he touches both the centre and the circumference, so that he is not only widely intelligent, but carries a council in his breast for the emergency of to-day; and alternates the contemplation of the fact in pure intellect, with the total conversion of the intellect into energy; Jove, and the thunderbolt launched from his hand. (*W* 10:277)

The speaker of the "Discourse" acknowledges that "much may be said to discourage & dissuade the young scholar from his career" (cf. *JMN* 9:237). Drawing on experience, he addresses the same grave charge—that of infidelity and atheism—that had been leveled against Emerson himself following the Divinity School Address of 1838, when he had shocked conservatives by offering as a model the scholar in his role as preacher—the preacher of soul, of the God Within. This segment of the "Discourse" was initially drafted in Journal W (where Emerson had asked, "Shall I say that I am driven to express my faith by a series of skepticisms?") and then rewritten. It was finally elaborated in a much-quoted passage of "Montaigne" that stands as an Emersonian *apologia pro vita sua*:

> Great believers are always reckoned infidels, impracticable, fantastic, atheistic, and really men of no account. The spiritualist finds himself driven to express his faith by a series of skepticisms. . . . The people's questions are not his; their methods are not his; and against all the dictates of good nature, he is driven to say, he has no pleasure in them.
> Even the doctrines dear to the hope of man, of the divine Providence, and of the immortality of the Soul, his neighbours cannot put the statement so, that he shall affirm it. But he denies out of more faith, and not less. He denies out of honesty. He had rather stand charged with the imbecility of skepticism, than with untruth. I believe, he says, in the moral design of the universe; it exists hospitably for the weal of souls; but your dogmas seem to me caricatures. Why should I make believe them?—Will any say this is cold and infidel? (*CW* 4:102–3; cf. *JMN* 9:228, 229)

It becomes clear that Emerson was writing from the heart when one turns from another recent journal entry to its similar elaboration in a later paragraph of "Montaigne." Voicing an old complaint that went back many years, he first wrote that he felt

> constrained by many lapses & ⟨dismaying⟩ failures to proportion my attempts to my means. Now I receive daily just so much vital energy as suffices to put on my clothes, ⟨to tie my shoes,⟩ to take a few turns in my garden & in my study with a book or a pen in my hand. If I attempt anything beyond this, if I so much as stretch out my hand to help my neighbor in his field, the ⟨good⟩ stingy Genius leaves me faint & sprawling;

97

Relics of things that have passed away
Fragments of stone reared by creatures of
                                    Clay.

Scholar goes for faith, but is a skeptic
He is here to say that God is
yet he denies all your isms
Well it is better that he sh^d speak the truth
He feels the yawning gulf between demand & supply,
    between vital power & the perception
        constructive
        genius   &   talent

Remedy in a vaster perception
Scholar a generalizer

Vast Skepticism & 136

"Scholar goes for faith, but is a skeptic"
Undated entry of spring or summer 1845, Journal W, p. 97; see *JMN* 9:228. The entry is elaborated in "Discourse at Middlebury College" and subsequently in "Montaigne"; see *CW* 4:102–4.

and I ⟨am farther to⟩ ↑must↓ pay for this vivacity by a prostration for two or three days following. These are costly experiments to try, I cannot afford two or three days when I count how many days it requires to finish one of my tasks; so I grow circumspect & disobliging beyond the example of all the misers. (*JMN* 9:194–95; cf. 9:228)

In "Montaigne" Emerson transformed this altogether personal complaint into just the kind of generalization he expected of the scholar. The "man of thought" who sees the world as "saturated with deity and with law" is ideally enabled to behold with serenity, the yawning gulf between the ambition of man and his power of performance, between the demand and the supply of power which makes the tragedy of all souls. . . . [T]he incompetency of power is the universal grief of young and ardent minds. They accuse the divine Providence of a certain parsimony. It has shown the heaven and earth to every child, and filled him with a desire for the whole; a desire raging, infinite. . . . Then for the satisfaction;—to each man is administered a single drop, a bead of dew of vital power, *per day*,—a cup as large as space, and one drop of the water of life in it. . . . In every house, in the heart of each maiden and of each boy, in the soul of the soaring saint, this chasm is found,—between the largest promise of ideal power, and the shabby experience. (*CW* 4:103–4)

So Emerson managed to continue the labor and keep the faith he demanded of the scholar. "Man helps himself by larger generalizations," he continues in both the "Discourse" and in "Montaigne." "The lesson of life is practically to generalize, to believe what the years and the centuries say against the hours"- -that "a great and beneficent tendency irresistibly streams" (*CW* 4:104; cf. *JMN* 9:224).

The "Discourse" itself concludes with a summarizing paragraph, partly drafted in Journal W, that repeats themes familiar in Emerson's writings since *Nature* and "The American Scholar," affirming

that the scholar must be much more than a scholar, that his ends give value to every means, but he is to subdue and keep down his methods; that his use of books is occasional, and infinitely subordinate; that he should read a little proudly, as one who knows the original, and cannot therefore very highly value the copy. In like manner he is to hold lightly every tradition, every opinion, every person, out of his piety to that Eternal Spirit which dwells unexpressed with him. He shall think very highly of his destiny. He is here to know the secret of Genius; to become, not a reader of poetry, but Homer, Dante, Milton, Shakspeare, Swedenborg. . . . If I could prevail to communicate the incommunicable mysteries, you should see . . . that ever as you ascend your proper and native path, you receive the keys of Nature and history, and rise on the same stairs to science and to joy. (*W* 10:288–89; cf. *JMN* 9:254–55)

ii. Uses of Greatness

As early as 1834, we recall, Emerson had written in his journal that the scholar of actual life is only *representative* of "that which he ought to be," namely, "the intellectual man"—later "the Thinker" and, in "The American Scholar," the ideal figure of *"Man Thinking"* (*JMN* 4:370; *EL* 1:226; *CW* 1:53). As recently as 1844, in "The Poet," he had idealized the scholar-poet as "the man without impediment, who sees and handles that which others dream of, traverses the whole scale of experience, and is representative of man, in virtue of being the largest power to receive and to impart" (*CW* 3:5). In actuality, however, no mere mortal—no poet or scholar—fully or permanently attains any such ideal, as Emerson, with his new sense of human limitation, knew all too well. "Our exaggeration of all fine characters," he wrote in "Nominalist and Realist," "arises from the fact, that we identify each in turn with the soul. But there are no such men as we fable; no Jesus, nor

Pericles, nor Cæsar, nor Angelo, nor Washington, such as we have made" (*CW* 3:134).

In late May of 1843 Emerson had written another relevant comment in his journal, under the inserted heading "*Men representative*": "Like a bird which alights nowhere, but hops perpetually from bough to bough, seems to me the Power which abides in no man and in no woman, but for a moment seems to speak from this one & for another moment from that one" (*JMN* 8:400). At some later time, when he decided to use these words in "Experience," he introduced them with two new sentences: "Of course, it needs the whole society to give the symmetry we seek. The parti-colored wheel must revolve very fast to appear white" (*CW* 3:34). Here he is drawing on his concept of "rotation," which appears again in "Nominalist and Realist" (the working title for which, according to *JMN* 12:xxxviii, was "Representative") and would reappear in the first of his lectures on "Representative Men."

"The rotation which whirls every leaf and pebble to the meridian," Emerson writes in "Nominalist and Realist," also "reaches to every gift of man, and we all take turns at the top." And since the components of our experience come to us in succession, it is only through rotation that we can conceive of Nature as a whole (*CW* 3:140, 142). "Rotation is the law of nature," he declares in "Uses of Great Men": "When Nature removes a great man, people explore the horizon for a successor; but none comes, and none will. His class is extinguished with him. In some other and quite different field, the next man will appear. . . . The power which [great men] communicate is not theirs. When we are exalted by ideas, we do not owe this to Plato, but to the idea, to which also Plato was debtor" (*CW* 4:11–12).

A further exploration of the concept of representation occurs only in a passage of the manuscript of the "Discourse" that names twelve representative figures:

> I delight in men adorned & weaponed with manlike arts, who could ↑alone or with a few like them↓ reproduce Europe & America[,] the results of our civilization. I delight in Euclid, who is geometry; in Plato, who is philosophy; in Swedenborg, who is symbolism; in Shakspeare, who is imagination & human life; in Raphael, master of all the secrets of form; in Chatham who carries joy and rage in his hand and lets forth the one spirit or the other at his pleasure; in Swift, whose pamphlet is war or peace[;] in Magliabecchi, whose knowledge was so vast that he had forgot more than most men ever knew[;] in Mirandola, who never forgot anything[;] in Adam Smith, with the wealth of Nations in his understanding; in Napoleon, who carries a campaign of Europe in his head; in Humboldt, who can represent in their order & symmetry the vast & the minute of the system of nature, so that if this world were lost out of space, he could almost report it from his brain. . . . (pp. 44–45)

Of these dozen historical figures, four—Plato, Swedenborg, Shakespeare, and Napoleon—are subsequently discussed in the lectures on "Representative Men."

As Emerson's attention shifted in the new lectures from celebration of ideal figures such as the Scholar and the Poet to portraits of six actual persons, he was following suggestions he himself had advanced as early as 1841. In opening his lectures on "The Times," it will be remembered, he had spoken of a projected "portrait gallery" of type figures from his own day (CW 1:170). And in "The Method of Nature" he proposed a "narrow" inspection of the biographies of a number of "great and wise men" in order to compare the actual performance of each "with his promise or idea" (CW 1:126)—that "idea after which all his facts are classified," as he had written in "Circles," that "helm which he obeys" (CW 2:180).[3]

Biographies of great men had long fascinated Emerson, who had been acquainted with Plutarch's *Parallel Lives* of eminent Greeks and Romans since his boyhood.[4] He had dealt to some degree with both Napoleon and Shakespeare in his early lectures on biography and English literature (EL 1:424, 287–319) and with Goethe in "Thoughts on Modern Literature," published in *The Dial* for October 1840 (W 12:309–36). As the new lectures of 1845–1846 began to take form in his mind in the spring of 1845 he wrote that he had "found a subject, *On the use of great men,* which might serve a Schleiermacher for monologues to his friends." He added that "in the first place, there should be a chapter *on the distribution of the hand into fingers"*—the same "old fable" he had used in "The American Scholar" to distinguish the general idea of Man from its embodiment in particular men—"or on the great value of these individuals as counterweights, checks of each other" (JMN 9:188). In the first lecture, entitled "Uses of Great Men," he declares that "The search after the great is the dream of youth, and the most serious occupation of manhood" (CW 4:3).

The example of Plutarch's *Parallel Lives* may well have reinforced Emerson's familiar method of organizing his lectures and chapters in pairs, as in *Essays: Second Series.* Now he would pair three sets of "counterweights": Plato as representative Philosopher with Swedenborg as a type of Mystic; Montaigne as Skeptic with Shakespeare as Poet; and Napoleon as "Man of the World"—a man of *action*—with Goethe, the Writer—"the king of all scholars," as Emerson had long thought of him (EL 3:22; W 12:327; cf. JMN 5:134). Even in our daily lives, he believed, we need such an alternation of polarities. "We balance one man with his opposite," according to "Uses of Great Men," "and the health of the state depends on the seesaw" (CW 4:16).

A further element in the lectures, as Emerson's friend Holmes long ago recognized in writing of the published version, is their autobiographical implications. In them he "shows his own affinities and repulsions," Holmes believed, "and, as everywhere, writes his own biography, no matter about whom or what he is talking."

> There is hardly any book of his better worth study by those who wish to understand, not Plato, not Plutarch, not Napoleon, but Emerson himself. All his great men interest us for their own sake; but we know a great deal about most of them, and Emerson holds the mirror up to them at just such an angle that we see his own face as well as that of his hero, unintentionally, unconsciously, no doubt, but by a necessity which he would be the first to recognize.[5]

iii. The Philosopher and the Mystic

When Emerson began to plan his lecture series on "Representative Men" he first projected discussions of Plato, Montaigne, and Swedenborg to accompany the new lecture on Napoleon he had given in April of 1845 (see *CW* 12:xxxii). A list of tentative titles in his Notebook Index Minor also includes Shakespeare and Saadi, Goethe, and Fourier as additional subjects, along with a still-untitled introductory lecture that became "Uses of Great Men" (*JMN* 12:580), but he later dropped Saadi and Fourier after deciding to pair Plato and Swedenborg, Montaigne and Shakespeare, Napoleon and Goethe. Manuscripts of the individual lectures have not survived, apart from a single leaf laid in Notebook BO Conduct and a few other leaves that appear in a printer's copy for *Representative Men* (1850). The published book also includes revisions of and additions to the lectures of 1845–1846; for example, some of the additions to "Plato, or the Philosopher" (*CW* 4:21–44) are drawn from Emerson's "Platoniana," described as "a loose set of related notes concerning Plato and his writings" that he assembled between 1845 and 1848 (*JMN* 10:468: headnote).

Although Plato has long been cited as "a major, lifelong source for Emerson," his "real interest in reading Plato," as Wallace E. Williams has pointed out, was "sporadic and not central until the 1840s" (*CW* 4: xxviii–xxix).[6] Quotations from Plato appear frequently in the journals of these years, along with passages from "the Indian scriptures"—"the Vedas, the Bhagavat Geeta, and the Vishnu Purana" (*CW* 4:28). In *Representative Men* Emerson hails this type of "the Philosopher" as "a balanced soul" who reconciles the diverse outlooks of East and West. Here he has in mind the familiar Emersonian principle of polarity, expressed most recently in "Nominalist and Realist" and now set forth in the contrasting terms of speculation versus action, unity versus diversity:

> The first is the course or gravitation of mind; the second is the power of nature. Nature is the manifold. The unity absorbs and melts or reduces. Nature opens and creates. These two principles reappear and interpenetrate all things, all thought: the one, the many. One is being; the other, intellect: one is necessity; the other, freedom: one, rest; the other, motion: one, power; the other, distribution: one, strength; the other, pleasure: one, consciousness; the other, definition: one, genius; the other, talent: one, earnestness; the other, knowledge: one, possession; the other, trade: one, caste; the other, culture: one, king; the other, democracy: and, if we dare carry these generalizations a step higher, and name the last tendency of both, we might say, that the end of the one is escape from organization, pure science: and the end of the other is the highest instrumentality, or use of means, or, executive deity. (*CW* 4:29–30; cf. *JMN* 9:307, 332–33; *JMN* 12:572)

In this characteristic statement Emerson is summing up an issue long-familiar in his own thinking. "Each student adheres by temperament and by habit to the first or to the second [of] these gods of the mind," he goes on to say. "By religion, he tends to unity; by intellect, or by the senses, to the many. A too rapid unification, and an excessive appliance to parts and particulars, are the twin dangers of speculation." During the 1840s, when his own faith was under challenge, as his thinking moved from a primarily inward and religious outlook to include a more outward and secular orientation, he evidently found a model in Plato for the "new philosophy" called for in "Experience": a philosophy that would allow for both faith and skepticism while avoiding their "twin dangers." Thus, in Emersonian terms, Plato was at once a Realist and a Nominalist.

> The unity of Asia and the detail of Europe, the infinitude of the Asiatic soul, and the defining, result-loving, machine-making, surface-seeking, operagoing Europe, Plato came to join, and, by contact, to enhance the energy of each. The excellence of Europe and Asia are in his brain. Metaphysics and natural philosophy expressed the genius of Europe; he substructs the religion of Asia as the base. (CW 4:31; cf. JMN 9:333)

Though this claim for the origins of Plato's thought may well be questioned, it is clear that the concept of a "balanced soul" was highly important to Emerson himself in 1845. Plato's achievements as "the broadest generalizer" (CW 4:23) qualified him as a scholar in the sense of a theorist and writer able "to show identity and connexion where men see nothing but fragments"—to borrow phrasing from the Middlebury "Discourse." Emerson's ideal Scholar is both philosopher and poet; Plato, as "the Representative of Philosophy," is likewise "more than a philosopher. Plato is clothed with the powers of the poet; stands upon the highest place of the poet," Emerson continues; "and, (though I doubt he wanted the decisive gift of lyric expression,) mainly is not a poet, because he chose to use the poetic gift to an ulterior purpose." Then follows a paragraph that might aptly be applied to Emerson himself as well as to Plato:

> Great geniuses have the shortest biographies. . . . They lived in their writing, and so their house- and street-life was trivial and commonplace. If you would know their tastes and complexions, *the most admiring of their readers most resembles them.* Plato, especially, has no external biography. If he had lover, wife, or children, we hear nothing of them. He ground them all into paint. As a good chimney burns its smoke, so a philosopher *converts the value of all his fortunes into his intellectual performances.* (CW 4:25; emphasis added)

So Emerson too had repeatedly converted *his* experience, *his* life, into lectures, essays, and poetry.

By the same token, Emerson's relatively brief treatment of what he saw as Plato's shortcomings touches on two charges made against himself, both in his own day and since: an undue "reverence for the intellect" and a supposed inconsistency (CW 2:101, 33). "The defect of Plato in power," he concludes,

> is only that which results inevitably from his quality. He is intellectual in his aim, and therefore in expression literary . . . [H]is writings have not, what is no doubt incident

to this regnancy of intellect in his work, the vital authority which the screams of prophets and the sermons of unlettered Arabs and Jews possess. . . .

In the second place, he has not a system. . . . He attempted a theory of the Universe. And his theory is not complete or selfevident. One man thinks he means this; and another, that; he has said one thing in one place, and the reverse of it in another place. (*CW* 4:42–43)

Emerson's belief that a scholar should be a poet as well as a philosopher is the informing idea behind his treatment of Swedenborg in "Swedenborg, or the Mystic" (*CW* 4:51–81). Less well known today than in Emerson's time, Swedenborg was an eighteenth-century scientist who in 1743, at age fifty-four, experienced a spiritual "illumination" that turned him to religious writing. Emerson had come to Swedenborg indirectly as a young man through the *New Jerusalem Magazine*, published by American Swedenborgians, and two writings of the "Swedenborgian druggist" Sampson Reed: the "Oration on Genius," which he read as a college senior, and *Observations on the Growth of the Mind* (1826). Later he acquired a number of works by Swedenborg himself that ultimately led him to temper his earlier enthusiasm. In *Representative Men*, where Swedenborg is paired with Plato, the Swedish thinker fares far less well than the Greek philosopher.[7]

One idea, the doctrine of "correspondence" that bulks so large in Emerson's *Nature*—the belief that natural facts are signs or symbols of spiritual facts and nature itself is the symbol of spirit—derived chiefly from Swedenborg, though it also had antecedents in Plato, the neoplatonists, and the German idealistic philosophy to which Emerson was introduced by Coleridge and Carlyle. (*Nature*, it will be remembered, was taken in some quarters as the work of a confirmed Swedenborgian.) "The American Scholar" praises Swedenborg as "the most imaginative of men, yet writing with the precision of a mathematician," having seen and shown "the connexion between nature and the affections of the soul. He pierced the emblematic or spiritual character of the visible, audible, tangible world" (*CW* 1:68).

As late as "The Poet" in 1844 Swedenborg "stands eminently for the translator of nature into thought. . . . Before him the metamorphosis continually plays. Everything on which his eye rests, obeys the impulses of moral nature." But in Emerson's further analysis, a "mystic" such as Swedenborg or Jacob Behmen cannot qualify as a true poet—that is, one whose imagination does not rest in the single meaning of a given object but continually "makes the same objects exponents of his new thought."

Here is the difference betwixt the poet and the mystic, that the last nails a symbol to one sense, which was a true sense for a moment, but soon becomes old and false. For all symbols are fluxional; all language is vehicular and transitive, and is good, as ferries and horses are, for conveyance, not as farms and houses are, for homestead. *Mysticism consists in the mistake of an accidental and individual symbol for an universal one.* (*CW* 3:20; emphasis added; cf. *JMN* 8:300)

And in "Swedenborg" Emerson finds it "remarkable" that such a man, "who by his perception of symbols saw the poetic construction of things and the primary relation of mind to matter, remained entirely devoid of the whole apparatus of poetic expression, which that perception creates. . . . [H]is books have no melody, no emotion, no humour, no relief to the dead prosaic level" (*CW* 4:80).

Emerson also holds that the Swedish writer's perception of nature is limited by being "mystical" and private rather than "human and universal": "He fastens each natural object to a theologic notion; a horse signifies carnal understanding; a tree, perception; the moon, faith; a cat means this; an ostrich, that; an artichoke, this other; and poorly tethers every symbol to a several ecclesiastical sense. The slippery Proteus is not so easily caught" (*CW* 4:68). Remembering Swedenborg's considerable contributions to science, Emerson wrote of his "access to the secrets and structure of nature, by some higher method than by experience." Then, in defining the term "mystic" as he applied it to Swedenborg, he equated Swedenborg's "illumination" with the traditional mystical assimilation of individual souls to "the original Soul, by whom, and after whom, all things subsist."

The path to such a union, which in Emerson's writings of 1841 he had called "ecstasy," is "difficult, secret, and beset with terror." By ecstasy, he now explains in "Swedenborg," the ancients meant "absence, a getting out of their bodies to think" (cf. *JMN* 12:558).

> All religious history contains traces of the trance of saints; a beatitude, but without any sign of joy; earnest, solitary, even sad; "the flight," Plotinus called it, "of the alone to the alone." . . . The trances of Socrates, Plotinus, Porphyry, Behmen, Bunyan, Fox, Pascal, Guion, Swedenborg, will readily come to mind. . . . This beatitude comes in terror, and with shocks to the mind of the receiver. . . . In the chief examples of religious illumination, somewhat morbid had mingled, in spite of the unquestionable increase of mental power. (*CW* 4:54–55; cf. "The Over-Soul," *CW* 2:167)

In the light of such a passage it seems inappropriate to regard Emerson himself as a true mystic, even if we allow for such occasional ecstatic moments as the "transparent eye-ball" experience that is described in *Nature*. Patrick F. Quinn, after reviewing the evidence both pro and con, concludes that he was "a mystic only in the very loosest sense of the term." As for Swedenborg, Quinn notes, Emerson emphasized not his "supreme love of God" but his work "as a kind of inspired scientist."[8] Given Swedenborg's "introverted faculties" and "dangerous discord with himself" (*CW* 4:73), he is the opposite of that "balanced soul," Plato.[9] He is "disagreeably wise," Emerson felt obliged to say, "and with all his accumulated gifts paralyzes and repels." His "entire want of poetry in so transcendant a mind" is a token of "disease," and "I think sometimes, he will not be read longer" (*CW* 4:80–81).

iv. The Skeptic and the Poet

As Emerson testifies concerning his first reading of Montaigne's *Essays* in 1825, "It seemed to me as if I had written the book myself in some former life, so sincerely it spoke my thought & experience. No book before or since was ever so much to me as that" (*JMN* 8:376; cf. *CW* 4:92).[10] In "Montaigne, or the Skeptic" (*CW* 4:83–105) he celebrates "the calendar day of our Saint Michel de Montaigne," praising him for taking and keeping a "position of equilibrium." Montaigne "drew an emblematic pair of scales" over his name "and wrote *Que sçais je* under it" (*CW* 4:94). But for all Emerson's love of Montaigne, the lecture has more to say about skeptics generally than about "this representative of Skepticism" and his writings.

The opening paragraphs of "Montaigne," which set forth familiar dualisms—"Infinite and Finite; Relative and Absolute; Apparent and Real"—are reminiscent of "Nominalist and Realist" and "Plato, or the Philosopher": every individual, Emerson says once again, is predisposed to one opposing side or the other. "The literary class," "the studious class" (read "the scholars"), believing in "the superiority of ideas," mistrust "the men of this world," who in turn regard a man of ideas as one "out of his reason"; still others, advocates of the "practical wisdom" set forth in "Experience" under the rubric of Surface, run into "indifferentism, and then into disgust." Characteristically, Emerson seeks to mediate among them, incidentally shedding further light on his understanding of the term *skeptic:* "The abstractionist and the materialist thus mutually exasperating each other, and the scoffer expressing the worst of materialism, there arises a third party to occupy the middle ground between these two, the skeptic, namely. He finds both wrong by being in extremes. He labours to plant his feet, to be the beam of the balance" (*CW* 4:88). Better "a wise skepticism" that will "suspend the judgment," Emerson contends, than dogmatically advancing rash conclusions when nothing more than "an approximate solution" is attainable, as with such debatable matters as marriage, the State, the Church, Labor, and Culture.

"The right ground of the skeptic," Emerson is careful to insist, is "not at all of unbelief, not at all of universal denying, nor of universal doubting, doubting even that he doubts; least of all, of scoffing and profligate jeering at all that is stable and good. These are no more his moods, than are those of religion and philosophy" (*CW* 4:90–91). Instead, the wise skeptic will have "a certain solid and intelligible way of living of his own, some method of answering the inevitable needs of human life; proof that he has played with skill and success; that he has evinced the temper, stoutness, and the range of qualities which, among his contemporaries and countrymen, entitle him to fellowship and trust"; while being "sufficiently related to the world," he will also be "a vigorous and original thinker." Such are the qualities that "meet in the character of Montaigne," "the frankest and honestest of all writers."

Though Emerson admired Montaigne as a thinker, he prized him even more as an essayist, an unparalleled maker of sentences.

> There have been men with deeper insight, but, one would say, never a man with such abundance of thoughts. He is never dull, never insincere, and has the genius to make the reader care for all that he cares for.
> The sincerity and marrow of the man reaches to his sentences. I know not any-

where the book that seems less written. It is the language of conversation transferred to a book. Cut these words, and they would bleed; they are vascular and alive. (*CW* 4:95; cf. *JMN* 7:374)

Concluding his treatment of the man with a question—"Shall we say that Montaigne has spoken wisely, and given the right and permanent expression of the human mind on the conduct of life?"—Emerson defers his answer, turning first to issues familiar in his own experience. "The wise skeptic," he acknowledges, is "a bad citizen" in that he remains uncommitted to any party. "He is a Reformer; yet he is no better member of the philanthropic association," for he takes a longer view of man's place in history. To minds "incapable of skepticism," Emerson observes, such uncommitted persons will always be "reckoned infidels, impracticable, fantastic, and really men of no account" when they withhold commitment and assent to popular causes and beliefs. Here, it will be recognized, he is adapting the phrasing of his "Discourse at Middlebury College," as he declares—with memories of the Divinity School controversy surely in his mind—that "Great believers are always reckoned infidels."

Again, considering various challenges to "the affirmative impulse" in men, himself included, Emerson instances "the absence of any appearance of reconciliation between the theory and the practice of life" and "the disproportion between the sky of law and the pismire of performance under it." The skeptic cannot reconcile these opposites, and even Montaigne, Emerson implies, can *not* give us ultimate wisdom concerning "the conduct of life." For a "natural believer" like Emerson, however, there remains a "final solution" which will transcend "those superficial views which we call Skepticism." Reaffirming once again his old belief in "the moral sentiment," he adapts for his concluding paragraphs another passage from the earlier "Discourse" in which he had set forth "the scholar's faith"—a faith, he now declares, that "avails to the whole emergency of life and objects."

> Through the years and the centuries, through evil agents, through toys and atoms, a great and beneficent tendency irresistibly streams.
> Let a man learn to look for the permanent in the mutable and fleeting; let him learn to bear the disappearance of things he was wont to reverence, without losing his reverence; let him learn that he is here not to work, but to be worked upon, and, that, though abyss open under abyss, and opinion displace opinion, all are at last contained in the eternal Cause. (*CW* 4:104–5)

In his next lecture, turning from a master of prose to a master of poetry, Emerson was reentering long-familiar ground. He had spoken twice on Shakespeare as part of his lectures on English literature in 1835; his presentations, it has been said, were "as much public readings as critical essays" (*EL* 1:288). In the following year he drew on the first of the two lectures for the "Language" chapter of *Nature*, and still later, when he prepared "Shakspeare, or the Poet," for the series on "Representative Men," he took background information on Shakespeare and other English poets and dramatists—some of it now known to be inaccurate or mistaken—from his notes and lectures of ten years before.

Emerson's initial topic in "Shakspeare, or the Poet" (*CW* 4:107–25) is the question of a writer's originality, a subject that had concerned him since the 1830s and one that he would explore once again in a lecture of 1859, "Quotation and Originality" (*W* 8:175–204). Early in his career as a public speaker he had determined to utter only his own thoughts; now he has come to realize that no mere mortal—no scholar—can be entirely original. "The greatest genius is the most indebted man," he declares, supporting his case by citing Shakespeare and his contemporaries who wrote for the London theater. There they found "audience and expectation prepared" and had access besides to a great body of old plays "in which any experiment could be freely tried." "The poet," Emerson writes, "needs a ground in popular tradition on which he may work, and which, again, may restrain his art within the due temperance. It holds him to the people, supplies a foundation for his edifice, and in furnishing so much work done to his hand, leaves him at leisure, and in full strength for the audacities of his imagination" (*CW* 4:111).

The rule in literature, Emerson asserts, is that a man who has "shown himself capable of original writing" may thenceforth "steal from the writings of others at discretion. Thought is the property of him who can entertain it." Indeed, "all originality is relative," and every thinker, whatever his field may be, is "retrospective"; it is so with Shakespeare, who sums up both his age and the past that age inherited. Though this writer for the public stage remained obscure among "the constellation of great men" in his time, Emerson continues, "literature, philosophy, and thought" have in later ages become "Shakspearized." (So in "The American Scholar" Emerson had remarked that "The English dramatic poets have Shakspearized now for two hundred years.") And though we know little about the poet's outer life, despite assiduous scholarly research, we have in his own words "his recorded convictions on those questions which knock for answer at every heart. . . . So far from Shakspeare's being the least known, he is the one person in all modern history known to us."

Though Emerson thinks highly of Shakespeare's dramatic merit, he regards it as secondary to his achievement "as poet and philosopher." The importance of his "wisdom of life" sinks "out of notice" the particular form which his writings took. "Not metres, but a metre-making argument," makes the poem, as Emerson had previously written; here he says that with Shakespeare's wisdom and humanity came "the equal endowment of imaginative and of lyric power. He clothed the creatures of his legend with form and sentiments, as if they were people who had lived under his roof, and few real men have left such distinct characters as these fictions. And they spoke in language as sweet as it was fit" (*CW* 4:121). In short, it is Shakespeare's "power of expression, or of transferring the inmost truth of things into music and verse," that makes him "the type of the poet."

How, then, "stands the account of man with this bard and benefactor, when in solitude, shutting our ears to the reverberations of his fame, we seek to strike the balance?" According to Emerson, Shakespeare was like Homer, Dante, and Chaucer in that he likewise

> saw the splendour of meaning that plays over the visible world; knew that a tree had another use than for apples, and corn another than for meal, and the ball of the earth than for tillage and roads: that these things bore a second and finer harvest to the mind, being emblems of its thoughts, and conveying in all their natural history a certain mute commentary on human life. Shakspeare employed them as colours to compose his picture. He rested in their beauty; and never took the step which seemed inevitable to such genius, namely, to explore the virtue which resides in these symbols, and imparts this power,—What is that which they themselves say? (*CW* 4:124)

Instead, says the Puritan in Emerson, he "converted the elements which waited on his command, into entertainments." Though this supreme representative of poetry might have tracked his symbols to their transcendent source, he was content to serve merely as "master of the revels to mankind."[11] What Emerson calls "The Egyptian verdict of the Shakspeare Societies comes to mind" as he continues: the man Shakespeare was no more than "a jovial actor and manager. I cannot marry this fact to his verse." In other words, Shakespeare too "shares the halfness and imperfection of humanity." He was not what Emerson would call a *spiritual* man; instead, this "best poet" led "an obscure and profane life, using his genius for the public amusement." As a consequence, Emerson concludes, "The world still wants its poet-priest" (*CW* 4:124–25).

v. The Man of the World and the Writer

In the lectures so far considered, including "Uses of Great Men," Emerson deals with old favorites from his reading—Shakespeare, Montaigne, and Swedenborg, who had contributed to his thinking and writing for many years—and also with Plato, a relatively recent enthusiasm. In all of these men, as Holmes long ago recognized, he saw something of himself, including on the one hand his own shortcomings and, on the other, the self he would like to be. Ideally, he too might become a balanced soul like Plato (though less coldly intellectual), a spiritual man like Swedenborg (though less rigid and theological, and more of a poet), a skeptic like Montaigne (though a thinker who would transcend his own skepticism), and even that poet-priest for whom he sought but did not find in the worldly Shakespeare. The juxtapositions in the several paired lectures seem somewhat arbitrary: Montaigne rather than Swedenborg might well have been paired with Plato, as philosopher and skeptic, and Swedenborg then placed instead with Shakespeare, since for Emerson the one needed to be more of a poet and the other more of a spiritualist. Even so, the issues and topics were all matters of great concern to him in 1845, and the lectures on "Representative Men" recapitulate his thinking of the early 1840s much as *Nature* and "The American Scholar" had summed up his prior intellectual development during the 1830s.

The next two lectures, pairing "Napoleon, or the Man of the World" (*CW* 4:127–48) with "Goethe, or the Writer" (4:149–66), provide sharper contrasts than any of their predecessors, embody more social criticism, and at the same time deal openly with a long-familiar Emersonian theme: a life of action versus the scholar's life of thought. Thus Napoleon's active participation in the world's affairs contrasts with Goethe's more contemplative role as "the scholar or writer." Extending the broad generalizations about contemporary society that Emerson had offered in his lectures on "The Times" in 1841, the lectures present Bonaparte as "a representative of the popular external life and aims of the nineteenth century. Its other half, its poet, is Goethe." Emerson joins the two as "representatives of the impatience and reaction of nature against the *morgue* of conventions—two stern realists, who, with their scholars, have severally set the axe at the root of the tree of cant and seeming, for this time, and for all time" (*CW* 4:156, 166).

Both lectures had their beginnings in the mid–1830s, when Emerson read widely in various accounts of Napoleon and, with the help of Margaret Fuller, learned German in order to deal at firsthand with the writings of Goethe and his circle. The figure of Napoleon, a man so unlike himself, continued to fascinate him, as we can see from the frequent allusions in both his journals and his public addresses. In "Literary Ethics," for example, he commends Bonaparte, in spite of his "defects or vices," for his realistic appraisal of facts and his shrewd application of means to ends. Early in 1845 Emerson was again reading about Napoleon in preparation for his lecture of the following April, which he later revised for the series on "Representative Men." The lecture effectively brings to bear a multitude of illustrations from Bonaparte's career; it is the most richly detailed of the entire series.

In the lecture as published in 1850 Napoleon appears as "far the best known, and the most powerful," among "the eminent persons of the nineteenth century." He "owes his predominance," in Emerson's view, "to the fidelity with which he expresses the tone of thought and belief, the aims of the masses of active and cultivated men" (*CW* 4:129). In the face of the "standing antagonism" that Emerson observes "between the conservative and the democratic classes" in both America and Europe, Napoleon, who is "thoroughly modern," particularly represents for him "the class of business-men," "the class of industry and skill." He had both the virtues and the vices of men of this class: "above all, he had their spirit or aim. That tendency is material, pointing at a sensual success, and employing the richest and most various means to that end; conversant with mechanical powers, highly intellectual, widely and accurately learned and skilful, but subordinating all intellectual and spiritual forces into means to a material success. To be the rich man, is the end" (*CW* 4:130).

Emerson had come to fear that "highly intellectual" men of his own time and country would likewise turn their own learning solely to the pursuit of material success. In his later writings, and particularly in his frequent addresses to young scholars on college campuses, he would continue to celebrate the intellect and the values of a life devoted to something more than what he here called "sensual success." "Our pursuit of wealth," he went on to say, has a "fatal quality": "it is treacherous, and is bought by the breaking or weakening of the sentiments; and it is inevitable that we should find the same fact in the history of this champion, who proposed to himself simply a brilliant career, without any stipulation or scruple concerning the means" (*CW* 4:144–45).

Following this mixed verdict, after a devastating survey of Napoleon's personal faults, Emerson declares that in the man's career we see "an experiment under the most favorable conditions, of the powers of intellect without conscience." In conclusion, as though still speaking from a pulpit, he offers this warning: "As long as our civilization is essentially one of property, of fences, of exclusiveness, it will be mocked by delusions. Our riches will leave us sick, there will be bitterness in our laughter, and our wine will burn our mouth. Only that good profits, which we can taste with all doors open, and which serves all men" (*CW* 4:148).

As Frederic Ives Carpenter has remarked, Emerson had once "considered Napoleon as the embodiment of pure evil—like many others of his time" until, "influenced by his reading of Goethe, he gradually achieved the more objective point of view" expressed in this lecture;[12] a full study of his continuing interest in both Napoleon and Goethe—and the implications of that interest—remains to be written.[13] His reading in Goethe also gave him a much more favorable view of the German author himself, whose life and writings seemed morally questionable in the eyes of many strict New Englanders of his day. In the 1830s, when Emerson was learning German, he entered in his journal many passages by and about Goethe that he had translated. In 1840, in "Thoughts on Modern Literature," he praised Goethe as a "poet, naturalist, and philosopher" who has "united in himself, and that in the most extraordinary degree, the tendencies of the era. . . . Whatever the age inherited or invented, he made his own" (*W* 12:322). In "Representative Men" Emerson enlarged on this judgment, finding Goethe "a man quite domesticated in the century, breathing its air, enjoying its fruits, . . . and taking away by his colossal parts the reproach of weakness, which, but for him, would lie on the intellectual works of the period" (*CW* 4:156).

In presenting Goethe as representative of "the class of scholars or writers" Emerson drew heavily on his "Discourse at Middlebury College" for the extended characterization of the scholar that comes near the beginning of "Goethe, or the Writer." He might well have called the lecture "Goethe, or the Scholar," except that Goethe is scarcely the altogether ideal figure of the scholar as Man Thinking that Emerson had delineated in 1837; instead, like Emerson's five other "Representative Men," he too is seen to "fail utterly in some one or in many parts to satisfy our idea," to borrow the earlier phrasing of "Nominalist and Realist." On the positive side, he is a man of true genius who does not speak merely from talent, for "the truth shines through: he is very wise, though his talent often veils his wisdom." Again, "He has the formidable independence which converse with truth gives. . . . The old Eternal Genius, who built the world, has confided himself more to this man than to any other." Still, Emerson must add, "I dare not say that Goethe ascended to the highest grounds from which genius has spoken. He has not worshipped the highest unity; he is incapable of a selfsurrender to the moral sentiment" (CW 4:163).

As for Goethe's formidable accomplishments in his widely varied endeavors—literary, scientific, and philosophical—Emerson offers this mixed verdict:

> There are nobler strains in poetry than any he has sounded. There are writers poorer in talent, whose tone is purer, and more touches the heart. Goethe can never be dear to men. His is not even the devotion to pure truth; but to truth for the sake of culture. He has no aims less large than the conquest of universal nature, of universal truth to be his portion: a man not to be bribed, nor deceived, nor overawed; of a stoical selfcommand and selfdenial, and having one test for all men, *What can you teach me?* All possessions are valued by him for that only; rank, privileges, health, time, being itself. (CW 4:163)

In sum, the man Goethe "is the type of culture, the amateur of all arts and sciences and events; artistic, but not artist; spiritual, but not spiritualist." Even "the worldly tone of his tales," Emerson supposes, "grew out of the calculations of self culture. It was the infirmity of an admirable scholar who loved the world out of gratitude." For "this man was entirely at home and happy in his century and the world," and in his "aim of Culture, which is the genius of his works, is their power." As for Emerson himself, though he had long subscribed to the vogue of self-cultivation then current in New England, there remained for him as a scholar an idea more exalted than Goethe's: "the idea of absolute eternal truth without reference to my own enlargement" (CW 4:165–66).

IV

THE SCHOLAR'S DILEMMA

❖

Though I sympathize with your sentiment and abhor the crime you assail[,] yet I shall persist in wearing this robe, all loose and unbecoming as it is, of inaction, this wise passiveness[,] until my hour comes when I can see how to act with truth as well as to refuse.

—Lecture of 1840 on "Reforms" (*EL* 3:266)

I waked at night, & bemoaned myself, because I had not thrown myself into this deplorable question of Slavery. . . . But then, in hours of sanity, I recover myself, & say, God must govern his own world, & knows his way out of this pit, without my desertion of my post which has none to guard it but me. I have quite other slaves to free.

—Entry of August 1852 in Journal GO (*JMN* 13:80)

If by opposing slavery I undermine institutions, I own I do not wish to live in a nation where slavery exists. The life of this world has but a limited worth in my eyes, & really is not worth such a price as the toleration of slavery.

—Entry (of 1854?) in Notebook WO Liberty (*JMN* 14:383)

11. THE SCHOLAR
AND REFORM, 1837–1844

❖

I must act with truth, though I should never come to act, as you call it, with
effect. I must consent to inaction. . . . Whilst therefore I desire to express
the respect and joy I feel before this sublime connexion of reforms, . . . I
urge the more earnestly the paramount duties of self-reliance.
                —"Introductory Lecture" on "The Times," 1841 (*CW* 1:177)

Ever since the mid–1830s, the scholar who would "live wholly from within" (*CW*
2:30) had continued to face perennial encroachments on his cherished privacy from
the world about him—especially challenges to take an active stand on pressing social
questions of the day. "Every decent and well-spoken individual affects and sways me
more than is right," Emerson wrote in "Self-Reliance," but when "malice and vanity
wear the coat of philanthropy"—as when "an angry bigot assumes this bountiful
cause of Abolition"—he is put off (*CW* 2:30). To an apostle of self-culture, neither
"men of one idea" among the reformers like "these poor Grahams & Garrisons &
Palmers" (*EL* 3:260; *JMN* 7:193) nor organized reform movements such as Anti-
Slavery societies seemed to require his active support. "All men plume themselves
on the improvement of society, and no man improves," he lamented: indeed, "Society never advances. It recedes as fast on one side as it gains on the other" (*CW* 2:48).
Emerson was repeating in "Self-Reliance" what he had said earlier in the concluding
lecture of "The Philosophy of History" series, where he also proclaimed that "the
best work of society is the formation of the Individual" (*EL* 2:174). Over the next few
years these views would be both reasserted and tested.

i. The Scholar's Problem

Emerson's first public comment on the issue of slavery came three months after
"The American Scholar," in November of 1837, when he was reluctantly persuaded to speak on that subject at the Second Church of Concord. But he had
long before determined that as a speaker he would present not what his audience
might expect to hear but what was fit for him to speak (*JMN* 4:372). In this case
the "major concern" of his address was less the evil of slavery itself than "the
preservation of the principle of free speech," then being threatened by "an almost
universal repression of abolition oratory."[1] Emerson was no partisan of slavehold-

ing, but as we know, he had been strongly affected by the murder of Elijah Lovejoy earlier in November, and he was disturbed by the refusal of most of the Boston churches to give a hearing to Anti-Slavery speakers. In Concord, by contrast, opposition to slavery was strong: Waldo's late brother Charles had delivered an Anti-Slavery speech in 1835; Lidian Emerson was an active member of the Women's Anti-Slavery Society; even Ezra Ripley and Aunt Mary Moody Emerson had been attracted to the cause. The Concord abolitionists, who had hoped for another forthright denunciation of slavery, were disappointed by the "cool and philosophical tone" of Waldo Emerson's address, according to Cabot; some of his friends told him that "his disgust at the methods or the manners of the philanthropists" had blinded him to the importance of their work.[2]

In the following spring, as his journal attests, Emerson was deeply troubled by another development, the enforced resettlement of the Cherokee Indians from their homes in Georgia to new lands beyond the Mississippi. At a meeting of townspeople he agreed to write in protest to President Van Buren, but his letter (*W* 11:87–96) was a "hated" one, as he called it, not because he objected to "the sentiment I write" but because the initiative came from his Concord friends rather than himself (*JMN* 5:475, 477, 479). As early as 1834, he had determined that as a dedicated scholar he would utter only his own word, not that of some other person (*JMN* 4:348–49), and writing at the bidding of others seemed to violate his self-imposed injunction. His mixed feelings about how to reply to requests such as this one are apparent in a journal passage of the time that he later used in his lecture on "The Heart" in January of 1838, shifting from the original first person discourse to third. When he is approached by "a zealot" representing some worthy cause—for example, "Temperance Reform," "the horrors of Southern slavery," or "the shameful neglect of the Schools"—he responds "with shame at my own inaction," for "None of these causes are foreigners to me. My Universal Nature is thus marked" (*JMN* 5:437; cf. *EL* 2:287). Though for the time he remained uncommitted, the shame of inaction in the face of social wrongs—slavery in particular—would long continue to trouble him. This was the scholar's persistent dilemma.

Emerson's attitude toward reform in general, as Len Gougeon has demonstrated in *Virtue's Hero: Emerson, Antislavery, and Reform,* reflected the traditional Unitarian emphasis on individual responsibility and especially the position taken by William Ellery Channing in opposition to organized action for social reform. Although Emerson himself had envisioned the scholar as a leader destined to "act upon" society, he also thought of him primarily as inspiring others through the power of his writing and speaking, as with "The American Scholar"—not as a champion of any one secular cause, such as the crusade against slavery or the Temperance movement, however noble its aims. As for religious reform, after the controversy engendered by his Divinity School Address of 1838, Emerson's single-handed attempt to breathe new life into contemporary Unitarian preaching and teaching, he was content to describe himself as "merely an observer, a dispassionate reporter, no partisan" (*JMN* 7:60).

A major factor in Emerson's preference for personal autonomy was his temperamental disinclination toward collective effort. Among the many projects for social reform undertaken during the 1840s were various experiments in communal living, one of them George Ripley's idea of establishing a Transcendentalist community at Brook Farm in West Roxbury, Massachusetts. Although Emerson was wary of such schemes, he somehow "wished to be convinced, to be thawed, to be made nobly mad by the kindlings before my eye of a new dawn of human piety." But Ripley wanted more from him than active participation or even moral support; he also asked for a cash investment, and to Emerson the project seemed merely "arithmetic & comfort"—"only a room in the Astor House hired for the Transcendentalists." As for himself, he wrote in his journal, "I do not wish to remove from my present prison to a prison a little larger. I wish to break all prisons. I have not yet conquered my own house." To accept "were to dodge the problem I am set to solve, & ↑to↓ hide my impotency in the thick of a crowd" (*JMN* 7:407–8).

Even so, Emerson hesitated, telling Margaret Fuller that he had given the idea "some earnest attention & much talk," though at the very name of a society "all my repulsions play, all my quills rise & sharpen" (*L* 2:364). To Ripley himself, on 15 December 1840, he finally wrote that he had decided, "very slowly & I may almost say penitentially," not to join, explaining in some detail that it would not be good for him or for his wife and mother, given their state of health, adding that he himself would not be good for the community. At the heart of his refusal was his conviction that "all I shall solidly do, I must do alone" (*L* 2:369–70). As he had already realized, his joining such a body would "traverse all my long trumpeted theory . . . that a man is stronger than a city, that his solitude is more prevalent & beneficent than the concert of crowds" (*JMN* 7:408). And there was still that unnamed "problem" that he was "set to solve."

ii. Three Lectures on Reform, 1839–1841

Between 1839 and 1841 Emerson was sufficiently concerned with the current topic of Reform to deliver three different lectures on that subject: "The Protest" in his series on "Human Life," "Reforms" in the series on "The Present Age," and "Man the Reformer," the one lecture he gave during the winter of 1840–1841, when he was occupied with his forthcoming *Essays*. Each of the three offers further definition of his own uneasy position during this period: though favoring reform in general, he objected to the manners and methods of particular reformers and preferred to think of himself as a self-reliant individual rather than as a member of any reform group.

Noting in June of 1838 that his young friend Caroline Sturgis "protests," Emerson added that to protest "is a good deal. In these times you shall find a small number of persons of whom only that can be affirmed" (*JMN* 7:23). His own one-man protest against the current state of religion, the Divinity School Address, followed in that same summer, arousing the ire of the Unitarian establishment and threatening his own self-confidence and faith. But in his lecture of January 1839 entitled "The Protest" he unrepentingly praised the impulse in "every young man and young woman . . . of moral and intellectual force" to contend "actively or passively against the opinions, practices, standards, that are current in the community." Still, each protester assails a different target, he went on to say: "Every reformer is partial and exaggerates some one grievance" (EL 3:90–91; cf. JMN 7:155). He again pointed to this prevalent narrowness of view in his lecture on "Reforms" in January of 1840. There, after taking favorable notice of "the great harvest" of projects for reform that has "remarkably distinguished the Present Age," he contrasted the reformers' idealistic "effort at the Perfect" with the "low inadequate form" of their actual organizations. "They mix the fire of the moral sentiment with personal and party heats, with measureless exaggerations, and the blindness that prefers some darling measure to justice and truth" (EL 3:256, 259).

What then should one do when urged to lend himself to some cause? (And as Emerson must have asked himself privately, What should a self-reliant scholar do?) Here is the lecturer's answer in 1840: "Accept the reforms but accept not the person of the reformer nor his law. Accept the reform but be thou thyself sacred, intact, inviolable, one whom leaders, one whom multitudes cannot drag from thy central seat. If you take the reform as the reformer brings it to you he transforms you into an instrument" (EL 2:260). "An instrument"—so Emerson had felt himself to be when urged by his well-intentioned neighbors in Concord to speak out against slavery and protest removal of the Cherokees. In the future, he promises, he will say "Nay, my friend, I do not work with these tools. . . . Though I sympathize with your sentiment and abhor the crime you assail yet I shall persist in wearing this robe, all loose and unbecoming as it is, of inaction, this wise passiveness until my hour comes when I can see how to act with truth as well as to refuse" (EL 3:266; cf. JMN 7:275).

Emerson, it should be noted, distinguishes between and among actions. Here and in another revealing paragraph of "Reforms," he uses act and action in their more conventional sense, not as equivalents for the active experience of living itself, as he had employed the same terms in his oration of 1837 when discussing action as a principal "resource" for the Scholar as Thinker. Ideally, thought and action should be reciprocally related. Why, he now asks himself and his audience, "should we be cowed by the name of action" when "the ancestor of every action is a thought"? Emerson is still speaking for the Scholar in 1840, though his tone is clearly more defensive than it had been in 1837. In "Reforms" and again in "Spiritual Laws" he assures himself that "to think" is itself "to act" (EL 3:267–68; CW 2:94). The ideal Scholar, as Man Thinking, actively thinks for society, and therefore his thought should precede social action. As for Emerson himself, until he can "see how to act with truth" he will remain a wisely passive scholar, "sacred and aloof from the common vices of the partisan," awaiting "a clear case on which he is called to stand his trial." Such a man "must and will be found faithful" in that which

14

hood of all that is common yet I dare
not believe that a mood so delicate can
be relied on like a principle for the wear & tear
of years. It will be succeeded by another & another
& the new will jar with the old. Yet
as it is genuine today, it will never be nothing.

A part of the Protest we are called to make
is to the Popular mode of virtuous endeavor. "Will you
not come to this Convention I nominate a Temperance
ticket? Let me show you the immense importance
of the step." Nay, my friend, I do not work with
those tools. The principles on which your
Church & State are built are false! a
portion of this virus & venom vitiates
the smallest detail even of your Charity
& religion. Though I am I sympathize with
your desire rather your adversaries
yet I shall persist in wearing this robe
all loose & unbecoming as it is of inaction.
This wise passiveness until my hour
comes when I can see how to act with
truth as well as to refuse   See p. 36. at bottom.

I proceed again in the humour of page 12
to say that it pleases the great Soul that
the present perception should arise
in the universal heart of man
of the Soul's allsufficiency So that
literature art persons space time
should be undervalued. Do not doubt that
this mood is one sign in Heavens eternal
zodiac or mistake the spirit of piety—

A Scholar's "robe . . . of inaction"
Entry of 21 October 1839, Journal E, p. 14; see JMN 7:274–75.

he calls action. "His scale of duty is different from yours," the lecturer tells his audience, but it will ultimately lead to some overt act (*EL* 3:268). Even so, what might constitute either a "clear case" or appropriate "action" by a scholar is left unspecified.

"Man the Reformer," the one lecture of the three devoted to Reform that Emerson revised for publication (see *CW* 1:145–60), was delivered on 25 January 1841 before the Mechanics' Apprentices' Library Association in Boston. This engagement provided a rather different audience for him, one to which he spoke clearly and directly in a manner that would characterize his later appearances before similar nonacademic groups. From the outset he addressed his listeners as individuals, assuming that each of them wished both to establish "clearer communication with the spiritual nature" and, in an age of reform, to be "a reformer, a benefactor," of the society in which he lives. As in "Literary Ethics," Emerson is seeking—for himself as well as for his individual auditors—a way of linking two diverse realms: "the finished man," he declares in his concluding paragraph, should "perform the high office of mediator between the spiritual and the actual world" (*CW* 1:145, 159).

Striking a now-familiar note, Emerson observes ironically that "the doctrine of Reform had never such scope as at the present hour"—even "State Street thinks, and Wall Street doubts and begins to prophesy!" Some reformers have proposed such extreme measures to counteract institutional evils that "the scholar flies for refuge to the world of ideas, and aims to recruit and replenish nature from that source." The abuses of a selfish society constitute "practical impediments" that threaten "virtuous young men" seeking to make their way, not only in trade but in "all the lucrative professions and practices." Every person is helplessly implicated in the social system, and "no one feels himself called to act for man, but only as a fraction of man." (The Scholar, Emerson had said in 1837, is no mere fraction— society's "delegated intellect"—but "Man Thinking.") What then can any individual do, whatever his station? If he cannot remake (re-form) society at large, he can at least begin with himself and learn "the lesson of self-help."

Here Emerson advocates some form of manual labor for everyone, regardless of occupation or class, as "a basis for our higher accomplishments, for he believes that "every man ought to stand in primary relations with the work of the world." Though "men of study generally" must especially guard themselves against "the taste for luxury," all persons should also reexamine their modes of living and institute a simple household economy. Not coincidentally, Emerson had recently settled on these same two measures as a way of "mending" his own domestic life, so as to make his manner of living both "honest and agreeable to my imagination" (*L* 2:370); now he tells of the "exhilaration and health" that are his when he goes into his garden with a spade and works with his own hands (cf. *JMN* 7:525). Though reformation, like human culture, thus begins with the individual, each person must recognize and foster not only his own potential but also that of his fellows, replacing egotistic selfishness with altruistic love. And what everyone must have, as "spring and regulator in all efforts of reform, is faith in Man," meaning what the Emerson as scholar had called man's infinitude and is referring to here as "the conviction that there is an infinite worthiness" in every individual "which will appear at the call of worth." Reawaken such a faith in and for each person, Emerson declares, and the selfishness that permeates society will give way to love; thus "a nobler morning" will dawn for all mankind.

"Man the Reformer" was evidently well received, for the sponsoring association requested that it be published; after some revision it appeared in *The Dial* for April 1841. A pirated English printing in "a cheap pamphlet" of 1842 pleased Carlyle, who informed Emerson of its "acceptance" in England, praising the address as "a *truly excellent* utterance, one of the best words you have ever spoken" (*CEC* 334). Carlyle found the argument congenial to his own thinking; Henry Thoreau, who lived with the Emersons from 1841 to 1843 and was indebted to both Carlyle and Emerson, put their ideas of labor and economy into practice at Walden Pond in 1845, when he built a cabin with his own hands, hoed his own beans, and followed his own admonition to "Simplify, simplify."

In other appearances of 1841, such as the "Introductory Lecture" in his series on "The Times," Emerson, as we have seen, identified himself more closely with reform if not with reformers. The reformer, as he declared in "The Method of Nature," "should aim at an infinite, not a special benefit." "Temperance, Anti-Slavery, Non-Resistance, No Government, Equal Labor"—all seem "fair and generous" causes, but "are poor bitter things when prosecuted for themselves as an end. . . . The imaginative faculty of the soul must be fed with objects immense and eternal" (*CW* 1:132–33), for all ends are transient and finite: "they are vents for the current of inward life which increases as it is spent. A man's wisdom is to know that all ends are momentary, that the best end must instantly be superseded by a better. But there is a mischievous tendency in him to transfer his thought from the life to the ends, to quit his agency and rest in his acts: the tool runs away with the workman, the human with the divine" (*CW* 1:129).

iii. Reform in Perspective

Emerson's next pronouncement on reform—specifically in education and in the treatment of workingmen and slaves—came almost incidentally in an address on "The Young American" (*CW* 1:222–44), delivered on 7 February 1844 before the Mercantile Library Association of Boston.[3] Once again he was speaking to members of a particular audience on their own terms, as in "Man the Reformer": this time a group of ambitious young men who were aspiring to commercial success. Even so, he also made some characteristically Emersonian pronouncements. As in "The American Scholar," he began with the observation that America needs a native rather than a European culture, though the tone here seems more like that of the later Walt Whitman than of the earlier Emerson: "We are sent to a feudal school to learn democracy," but at last "America is beginning to assert itself to the senses and to the imagination of her children, and Europe is receding in the same degree." In the body of the address he set forth an optimistic vision of the national future phrased especially for his practical-minded Yankee listeners.

One principal influence for change among his countrymen, the lecturer declares, had been the rapid building of railroads, fostering the growth of cities like Boston and at the same time opening new land for cultivation. Along with other citizens of Concord, Emerson was fascinated by the new railroad then approaching their town from the city, but he was not insensitive to exploitation of Irish immigrant laborers as the work progressed. The labor demanded of them is "excessive," he charges, "and the sight of it reminds one of negro-driving." More positively, he goes on to say, the new railroads are important "in creating an American sentiment" as they acquaint the people with "the boundless resources of their own soil," and with settlement of the West there has come "a new and continental element into the national mind." "Every American should be educated with a view to the values of land," Emerson urges his audience, holding as in "Man the Reformer" that farming can "repair the errors of a scholastic and traditional education, and bring us into just relations with men and things." The need for educational reform was much on his mind during the early 1840s.

Although clearly conscious of the immediate cost to some individuals of new material developments in American national life, Emerson was inclined in speaking to this audience to emphasize the benefits those developments would bring over the years to society as a whole. Commerce, here and elsewhere, had operated like a force of nature itself, he told his listeners, and that force, while it might seem harsh, is ultimately beneficent:

> there is a sublime and friendly Destiny by which the human race is guided,—the race never dying, the individual never spared,—to results affecting masses and ages. Men are narrow and selfish, but the Genius, or Destiny, is not narrow, but beneficent. It is not discovered in their calculated and voluntary activity, but in what befalls, with or without their designs. Only what is inevitable interests us, and it turns out that love and good are inevitable, and in the course of things. (CW 1:230)

Although this line of thinking seems akin to that nineteenth-century doctrine of "Manifest Destiny" so often used by American politicians to justify westward expansion, it is even more expressive of the scholar's own long-range cosmic outlook. "My whole philosophy," Emerson had told Carlyle in 1841, "teaches acquiescence and optimism" (CEC 304). Such teaching would become increasingly prominent in his later writings, notably in the essay on "Fate" in The Conduct of Life (1860).

In "The Young American" Emerson continues with the hope that Trade, as "the principle of Liberty" that "planted America and destroyed Feudalism," will in the long run make and keep peace and abolish slavery; he makes no recommendation, however, of more immediate action toward these ends. As for other social reforms, he glances in his concluding paragraphs at current communitarian experiments as pointing toward a better society, whatever their present shortcomings. In politics he hopes that "feudal governments in a commercial age" would eventually give way to a genuine aristocracy of ability, with national leaders guided by "the Spirit who led us hither, and is leading us still."

In contrast to "The Young American," which looks hopefully to the future, Emerson's lecture on "New England Reformers" (CW 3:149–167) considers the historical background of the reform movement. The lecture was given on 3 March 1844 at Amory Hall in Boston, a public room where the Church of the Disciples—an independent religious society with his friend James Freeman Clarke as its minister—held its regular Sunday meetings. Emerson first thought of his address there as a "Sermon," though it may actually have grown out of his fifth lecture in the "New England" series (JMN 12:564; cf. 12:xx). He did not "think to do much that is new" in the lecture (L 3:242), and in fact it substantially recapitulates what he had been writing and speaking about contemporary society during the late 1830s and early 1840s. Within "the last twenty-five years," he notes at the outset, "the Church, or religious party," had been "falling from the church nominal, and is appearing in temperance and non-resistance societies, in movements of abolitionists and of socialists, and in very significant assemblies, called Sabbath and Bible Conventions."[4] In short, the recent impulse toward reform, in his view, was a secular manifestation of the old New England religious spirit. Whatever the eccentricities and excesses among reformers generally, in Emerson's words, "there was sincere protesting against existing evils. . . . No doubt, there was plentiful vaporing, and cases of backsliding might occur. But in each of these movements emerged a good result, a tendency to the adoption of simpler methods, and an assertion of the sufficiency of the private man" (CW 3:150).

After glancing at the need for reform in politics and in trade, Emerson next deals at some length with what in "The Young American" he had called "the errors of a scholastic and traditional education" (CW 1:226). Here he incorporates passages originally written nearly five years before, both in his journal and also in a lecture on "Education" in his series on "The Present Age." A persistent Emersonian theme is the charge that professional educators lack the scholar's own democratic faith in the potentiality of each and every student. But though Emerson had spoken expansively in the earlier lecture of his doctrine of "God in man" and its corollary, "the infinitude of the private man," as the basis for that faith, he now writes more cautiously of "divine sentiments in man" and the private man's "sufficiency." Here he repeats his earlier objection to an education in words rather than things, turning into passive voice ("It was complained that . . .") much of what he had written in his own person after listening in 1839 to "a sad discourse" by Horace Mann that was "full of the modern gloomy view of our democratical institutions" (JMN 7:237–38).[5]

To Emerson's regret, modern scholars are mere "students of words: we are shut up in schools, and colleges, and recitation-rooms, for ten or fifteen years, and come out at last with a bag of wind, a memory of words, and do not know a thing." As remedial measures, he again advocates working with one's hands "in the field" (as in "Man the Reformer"), recommends the "experimental" teaching of science, and calls for abandonment of "our scholastic devotion to the dead languages," that "warfare against common sense" which requires drill in Latin and Greek of every student, regardless of his talents and interests. Emerson himself was steeped in classical literature; what he objected to was concentration on language for its own sake, sacrificing the spirit to the letter.

Unfortunately, "our system of education," in Emerson's words, is really "a system of despair," and our professional scholars themselves "betray a destitution of faith," as he had written of "students" in the first of his lectures on "The Times" in 1841. Renouncing "all high aims" for our instruction, we merely "adorn the victim with manual skill, his tongue with languages, his body with inoffensive and comely manners. So have we cunningly hid the tragedy of limitation and inner death." Even our scholar-teachers, being products of this same kind of training, are doubtful of its value. In their own experience,

> the scholar was not raised by the sacred thoughts amongst which he dwelt, but used them to selfish ends. He was a profane person, and became a showman, turning his gifts to a marketable use, and not to his own sustenance and growth. It was found that the intellect could be independently developed, that is, in separation from the man, as any single organ can be invigorated, and the result was monstrous. A canine appetite for knowledge was generated, which must still be fed, but was never satisfied, and *this knowledge not being directed on action*, never took the character of substantial, humane truth, blessing those whom it entered. It gave the scholar certain powers of expression, the power of speech, the power of poetry, of literary art, but it did not bring him to peace, or to beneficence. (CW 3:159; emphasis added)

"When the literary class betray a destitution of faith," Emerson continued, "it is not strange that society should be disheartened and sensualized by unbelief." Although he was speaking of the entire "literary class," his long identification of himself as a writer and scholar, his more recent questioning of his own faith, and his significant reference to "action" may suggest once more some degree of "sad self-knowledge." However that may be, he sets forth here this "remedy" for unbelief:

> Life must be lived on a higher plane. We must go up to a higher platform, to which we are always invited to ascend; there, the whole aspect of things changes. I resist the skepticism of our education, and of our educated men. I do not believe that the differences of opinion and character in men are organic. I do not recognize, beside the class of the good and the wise, a permanent class of skeptics, or a class of conservatives, or of malignants, or of materialists. (CW 3:159)

In later paragraphs of the lecture, picking up terms from his lecture on "The Times"—"the establishment" and "the movement party"—Emerson returns to his central topic, New England reformers in general. He levels two main charges against his contemporaries among them: first, as he had often said, they are "partial" in their devotion to "some single improvement" of society rather than its "total regeneration"; second, they rely on "Association"—group organizations—while remaining incapable as individuals of inward wholeness. Gougeon has emphasized the influence here of William Ellery Channing, citing various journal entries of these years that "present virtual echoes of Channing's statements concerning the perils of myopic associationism where all other concerns are subordinate to one principal cause."[6] Like Channing, who had died in 1842, Emerson had long believed that reform must begin with the individual; what is needed to bring it about, he now declares, is "that faith in man, which the heart"—not the intellect—"is preaching to us in these days."

iv. Toward Engagement

A significant shift in Emerson's independent position with respect to reform is evident in his address at Concord of 1 August 1844, delivered by invitation at a meeting of abolitionists from thirteen Massachusetts towns in celebration of the tenth anniversary of emancipation in the British West Indies (W 11:97–147). Since his address of 1837 on slavery, which had not pleased his Concord listeners, Emerson had occasionally attended other local Anti-Slavery rallies, but not as a speaker. His acceptance in 1844 of the new invitation to speak meant an end to his carefully maintained disengagement from the abolitionist cause; it also obliged him to acquaint himself more fully with the history of that cause and its implications for a scholar. Quoting Emerson's own words, Joseph Slater has remarked that "many July days must have been, as he said, 'occupied with this history'—many hours in his study and many solitary, meditative walks 'in the pastures and along the edge of woods'" (97).[7] From his reading and thinking Emerson had evidently learned to discard "the old indecent nonsense about the nature of the negro," which to some degree had been reflected in his own thinking. As he declares in the oration, "It now appears that the negro race is, more than any other, susceptible of rapid civilization" (140–41).

One consideration affecting Emerson's decision to speak on emancipation was his strong opposition to the proposed annexation of the Republic of Texas to the United States; like many Northerners, he saw it as a scheme both to extend slaveholding into the Southwest and to increase the proslavery power of the South within the national government. Although he believed that Americans would ultimately "overrun that tract, & Mexico & Oregon also," he wished for the present to "resist the annexation with tooth & nail" (JMN 9:74). In the Congress, where John Quincy Adams had fought for the right to discuss the issue of slavery, Emerson's long-admired Daniel Webster was now proving to be a man of expediency rather than a principled leader; had Webster only "given himself to the cause of Abolition of Slavery in Congress," Emerson felt, "he would have been the darling of this continent" (*JMN* 9:90–91). But as the scholar once sadly observed, among those who go to Congress, "none comes back innocent" (*JMN* 11:417).

Emerson's growing disappointment with such politicians as Webster is reflected in his discussion of "Politics" in the *Essays* of 1844. Building upon his earlier distinction in lectures on "The Times" between the party of the Future and the party of the Past, he had come to identify them respectively with the Democrats and the Whigs, the leading American political parties of the 1840s. In his judgment, both were deficient, though for different reasons: "one has the best cause, and the other contains the best men" (cf. *JMN* 8:314).

> The philosopher, the poet, or the religious man, will, of course, wish to cast his vote with the democrat. . . . But he can rarely accept the persons whom the so-called popular party propose to him. . . . They have not at heart the ends which give to the name of democracy what hope and virtue are in it. The spirit of our American radicalism is destructive and aimless: it is not loving; it has no ulterior or divine ends; but is destructive only out of hatred and selfishness.

The opposing movement had its own drawbacks, as Emerson had already noted in his lectures on "The Times." Though the conservative party of the day "is composed of the most moderate, able, and cultivated part of the population," he now writes, it is "timid, and merely defensive of property. It vindicates no right, it aspires to no real good, it brands no crime, it proposes no generous policy, it does not build, nor write, nor cherish the arts, nor foster religion, nor establish schools, nor encourage science, nor emancipate the slave, nor befriend the poor, or the Indian, or the immigrant" (*CW* 3:122–23).

The essayist's reluctant inference is that "from neither party, when in power, has the world any benefit to expect in science, art, or humanity, at all commensurate with the resources of the nation." Yet Emerson also expresses in "Politics" his persistent idealistic faith in the possibility of future improvement. "They only who build on Ideas, build for eternity," he declares, while the forms of government that exist in the present merely express whatever degree of civilization has been attained by the societies that permit them—a condition that will necessarily vary from nation to nation and from time to time. "Every actual State," he holds, "is corrupt," and "Good men must not obey the laws too well"—an antinomian position he would come back to in the 1850s after passage of that "filthy enactment," the Fugitive Slave Law.

If elected leaders persist in remaining silent, then private citizens—scholars included—must speak out; so Emerson had now come to think. In the oration of August 1844, clearly outraged by the jailing and kidnapping of free black citizens of Massachusetts in southern ports, he castigates "the tameness and silence" of the state's congressional delegation as well as the deplorable inaction of Massachusetts authorities. England had set an admirable moral example by freeing its slaves; the

American government, disregarding the inevitable "tendency of things" toward morality and freedom, was merely temporizing. "There is a blessed necessity by which the interest of men is always driving them to the right," Emerson affirms in conclusion, voicing once more the optimism toward the future he had expressed in both "The Young American" and the more recent "Politics." "The sentiment of Right, once very low and indistinct, but ever more articulate, because it is the voice of the universe, pronounces Freedom."

With this ringing declaration in support of freedom and morality the scholar had put off his "robe of inaction," the "wise passiveness" of earlier years, having seen at last "how to act with truth" by speaking out publicly against slavery. As Gougeon has rightly observed, Emerson had now "made the transition from Anti-Slavery to abolition, and his association with organized abolitionists would continue to grow from this point forward."[8] The oration of 1844 was enthusiastically received in Concord. In early September Emerson printed it in pamphlet form and furnished proofsheets for a later edition in London; elsewhere, Horace Greeley reprinted the oration in his *Daily Tribune* and Nathaniel Rogers carried it in the abolitionist *Herald of Freedom*. Although the Boston *Courier* concluded that Emerson had now "identified himself with the abolitionists,"[9] Rogers objected that he had not gone far enough: "Let us have Abolition and not Emancipation," he wrote in reviewing the oration. Remarking that "the scholar knows only a sort of lettered humanity," Rogers suggested to "the gifted author of the Address, that a tour of anti-slavery field service would be most helpful to his own powers of writing and speech" (CW 3:xxx).

As we shall see, Emerson, a subscriber to the *Herald*, did not forget this pointed advice. Although he had reservations about the oration itself, describing it to Carlyle as "an intrusion . . . into another sphere & so much loss of virtue in my own" (CEC 273), he had nevertheless made a public commitment. But the scholar had not escaped his persistent dilemma. Throughout the troubled years leading up to the Civil War, the question of his further response to the issue of slavery would be a particularly troubling component of that "problem" he felt himself "set to solve."

12. NEW AND LARGER CIRCLES, 1845–1850

◆

> Our life is an apprenticeship to the truth, that around every circle another can be drawn.
>
> —"Circles" (CW 2:179)

The year 1844 can now be seen as a notable turning point in Emerson's thinking. By that time, freed from the troublesome burden of *The Dial,* he had been able to complete his long-projected second volume of essays. In composing the essay on "Experience" he had assimilated his skepticism of the earlier 1840s, recognizing that "the new philosophy" required him to take in new ideas along with his old faith. In "Nominalist and Realist," an essay closely related to "Experience," he was already laying new intellectual groundwork for the lectures on "Representative Men" that he was to give in 1845–1846. And in "Politics," though he voiced his usual optimism concerning the future of the United States, he also made it plain that in his judgment the major American political parties were failing to address the immediate needs of the country. "Politics" and "New England Reformers" were the immediate antecedents of his address of 1844 on "Emancipation in the British West Indies." In events of the day he had at last found a clear case for a scholar's "action": he would speak publicly on Great Britain's emancipation of slaves as a praiseworthy example for the United States to follow.

Contemporary reviews of *Essays: Second Series,* which came in slowly from both American and British sources, were for the most part disappointing. A number of them expressed reservations about either the content or the rhetoric of the new essays (see *CW* 3:xxxii–xxxvii); even Carlyle in a letter and Margaret Fuller in a published review wished for more coherence between both the volume's successive paragraphs and its component essays.[1] During the winter of 1845–1846 Emerson spoke in Boston on "Representative Men"; he repeated some or all of these new lectures in other New England cities and towns during both 1846 and 1847. Meanwhile, he had been preparing his first volume of verse, which appeared in December 1846; it included poems mentioned in these pages as marking stages in his intellectual development: "The Rhodora" and "Each and All" from the early 1830s, "The Problem" from 1839, and "Uriel" and "Threnody" from the 1840s. In October of 1847, when he brought out a second edition of the *Essays* of 1841, he added short poems as mottoes for each of the chapters.

ii. The Scholar in Wartime

As we know from Emerson's journal entries of the 1840s, he had come to resent the failure of Northern senators and congressmen to take a strong stand against Southern pressure not only to maintain slavery as an institution but also to increase proslavery power in Washington by admitting new slaveholding states to the Union. He was particularly embittered by the insulting treatment offered to his friend and respected fellow townsman Samuel Hoar in Charleston, South Carolina. Hoar had gone there in an effort to protect the rights of black citizens of Massachusetts who were being threatened with detention and possible enslavement if they landed in South Carolina ports. When Hoar was forcibly expelled from the state in accordance with a vote of the South Carolina legislature and under immediate threats from a mob, Emerson like other citizens of Massachusetts began viewing North-South relations in a new light.

Until 1844, as we know, Emerson's movement toward active engagement with the issue of slavery had been a gradual one. In the contemporary drive for reforms of all kinds he had discerned a secular manifestation of the traditional New England religious spirit. Since his years as a minister in Boston he had repeatedly championed the right of Anti-Slavery agitators to be heard, even while he remained publicly uncommitted to their cause—or indeed to any particular reform, though he fully recognized what he referred to as "the horrors of Southern slavery." Reacting unfavorably to the narrow parochialism of all too many zealous reformers, he continued through the early 1840s to maintain his conception of the scholar as a wholly disinterested observer and "dispassionate reporter," as he had put it in 1839. Even so, he was growing more and more concerned with social issues and social criticism, as he had indicated as early as 1836–1837 in "The Philosophy of History" lectures. This concern continued with the later series on "The Present Age" in 1839–1840 and his lectures on "The Times" in 1841–1842, when he allied himself with what he called "the movement party" rather than the conservative "establishment."

Emerson's growing sympathy for blacks, clearly expressed in the address of 1844, was further manifested in November of 1845, just as he was writing and scheduling his new lectures on "Representative Men," when he declined an invitation to address the New Bedford Lyceum because its members had voted to bar non-whites from its audience. Thinking as he did that "the Lyceum exists for popular education" and actively working in it for that end, Emerson wished to "exclude nobody" from its programs but hoped instead to welcome even "the humblest and most ignorant." The decision in New Bedford, he told an official there, was a "direct contradiction to the obvious duty and sentiment of New England, and of all freemen in regard to the colored people" (L 3:312).[2] When William Lloyd Garrison printed Emerson's letter in The Liberator for 16 January 1846, his new commitment to the Anti-Slavery cause became all the more evident. Meanwhile, the federal government was moving to annex what for almost ten years had been the slaveholding Republic of Texas. Relations with Mexico were deteriorating, and actual hostilities along the Mexican border began in April 1846. In May the United States declared war against that country, and major fighting between the two nations continued during the remaining months of 1846 and into 1847; American troops entered Mexico City on 14 September 1847. A peace treaty was finally concluded in February of 1848, after Texas had already become part of the Union.

As hostilities began in 1846 between the United States and Mexico, Emerson grew more and more discouraged by the turn of national and international events. He was no antiwar activist, however, and rather than taking a public stand in opposition to "Mr. Polk's war," he was tempted to do what certain young male Americans would be doing in the 1960s when they too opposed their country's military commitments: quietly go "toward Canada" (*JMN* 10:29).[3] The tone of Emerson's journal entries of the mid–1840s, intended for his eyes alone, may well surprise any reader who still thinks of him primarily in the light of "The American Scholar," the Divinity School Address, or such essays of the earlier 1840s as "Spiritual Laws" and "The Over-Soul." Observing the national scene, he now seems far more down-to-earth, tough-minded, even disillusioned and cynical.

Here is a sampling of Emerson's private comments made during the war years:

> The name of Washington ↑City↓ in the newspapers is every day of blacker shade. . . . It seems to be ⟨a⟩ settled that no act of honor or benevolence or justice is to be expected from the American Government, but only this, that they will be as wicked as they dare. No man now can have any sort of success in politics without a streak of infamy crossing his name.
>
> Things have another order in these men's eyes. ⟨Solid⟩ ↑Heavy↓ is hollow & good is evil. A western man in Congress the other day spoke of the opponents of the Texan & Mexican plunder as "Every light character in the house," & [a Boston banker] speaks of "the solid portion of the community," meaning, o[f] course, the sharpers. I feel, meantime, that those who succeed in life, in civilized society, are beasts of prey. It has always been so. (*JMN* 10:29)
>
> We live in Lilliput. (*JMN* 10:30)
>
> If capital punishment is abolished, private vengeance comes in. If Eng[land]., France, America, are forbidden war with each other, they spend their ferocity on Sikhs, Algerines, & Mexicans & so find a vent for their piratical population. You shall not as feudal lords kill the ⟨ch⟩serfs, but now as capitalists you shall in all love & peace eat them up as before. (*JMN* 10:36; cf. 9:424–25)
>
> We devour Mexico as the stomach arsenic, but it brings us down at last. (*JMN* 10:36, cf. 9:430–31)
>
> Nationality is babyish for the most part[.] (*JMN* 10:76)
>
> Patriotism is balderdash. (*JMN* 10: 161)

The more dramatic outward gestures that some of Emerson's contemporaries were making in protest against the war struck him as wasted effort; for all his idealism he was shrewd enough to realize that a war-minded president and Congress would pay little attention to a few Northerners who lacked the power of either numbers or the purse. And Southerners in and out of Washington could afford to be "cool & insolent" to the North, as he had observed when the war broke out, knowing just as the Southerners did "why Massachusetts & New York are so tame"—apart from a few angry voices. The reason was sheer economic self-interest. "Cotten thread holds the union together," he wrote in 1846, and "unites John C. Calhoun & Abbott Lawrence. Patriotism for holidays & summer evenings with music & rockets, but cotten thread is the union" (*JMN* 9:431, 425).

Even Henry Thoreau's now celebrated decision, taken late in July of 1846, to go to jail rather than pay his Massachusetts tax, failed to "reach the evil" it opposed, Emerson thought at the time, since support of the war was actually coming from federal levies on articles of ordinary commerce—meaning Northern-sponsored tariffs on imported goods—rather than state taxes. As for the abolitionists, who opposed the war primarily because it would lead to the creation of more slaveholding states and so increase the proslavery vote in Congress, they should indeed resist, he felt, simply "because they are literalists; they know exactly what they object to, & there is a government ⟨to which⟩ possible which will content them. Remove a few speci⟨al⟩fied grievances, & this present commonwealth will suit them. They are the new Puritans, & as easily satisfied." But "nothing will content" a man like Thoreau, as Emerson well knew. "No government short of a monarchy consisting of one king & one subject, will appease you," he wrote with Thoreau in mind. "Your objection then to the state of Massachusetts is deceptive" (he had first written "is then absurd"). "Your true quarrel is with the state of Man" (*JMN* 9:447).

It was Emerson's own standing quarrel "with the state of Man" that for most of his life kept him from enrolling in more limited crusades, whether against the government, the Mexican War, or even American slavery, much as he despised its existence. Although he had finally come to advocate in public the emancipation of American slaves, he was not about to enroll among the abolitionists or violate his principles by using scheduled lecture engagements as occasions for fulminating against either slavery or the Mexican War. Even so, he remained gravely troubled by the conflicting demand of his self-dedication as an observant but detached scholar and his feelings as a concerned citizen who deplored the injustice and immorality of both war and slaveholding. If the nineteenth century was divided in spirit between scholars and men of the world, as he had declared in contrasting Goethe with Napoleon, in wartime America the businessmen and politicians who supported the South and the war were clearly dominant, the "true scholars" being a lonely minority.

What then *were* the duties at such a time for Emerson as an American Scholar, especially since he had become a prominent public figure?[4] Though Emerson continued to speak out against slavery, as he did in an address before the Massachusetts Anti-Slavery Society on 4 July 1846 in Dedham, he knew himself powerless to alter the course of a now-declared war or to prevent its inevitable political sequel: increased representation for the proslavery forces in Congress. In "this emergency," as Emerson called his personal situation, he felt the need of some definite objective—"a whip for the top," as he called it. In February 1847, thanks to his growing reputation abroad as well as at home, he received a possible answer to that need: a challenging invitation to lecture in Great Britain.

Going abroad, as Emerson well knew, would of course take him away, on altogether legitimate business, from the immediate problems of war and slavery in America. But he was slow to agree, and as he continued to ponder both his proper duty at home and the tempting invitation from England, he made a significant analysis of his problem. "A Scholar," he declared, in a journal entry made late in March of 1847, "is a candle which the love & desire of men will light. Let it not lie in a dark box." But such a candle must somehow "be set aglow," preferably by "the stimulus of a stated task." Confessing that he had wished for a professorship or even—"Much as I hate the church"—a pulpit, he granted that "perchance" Nathaniel Rogers had spoken "more truly than he knew" when in 1844 he "recommended an Abolition-Campaign" to the scholar and added that no doubt "a course of mobs" would do him "much good." Emerson's real preference, he admitted, would be to "withdraw myself for a time from all domestic & accustomed relations & command an absolute leisure with books—for a time" (*JMN* 10:28–29). But this would seem to mean leaving the candle unlit; could it not be made to shine once again if it were carried across the Atlantic?

On further reflection the scholar came to regard the proposal more favorably. He had unpublished material at hand; he had already outlined a possible new course of lectures, on "Mind & Manners in the XIX Century" (*JMN* 9:403, 443), in which he might carry forward the cultural analysis begun in his earlier lecture series and continued most recently in the concluding lectures of "Representative Men." Once decided, Emerson wrote on 31 July 1847 to Alexander Ireland, his English correspondent in Manchester, accepting the invitation, and on 5 October he sailed from Boston for Liverpool to begin his second visit to England. While he was away, Henry Thoreau, who had previously lived with the Emersons, became caretaker in Concord.

ii. The Scholar in England and Scotland, 1847–1848

During Emerson's first travels in Europe in 1832–1833 he had habitually referred to himself as an aspiring student; early in 1847 he began an entry in his new Journal AB with the motto "Ancora imparo"—"I still learn," adding the comment "Scholar perpetual" and closing the entry by repeating the initial phrase: "Ancora imparo. I carry my satchel still" (*JMN* 10:6–7; cf. "Michel Angelo Buonaroti," *EL* 1:103). From the beginning he thought of the second European trip as a further learning experience. Before his departure, with travel to France as well as to England in prospect, he prepared himself by subscribing to a French-language newspaper and taking lessons in French conversation.

Always the scholar as man of letters, Emerson hoped that during his absence

"A Scholar is a candle"
Entry of ca. 25 March 1847, Journal AB, p. 61; see *JMN* 10:28–29.

abroad he might gain new material for his writing and lecturing, but he also sought to gain a new perspective on the events at home that had so discouraged him. "We go to Europe to see aristocratic society with as few abatements as possible," he wrote. "We go to be Americanized, to import what we can. This country has its proper glory, though now shrouded & unknown. We will let it shine" (*JMN* 10:161). The scholar could indeed be set aglow once again. As a representative American, he would be a cultural ambassador, first from the New World to the Old; then from the Old World back to the New.

Emerson's arrival at Liverpool on 22 October was complicated by Alexander Ireland's inability to meet him as intended; there was also a delay in receiving a letter from Carlyle inviting him to hasten to London. But he was soon settled in Manchester, with time before his lecturing began there to spend four days with the Carlyles. While in London he also saw the American minister to Britain, George Bancroft, and took breakfast with the celebrated Samuel Rogers. Then, during November, he lectured alternately in Manchester and Liverpool, presenting all the components of "Representative Men" except "Plato, or the Philosopher," which he read only privately to a small group of friends. He also gave additional lectures on "Eloquence" and "Domestic Life" and two new offerings: "Books or a Course of Reading" and "The Superlative in Manners and Literature." Both Swedenborgians and orthodox Church of England clergymen were openly troubled by Emerson's supposedly transcendental ideas, and press reviews of his first lectures were somewhat mixed. Although he lamented chiefly that these accounts "report my lectures and London papers reprint so fully, that they are no longer repeatable," he soon learned that local committees wanted those they had already "heard of" and advertised (*L* 3:452; 4:4); he proceeded thereafter to give both old offerings and new.

During the winter months of 1847–1848, when Emerson visited other English provincial cities, he delivered individual lectures rather than a related series: "Napoleon," "Domestic Life," "Shakspeare," "Books," "Eloquence," "Uses of Great Men," and another new composition, "The National Characteristics of the Six Northern States of America," evidently intended to present the Northern cause to his English listeners at a time when British manufacturing interests tended to be sympathetic toward the cotton states of the South. Back in Manchester on Christmas Day, Emerson reviewed his lecturing to date in a long letter to his wife, who had written to ask him for "full and 'private' letters" about his stay in England. He was "so harried by this necessity of reading Lectures" that he scarcely expected to comply "for a fortnight or three weeks," but the Christmas letter itself is revealing.

"What reconciles me to the clatter & routine," Emerson told Lidian, "is, the very excellent opportunity it gives me to see England."

I see men & things in each town in a close & domestic way, I see the best of the people, (—hitherto, never the proper aristocracy, which is a stratum of society quite out of sight & out of mind here on all ordinary occasions,)—the merchants the manufacturers the scholars the thinkers—men & women,—in a very sincere & satisfactory conversation. I am everywhere a guest. Never call me solitary or Ishmaelite again. I begun here by refusing invitations to *stay* at private houses; but now I find an invitation in every town, & accept it, to be at home. . . . My admiration & my love of the English rise day by day. (*L* 3:454)

As this passage suggests, his acquaintance in the provinces was chiefly with the middle class, not with the aristocrats or with farmers and factory workers.

During January and February 1848 Emerson lectured both in northern England and in Scotland. At Edinburgh, where his host was Dr. Samuel Brown, a scientist with whom he had corresponded, he read a new lecture on "Natural Aristocracy" along with "The Genius of the Present Age," "Shakspeare," and "Eloquence." While in the city he met Thomas De Quincey, the writers Francis Jeffrey and John Wilson ("Christopher North"), the publishers Robert and William Chambers, and the painter David Scott, to whom he sat for a portrait (reproduced as the frontispiece to this volume). In Glasgow he read "Domestic Life"; in Dundee, "The Spirit of the Times" and "Eloquence"; and in Perth, both "Eloquence" and his most popular lecture in Britain, "Napoleon." On his way back to London he called at Ambleside on Harriet Martineau, who had visited him in Concord, and again paid his respects to Wordsworth.

In London from early March until early May, having taken lodgings with his British publisher, John Chapman, Emerson enjoyed seeing the new Houses of Parliament, Hampton Court, Kew Gardens, and the British Museum. He made a longer excursion to Oxford University as a guest of Arthur Hugh Clough, visiting the Bodleian Library and meeting a number of Oxford dignitaries. In London he became something of a social lion. The Bancrofts gave a dinner in Emerson's honor, presenting him to London society, the best London clubs offered him membership privileges, and for the first time he began to move in aristocratic circles. "I have seen a good deal of society of the upper & of the best middle class," he reported on 21 April to his Boston friend Abel Adams (*L* 4:59). He also attended musical events, scientific lectures, and sessions of the House of Commons and saw and admired Turner's paintings. He talked with leading scholars of the day, in London as at Oxford, and came to know most of the prominent English writers, among them Dickens and Tennyson.[5]

Emerson's letters and journals up to this point show him to have been strongly and favorably impressed by London itself and by the power and wealth of industrialized England generally, though he was well aware of its dirt and grime, of the "eminently prosaic or unpoetic" character of its people (*JMN* 10:341), and of the hard lot of its women and children; he had also taken note of the provinciality and poverty of Scotland across the northern border. The moderate English "working climate," the efficient British factories and railways, and the *Times* newspaper in London, which he read devotedly, all received his enthusiastic praise. "If I stay here long," he wrote, "I shall lose all my patriotism, & think that England has absorbed all excellences" (*JMN* 10:244). And to Margaret Fuller, on the eve of his departure for France on 6 May, he wrote that he was leaving "with an increased respect for the Englishman. His stuff or substance seems to be the best of the world. I forgive him all his pride. My respect is the more generous that I have no sympathy with him, only an admiration" (L 4:62).

iii. The Scholar and the Times, 1848

"I have been exaggerating the English merits all winter, & disparaging the French," Emerson acknowledged after his arrival in Paris. "Now I am correcting my judgment of both, & the French have risen very fast" (JMN 10:327; cf. L 4:76). At the very beginning of his brief stay in France, which lasted only from 6 May to 2 June, he found Frenchmen to be "expressive" and "intensely masculine"; they are "all soldiers, all speakers," and every man has the "àplomb which these need. . . . A certain ingenuity & verbal clearness of statement they require & that satisfies them that they have a new & lucid & coherent statement though it is artificial, & not an idea." The very climate of Paris seemed different from that of London, and its architecture appeared to be "far more original, spirited, national" (JMN 10:261–62, 263, 265). But his changing appraisal of the Parisian French was most significantly related to his growing appreciation of their political and social outlook, so different from that of rich and conservative Englishmen, who intensely disliked French socialism.

Emerson had gone to Paris in the face of warnings from his well-to-do English friends about the dangers he might encounter in the city, where radical agitation had continued after the overthrow in the previous February of Louis Philippe, the so-called "Citizen King." Londoners, he observed, meaning the upper classes, had no use for the new provisional government, labeling as "an ass & a rogue" the moderate Alphonse de Lamartine, the French poet and historian who had become one of its ministers and its most prominent orator. Alfred Tennyson "affected to think" that Emerson would "never come back alive from France, which he, in common with all his countrymen, distrusts & defies" (JMN 10:295, 538–39; L 4:74). Emerson, a confirmed individualist, had long kept his distance from socialistic movements, beginning with Brook Farm and its later transformation into a Fourier-istic phalanx, and he was not prepared when he went abroad to embrace any form of French socialism. "The oracle is dumb" concerning socialism, he had written while still in England. "When we would pronounce anything truly of man, we retreat instantly on the individual. . . . When I see changed men, I shall look for a changed world" (JMN 10:310–11).[6] But what he saw and heard while in France proved to be both provocative and surprisingly instructive.

In Paris Emerson went to the Louvre, attended performances by the actress Rachel and lectures at the Collège de France, dined with Alexis de Tocqueville, and visited the Comtesse d'Agoult, who as "Daniel Stern" was at work on her history of the revolution of 1848.[7] At the National Assembly he listened to an address on Poland by Lamartine, who was opposed by extremists of both the right and the left. With English friends he went to two of the radical socialist clubs, those of Armand Barbès and Louis Blanqui, to hear protests against "the extreme inequality of property" in France; as he knew, there were "depots of arms" in the clubs, ready to be used. This was on the very eve of the radicals' abortive attempt on 15 May to overthrow the new government, a *rappel* which he witnessed. "I have seen Barbé's role in his *Club de la Revolution,* & Blanqui in his *Club des Droits de l'homme,*" Emerson wrote afterward, "and today they are both in the dungeon of Vincennes" (*JMN* 10:321, 323).

What Emerson heard in the clubs made a lasting impression, deepening his understanding of current issues. In a letter to his wife on 17 May he declared that "the deep sincerity of the speakers who are agitating social and political questions, and who are studying how to secure a fair share of bread to every man, and to get God's justice done through the land, is very good to hear" (*L* 4:73–74). As a well-informed American, Emerson knew before leaving home that the year 1848 was a time of great unrest in many parts of Europe, where the peoples of Poland, Hungary, and Italy were rising in revolt against oppressive rulers. Margaret Fuller was then in Rome, reporting to Horace Greeley's New York *Tribune* on the attempted Italian revolution, and American newspapers generally had been giving prominence to dispatches from abroad. Emerson was directly familiar with the demands of the Chartists in England for electoral reforms (*JMN* 10:567), having followed Carlyle's suggestion, shortly after he reached London, that he go to one of their meetings, but he was put off by the appearance of those attending.

During the first week of April, when a Chartist march on the Houses of Parliament was in prospect, Emerson heard rumors of "a ↑Chartist↓ revolution on Monday next, and an Irish revolution in the following week." "The right scholar," he thought, would feel that "now was the hour to test his genius. His kingdom is at once over & under these perturbed regions. Let him produce its Charter now, & try whether it cannot win a hearing, & make felt its infinite superiority today, even today." (*JMN* 10:310–11). But the scholars he came to know in succeeding weeks, both English and French, proved unequal to such a task. "The writers are bold & democratic" in what they say and write, he observed while in Paris. When revolution actually comes, however, they prove not to be "Chartists & Montagnards," for at that crucial point they merely "talk & sit with the rich, & sympathize with them." The Chartists in particular "have such gross & bloody chiefs to mislead them, and are so full of hatred & murder," Emerson continued, "that the scholar recoils;—and joins the rich. That he should not do" (*JMN* 10:325).

Once again, what *should* scholars properly be doing? Further, Emerson was surely asking himself, now that he had responded so favorably to "the deep sincerity" of the French radicals, what should a visiting *American* scholar be doing? Note the telling shift from third person to first as this same journal passage continues. The scholar, he went on to say,

should accept as necessary the position of armed neutrality abhorring the crimes of the Chartist, yet more abhorring the oppression & hopeless selfishness of the rich, &,

still *writing the truth,* say, the time will come when these poor enfans perdus of revolution will have instructed their party, if only by their fate, & wiser counsels will prevail,
& the music & the dance of liberty will take me in also. Then I shall not have forfeited
my right to speak & act for the Movement party. Shame to the fop of philosophy who
suffers a little vulgarity of speech & of character to hide from him the true current of
⟨t⟩Tendency, & who ⟨hides retrea⟩ abandons his true position of being priest & poet
of these impious & unpoetic ⟨workmen⟩doers of God's work. (*JMN* 10:325–26)

Emerson did in fact "speak & act for the Movement party" in the concluding
lecture of the series that he was shortly to give in London, adapting this revealing
passage for "Natural Aristocracy" (cf. *W* 10:63–64).

As a disengaged scholar, Emerson was still uncommitted to any organized
movement for reform, including English Chartism and French socialism as well as
American abolitionism, but what he saw and heard while in France had made him
far more sympathetic to the political and social goals of the European reformers, if
not to their belligerent activism. His recommendation to scholars generally of a
posture of "armed neutrality" was quite in keeping with the position he had assumed during the earlier 1840s: as an optimistic member of "the Movement party"
in the United States, he had spoken in a similar vein of remaining apart from
specific reform movements, being dubious about their single-minded leaders but
confident nevertheless that an inevitable cosmic "Tendency" would eventually
bring an end to American slavery. Though he had become noticeably less optimistic about the Anti-Slavery cause by the mid–1840s, he was still not prepared while
in Europe to do what writers at home such as Whittier and Lowell had already
done: draw a parallel between the situation of American slaves and that of the
oppressed classes of Europe.

Emerson's experiences in Paris not only gave him a more balanced view of both
France and England but also affected the content and the tone of the lectures he
delivered in London following his return there on 3 June 1848. He had agreed only
reluctantly to speak in London, feeling obliged if he did so to prepare lectures
previously unheard in England and Scotland (and so unreported in the London
papers), but he could not ignore a petition signed by prominent Londoners such as
Carlyle and Dickens who wished to hear him lecture. As he told Margaret Fuller
before accepting, he had already begun work on "some papers" which might
ultimately serve "as a kind of Book of Metaphysics to print at home"; preparation
for the lectures obliged him to cut short his visit to Paris, which was spoiled
because of his need to work on the "portfolio of papers" that accompanied him
there (*L* 4:63, 78).

Three days after his return to London, Emerson read six lectures before the
Literary and Scientific Institution in Portman Square. His general subject was
"Mind and Manners in the Nineteenth Century," the title he had in mind before
leaving Concord. On the evening of 8 June a weary lecturer informed his wife that
he had not only been "writing all day" after reading his second lecture but must
also "work all day tomorrow on my third." For the series to date he had attracted "a

very moderate audience & I was right of course in not wishing to undertake it for I spoil my work by giving it this too rapid casting." Eight days later, in another letter to Lidian, a still-pressed Emerson told her that his last lecture "is tomorrow, & is far from ready" (L 4:80, 83).

The first three London lectures, which Emerson spoke of at the outset as "sketches" for a larger project, "The Natural History of Intellect," evidently grew out of the "papers" he had begun in London and carried to France. Their titles were "Powers and Laws of Thought," "Relation of Intellect to Natural Science," and "Tendencies and Duties of Men of Thought." He had long been interested in formulating what he called in 1835 "the original laws of the mind" (JMN 5:270), returning to the subject in various lectures of the later 1830s such as "The Head" and in 1841 with his essay on "Intellect" and his address on "The Method of Nature." Listening to scientific lectures while he was in London may have stimulated his desire to draw analogies between the laws of nature and the laws of mind, an objective that would continue to engage him over many years.[8]

As for the three other lectures, "Politics and Socialism," "Poetry and Eloquence," and "Natural Aristocracy," Emerson had previously spoken on "Eloquence" during the winter of 1846–1847, before leaving home, and in Manchester a year later he had drafted an early version of "Natural Aristocracy" for delivery in Edinburgh and elsewhere. "Politics and Socialism," an altogether new lecture, was directly related to what he had recorded of his recent experiences in both London and Paris.[9] The entire "Mind and Manners" series was directed particularly at scholars, himself included. "My rede," he declared as he worked on the lectures, "is to make the student independent of the century," showing him that "his class offer one immutable front in all times & countries"; because they transcend place and time they "cannot hear the drums of Paris, cannot read the London journals." He likened them to "the Wandering Jew or the Eternal Angel that survives all, & stands in the same fraternal relation to all," while the world at large, which "is always childish," puts its trust in such passing developments as "a revolution or a new constitution." Taking his customary idealistic view, Emerson put his own faith in that "permanent good" which "is for the soul only & cannot be retained in any society or system" (JMN 10:328).

Such a message, as might be expected, struck some of Emerson's listeners as simply impractical; Carlyle, for example, dismissed the entire series as "pleasant moonshiny discourses." Emerson's British friend J. J. Garth Wilkinson, the translator of Swedenborg (whom Emerson thought to be turning from Swedenborg to Fourier), disliked a characteristic Emersonian remark in "Politics and Socialism" that the socialists "are not the creatures they believe themselves," being in fact "unconscious prophets of a true state of society . . . which the tendencies of nature lead unto." Lord Morpeth, by contrast, protested to Emerson concerning a passage in "Natural Aristocracy" that deplored upper-class insensitivity to the plight of the poor. Those most favorably impressed, it would seem, were the younger scholars whom Emerson especially wished to reach—for example, Oxonians such as Clough and his friend Matthew Arnold, who later wrote of Emerson's message during the 1840s as "a strain as new, and moving, and unforgettable, as the strain of Newman, or Carlyle, or Goethe."

Larry J. Reynolds, in touching on these differing responses, has offered a balanced appraisal of the "Mind and Manners" series. "From one point of view," as he says, the lectures were "conservative, in the sense that they belittled the importance of political and social change. From another point of view, however, Emerson's own, they advocated a radicalism far more profound than any being voiced by his European contemporaries." And "at the heart of Emerson's idealism," as Reynolds has rightly observed, "is the call for spiritual regeneration, for new men, not new social orders" (42).[10]

iv. From London to Concord

Before leaving England on 15 July Emerson was persuaded to give three lectures at more popular prices, this time at Exeter Hall in late June, when he spoke once again on "Napoleon," "Domestic Life," and "Shakspeare"; on 26 June he also returned to Portman Square to read "The Superlative in Manners and Literature."[11] These additional lectures served to pay his passage home (L 4:103). There was still time before his departure for several excursions into the English countryside, including a visit to Cambridge; at Stonehenge he had a remarkable conversation with Carlyle that he would later describe in his *English Traits* (1856).

From the time of their first reunion meeting in October 1847, when Emerson and Carlyle had differed strongly over their estimates of Carlyle's hero Oliver Cromwell, their long relationship had become sadly strained, though their correspondence while Emerson was traveling in the provinces remained distantly polite. When Emerson returned to London in April of 1848 he preferred to take rooms with John Chapman rather than stay with the Carlyles. His letters and journals of the next two months reported his dissatisfaction with Carlyle's reactionary opinions and vitriolic conversation; conversely, Carlyle repeatedly dismissed Emerson's moderate views and complained to friends about both sets of his London lectures. But the weekend in the country that they spent together, shortly before Emerson sailed for home, proved to be, in Joseph Slater's well-chosen words, "a recapitulation and a coda; it was also a resolution of discord." By this time, having learned "the worst about each other," they "were not to be shocked or shaken by the deepest disagreement" (CEC 39, 43).

Back in Concord in late July, Emerson began to appraise his situation. Financially, the trip abroad had left him in debt, but he hoped, "first or last, to make the whole Excursion pay itself" (L 4:103). In November 1848 he resumed lecturing with selected components of the series on "Representative Men"; in 1849 and 1850 he offered new lectures, variously titled, on England and the English and on London, anticipating his book of 1856 on *English Traits*. He also revised and read some of the lectures from the "Mind and Manners" series during these same years; it was probably "Natural Aristocracy" that Herman Melville listened to with approval at the Freeman Place Chapel in Boston on 5 February 1849, when his interest in Emerson began.[12] In the spring of 1849 Emerson published as *Nature, Addresses, and Lectures* the long-planned selection of his earlier writings, some of which had been repeatedly pirated in England; the chosen lectures in particular required careful pruning and revision. And in the following summer and fall he was at work turning the more recent lectures of 1845–1846 into *Representative Men* (1850). All of these activities of course helped to remedy his financial difficulties.

It is impossible to comment in detail about the extent of Emerson's revisions for *Representative Men*, since few identifiable leaves of the lecture manuscripts have survived. But a number of additions are evident—notably "Plato: New Readings" (CW 4:45–50), occasioned by publication of the first two volumes of the new Bohn edition of Plato, with translations by Henry Cary and Henry Davis. As we know from Emerson's notebook "Platoniana," he had been accumulating other material from his later reading concerning Plato and Socrates; some of his notebook entries were incorporated in a revised version of "Plato, or the Philosopher," the one lecture of the series that he had read only once while abroad. Other additions to the book resulted from his acquisition of newly translated works of Swedenborg and from miscellaneous information he had picked up in England: for example, his reference to copies of Montaigne's *Essays* owned by Shakespeare and Ben Jonson that had been shown to him at the British Museum (CW 4:92–93; JMN 10:295).

In early January of 1850 *Representative Men* appeared almost simultaneously both in Boston and in London (the English edition was quickly pirated). In Great Britain, where the book was reviewed "widely but not generously,"[13] it was frequently compared—to Emerson's disadvantage—with Carlyle's *Heroes and Hero-Worship*, which present-day critics regard as altogether different in both conception and style. "The English journals ⟨as⟩ snub my new book; as indeed they have all its foregoers," Emerson responded, adding wryly that "The fate of my books is like the impression of my face. My acquaintances, as long back as I can remember, have always said, 'Seems to me you look a little thinner than when I saw you last'" (JMN 11:214–15). In America the book sold well, despite the usual objections to Emerson's unorthodox religious views and his supposed obscurity, it became the most popular book he had yet published. As for Emerson himself, he had declared long before that Jesus was the representative man he should have sketched but felt unequal to the challenge; in later years, following the appearance of Renan's *Vie de Jésus* in 1863, he repeated his admission (JMN 9:139; 15:224).

Representative Men remained popular well into the present century, when Emerson and his writings for a time fell out of both popular and critical favor. It is now seen as marking a transition from the inwardness of his earlier writings to the more outward orientation of his later lectures and books, notably *English Traits*, and by his greater freedom of expression, reflecting more directly than its predecessors his manner of speaking from the platform. On the negative side is a charge of "pervasive intellectual impotence" that has been raised most forcefully by Ann Douglas Wood. "None of Emerson's chosen 'representative men' are Americans," she has written. "He sidesteps all the figures who were held up to his generation as heroes"—notably George Washington. Instead, they are

> all, with the possible exception of Napoleon, intellectuals or artists. Although none of them are specifically reformers or anti-reformers, they fall, with a frightening neatness indicative of Emerson's divided state, into two categories: those who observe the universe and grow sterile through non-participation, and those who use it and are corrupted through their involvement. . . . [H]e is meticulously careful to follow an account of these men's strengths with a summary of their weaknesses . . . [that] deflates every heroic figure he blows up.

In short, "Emerson does not finally solve the dilemma that produced the lectures," Douglas continues, "namely, the problem of the intellectual as hero."[14] It was the old problem that had confronted him for more than a decade, when his vision of the American Scholar as heroic spokesman and leader had been dimmed in the aftermath of the Divinity School controversy; it would come home to him again in the decade of the 1850s as the American nation drifted inexorably toward disunion and civil war. The "position of armed neutrality" that Emerson had been advocating for the scholar during the 1840s was shortly to meet its greatest challenge.

13. THE SCHOLAR AND PUBLIC AFFAIRS, 1850–1865

And this ⟨ferocious⟩ ↑filthy↓ enactment was made in the 19th Century, by people who could ⟨wr⟩ read & write.
I will not obey it, by God.

> —Undated entry concerning the Fugitive Slave Law
> in Journal GO, p. 145 (*JMN* 11:412)

During the years between 1850 and 1865 Waldo Emerson reached the height of his fame. He published three notable books of his own: *Representative Men* (1850), *English Traits* (1856), and *The Conduct of Life* (1860). Following the death by shipwreck of Margaret Fuller, her Italian husband, and their child in July of 1850, he also helped materially in preparing the two-volume *Memoirs of Margaret Fuller Ossoli* (1852). As a popular lecturer he traveled regularly, not only in New England and the middle states but in what is now the Midwest, beginning with his response in 1850 to a petition from residents of Cincinnati requesting him to lecture there. Emerson had come back from abroad with the hoped-for new perspective on his country and himself that he had sought in Europe. Having learned from his demanding schedule of engagements in provincial English cities and in Scotland to move easily from town to town and to converse readily with a wide variety of men and women, a more sociable scholar was now better prepared for the long winters of travel that lay before him.

In the early 1850s, when debate over slavery in the United States was growing ever more intense and divisive, Emerson was torn once again by an old question: How far in the direction of activism should a scholar properly go? Should he at last follow the lead of William Lloyd Garrison and Nathaniel Rogers to become an out-and-out abolitionist? Garrison, he remarked in 1850, was still single-minded, "neigh[ing] like a horse when you suggest a new consideration, as when I told him, that, the fate-element in the negro question he had never considered"; even so, Rogers' recommendation of "a course of mobs . . . to correct my quaintness & transcendentalism" might have served Emerson as helpfully as "the water cure for paralyzed stomachs" (*JMN* 11:231). At that time, before the Fugitive Slave Law went into effect, he could still write that "men of thought" will "refuse the necessity of mediocre men, that is, to take sides." Abhorring both "whiggism" and "rebellion," they thereby maintain their own equilibrium, their own self-poise

(*JMN* 11:263). But this was not to be the scholar's own final position. Reluctantly but inexorably, he was drawn into the arena of public affairs.

i. "This filthy enactment"

As Emerson had predicted before going abroad, the admission of Texas to the Union and the increasing power in Congress of the Southern states meant a renewed drive for proslavery legislation after the Mexican War was concluded in 1848. Still cherishing his ideal of the detached scholar but outraged by ensuing events, Emerson took a more and more active position against slavery, abandoning his posture of "armed neutrality" and moving steadily toward the abolitionist camp. Although he never joined an abolitionist organization, as Len Gougeon has noted, "he effectively became an abolitionist, in the eyes of both his friends and his enemies."[1] Despite his distinction between occasional pronouncements on public issues and his regular lecturing, his views on slavery made him unwelcome as a lecturer even in some Northern cities as well as in the Southern states.[2] This was especially true in the late 1850s, after his endorsement of John Brown and his acts of violence in Kansas and Virginia—an endorsement that seemed surprising for a peace-loving scholar.

What finally "radicalized" Emerson, to use our present-day term, was passage by the Congress in 1850 of the Fugitive Slave Law, a "detestable" piece of legislation, as he rightly called it, that obliged Northerners to aid in returning runaway slaves instead of expediting their flight for freedom. This requirement, Emerson noted in December 1850, "makes slavery the single topic of conversation in this Country" (*JMN* 11:323). Since 1793 there had been a similar federal law, but it was loosely enforced in Northern states; in some cases, as in Massachusetts, state and local officials were actually forbidden by state legislation to help capture runaways. But the new and more rigorous act, passed as part of the Compromise of 1850 as a concession to the South, set heavy penalties for anyone, Southerner or Northerner, who sought to help an escaping black fugitive. Many leading Northerners angrily protested, Emerson among them. He filled eighty-six consecutive pages of his Journal BO (1850–1851) with his searing denunciation of this "filthy enactment" and of the "treachery" of his old hero Daniel Webster, then senator from Massachusetts. In Emerson's eyes Webster had sacrificed principle to politics by appeasing Southern slaveholders out of a base regard for the economic interests of the Northern businessmen to whom he was beholden. As a leader in the Senate, Emerson charged, Webster had not only reenacted the old law but also given it "*force,* which it never had before," so brought the North—Massachusetts in particular—down "to the cannibal level" of the South (*JMN* 11:354–55).

In April 1851 matters came to a head in Emerson's own state with the arrest of the fugitive slave Thomas M. Sims. Lemuel Shaw, Chief Justice of the Massachusetts Supreme Court, who was personally opposed to slavery, nevertheless felt obliged under the new law to refuse the man's release from jail on habeas corpus, and Sims was subsequently returned to slavery. What Shaw should have done, in Emerson's view, was to declare the law unconstitutional. Shaw's decision would seem to be the instance Emerson had in mind when he wrote, "We are glad at last to get a clear case, one on which no shadow of doubt can hang" (*JMN* 11:361, 411). Out of the journal came passages for his first address on "The Fugitive Slave Law," given by invitation in Concord on 3 May 1851 (*W* 11:177–214) and repeated in Fitchburg and Cambridge. "The last year has forced us all into politics," he declares at the outset, speaking for himself as well as for his listeners. "We do not breathe well. There is infamy in the air," he continues.

> I have a new experience. I wake in the morning with a painful sensation, which I carry about all day, and which, when traced home, is the odious remembrance of that ignominy which has fallen on Massachusetts, which robs the landscape of beauty, and takes the sunshine out of every hour. I have lived all my life in this state, and never had any experience of personal inconvenience from the laws, until now. They never came near me to any discomfort before.

Even those "who take no interest in the ordinary questions of party politics" share these same feelings, and "the whole population will in a short time be as painfully affected" (*W* 11:179–80).

Other Northerners, Emerson declares, have expressed their "mortification at the late events in Massachusetts, and at the behavior of Boston," where Webster was praised by prominent citizens for his support of the Fugitive Slave Bill and a hundred guns were fired to celebrate its passage. Developments since then have conspicuously shown the "nature and impracticability" of the law. It is contravened, Emerson argues, on five counts: by the sentiment of duty, which requires a man to break any law which is immoral; by the sentiments of piety and charity; by other written laws; by "the mischiefs it operates"; and by the very history of the statute itself. Each point is buttressed in the address by a variety of materials, ranging from somewhat toned-down journal passages to supporting quotations drawn from the writings of noted jurists. Dealing with the history of the Fugitive Slave Law led Emerson to condemn Webster for his leading role in bringing about its passage. Speaking as a member of the Movement party, the party of the future, Emerson scathingly labels Webster as "a man who lives by his memory, a man of the past, not a man of faith or of hope."

This is Emerson's verdict on Webster's limitations as a nineteenth-century statesman:

> Happily he was born late,—after the independence had been declared, the Union agreed to, and the constitution settled. What he finds already written, he will defend. Lucky that so much had got well written when he came. For he has no faith in the power of self-government. . . . Not the smallest municipal provision, if it were new, would receive his sanction. In Massachusetts, in 1776, he would, beyond all question,

have been a refugee. He praises Adams and Jefferson, but it is a past Adams and Jefferson that his mind can entertain. A present Adams and Jefferson he would denounce. (*W* 11:204; cf. *JMN* 11:404–5)

Emerson turns next to the larger question of the Union and its chances for survival, given the unhappy fact that in 1851 "there are really two nations, the North and the South." As he sees the situation,

> it is not slavery that severs them, it is climate and temperament. The South does not like the North, slavery or no slavery, and never did. The North likes the South well enough, for it knows its own advantages. . . . If they continue to have a binding interest, they will be pretty sure to find it out; if not, they will consult their peace in parting. But one thing appears certain to me, that, as soon as the constitution ordains an immoral law, it ordains disunion. The law is suicidal, and cannot be obeyed. The Union is at an end as soon as an immoral law is enacted. And he who writes a crime into the statute-book digs under the foundations of the Capitol to plant there a powder-magazine, and lays a train. (*W* 11:206; cf. *JMN* 11:408)

What, then, shall we do? "First, abrogate this law," Emerson urges; "then, proceed to confine slavery to slave states, and help them effectually to make an end of it." He would do in the United States what the British did in the West Indies: buy the slaves. "I say buy,—never conceding the right of the planter to own, but that we may acknowledge the calamity of his position, and bear a countryman's share in relieving him; and because it is the only practicable course, and is innocent." The necessary funds could be raised, he is sure, through a combination of taxes, deferred governmental expenditures, and popular subscription. Meanwhile, "One thing is plain, we cannot answer for the Union, but we must keep Massachusetts true. . . . Massachusetts is little, but, if true to itself, can be the brain which turns about the behemoth." In short, "Let us respect the Union to all honest ends. But also respect an older and wider union, the law of Nature and rectitude. Massachusetts is as strong as the Universe, when it does that."

Emerson's address was well received in Concord, where Anti-Slavery sentiment was strong, but when he delivered it at Cambridge in support of his friend John G. Palfrey, a Unitarian clergyman who was the unsuccessful Free-Soil candidate for Congress in his district, he met angry opposition. As William Lloyd Garrison's *Liberator* reported, "students from Harvard College did what they could to disturb the audience and insult the speaker, by hisses and groans, interspersed with cheers for Webster, Clay, Fillmore, Everett, and 'Old Harvard.'"[3] It was disputed at the time whether the disturbance was caused by Southern students or Northern sympathizers with the Southern cause. E. P. Whipple remarked later that Emerson "seemed absolutely to enjoy" the hissing, but James Elliot Cabot disagreed, holding that "he must have been profoundly grieved to see men of his own order—young men, too, whom above all others he would have wished to influence—so utterly wrong-headed." As an eyewitness told Cabot, Emerson maintained his dignity and composure. "He stood with perfect quietness until the hubbub was over, and then went on with the next word. It was as if nothing had happened: there was no repetition, no allusion to what had been going on, no sign that he was moved, and I cannot describe with what added weight the next words fell."[4]

ii. The Persistent Dilemma

Following Emerson's return from abroad in 1848, when he was occupied with seeing two books through the press—first *Nature, Addresses, and Lectures* and then *Representative Men*[5]—he made use in his lecturing during 1849 and 1850 of either material already in manuscript or new discussions based on his experiences in England.[6] During these years he suffered a number of personal losses: his friends Ellen Hooper and David Scott—the "natural priest" who had painted his portrait in Edinburgh (*JMN* 11:111, 53)—died in 1849 and Margaret Fuller in 1850; his mother's death would come in 1853. During 1851, as the basis for his contribution to the *Memoirs of Margaret Fuller Ossoli,* he filled a notebook with quotations from her diary and correspondence along with original biographical material (*JMN* 11:455–509); the two-volume *Memoirs,* with additional contributions by William Henry Channing and James Freeman Clarke, appeared in the following February. On 7 October 1851, in a letter subsequently printed in the New York *Daily Tribune,* Emerson told Lucy Stone that his work on the *Memoirs* would keep him from attending the Woman's Rights Convention being held at Worcester; he noted that he had signed the call for the convention and still sympathized with its objectives (*L* 4:260–61).

By February 1851 Emerson was planning another new lecture series (*JMN* 11:339), including lectures that he first delivered at Pittsburgh in March and again in Boston during the following winter. Components of this series, "The Conduct of Life," became his staple offerings for a number of years; in 1860 he published the lectures, with revisions and additions, as a book with that same title.[7] He lectured eighty-two times during 1852, traveling north to Montreal and west as far as St. Louis. At Concord on 11 May he gave a brief welcoming address in honor of Louis Kossuth, hero of the Hungarian revolution of 1848–1849 (*W* 11:395–401; cf. *JMN* 10:466–67). Calling Kossuth "the man of Freedom," he also hailed him as "the man of Fate," saying that "you do not elect, but you are elected by God and your genius to the task." Kossuth, who was visiting the United States in search of tangible help for Hungary, may well have troubled Emerson by his pointed response. Though some "distinguished men" endeavor to "make their way throughout the world merely by their moral influence," Kossuth observed, "I have never yet heard of a despot who has yielded to the moral influence of liberty. . . . The doors and shutters of oppression must be opened by bayonets."[8]

By December 1852, as Emerson reported to his brother William from Cincinnati, he was anxious "to be at home, where I have now accumulated tasks. For my English notes have now assumed the size of a pretty book, which I am eager to complete; and some other papers have got nearly ready for printing" (*L* 4:332). But in 1853 he was once more on the lecture circuit, making a total of fifty-six appearances that included a return visit to St. Louis. The "English notes" Emerson referred to were brought together in Notebook ED ("England"), which he had compiled in 1852 and 1853 from his earlier journals and correspondence of 1832–1833 and 1847–1848 (*JMN* 10:494–568), looking forward to the publication of *English Traits* in 1856. Why the appearance of a book that Emerson was "eager to complete" was delayed for nearly four years can be explained partly by the continuing need to maintain his income through lecturing, but there were other factors, notably the further political developments of the 1850s.

iii. The Scholar and Abolition

A journal entry of August 1852 expresses Emerson's still-persistent dilemma as he reacted to the more recent current of events:

> I waked at night, & bemoaned myself, because I had not thrown myself into this deplorable question of Slavery, which seems to want nothing so much as a few assured voices. But then, in hours of sanity, I recover myself, & say, God must govern his own world, & knows his way out of this pit, without my desertion of my post which has none to guard it but me. I have quite other slaves to free than those negroes, ↑to wit,↓ imprisoned spirits, imprisoned thoughts, far back in the brain of man,—far retired in the heaven of invention, &, which, important to the republic of Man, have no watchman, or lover, or defender, but I.— (*JMN* 13:80)

Here two cardinal principles of Emerson's thinking can be seen coming into conflict: his strong moral sense and his equally strong commitment to the ideal of the detached scholar. What he liked to call "the moral sentiment" was central to his nature, and he had long since denounced slavery as morally wrong. But through the 1840s, as he put it in "The Young American" (1844), he had remained optimistic that in due course, with the guidance of "the Spirit who led us hither, and is leading us still," his countrymen would voluntarily put an end to slavery; this was "the fate-element in the negro question" he had asked Garrison to consider.

Even in 1852, despite Emerson's anger over the Fugitive Slave Law, he could still write that "God must govern his own world, and knows his way out of this pit." Moreover, he believed sincerely that the scholar has "quite other slaves to free than those negroes." Consciously or otherwise, in saying that "imprisoned spirits, imprisoned thoughts . . . important to the republic of Man, have no watchman, or lover, or defender, but I," Emerson was echoing his own idealistic words of the 1830s on the scholar as Watcher; his reference to "the republic of Man" even recalls both his definition of the American Scholar as "*Man Thinking*" and his later remarks about the idealist's quarrel with "the state of Man." Though powerfully moved in 1852 to go beyond his public denunciation of the Fugitive Slave Law and become an active campaigner for abolition, he nevertheless reaffirmed both his

119

I waked at night, & bemoaned myself, because I had not thrown myself into this deplorable question of Slavery, which seems to want nothing so much as a few assured voices. But then, in hours of sanity, I recover myself, & say, God must govern his own world, & knows his way out of this pit, without my desertion of my post which has none to guard it but me. I have

The Scholar's Dilemma
Undated entry of early August 1852, Journal GO, p. 119; see *JMN* 13:80.

optimistic faith in the ultimate power of divine guidance and his old commitment to scholarly objectivity.

By 1854, however, the scholar had begun to shift his ground, moving further in the direction of Anti-Slavery activism. Speaking in New York on 7 March 1854, "the fourth anniversary of Daniel Webster's speech in favor of the bill," Emerson delivered his second address on the Fugitive Slave Law (*W* 11:215–44). On that occasion, as he said, he was addressing "the class of scholars or students,—that is a class which comprises in some sort all mankind, comprises every man in the best hours of his life; and in these days not only virtually but actually," thanks to "the silent revolution which the newspaper has wrought." "I do not often speak to public questions," Emerson told his listeners in New York; "—they are odious and hurtful, and it seems like meddling or leaving your work." And then, reaffirming his sentiments of 1852, he added that "I have my own spirits in prison;—spirits in deeper prisons, whom no man visits if I do not" (cf. *JMN* 13:409).

As Emerson goes on to explain, "My own habitual view is to the well-being of students or scholars. And it is only when the public event affects them, that it very seriously touches me. And what I have to say is to them. For every man speaks mainly to a class whom he works with and more or less fully represents. It is to these I am beforehand related and engaged, in this audience or out of it—to them and not to others" (*W* 11:217–18). His message to such persons is hortatory. The true lovers of liberty, he feels (perhaps remembering Kossuth), "may with reason tax the coldness and indifferentism of scholars and literary men," particularly those persons in the universities (he was surely thinking of Harvard) who are "lovers of liberty in Greece and Rome and in the English Commonwealth," but "lukewarm lovers of the liberty of America in 1854" (*W* 11:242). By this time, he had come to believe, scholars too must join in active opposition to slavery.

The printed text of Emerson's address in New York is prefixed by two passages of verse, one from John Greenleaf Whittier's scathing dismissal of Webster in "Ichabod" ("from those great eyes / The soul has fled") and one from Robert Browning's "The Lost Leader." The body of the lecture begins with a survey of the downward course of Webster's career in the years before his death in 1852, charging that Webster, "by his personal influence, brought the Fugitive Slave Law on the country." Then follows a denunciation both of slavery itself and of those who have followed Webster's lead in furthering its continuance. The Fugitive Slave Law "did much to unglue the eyes of men, and now the Nebraska Bill leaves us staring." Emerson's latter reference is to congressional legislation then pending, the Kansas-Nebraska Bill, which would become law on the following 30 May and would lead to bloody fighting in those former territories over the slavery issue.

In January of 1854 Senator Stephen A. Douglas of Illinois, chairman of the Senate Committee on Territories, had reported a bill providing that the question of slavery in states yet to be formed from territories west of Iowa and Missouri should be left to the decision of their settlers; a subsequent amendment then repealed that section of the Missouri Compromise of 1820–1821 which had provided that slavery would be banned altogether in those territories. The expectation was that the new state of Kansas would be a slave state while Nebraska would be free. The bill passed as amended, with the backing of Southern congressmen, and was signed by President Franklin Pierce. The sequel was an immediate attempt by both proslavery and Anti-Slavery forces to send enough emigrants to Kansas to determine the vote there. The popular expression "bleeding Kansas" describes the armed clashes that resulted, in which John Brown, a native New Englander and an ardent abolitionist, took a prominent part.

"I respect the Anti-Slavery Society," Emerson said at the conclusion of his New York address, with these developments in mind. "It is the Cassandra that has foretold all that has befallen, fact for fact, years ago; foretold all, and no man laid it to heart." The Society, he predicted,

> will add many members this year. The Whig Party will join it; the Democrats will join it. The population of the free states will join it. I doubt not, at last, the slave states will join it. But be that sooner or later, and whoever comes or stays away, I hope we have reached the end of our unbelief, have come to a belief that there is a divine Providence in the world, which will not save us but through our own coöperation. (W 11:244)

God may indeed know the way "out of this pit," as Emerson had written earlier, but men—scholars included—must do their own part as well. "Armed neutrality" would no longer serve, even if the scholar's new activism affected his customary devotion to those other "imprisoned spirits" he was previously committed to serve.

Events of the later 1850s continued to involve Emerson more and more deeply in the crusade for American liberty that he had now actively joined. "If by opposing slavery I undermine institutions," he wrote in Notebook WO Liberty, "I own I do not wish to live in a nation where slavery exists. The life of this world has but a limited worth in my eyes, & really is not worth such a price as the toleration of slavery" (JMN 14:383);[9] in a letter to his brother William, he would in fact write of "looking into the map to see where I shall go with my children when Boston & Massachusetts surrender to the slave-trade" (L 5:23). On 25 January 1855, speaking in Boston on "American Slavery" before the Massachusetts Anti-Slavery Society, he again proposed that the American government buy the slaves (L 4:484 n. 14); he repeated the address later in the same year at New York, Philadelphia, and other cities. And on 20 September, addressing the 1855 Woman's Rights Convention in Boston, he noted that "all my points would sooner be carried in the State"— including abolition of slavery—"if women voted" (W 11:420).

In May of 1856 Emerson agreed wholeheartedly when his friend Charles Sumner, the Free-Soil senator from Massachusetts, spoke out against the proslavery outrages that had been taking place west of the Mississippi. Sumner's speech on "The Crime Against Kansas" was answered on the floor of the Senate by a Southern congressman who attacked him brutally. When word of their encounter reached Concord, Emerson, ever loyal to his friends, is said to have responded "as if he personally had been attacked,"[10] for the event affected him in much the same way as abuse of Samuel Hoar in South Carolina had angered him during the 1840s. Discussing "The Assault on Mr. Sumner" at a public meeting in Concord on 26 May (W 11:245–52; cf. JMN 14:407 n. 114), he stated flatly that "every sane human being" was now "an abolitionist, or a believer that all men should be free." The entire slaveholding South he stigmatized as "a barbarous community" where "man is an animal"; and since barbarity and civilization cannot "constitute one state," as he argued, America was facing a momentous choice: either "we must get rid of slavery, or we must get rid of freedom" (W 11:250, 247).

By this point Emerson had put the cause of abolition well ahead of any desire to preserve the Federal Union. Hearing that his friend Oliver Wendell Holmes, speaking in New York, had taken the opposite position and allegedly "denounced the abolitionists of New England . . . as 'traitors to the Union'"—so the Boston Daily Advertiser had reported—Emerson expressed his relief when Holmes denied the allegation. "I divide men as aspirants & desperants," he wrote in a characteristic letter of March 1856 in which he spoke once again for "the pathetically small minority of disengaged or thinking men" who "stand for the ideal right, for man as he should be." The letter deserves generous quotation. "A scholar," he told Holmes,

> need not be cynical to feel that the vast multitude are almost on all fours; that the rich always vote after their fears[;] that cities churches colleges all go for the quadruped interest, and it is against this coalition that the pathetically small minority of disengaged or thinking men stand for the ideal right, for man as he should be, &, (what is essential to any sane maintenance of his own right) for the right of every other as for his own. When masses then as cities or churches go for things as they are, we take no note of it, we expected as much. . . . [B]ut when a scholar, (or disengaged man,) seems to throw himself on the dark[,] a cry of grief from the aspirants['] side is heard exactly proportioned in its intensity to his believed spiritual rank. (From a rough draft, as emended by Emerson, in L 5:17–18)

On a separate sheet apparently associated with this letter, Emerson added that "the Union with Slavery . . . is dead & rotten."

As for Emerson himself, his gradual movement from scholarly disengagement to active involvement in the Anti-Slavery cause continued to gather momentum after publication of English Traits in the following August. On 10 September 1856, at a Kansas Relief Meeting in Cambridge, he gave a "Speech on Affairs in Kansas" since passage of the Kansas-Nebraska Act (W 11:253–63). Lawful emigrants to a national territory, he declared, have been "set on by highwaymen, driven from their new homes, and numbers of them killed and scalped" in the course of "a systematic war to the knife"—a war in which the Federal government itself "armed and led the ruffians against the poor farmers," and to which neither Congress nor the President had objected. His bitter appraisal: "I do not know any story so gloomy as the politics of this country for the past twenty years."

On this same occasion Emerson observed that in what he called "the universal cant," even language itself reverses its normal meanings. "The corruption of man is followed by the corruption of language," Emerson had written long before in *Nature* (*W* 1:20); now, he observes, "*Representative Government* is really misrepresentative; *Union* is a conspiracy against the Northern States which the Northern States are to have the privilege of paying for; the *adding of Cuba and Central America* to the slave marts is *enlarging the area of Freedom. Manifest Destiny, Democracy, Freedom,* fine names for an ugly thing" (*W* 11: 259). As a result, he declares, nineteenth-century Americans face a greater danger than did their forebears at the time of the American Revolution. If the population then was small, the people "were united, and the enemy three thousand miles off. But now, vast property, gigantic interests, family connections, webs of party, cover the land with a network that immensely multiplies the dangers of war."

During the later 1850s Emerson continued his regular winter lecturing, speaking on a variety of subjects that included several new topics, such as "Beauty" and "Courage" as well as a single lecture entitled "Conduct of Life"; in February 1857 he repeated at Cincinnati the lecture on "The Scholar" that he had given in 1854 and 1856 at Williamstown and Amherst. In view of the kind of legislation passed by the Congress, the attack on Sumner, and the recent bloody events in Kansas, he and many of his friends in both Concord and Boston gravitated toward the newly formed Republican party because of its announced opposition to slavery. Emerson was temperamentally unable to become an enthusiastic partisan, however, and though he accepted appointment in 1856 as an alternate delegate to the party's first national nominating convention, he declined to attend when vacancies occurred. As a citizen, he persistently refrained from signing petitions and delivering speeches even on behalf of candidates and causes that he approved.

A notable setback to the Anti-Slavery cause came in 1857, when the Southern majority on the United States Supreme Court held, in the case of Dred Scott, that slaves had no standing in federal courts; moreover, the Court declared that the Congress had no power to prohibit slavery in the western territories. Northern opponents of slavery were outraged, Emerson among them. He was favorably impressed when John Brown visited Concord in 1857 and 1859, being convinced of the rightness of Brown's violent resistance to proslavery settlers in Kansas. But he surprised his close associates by making an unexpected public defense of Brown's armed attack on the government arsenal at Harpers Ferry, Virginia, in October 1859, accepting his latest resort to bloodshed as equally justified. Brown was convicted of treason and murder for his actions at Harpers Ferry, which he had intended as a signal for a slave insurrection.

On 18 November 1859, at a meeting in Boston for the relief of Brown's family (*W* 11:265–73), Emerson spoke of him as "the rarest of heroes, a pure idealist, with no by-ends of his own."[11] He thought of Brown as one who "believed in his ideas to the extent that he existed to put them all into action; he said 'he did not believe in moral suasion, he believed in putting the thing through'" (*W* 11:268, 270). Such words must have struck home for Emerson, a fellow idealist who had been uncertain for so many years about the scholar's proper role in public affairs; in quoting Brown he may even have remembered Kossuth's remark in 1852 that "The doors and shutters of oppression must be opened" not by "moral influence" but "by bayonets." On 2 December, on the day and hour when Brown's sentence to be hanged was carried out, Emerson spoke at a memorial service in Concord, and on 6 January he briefly addressed a meeting at Salem, where funds were being raised for the families of Brown and his men (W 11:275–81).

Public awareness of Emerson's support of Brown and Brown's acts of violence provoked stormy objections, leading to cancellation of a scheduled lecture engagement in Philadelphia; there were angry protests as well against his two appearances in Cincinnati during early February 1860. According to Emerson's friend and host in that city, Moncure Conway, "a wealthy Conservative" asked Emerson about a report that before Brown's conviction he had declared in a lecture that "If Brown should suffer, he would 'make his gallows glorious like a cross.'"[12] "Emerson asked that the reported words should be repeated," Conway wrote, "and then remarked, 'That's about what I said.' The questioner, much shocked, said, 'Surely you do not approve the bloody raid of John Brown upon the families of Virginia.' Emerson slowly replied, 'If I should tell you why I disapproved, you might not like it any better.'"[13]

In the following June Emerson was saddened by the death of Theodore Parker, a staunch and outspoken ally in the fight for freedom. "I can well praise him at a spectator's distance," Emerson wrote in his journal, "for our minds & methods were unlike,—few people more unlike" (JMN 14:352–53). Addressing a memorial meeting in Boston (W 11:283–93), he spoke of Parker's life as "part of the history of the civil and religious liberty of his times," for his ministry fell "on the years when Southern slavery broke over its old banks, made new and vast pretensions, and wrung from the weakness or treachery of Northern people fatal concessions in the Fugitive Slave Bill and the repeal of the Missouri Compromise." Parker's "commanding merit as a reformer," Emerson believed, is "that he insisted beyond all men in pulpits—I cannot think of one rival—that the essence of Christianity is its practical morals; it is there for use, or it is nothing" (W 11:289). So Emerson himself, ever an apostle of the moral sentiment, had come to define Parker's understanding of Christianity if not his own.

iv. The War Years, 1861–1865

Having voted for Abraham Lincoln in the presidential election of November 1860, Emerson hailed the news of Lincoln's "sublime" victory, calling it "the pronunciation of the masses of America against Slavery" (JMN 14:363). But the issue was by no means settled. Conservative Northern Unionists continued to favor compromise with the South, and in some Northern cities, including Boston, there were instances of mob violence against both abolitionists and free blacks. Further trouble erupted at the annual meeting of the Massachusetts Anti-Slavery Society, held in Boston on 24 January 1861. Emerson was invited to participate by the abolitionist Wendell Phillips, whom he greatly admired. "Esteeming such invitation a command, though sorely against my inclination & habit, I went," Emerson wrote, "and, though I had nothing to say, showed myself. If I were dumb, yet I would have gone & mowed & muttered or made signs." When called upon to say a few words he was hooted down. "The mob roared whenever I attempted to speak," he added in his journal entry, "and after several ⟨attempts⟩ beginnings, I withdrew" (JMN 15:111).

Meanwhile, among the Southern states, South Carolina had seceded in December of 1860 and others soon followed, forming their own Confederate government in February 1861. News of the outbreak of hostilities in April, shortly after Lincoln's inauguration, surprised Emerson but served him as a kind of relief. "We have been very homeless, some of us, for some years past,—say since 1850," he declared in a new lecture, "Civilization at a Pinch," "but now we have a country again. . . . Now we have forced the conspiracy out-of-doors. Law is on this side and War on that. It was war then, and it is war now; but declared war is vastly safer than war undeclared."[14]

As Gougeon has remarked, Emerson at first attributed the coming of war to "an inevitable ameliorative fate," but as the conflict dragged on, he came to reaffirm his belief of the 1850s, "that the reform of society would be wrought through the persistent and cooperative efforts of heroic individuals working with and through, the fatalistic forces at hand." The scholar's interest in the war, Marjory Moody has observed, "was chiefly philosophical and moral, rather than political or military. In the first year of the conflict, moreover, the biggest problem which Emerson wanted to see solved was that of emancipation."[15]

"If Mr. Lincoln appear slow and timid in proclaiming emancipation," Emerson granted, "it is to be remembered that he is not free as a poet to state what he thinks ideal or desirable, but must take a considered step, which he can keep."[16] But as he put it in August 1861, first in his journal and then in a lecture on "American Nationality," the idea of a war for the Union "is not broad enough, because of Slavery, which poisons it." Once again he proposed his idea of "emancipation with compensation," applying it now "to the Loyal States" (JMN 15:141).[17] "The first advantage of the War," in his judgment, "is the favorable moment it has made for the cutting out of our cancerous Slavery. Better that ⟨defe⟩ war & defeats continue, until we have come to that amputation" (JMN 15:145).

Emerson had written in a similar vein in a letter to Cabot, though he also remarked that the war "threatens to engulf us all—no preoccupation can exclude it, & no hermitage hide us." All citizens—scholars included—must do what they can for the cause of freedom, he declared, hoping "that 'scholar' & 'hermit' will no longer be exempts, neither by the country's permission nor their own, from the public duty" (L 5:253). At fifty-eight, Emerson the scholar was too old for military service, but he could continue to speak out. He and his family did not escape hardships caused by the war. A letter of 21 January 1862 to William Emerson aptly set forth their situation and his own response. The new year, he wrote, "has found me in quite as poor plight as the rest of the Americans. Not a penny from my books since last June,—which usually yield 5, or $600.00 a year." There had been no bank dividends or income from Lidian's Plymouth property. Moreover,

> almost all income from lectures has quite ceased: so that your letter found me in a study how to pay 3, or 400.00 with $50. . . . My fortunes must repair themselves by a new book, whenever books again sell. . . . Meantime, we are all trying to be as unconsuming as candles under an extinguisher, and tis frightful to think how many rivals we have in distress & in economy. But far better that this grinding should go on bad & worse, than that we be driven by any impatience into a hasty peace, or any peace restoring the old rottenness. (L 5:263–64)

In thinking of a possible "new book" Emerson made notes in his journal during 1862 and again in 1863 of materials it might include: among them, several of his "Antislavery Discourses" and his speeches on "Affairs in Kansas" and on such heroic activists as Sumner, Parker, and John Brown (JMN 14:167, 362–63); these were first collected after his death, along with other addresses, in Miscellanies. Early in 1862 he was able to arrange a few lecture engagements in nearby Massachusetts towns, at the Smithsonian Institution in Washington, and in Brooklyn. Speaking in Washington on "American Civilization," he called for emancipation as "the demand of civilization, the inevitable conclusion reached by the logic of events."[18]

While Emerson was in the capital Senator Sumner introduced him to President Lincoln (who had previously heard him as a lecturer), to Secretary of State William Henry Seward, and to other cabinet members; he attended church with Seward and again visited Lincoln. "The President," he wrote, "impressed me more favorably than I had hoped. A frank, sincere, well-meaning man, with a lawyer's habit of mind, good clear statement of his fact, correct enough, not vulgar, as described, but with a sort of boyish cheerfulness." In conversation he showed "a fidelity a conscientiousness very honorable to him" (JMN 15:187).

Although Emerson complained at the government's slowness in freeing slaves within Union territory, he was delighted when Lincoln at last issued his preliminary emancipation proclamation in the following September, commenting privately that "It works when men are sleeping, when the Army goes into winter quarters, when generals are treacherous or imbecile" (JMN 15:291). In an address in Boston he publicly admitted that he had underestimated the President's "capacity and virtue," declaring that through his proclamation Lincoln had been permitted by Divine Providence "to do more for America than any other American man." With the blot of slavery finally "removed from our national honor," he went on to say, Americans "shall cease to be hypocrites and pretenders" and "what we have styled our free institutions" will at last be free in truth (W 11:317, 321). Such were the goals that had made an activist of the scholar.

Emerson was able to extend his schedule of lecturing early in 1863, when he spoke first in Toronto and then traveled to states as far west as Illinois and Wisconsin. In July and August he addressed students at Dartmouth and Waterville Colleges on a familiar topic, "The Scholar," the first of his several addresses on scholarship and letters delivered to academic audiences over the next few years. By the President's appointment, which had come as a sequel to their meeting in Washington, he served as a member of the Board of Visitors of the United States Military Academy at West Point, where he was much taken with the Academy and with the self-reliance of its young cadets (*JMN* 15:215). To the literary societies at Dartmouth and Waterville, mentioning the cadets as examples, he advocated self-reliance and self-help as "first steps to power. Learn of Samuel Johnson or David Hume, that it is a primary duty of the man of letters to secure his independence" (*W* 10:251).

In the dark days before Gettysburg, the turning point of the war, Emerson castigated those Whigs and Democrats of the North who still opposed the fighting and talked of suing for peace. Remembering the men whose lives were being sacrificed in battle, he shuddered to think that the very politicians who had helped to bring on hostilities might return "to rule again" when the war was ended. For this reason he held, then and later, that "in our future action touching peace, any & every arrangement short of forcible subjugation of the rebel country, will be flat disloyalty" (*JMN* 15:211, 301). When peace came at last in 1865 he felt that Lincoln had been too lenient with the enemy and that General Grant's terms for Lee's surrender were far too easy;[19] he subsequently became a radical reconstructionist like his friend Sumner.

Thus the peace-loving scholar of the 1830s and 1840s had finally metamorphosed during the 1850s into an active crusader for abolition, ultimately supporting Lincoln's Emancipation Proclamation and the Union war effort as necessary means of bringing it about. Emerson's growing animus against the Southern slave power had been matched by his increasing revulsion against American materialism generally and his bitterness toward Daniel Webster and other Northern politicians—men whose fealty to commercial interests had led them again and again to compromise with the South, sacrificing morality and justice for mere political expediency.[20] Throughout the war years he spoke out repeatedly as a champion of national honor, envisioning a new era of freedom and justice for all Americans.

After the war had ended, when Emerson was free to resume a scholar's peace-time tasks, he expressed opinions on public affairs only in his journal or to a few friends, not as a crusader, for his role as an active advocate had ended: first with the Emancipation Proclamation and then with the Union victory. Shortly after that victory, in April of 1865, he had addressed his neighbors at Concord's memorial service for the martyred Abraham Lincoln (*W* 11:327–38). Tracing the course of the late President's career, he paid tribute to his extraordinary leadership. "This man grew according to the need. . . . Rarely was man so fitted to the event. . . .

[B]y his courage, his justice, his even temper, his fertile counsel, his humanity, he stood a heroic figure in the centre of a heroic epoch." "Had he not lived long enough," Emerson asked, "to keep the greatest promise that ever man made to his fellow men,—the practical abolition of slavery?" Reaffirming his faith in that serene Power "which rules the fate of nations," the scholar declared that "Providence makes its own instruments, creates the man for the time, trains him in poverty, inspires his genius, and arms him for his task." Perhaps "this heroic deliverer could no longer serve us," he ventured to say, for "the rebellion had touched its natural conclusion, and what remained to be done required new and uncommitted hands,— a new spirit born out of the ashes of the war."

V

THE SAGE OF CONCORD

Talent alone cannot make a writer. There must be a man behind the book. . . . If he cannot rightly express himself today, the same things subsist, and will open themselves tomorrow. There lies the burden on his mind,— the burden of truth to be declared,—more or less understood, and it constitutes his business and calling in the world, to see these facts through, and to make them known.

—"Goethe, or the Writer" (CW 4:162)

14. ENGLAND AND AMERICA, 1847–1856

I told Carlyle . . . that, though . . . I was dazzled by the wealth & power & success everywhere apparent [in England],—yet I knew very well that the moment I returned to America, I should ⟨r⟩lapse again into the habitual feeling which the vast physical influences of that continent inevitably inspire of confidence that there & there only is the right home & seat of the English race; & this great England will dwindle again to an island which has done well, but ⟨is⟩ has reached its utmost expansion.

>—Undated entry of July 1848 in Journal LM, p. 100,
> written at sea during Emerson's return from England
> (*JMN* 10:335–36); cf. *English Traits*, *W* 5:275–76

Despite Emerson's demanding schedule of lectures, beginning in the fall and winter of 1848–1849, and his increasing prominence as an Anti-Slavery spokesman during the 1850s, he managed to complete both *English Traits* and *The Conduct of Life* before the outbreak of war in 1861. At home in Concord during these years he greatly enjoyed the companionship of his growing children, the rewards of his garden, and the meetings of Concord's Social Circle.[1] At Boston he helped to organize the *Atlantic Monthly* in 1857 and to found two new clubs: the short-lived Town and Country Club in 1849 and the celebrated Saturday Club in 1856; one of the papers in *Society and Solitude* (1870) is on "Clubs" (*W* 7:223–50). In 1858 he spent two weeks in the Adirondacks with other members of the Saturday Club, reporting their excursion in a blank-verse "journal" (*W* 9:182–94) that he later printed in his second volume of poems, *May-Day* (1867). As a lover of poetry and of his country Emerson had long been looking for the poet of America he had called for in *Essays: Second Series;* in 1855, having received a copy of Walt Whitman's *Leaves of Grass,* he was moved to write to its author, praising him for his originality and experimentation and saluting him "at the beginning of a great career." A personal relation soon developed that lasted, not always without strain, until Emerson's death.[2]

i. "A Plea for the Scholar"

While still in England during 1847–1848, Emerson habitually drew comparisons and contrasts between Englishmen and Americans; he continued to do so following his return to Concord. When he and Henry Thoreau happened in 1850 to talk of national characteristics and to compare Americans and American scholars with their English contemporaries, Emerson maintained that Americans, unlike the English, were not yet "ripened," adding that "I like the English better than our people, just as I like merchants better than scholars," for with solid English merchants there was "no cant" but rather "great directness, comprehension, health, & success." His own "quarrel with America," he added, "was, that the geography is sublime, but the men are not" (*JMN* 11:284). Two years later, in referring to William Johnston's *England As It Is* (1851), he remarked that "we Americans read with a secret interest" whatever such a book may say about both England and America, "for we know that we are the heir," that "we are the Englishman," by "gravitation, by destiny, & laws of the Universe" (*JMN* 13:84).

This same idea of America as a still-immature heir to a fully mature England influenced the writing of Emerson's own *English Traits*. Before turning to that book, it will be useful to look briefly at "A Plea for the Scholar," an unpublished address that he first gave at Williams College in August of 1854 and repeated at Amherst College a year later, just at the time when the book on England was taking form. In the address, which once again explores the relation of scholars to their society, he touched incidentally on attributes that the United States had already taken over from the English: "the vulgarity of this country," he said, "came to us, with commerce, out of England." According to Cabot's summary of the address, Anglo-Saxon society—American as well as British—is "a great industrial corporation," a "walking ledger"; to attain "success" within it, "You must make trade everything." But in truth, "this devotion to means is an absurdity," for it defeats "the true ends of living."[3] As the later book would charge, such a result had already come about in nineteenth-century England; as Emerson feared, it was occurring in the United States as well.

Men "expiate their own shortcomings" by educating their children, Emerson told his student audiences. Indeed, fathers successful in trade have been supportive of "schools, a clergy, art, music, poetry, the college" not simply to turn out duplicates of themselves but rather to produce "guides and commanders" for their nation. Therefore the college itself, instead of functioning merely "to make you rich or great," should "show you that the material pomps and possessions, that all the feats of our civility, were the thoughts of good heads." For all powers are basically intellectual; "it is thoughts that make men great and strong." Here, of course, the idealistic scholar was reasserting his old belief in the primacy of ideas and the preeminence of thinking men. It is simply Anglo-Saxon "vulgarity," he said, to believe "that naked wealth, unrelieved by any use or design, is merit"; he was to amplify these points in chapters on "Wealth" in both *English Traits* and *The Conduct of Life*.

In the lecture a searching question follows: "Who is accountable for this materialism?" Emerson's answer—"Who but the scholars?"—may seem surprising, though in fact it anticipates the argument of his chapter on "Literature" in *English Traits*. As he explains in "A Plea for the Scholar," it is the duty of scholars and writers, outnumbered in society though they obviously are, to set an example for mankind: "The world is always as bad as it dares to be, and if the majority are evil it is because the minority are not good." Though lecturers and poets readily gratify the public's wish to be amused, by doing so they are shirking their responsibility as thinking men, for what the people really want are leaders, and "intellect is the thread on which all their worldly prosperity is strung." Here Emerson is once more emphasizing the duty and discipline of a scholar as he had first conceived it in the 1830s. Should he himself set a bad example by limiting his discussion to the "secular and outward benefits" of scholarship, he would have to confess that "I speak badly for the scholar." And to anyone who would value the intellectual life solely for the tangible results it might produce, he had this to say: "All that is urged by the saint for the superiority of faith over works is as truly urged for the highest state of intellectual perception over any performance." These words afford an excellent preface to *The Conduct of Life* as well as to *English Traits.*

ii. The Genesis of *English Traits*

During 1854 and 1855, the years of Emerson's "Plea for the Scholar" at Williams and Amherst, he traveled more and more widely on the lecture circuit, making well over fifty appearances in each lecture season. The fact that many of his engagements were once again in cities well beyond New England attests to his growing reputation throughout the northern states. At Philadelphia in January 1854 he began a new series, "Topics of Modern Times," that included such materials as "The Norsemen" and "English Influence on Modern Culture." These offerings, along with an existing lecture on "The Anglo-American" and later lectures on "English Character and Influence" and "Characteristics of the English People," were evidently derived from his continuing work on *English Traits* and also contributed to it. As Robert Burkholder has remarked, "Emerson delivered lectures on English topics more than forty times in various parts of the country" between 1848 and 1856. "The notices of these lectures not only informed the public what he was working on but also whetted the popular appetite for more of his views."[4]

From Philadelphia in 1854 Emerson continued as far west as Michigan, Illinois, and Wisconsin, returning through Ohio and New York to New England. During the next fall and early winter, when he lectured primarily in New England and in upper New York and spoke several times against slavery, he also introduced a lecture on "Beauty" that he frequently repeated and would later include in *The Conduct of Life.* As for the long-delayed book about England and the English, he finally sent the first chapter to his publisher on 9 October 1855, promising early delivery of the remaining "sixteen or seventeen chapters" (L 4:533). But being perennially in need of money, he was again lecturing in November and December, mostly within Massachusetts, and in late December he returned to the Mississippi valley and then to Michigan and Ohio, once more concluding the season in New England.

Though more chapters must have been submitted during October, Emerson was unhappily laboring over the book while on his travels and still had "the weary refractory concluding chapters" to write after his return to Concord, when he was troubled by the unhappy course of national events. "But what times are these," he wrote to William Emerson on 2 June 1856, "& how they make our studies impertinent, & even ourselves the same!" (L 5:23). Work was at last completed in June of 1856 and *English Traits* was published on 6 August. Sales were brisk from the beginning, leading Emerson to remark to William that "The poor book has long been a bore & an obstruction to me; 'tis time it should be something else"— that is, a source of income, for he "was never so balked of money as in the last two years" (L 5:30).

As suggested by the opening chapter of *English Traits,* Emerson's initial interest in the English had been literary: his "narrow and desultory reading" during his younger years inspired in him "the wish to see the faces of three or four writers,— Coleridge, Wordsworth, Landor, De Quincey, and the latest and strongest contributor to the critical journals, Carlyle," though as he went on to say, "The young scholar fancies it happiness enough to live with people who can give an inside to the world; without reflecting that they are prisoners, too, of their own thought, and cannot apply themselves to yours" (W 5:4). Drawing on his journals of 1832–1833, he recalled his conversations with these men, which he found much more significant than his "visits to places." He left unmentioned the series of ten lectures on "English Literature" he had given at Boston in 1835–1836, making abundant use of secondary sources to supplement his own reading. One of these lectures, "Permanent Traits of the English National Genius," is an obvious forerunner of *English Traits.* So too are his lectures of 1843 on "New England": as Philip Nicoloff has pointed out, the individual titles of that series anticipate "in order and in subject matter" the "core chapters" of the later book.[5] For Emerson, the relation of American attributes to those of the English and the future prospects of both England and the United States were major concerns of his thinking throughout the 1850s.

Although *English Traits* is basically a report of the mature scholar's direct observations of the English in 1847–1848, his ultimate pronouncements on their institutions and national character were significantly influenced by his reading over the years and given depth and perspective by the passage of time. As Nicoloff has demonstrated, his ideas on history and race set forth in chapters 3 and 4 reflect his familiarity with Greek and oriental thought, with various contemporary philosophies, and with current scientific ideas—particularly in the fields of geology and biology—that he knew both through his reading and through lectures by and conversations with eminent British scientists. Even his own practice in the cultivation of garden pears seems to have affected his belief in the virtues of hybrid stock. "Nature loves crosses, as inoculations of barbarous races prove," he had written as early as 1847; "marriage is crossing," and "Milton, Bacon, Gray, are crosses of the

Greek & Saxon geniuses" (*JMN* 10:45). So now, in his fourth chapter, "Race," he remarks that "We are piqued with pure descent, but nature loves inoculation. . . . The best nations are those most widely related," and the "composite character" of the English "betrays a mixed origin" (*W* 5:50).

Emerson of course knew Carlyle's examination of English politics in *Past and Present*, which he had reviewed in 1843 for *The Dial*, and was familiar through their correspondence and recent conversations with Carlyle's dark views of the current state of affairs in England. In December of 1848, when he was preparing his first lectures on England and the English and addressing the question "Why England is England?" that he was to pose there and again in his own book (*W* 5:35), he was reading "up & down in English history and topography" in order to "verify & fix such memoranda as I brought home from my journeying" (*L* 4:125). He had also carried with him a number of works he would use in *English Traits*, including Laing's translation of *The Heimskringla*, Wood's *Athenae Oxonienses*, which was given him by Carlyle, and two other works that Carlyle had particularly recommended: Bede's *Ecclesiastical History of England* and Lowth's *Life of William of Wykeham* (*JMN* 10:336, xx). In 1852 he was taking notes from both Johnston's *England As It Is* and, with a discussion of higher education in mind, Bristed's *Five Years in an English University* (*JMN* 10:229, 250, 275). This is to say that the book as it finally appeared was the product of direct observation, years of widely varied reading, and mature reflection.

iii. A Critique of Materialism

Five chapters of *English Traits*—"Ability," "Manners," "Truth," "Character," and "Cockayne" (5–9)—offer a generally favorable view of the English, reflecting opinions Emerson had formed while lecturing in provincial cities and coming to know members of the industrious middle class. But for some readers the following chapter on "Wealth" (10) marks a turning point in the book: after celebrating the positive achievements that English initiative had made possible, Emerson notes the evils that have come with industrialization and asks, in a passage reminiscent of his address at Williams and Amherst, whether the nation has made the wisest use of its surplus capital:

> Her prosperity, the splendor which so much manhood and talent and perseverance has thrown upon vulgar aims, is the very argument of materialism. Her success strengthens the hands of base wealth. Who can propose to youth poverty and wisdom, when mean gain has arrived at the conquest of letters and arts; when English success has grown out of the very renunciation of principles, and the dedication to outsides? (*W* 5:170)

Emerson renders similarly mixed judgments as he takes up in turn "Aristocracy," "Universities," "Religion," "Literature," and "The Times" (Chapters 11–15). "On general grounds," he declares, "whatever tends to form manners or to finish men, has a great value," and on this score the English class structure and system of education have gone "to form what England values as the flower of its national life,—a well-educated gentleman." But the old aristocracy is giving way to a rising class of educated men, "bred into their society with manners, ability and the gifts of fortune," who "in vigor and color and general habit" outstrip "their contemporaries in the American colleges"; in Emerson's judgment "they read better than we, and write better." He had found England to be "full of manly, clever, well-bred men who possess the talent of writing off-hand pungent paragraphs, expressing with clearness and courage their opinion on any person or performance. . . . The English do this, as they write poetry, as they ride and box, by being educated to it." Such able individuals now constitute "an untitled nobility" possessing "all the power without the inconveniences that belong to rank."[6]

Emerson's severe strictures on English religion and literature demand special attention, for they lie at the very heart of his evaluation of materialistic nineteenth-century society in both England and America. Believing as he did that without spiritual vision a people will inevitably perish, he had stressed as early as his Address on Education in 1837 the ideals that a nation's scholars—its clergy, its literary men, its teachers of youth—ought to represent (*EL* 2:202); during the 1850s he had come to blame the scholars for their failure to counteract the typical Anglo-Saxon preoccupation with material wealth. In the chapter on "Religion" (*W* 5:214–31) he notes that "for a thousand years" the English clergy "have been the scholars of the nation." What do these men and their church represent in nineteenth-century England? The Established Church, through its "unbroken order and tradition," serves as "a political engine," allied "with the throne and with history." To its credit, it is "marked by the grace and good sense of its forms, by the manly grace of its clergy," but it must be seen as "the church of the gentry" rather than "the church of the poor." In Emerson's view, the spirit that once dwelt within it has since "glided away to animate other activities," and to a country where taste is tyrannical, the only gospel it now preaches is, "By taste are ye saved."

What Emerson found absent from decorous English worship was "the power of the religious sentiment," which in earlier times had "put an end to human sacrifices, checked appetite, inspired the crusades, inspired resistance to tyrants, inspired self-respect, set bounds to serfdom and slavery, founded liberty," and "created the religious architecture" of churches and cathedrals—"works to which the key is lost" in nineteenth-century England, together with "the sentiment which created them." This passage, based on two previous journal entries concerning English church architecture as an expression of the religious sentiment (*JMN* 10:279; 11:81), also recalls Emerson's poem of 1839 called "The 'Problem,'" with its admiring reference to "England's abbeys." As for sects outside the Church of England, "they are only perpetuations of some private man's dissent" ("the lengthened shadow of one man," as Emerson had put it in "Self-Reliance"), and true religion in England must be looked for elsewhere: in doers of good "from the days

Another lesson I learned from England, was, the power of the religious sentiment; the belief in the immortality of the soul, & the rest, — which inspired the Crusades, inspired the religious architecture, — York, Newstead, Westminster, Winchester, Ripon, Beverley, & Dundee (works to which the key is lost, with the sentiment that created them; & inspired the English Bible, the Chronicle of Richard of Devizes,

A Lesson Learned from England
Undated entry in Journal London, p. 191, on the power of the religious sentiment; see *JMN* 10:279.

of Alfred to those of Romilly, of Clarkson and of Florence Nightingale, and in thousands who have no fame."

More than Emerson's reading about the English gave him his perspective on their religion,[7] for something of what he saw in contemporary England he had already been witnessing in New England. There too, as he declared in 1844, the "religious party" was "falling from the church nominal" and appearing in such American reform movements as the Anti-Slavery Society (CW 3:149). In his earlier strictures against "corpse-cold Unitarianism" at home and his own attempt at religious reform in his Divinity School Address of 1838 he had of course attempted to counter this development; his abandonment of his Boston pulpit and his eventual commitment to a secular campaign against slavery illustrate the very tendency—international in its scope—of which he was writing.

Directly related to the scholar's reservations about religious life in the England of his day is his conviction that English literature, having reached its greatest flowering in the sixteenth and seventeenth centuries, was also in a state of decline. His specific reasons for such a belief are set forth in chapter 14 (W 5:232–60)—the longest chapter of the book and perhaps its most controversial. "For two centuries," Emerson maintains, "England was philosophic, religious, poetic"; now, in marked contrast, it has become practical, materialistic, and scientific. Believing as he did that "Mixture is the secret of the English island," he calls attention to the mingling of Saxon and Latin words in the English language itself, to the dual English heritage of Hebrew and Greek genius, and especially to that union of sense and intellect that he discerned in the greatest English writers—particularly the poets: "The Saxon materialism and narrowness, exalted into the sphere of intellect, makes the very genius of Shakspeare and Milton. When it reaches the pure element, it treads the clouds as securely as the adamant. Even in its elevations materialistic, its poetry is common sense inspired; or iron raised to white heat" (W 5:234).

Among the earlier prose writers of note, Emerson singled out his old favorite Francis Bacon as an example of what he called "the English duality." Dismissing Bacon's scientific experiments as "exquisite trifles" in comparison with those of later scientists and inventors, he wrote that this man "drinks of a diviner stream, and marks the influx of idealism into England." Ever the idealist himself, as we know, Emerson had long taken idealism to be the converse of materialism in every sense of that word. His point about Bacon is that "in the structure of his mind" Bacon "held of the analogists, of the idealists, or (as we popularly say, naming from the best example) Platonists." But as he had regretfully written in his journal, "the Platonism died in the Elizabethan" (JMN 10:511; 11: 194), and for Emerson its absence in most modern Englishmen explains the resurgence of "Saxon materialism and narrowness" that he deplored in nineteenth-century England.

Here is the key passage of chapter 14, revised from an earlier journal entry:

> Whoever discredits analogy and requires heaps of facts before any theories can be attempted, has no poetic power, and nothing original or beautiful will be produced by

him. Locke is as surely the influx of decomposition and of prose, as Bacon and the Platonists of growth. The Platonic is the poetic tendency; the so-called scientific is the negative and poisonous. 'T is quite certain that Spenser, Burns, Byron and Wordsworth will be Platonists, and that the dull men will be Lockists. Then politics and commerce will absorb from the educated class men of talents without genius, precisely because such have no resistance. (*W* 5:239–40; cf. *JMN* 13:356)

As we have seen, Emerson's old animus against John Locke dates from his student days at Harvard, when he stigmatized Locke and the rationalists as "Reasoning Machines" (*JMN* 2:238). When he and his friends founded in 1836 what became the misnamed "Transcendental Club," they objected to the practice of taking Locke's "sensuous philosophy" as a basis for Unitarian theology; in 1842, in "The Transcendentalist," Emerson compared Locke's thought unfavorably with that of Immanuel Kant (*CW* 1:206–7). So in *English Traits*, lamenting what he regarded as the decline of English intellectual life after Bacon's time, he wrote of "a descent of the mind" from its former heights "into lower levels," its "loss of wings," and of the consequent absence in England of "high speculation": "Locke, to whom the meaning of ideas was unknown, became the type of philosophy, and his 'understanding' the measure, in all nations, of the English intellect. His countrymen forsook the lofty sides of Parnassus, on which they had once walked with echoing steps, and disused the studies once so beloved; the powers of thought fell into neglect" (*W* 5:243).

Continuing in this vein, the scholar charges that while the materialistic English accumulate facts, they lack that insight into general laws that he found to be characteristic of both the ancient Greeks and the modern Germans. His point about the decline of intellect in England is illustrated with brief references to the prose of Milton, Burke, and Samuel Johnson followed by a longer discussion of his contemporary Henry Hallam, "a learned and elegant scholar" whom he had met while in London; Hallam's monumental *Introduction to the Literature of Europe* (1837–1839) was in his library. Hallam's "eye does not reach to the ideal standards" when he makes his literary judgments, Emerson complains. In these pronouncements "The expansive element which creates literature is steadily denied. Plato is resisted, and his school. . . . He passes in silence, or dismisses with a kind of contempt, the profounder masters: a lover of ideas is not only uncongenial, but unintelligible."[8] In such a mind, writes Emerson, in phrasing much like that of his Introduction to *Nature* twenty years earlier, one finds a "type of English genius": "It is wise and rich, but it lives on its capital. It is *retrospective*. How can it discern and hail the new forms that are looming up on the horizon, new and gigantic thoughts which cannot dress themselves out of *any old wardrobe of the past?*" (*W* 5:246; emphasis added; cf. *CW* 1:7).

Turning from Hallam to other contemporary writers, Emerson observes that "The essays, the fiction and the poetry of the day have the like municipal limits." He then offers brief comments on the narrow vision of Dickens, Bulwer, Thackeray, and the materialistic Macaulay; he finds limitations even in Coleridge, with his "vast attempts but most inadequate performings," in Carlyle, "driven by his disgust at the pettiness and the cant, into the preaching of Fate," and in Garth Wilkinson, whose mind is powerful but lacks "a manifest centrality." "Even what is called philosophy and letters is mechanical in its structure, as if inspiration had ceased," the scholar charges, and indeed he detects a "mortal air" in "the tone of colleges and of scholars and of literary society" (cf. *JMN* 13:417). Universities "must be retrospective," he grants, adding that they are "of course hostile to geniuses," much "as churches and monasteries persecute youthful saints. Yet we all send our sons to college" (*W* 5:212).

"One of my chief lessons in England," Emerson had written in 1849, "was the confirmation of a frequent experience at home that in literary circles the men of the most trust & consideration, bookmakers, editors, university deans & professors, bishops too, were by no means men of the ⟨most⟩ ↑largest↓ literary talent, but usually of a low & ordinary intellectuality but of a sort of mercantile activity & working talent" (*JMN* 11:81; cf. 10:300).[9] English science he found limited as well, except for the distinguished work of a few men of ideas like John Hunter, Robert Brown, and Richard Owen. As he had said in his early lectures on science and again in *Nature,* so he declares once more in *English Traits:* the true scientist must be "alive to the heart as well as to the logic of creation." But most English science, he finds, "puts humanity to the door." Moreover, it "wants the connection which is the test of genius," and "is false by not being poetic."

Modern English poetry, in the scholar's critical reading, "is degraded and made ornamental. Pope and his school wrote poetry fit to put round frosted cake," and most nineteenth-century verse is "low and prosaic," for its writers "have lost sight of the fact that poetry exists to speak the spiritual law." One great exception is Wordsworth, who, "alone in his time"—as Emerson wrote in a later chapter—"treated the human mind well, and with an absolute trust. His adherence to his poetic creed rested on real inspirations. The Ode on Immortality is the high-water mark which the intellect has reached in this age" (*W* 5:298). Wordsworth and Tennyson—for Emerson, a lesser poet—are each endowed in points where the other is lacking: thus Tennyson has music and color, but "he wants a subject, and climbs no mount of vision."

In spite of these reservations about the contemporary English mind and its limitations, Emerson in 1856 was not without hope for England, for he believed in the "retrieving power" of "a minority of profound minds . . . capable of appreciating every soaring of intellect and every hint of tendency." Though in his judgment "the constructive power seems dwarfed and superficial" among the English, "the criticism is often in the noblest tone and suggests the presence of the invisible gods." Moreover, as he wrote near the conclusion of the chapter on "Literature," "the power of the English State" is derived from the mutually interacting polarity of "the perceptive class" and "the practical, finality class"—in other words, it is a product of that very English duality "of genius and of animal force," with both "their discord and their accord," that provides the leitmotiv not only of the chapter but of the book as a whole.

In addition to the "Speech at Manchester" that closes the book with chapter 19, Emerson's "refractory concluding chapters" report his expedition with Carlyle to Stonehenge (16), acknowledge in "Personal" his debts to the many friends he had made in England (17), and attempt in "Result" to provide an overall summary of his impressions of the country and its people (18). In "Result" he hails England, whatever her shortcomings, as "the best of actual nations" and London as "the epitome of our times." But to Carlyle at Stonehenge, looking to the future, he had expressed his conviction that in America rather than in England must be "the seat and centre of the British race" because "no skill or activity can long compete with the prodigious natural advantages of that country, in the hands of the same race; and . . . England, an old and exhausted island, must one day be contented, like other parents to be strong only in her children" (*W* 5:275–76; cf. *JMN* 10:335–36). Here as elsewhere he assumed a continuing dominance of Anglo-Saxon stock in both England and the United States, frequently referring to Americans as the children and heirs of the English. "The American people," he granted, "do not yield better or more able men, or more inventions or books or benefits," but he regarded American society as "more democratic, more humane" than that of class-ridden England.

Within England itself, Emerson went on to say in "Result," he had encountered a narrow provincialism: the English "cannot see beyond England, nor in England can they transcend the interests of the governing classes," and the vaunted "'English principles' mean a primary regard to the interests of property." Neither at home nor abroad are English policies always generous or just, though there have been notable exceptions: "They have abolished slavery in the West Indies and put an end to human sacrifices in the East." Their great variety of power and talent, their "many-headedness," results from "the advantageous position of the middle class, who are always the source of letters and science." But the English people generally, though "right in their feeling," are "wrong in their speculation," and the English mind remains "in a state of arrested development" because it is currently occupied mainly with "a corporeal civilization, on goods that perish with the using," rather than with things of the spirit.

Concluding on a more positive note, Emerson declares that "the right measures of England are the men it bred," for "it has yielded more able men in five hundred years than any other nation," and the English have consistently "given importance to individuals, a principal end and fruit of every society." In sum, England is for Emerson "the land of patriots, martyrs, sages and bards, and if the ocean out of which it emerged should wash it away, it will be remembered as an island famous for immortal laws, for the announcements of original right which make the stone tables of liberty."

iv. The Reception of *English Traits*

To Emerson's surprise and pleasure, *English Traits* quickly proved to be the most popular book he had yet published. Within a month of its American appearance in August 1856 it had gone into a second printing, and by April 1857 it was in its "Eighth 1000" (*L* 5:34; *JMN* 14:452). In England, where the "new work" by the man regarded there as "the serene sage of Concord" had been eagerly awaited, public demand led to four printings of 6,000 copies each during September and October 1856.[10] According to Burkholder's study of its contemporary reception, the nearly fifty reviews that were published in Britain and America during 1856 and 1857 made *English Traits* "one of Emerson's most noticed books." The one response that may have pleased him most came in a letter from Carlyle: "Not for seven years and more have I got hold of such a Book," Carlyle wrote; it is "by a real *man*, with eyes in his head; nobleness, wisdom, humour and many other things in the heart of him" (*CEC* 517).

Not all of the appraisals were so friendly in tone, however. Walter Savage Landor, irritated by Emerson's account in chapter 1 of their long-ago conversation, published a twenty-two-page *Letter from W. S. Landor to R. W. Emerson* (1856) in defense of his views, and in most of the British periodical notices Burkholder has detected a barely concealed "sense of nationalistic anger" over Emerson's supposedly unfavorable attitude toward the English people and their institutions. The American reviewers, though generally "kinder," went to the opposite extreme: many of them felt that the book unduly praised the English, and an old hostility toward Emerson himself reappeared among Southerners and Southern sympathizers. That *English Traits* should not be judged in such broad terms, as either wholly flattering or wholly antagonistic, seemed evident to Nathaniel Hawthorne, who was then serving as American consul in Liverpool. Writing from England on the basis of his own experience among the English, he told Emerson that "these are the truest pages that have yet been written about this country." Though afraid that the book "will please the English only too well," he added that "they will never comprehend that what you deny is far greater and higher than what you concede."[11]

Although neither national biases nor preexisting attitudes toward Emerson have unduly colored later criticism of *English Traits*, there are several points of discussion that have persisted over ensuing years. Praise of his shrewd eye and witty characterizations has for the most part replaced objections by his contemporaries to the book's supposed obscurity, but reservations about its organization are still common.[12] As for Emerson's point of view, it must be granted that he wrote mostly about the middle and upper classes, for he had little opportunity while in England and Scotland to visit their most depressed and degraded areas or even to meet rural and urban laborers. His somewhat murky ideas of race that Nicoloff has explored now seem curiously dated. Nicoloff may have claimed too much in contending that Emerson had worked out a general theory of national life cycles, involving youthful vigor, complacent maturity, and inevitable decline, that would be applicable to every country. The late Howard Mumford Jones objected even to the idea "that Emerson was demonstrating the coming decadence of Great Britain," but it seems clear enough that the scholar saw the United States as England's future replacement on the world stage, with all the benefits and dangers that would inevitably come with such a position of prosperity and power.[13]

To the historian Henry Steele Commager, *English Traits* is at once autobiographical, prophetic, and doubly critical: it "tells us not only about Emerson, but about his New England, for the comparison between the Old England and the New is always there, implicit or explicit." And Emerson's appraisal of Old England, in Commager's view, was as prescient as Tocqueville's of America, for "Emerson saw in England more than England; he saw, though indistinctly, what America might become. . . . A century later, . . . America became what England was, not merely in ostentatious things like the exercise and abuse of world power, but in the respect for wealth, strength, position, in social and economic conservatism, in self-satisfaction and complacency."[14] And, as this present chapter has demonstrated, *English Traits* is indeed "autobiographical" as well as prophetic, bringing together not only what the scholar saw while in England but what he came to believe both before and after his visit there.[15]

Two chapters mentioned in Carlyle's letter about the book will illustrate this last point. Carlyle liked the "Chapter on the Church," he told Emerson, but did not "much seize your idea in regard to 'Literature,' tho' I do details of it, and will try again" (*CEC* 517). As we know, Emerson's charge that the English church, both Anglican and dissenting, lacked the religious sentiment parallels closely his earlier complaints of coldness and lack of spirituality in New England Unitarianism. And though the central idea of the still-controversial chapter on "Literature" somehow escaped Carlyle, we remember that Emerson had originally been attracted to his Scottish friend in the belief that Carlyle too had taken a "brave stand . . . for Spiritualism" (*CEC* 91). Ever since the 1830s, *spiritualism* had meant for Emerson an exaltation of idealism over materialism, poetry over science, Plato over Locke. And for a "scholar or spiritual man" such as he, that conviction would determine his vision—past, present, and future—of both England and America.[16] "By destiny, & laws of the universe," America would eventually inherit England's role; what was needed was the "ripening" of his still immature countrymen. In turning to the subject he called "the conduct of life" he would be addressing that need.

15. OTHER SLAVES
TO FREE, 1851–1860

❖

> There are two forces in Nature, by whose antagonism we exist; the power of Fate, Fortune, the laws of the world, the order of things, . . . the material necessities, on the one hand,—and Will or Duty or Freedom on the other.
> —"The Fugitive Slave Law," as read on 7 March 1854
> in New York City (*W* 11:231)

Although Emerson did not publish *The Conduct of Life* until four years after the appearance of *English Traits* in 1856, by the early 1850s he had already drafted much of the material that he would be using in both books. *English Traits*, as we know, originated in the individual lectures on England and the English that he delivered in the fall of 1848, following his return from abroad; the book took form slowly over the next six years, when the demands of lecturing required most of his time and energy. A new development began in March 1851, when he assembled for delivery at Pittsburgh a series of six lectures, most of which he had already read singly, that opened with "England" and continued with "Laws of Success," "Wealth," "Economy," "Culture," and "Worship." In the following October he began to revise this series, adding new material. In December, when he spoke in Boston, he presented the course as "The Conduct of Life," having replaced "England" and "Laws of Success" with "Fate" and "Power" but continuing with new versions of "Wealth," "Economy," "Culture," and "Worship."[1]

The theme for the revised course, "The Conduct of Life," has a history of its own that is related to Emerson's evolving conception of the scholar's office. "The question of the Times is to each one a practical question of the Conduct of Life," he wrote in 1850. "How shall I live?" (*JMN* 11:218; cf. *W* 6:3).[2] Enactment in that same year of the infamous Fugitive Slave Law, which as a private individual he vowed to disobey, brought home to him once more the old question of his public role as a scholar: How should Waldo Emerson, by then an internationally known public figure, conduct his own professional life? Had it finally become his immediate duty to work actively against negro slavery in the United States, or was it still his primary obligation to minister to "quite other slaves," those "imprisoned spirits, imprisoned thoughts," that he had so long sought to free?

As we have seen, Emerson's chosen course throughout the 1850s was to do both: he would speak out strongly against slavery in occasional addresses, but through his regular lecture tours he would continue to pursue his customary scholarly aims; meanwhile, he would also be laboring to complete first *English Traits* and then *The Conduct of Life*. But public opinion at the time, both national and local, was becoming increasingly divided over the slavery issue and those individuals who took positions concerning it, and Emerson's own Anti-Slavery addresses and his open support of John Brown were making him a more and more controversial choice as a speaker. The engaged scholar of the troubled 1850s in America was scarcely the "serene sage of Concord" that an English periodical of the time envisioned.

i. Nature and Thought

While Emerson was publicly protesting against the Fugitive Slave Law, castigating those sectional and material-minded interests whose maneuvering had brought about its enactment, he was also examining in a more philosophical light the challenges to human freedom represented by "Fate, Fortune, the laws of the world," as he put it in 1854 (*W* 11:231). His lectures on "The Conduct of Life," which posit a polar opposition of Freedom with Fate and of Fate in turn with Power, appraise the conduct of men who seek to counter Fate, observing them on a series of ascending platforms of Power. The movement upward from the materialistic platforms of "Wealth" and "Economy" to the heights of "Culture" and "Worship" is something like the "progressive arrangement" that Emerson had followed in *Nature*, where the ascent begins with "Commodity" and proceeds upward to "Spirit" and onward to "Prospects," but the tone of these lectures is that of an older and less sanguine thinker.

As Stephen Whicher has so tellingly demonstrated in his book of 1953, the polarity of Freedom and Fate had long concerned Emerson. There is a foreshadowing of "Fate" in his early lecture on "Tragedy," part of the "Human Life" series of 1838–1839, where he identified "laws of the world" as constituting one kind of fate and also distinguished the idea of Fate itself from the optimistic "doctrine of Philosophical Necessity." Concluding with a passage that he could well have headed "The Conduct of Life," he recommended that a person facing misfortune should remain "cool and disengaged." Relief will come, he said, with the passage of time, the resilience of temperament, "the just application of the intellect to the facts," and the beauties of nature; moreover, there will be certain compensations: "in moral activity, in the growth of the interior life, in the development of the slow but precious fruit of character" (*EL* 3:113–15). When shortening this lecture for its later publication in *The Dial*, Emerson restated his recommendations, writing of the intellect as "a consoler which delights in putting an interval between a man and his fortune and so converts the sufferer into a spectator and his pain into poetry" ("The Tragic," *W* 12:416). This idea—reminiscent of all that he had said in the 1830s about the conversion of experience into thought—is echoed in "Fate" and the lectures and chapters which followed it.

Believing as he did in the "infinitude" of a self-reliant, God-reliant individual, the Emerson of 1841 could declare in "Circles" that "The only sin is limitation. As soon as you once come up with a man's limitations, it is all over with him" (CW 2:182–83). But three years later, in "Experience," when he acknowledged that his "new philosophy" would incorporate "limitations of the affirmative statement" along with his old faith (CW 3:43), Emerson had come to acknowledge Temperament as "the veto or limitation-power" in one's constitution and to write of human life itself as "a mixture of power and form" that "will not bear the least excess of either" (CW 3:32, 35). This dualistic formulation anticipates the pairing of Power with Fate in "The Conduct of Life."

During the early 1840s Emerson had been reading of fate in Indian mythology and in Greek tragedy—works which contributed to "Experience" and ultimately to "Fate." His interest in mythology continued to broaden as he turned later in that decade to translations from both Persian and Norse literature. He was also keeping abreast of recent developments in science and technology, reading books that would provide material for the chapters on "Land" and "Race" in *English Traits* and modify his earlier conceptions of both nature and human freedom.[3] In August of 1847, shortly before his departure for England, he made a retrospective journal entry on what he called "Circumstance" as it affects the self: "Once we thought the ⟨Man⟩ ↑positive power↓ was all, now we learn that ⟨cir⟩ the negative power, namely, the Circumstance is half. . . . Circumstance! Yes that is Nature. Nature is what you may do. There's much you may not. The Circumstance, and the life" (*JMN* 10:143; cf. *W* 6:14–15).

As Emerson reacted more and more strongly against American slavery and recognized with bitterness the proslavery power of Southern congressmen and of Northern "Cotton Whigs"—men who knew well enough where their material interests lay—he identified those very interests as another form of constraint: they have come to rule man himself. "Things are in the saddle," riding mankind, he wrote in 1846, admonishing the material-minded to "serve law for man," not "law for thing" ("Ode: Inscribed to W. H. Channing," *W* 9:78). The same unhappy inversion of values that he witnessed in America had already gone further in industrialized England: what he saw there in 1847 and 1848 led him to describe that country as "a roaring volcano of Fate, of material values," and "a terrible machine" that "has possessed itself of the ground, the air, the men and women," so that "hardly even thought is free" (*W* 5:255, 103). By 1851, as Phyllis Cole has observed, he was writing long journal entries on two subjects: "the limitations of Fate and the immorality of political compromise." Moreover, "metaphors of material obstruction and enclosure" were appearing frequently in his comments on both English and American society.[4]

How Americans might escape the fate of Britons and turn the oppressive demands of their own materialistic culture into opportunities for freedom and personal development is a major theme of "The Conduct of Life" series, which took form concurrently with *English Traits*.[5] In his initial lecture, drawing on journal entries of 1850, Emerson begins by acknowledging the difficulties we face: in our attempts to answer the practical question "How shall I live?" we soon encounter a seeming contradiction: even as we affirm our individual liberty we must also "accept an irresistible dictation" and acknowledge the limitations imposed by "Fate, or laws of the world" (W 6:3–4; cf. JMN 11:210, 214, 220).[6] To make the case for Fate before offering his counterarguments for Freedom, he then cites one grim example after another to demonstrate that "Nature is no sentimentalist." "Running through entire nature," he declares, is the element "known to us as limitation. Whatever limits us we call Fate" (W 6:20). Again, "The book of Nature is the book of Fate. She turns the gigantic pages,—leaf after leaf,—never re-turning one. . . . The face of the planet cools and dries, the races meliorate, and man is born. But when a race has lived its term, it comes no more again" (W 6:15; cf. JMN 11:420; 10:353).

Then comes the turn in Emerson's argument: "We must respect Fate as natural history, but there is more than natural history." Man is a dual creature, made up of mind and spirit as well as flesh and matter. Though his very body "betrays his relation to what is below him" in nature, "the spirit which composes and decomposes nature" is also within him, giving him his power of thought, his intellect. "Intellect annuls Fate. So far as a man thinks, he is free" (W 6:22–23; cf. JMN 11:388, 12:584). As man matures, he will come to look upon Fate as "a name for facts not yet passed under the fire of thought"—a familiar Emersonian phrase; thus, "every jet of chaos which threatens to exterminate us is *convertible by intellect into wholesome force*. Fate is unpenetrated causes" (W 6:31–32; emphasis added).

Emerson's reading in science during the 1840s had served to support his basically optimistic faith that change and progressive development, what he liked to call "metamorphosis" and "melioration," are operative in nature and man alike. Here he applies these same principles to the concept of Fate and also to the problem of evil, going beyond the idea he had voiced in the Divinity School Address: that evil is "merely privative" (CW 1:78).

> If Fate is ore and quarry, if evil is good in the making, if limitation is power that shall be, if calamities, oppositions, and weights are wings and means,—we are reconciled.
>
> Fate involves the melioration. No statement of the Universe can have any soundness which does not admit its ascending effort. The direction of the whole and of the parts is toward benefit, and in proportion to the health. Behind every individual closes organization; before him opens liberty,—the Better, the Best. (W 6:35)

In History itself Emerson sees the never-ending action and reaction of Nature and Thought; they are like "two boys pushing each other on the curbstone of the pavement. Everything is pusher or pushed; and matter and mind are in perpetual tilt and balance. . . . Every solid in the universe is ready to become fluid on the approach of the mind, and the power to flux it is the measure of the mind" (W 6:43; cf. JMN 11:404, 450; JMN 12:612; JMN 11:437). But superior to this pervasive duality, according to Emerson's old faith, is an ultimate unity, that "Blessed Unity which holds nature and souls in perfect solution, and compels every atom to serve an universal end" (W 6:48). And here he appeals once again to that "doctrine of Philosophical Necessity" he had referred to in his early lecture on "Tragedy." In his essay of 1844 on "Politics" he had declared that "We must trust infinitely to the beneficent necessity which shines through all laws" (CW 3:124); here in concluding "Fate," he writes, in Aeschylean phrase, "Let us build altars to the Beautiful Necessity, which secures that all is made of one piece" and which, "rudely or softly," educates man to "the perception that there are no contingencies; that Law rules throughout existence; a Law which is not intelligent but intelligence;—not personal nor impersonal," a Law that "dissolves persons" and "vivifies nature; yet solicits the pure in heart to draw on all its omnipotence" (W 6:48–49; cf. JMN 11:95; TN 1:83–84).

ii. Platforms of Power

Emerson's second lecture, "Power," is a further product of his conviction, expressed as early as *Nature*, that the world we live in is essentially plastic and fluid (CW 1:44). Even material things must change, however slowly, as nineteenth-century geologists were teaching, and the meliorating force within all living creatures—Emerson thought of it as *Spirit* or simply as *Power*—impels them to grow and improve. But "Power ceases in the instant of repose," as he declared in "Self-Reliance"; "it resides in *the moment of transition* from a past to a new state, in the shooting of the gulf, in the darting to an aim" (CW 2:40; emphasis added). In human history the same principle applies: according to a journal entry of 1847 that he adapted for the lecture on "Power," "the great moment" in man's progressive development comes "when the savage is just ceasing to be a savage with all his Pelasgic strength directed on his opening sense of beauty; you have a Pericles & Phidias, not yet having passed over into the Parisian civility. Every thing good in nature & the world is in that moment of transition" (JMN 10:82; cf. W 6:70–71). In *English Traits* he had identified the age of Elizabeth and Shakespeare as a similar period of transition when strength and beauty were still in equilibrium.

What troubled Emerson, however, was finding a way to foster man's development without sacrificing his "Pelasgic strength" to enervating "civility." As he wrote in "Experience," "Human life is made up of the two elements, power and form, and the proportion must be invariably kept, if we would have it sweet and sound. Each of these elements in excess makes a mischief as hurtful as its defect" (CW 3:38). In every chapter of *Representative Men* he underscored this need for balance: the best example is the essay on Plato, which envisions in Periclean Athens an ideal balance of power and form, of strength and beauty; there Emerson declared that Plato, himself "a balanced soul," honored both "the ideal, or laws of the mind, and Fate, or the order of nature" (CW 4:31, 26). But by the nineteenth century, he regretfully concluded, human attributes had run to extremes. Two unlike figures, Napoleon—a man of power and strength, a *do*-er—and Goethe—a man of beauty and form, a *say*-er—had divided the modern world between them. How could the new American nation, still in a period of transition, learn to avoid the extremes and combine the best qualities of both?

These considerations lie behind the upward progression in "The Conduct of Life" from "Power" to "Culture" and "Worship." The three lectures that immediately followed "Fate"—"Power," "Wealth," and "Economy"—reflect Emerson's old admiration for men of action, such as those contemporary entrepreneurs both English and American who had established mills and mill towns and built the railroads that connect them: "We know in Massachusetts who built New Bedford, who built Lynn, Lowell, Lawrence," and other centers of industry and commerce, he had written approvingly in "Fate" (*W* 6:42–43; cf. *JMN* 11:297, 394). By contrast, the scholars of his day in both America and England tended to be lesser men, possessing mere "working talent" rather than the power that comes with real genius (*W* 6:79–80; cf. *JMN* 10:300, 11:81); "I like merchants better than scholars," he had confessed in 1850 (*JMN* 11:284).

When Emerson turns from "Fate" to "Power" in "The Conduct of Life" series he begins by calling life itself "a search after power" (*W* 6:53). Success in its pursuit, he maintains, requires a healthy and vigorous constitution—something he himself had lacked since his youth. "There is always room for a man of force," he declares, observing realistically that "strong transgressors" like Jefferson and Jackson can be especially effective in government and that men with "a trace of ferocity" may prosper notably in trade. Indeed, "It is an esoteric doctrine of society that a little wickedness is good to make muscle, as if conscience were not good for hands and legs" (*W* 6:66; cf. *JMN* 10:340). And it must be granted that such men exemplify the commendable habits of "concentrating our force" and learning "the power of use and routine," which are universally valuable.

But "We can easily overpraise the vulgar hero," as Emerson is careful to add in concluding "Power." "Physical force has no value where there is nothing else," and this is true also "of spirit, or energy." Moreover, "there are sublime considerations which limit the value of talent and superficial success" (*W* 6:80, 70). Here Emerson was looking forward to the lectures on "Culture" and "Worship," but first he needed to deal with "Wealth" and "Economy," again with the idea of balance in mind. His discussion of "Wealth" begins with a series of homely examples that illustrate man's "applications of mind to nature" (*W* 6:86). "Men of sense," he writes, "esteem wealth to be the assimilation of nature to themselves, the converting of the sap and juices of the planet to the incarnation and nutriment of their design. Power is what they want, not candy;—power to execute their design, power to give legs and feet, form and actuality to their thought." These men are literally "idealists": each of them works "after his thought," and "would make it tyrannical, if he could. He is met and antagonized by other speculators as hot as he. The equilibrium is preserved by these counteractions" (*W* 6:93–94).[7] Then Emerson's argument takes a new turn: "I have never seen a man as rich as all men ought to be, or with an adequate command of nature." His point is that "Wealth, or surplus product," should be in the hands of those who have the ability and desire to "animate all their possessions," opening a path for others by making their treasures available to the public: "For he is the rich man in whom the people are rich, and he is the poor man in whom the people are poor; and how to give all access to the masterpieces of art and nature, is the problem of civilization" (W 6:95, 97).

Emerson's injunction to individuals in "Economy" is that their getting and spending ought to be directed by "that law of nature whereby everything climbs to higher platforms. . . . The true thrift is always to spend on the higher plane"; to invest so that a man "may spend in spiritual creation and not in augmenting animal existence" (W 6:126). This appeal to the principle of melioration affords a bridge to the key chapter on "Culture," which opens with the remark that "Whilst all the world is in pursuit of power, and of wealth as a means of power, culture corrects the meaning of success" (W 6:131). During the 1830s, when Emerson was developing his doctrine of self-reliant individualism, he had given a series of lectures on "Human Culture"; now he brings the two subjects together, telling "the student we speak to" that culture is based on individuality, "the cardinal necessity by which each individual persists to be what he is": "The end of culture is not to destroy this, God forbid! but to train away all impediment and mixture and leave nothing but pure power. Our student must have a style and determination, and be a master in his own specialty. But having this, he must put it behind him. He must have a catholicity, a power to see with a free and disengaged look every object" (W 6:134–35). Such "power to see with a free and disengaged look" is of course a distinguishing mark of Emerson's "true scholar."

The following paragraphs explain how culture combats the self-centered narrowness that afflicts individuals—scholars among others. The core of the lecture links culture with education as the key to melioration in the individual and reform in society. "We shall one day learn to supersede politics by education," Emerson predicts. "What we call our root-and-branch reforms, of slavery, war, gambling, intemperance, is only medicating the symptoms. We must begin higher up, namely in Education" (W 6:140–41; cf. JMN 11:416, 12:598). The cultivated person, he writes, "must have an intellectual quality in all property and all action, or they are naught," and culture must open for him "the sense of beauty. A man is a beggar who only lives to the useful, and however he may serve as a pin or rivet in the social machine, cannot be said to have arrived at self-possession" (W 6:158–59). Though characteristics retained from man's animal ancestry may impede the process of human melioration, culture can help to effect a genuine metamorphosis, so that a "new creature" may ultimately "emerge erect and free." It is through his culture that man will "convert all impediments into instruments, all enemies into power" (W 6:165–66).

The final lecture of the series, "Worship," advances the concept of the moral sentiment, the very idea that Emerson found so sadly lacking in contemporary

England and America. Here he drew upon journal entries of 1847 and possibly "a Sunday discourse" on Worship that he had read at Nantucket in May of that year; it, too, emphasizes "the cardinal topic of the moral nature."[8] "The whole state of man is a state of culture," according to the lecture, "and its flowering and completion may be described as Religion, or Worship." But religion "cannot rise above the state of the votary. . . . The god of the cannibals will be a cannibal, of the crusaders a crusader, and of the merchants a merchant" (*W* 6:204–5). Emerson regarded the nineteenth century, for good or for ill, as another transition period, a time when the old faiths "seem to have spent their force"; the religions of the day appeared to him "either childish and insignificant or unmanly and effeminating. The fatal trait is the divorce between religion and morality" (*W* 6:207). Both merchants and scholars, he charged, have succumbed to "a great despair"; they "have corrupted into a timorous conservatism and believe in nothing." Instead of faith in the intellectual or the moral universe there is faith only in material objects "and in public opinion, but not in divine causes" (*W* 6:208; cf. *JMN* 10:143–44, 14:400).

Emerson's response to the prevailing materialism of his contemporaries is to affirm that "the moral sense reappears to-day with the same morning newness that has been from of old the fountain of beauty and strength," and that it can bring "vast and sudden enlargements of power" (*W* 6:212–13). "All the great ages," he holds, "have been ages of belief," and worship "stands in some commanding relation to the health of man and to his highest powers, so as to be in some manner the source of intellect." There being "an intimate interdependence of intellect and morals," the new religion "must be intellectual" and the new church will be "founded on moral science" (*W* 6:216–17, 240–41). As for the individual worshiper, development of character brings "an increasing faith in the moral sentiment," which reflects the divine order of things—the eternal Necessity that governs both man and nature in a universe of Law. "Man is made of the same atoms as the world is, he shares the same impressions, predispositions and destiny. When his mind is illuminated, when his heart is kind, he throws himself joyfully into the sublime order, and does, with knowledge, what the stones do by structure." Here, as in the concluding paragraphs of "Fate," Emerson holds that "a voluntary obedience, a necessitated freedom," is "the last lesson of life" (*W* 6:227, 240).

iii. Toward *The Conduct of Life*

There is evidence to show that not all of Emerson's listeners to "The Conduct of Life" liked or even understood what he had to say. As he himself acknowledged, "Some of my friends have complained . . . that we discussed Fate, Power and Wealth on too low a platform," conceded too much to "the evil spirit of the times," and risked overstating the arguments that the lectures were intended to counter. But he made no apology. With "Fate" particularly in mind, he replied instead that

"A just thinker will allow full swing to his skepticism. I dip my pen in the blackest ink, because I am not afraid of falling into my inkpot" (*W* 6:201). It would seem, however, that Emerson was actually more of a fatalist in the 1850s than he cared to say publicly. In 1853, discouraged by "the bounded world" and the "quadruped estate" of human beings within it, he had written in a letter to Caroline Sturgis Tappan that though he rejected a "foolish & flippant" Fatalism, he affirmed that "Fatalism held by an intelligent soul who knows how to humour & obey the infinitesimal pulses of spontaneity, is by much the truest theory in use. All the great would call their thought fatalism, or concede that ninetynine parts are nature & one part power, tho' that hundredth is elastic, miraculous, &, whenever it is in energy, dissolving all the rest" (*L* 4:376–77).

As for the reactions of Emerson's listeners, David Mead has shown that contemporary newspaper accounts of Emerson's tours of the 1850s sometimes complained that his lectures were obscure, difficult to follow, and even un-Christian.[9] In a more recent study, Mary Kupiec Cayton has suggested that in fact he "may have been systematically misconstrued by his audience." While reports of what Emerson said in "The Conduct of Life" series closely parallel the versions that he himself later printed, she finds that these accounts consistently fail to grasp the full implication of his words. Her explanation is that when listeners were given such seemingly "familiar and practical" topics as "Power," "Wealth," and "Culture" without having a clear understanding of Emerson's overall design, they could easily mistake the lectures as "endorsement of the existing order" rather than, "as Emerson intended, a subtle indictment of its shortcomings."[10] That twentieth-century readers of the published texts have also been known to mistake his intentions lends a measure of support to the Cayton thesis.[11]

Emerson had long objected that detailed reporting of his lectures by metropolitan newspapers undercut their appeal to potential listeners; if he saw these accounts of "The Conduct of Life" series he may even have sought to clarify some of his statements as he traveled among Northern cities and towns, for as late as the spring of 1860 he was still offering several of the component lectures and introducing various revisions. But when he at last came to prepare the lectures for publication, he retracted nothing essential, arguing that he had simply been true to fact and denying "any fear that a skeptical bias can be given by leaning hard on the sides of fate, of practical power, or of trade, which the doctrine of Faith cannot downweigh. . . . We may well give skepticism as much line as we can. The spirit will return and fill us" (*W* 6:202).

Emerson's principal additions and changes were made in order to expand "The Conduct of Life" to book length. He enlarged several of the lecture manuscripts, particularly those of "Fate" and "Wealth" (in which he incorporated "Economy"), and added other new material—mostly revised versions of existing lectures that had not been part of the series. But over Lidian Emerson's objections, as their son remembered, he also did some severe "pruning and refining," sacrificing "good anecdotes and lighter touches" that he had originally included so as "to hold the attention of Lyceum audiences" (*J* 9:287). The result was a volume of nine chapters that fairly represents much of Emerson's thinking, after a quarter-century as a scholar and lecturer, on the condition and prospects of the contemporary scholar. Deliberately excluded, however, was any expression of opinion on the evils of slavery or on other issues that were dividing a country already on the eve of civil war; instead, the emphasis in most of the chapters is on personal conduct, that perennial concern of eighteenth- and nineteenth-century moralists.

Several major additions to "Fate" derive from entries that Emerson made during or after June 1859 in his Notebook EO (*TN* 1:88–92), where he wrote that "Fate is an algebraic X to cover the First Cause" and "Fate means the force of natural laws considered in relation to the wishes of man." Some of the other entries in EO seem designed to relate this first chapter more closely to the chapters which follow it: for example, there are notes on the dualistic interrelation of Fate and Power that anticipate this key passage in the published text: "But Fate has its lord; limitation its limits,—is different seen from above and from below, from within and from without. For though Fate is immense, so is Power, which is the other fact in the dual world, immense. If Fate follows and limits Power, Power attends and antagonizes Fate" (*W* 6:22; cf. *TN* 1:89, 91). Not only does Fate have its limits, Emerson is saying, but one's view of Fate—whether from above or below, from within or without—is subjective, depending on what he liked to call the angle of vision (*JMN* 10:76, 133, 173; *W* 12:10).

Emerson also wrote in EO that "The revelation of thought takes us out of servitude into freedom" and "So does the sense of right[.] They are exertions of will, a blending of these two" (*TN* 1:90). This is the germ of an important seven-paragraph passage in "Fate" on Thought, on the moral sentiment, and on will (*W* 6:25–30). During 1859, in his Journal CL, Emerson drafted a preliminary version of this passage, based on the earlier notebook entry, with particular emphasis on Fate and Necessity and also on thought and will (*JMN* 14:305–307). This version begins by distinguishing Fate from "the Necessary & Eternal," defining Fate as "the name we give to the action of that one eternal all-various Necessity on the brute myriads whether in things, animals, or in men in whom the intellect pure is not yet opened. . . . The great day in the man is the birth ⟨of mind in him⟩ of perception, which instantly throws him on the party of the Eternal." "There is no limitation about the Eternal," according to Emerson. Moreover, "Thought, Will is co-eternal with the world; and, as soon as intellect is awaked in any man, it . . . shares so far of the eternity,—is of the Maker not of the Made."

So in "Fate," adapting the phrasing of the journal, Emerson declares, "The day of days, the great day of the feast of life, is that in which *the inward eye opens* to the Unity in things, to the omnipresence of law:—sees that what is must be and ought to be, or is the best" (*CW* 6:25; emphasis added). Long before, in *Nature*, he had written in a similar vein: "The best, the happiest moments of life" come when "the eye of Reason opens" (*CW* 1:30). As he continues his discussion of Thought in "Fate" he introduces another idea of the 1830s: the essentially passive relation of

"The great day . . . is the birth of perception"
Undated entry of spring or early summer 1859, Journal CL, pp. 39–40; see *JMN* 14:305.
Note also Emerson's distinction between "Fate" and "the Necessary & Eternal."

the individual person to the impersonal Universe: "This beatitude dips from on high down on us and we see. . . . This insight throws us on the party and interest of the Universe, against all and sundry; against ourselves as much as others. A man speaking from insight affirms of himself what is true of the mind. . . . It is not in us, but we are in it. It is of the maker, not of what is made" (*W* 6:25–26).

Since insight "does not overvalue particular truths," we "hear eagerly every thought and word quoted from an intellectual man"—which is to say, from Emerson's "true scholar." "But in his presence our own mind is roused to activity, and we forget very fast what he says, much more interested in the new play of our own thought than in any thought of his" (*W* 6:26). In other words, this passage of "Fate" reaffirms the long-standing Emersonian belief that the scholar's function in society is to awaken the intellect in others, whether his medium be poetry or prose, lecturing or preaching, and so to free their "imprisoned spirits, imprisoned thoughts." For "Just as much intellect as you add, so much organic power. He who sees through the design, presides over it, and must will that which must be" (*W* 6:27).

iv. The Added Chapters

The new chapters that Emerson added to his book contribute to its theme of personal conduct, though at some cost to the structural device of successive platforms that had helped to unify the original lecture series. His new fifth chapter, "Behavior," placed between "Culture" and "Worship," seems to incorporate a lecture on "Manners" that he had first given in Boston on 20 April 1859 and recently repeated.[12] The chapter deals with the outward expression of spirit in "the figure, movement and gesture" of men and women, which correlates with their "capacity for culture" (W 6:169, 176). Reaffirming what he had written on self-expression in the 1830s and early 1840s, he declares now that in society, "the stage on which manners are shown," individuals affect one another less by what they say than "by their personality, by who they are, and what they said and did heretofore." True self-possession comes with cultivation; self-reliance is both "the basis of behavior" and "the guaranty that the powers are not squandered in too much demonstration"—the mark of "a superficial culture" (W 6:190–91).

The new seventh chapter, "Considerations by the Way," follows "Worship."[13] As Edward Emerson remarked, his father's "considerations" there are not with an abstract theme "but, below the clouds, with the day and its chances" (W 6:400–401). Once again, the immediate focus is on the self-reliant, self-possessed individual who stands or falls "on strength of his own"; such persons, though always in the minority, will be the true benefactors of mankind (W 6:246, 248). "All revelations, whether of mechanical or intellectual or moral science, are made, not to communities, but to single persons," Emerson declares; the majority, on the other hand, "are unripe, and have not yet come to themselves, do not yet know their opinion," and among them, what he liked to call "the quadruped interest" is "very prone to prevail" (W 6:251, 252; cf. JMN 13:377, L 5:17). How, then, must this small minority whom he is once more addressing—clearly "the class of scholars or students," as in 1854 (W 11:217)—conduct their lives? Emerson's initial answer, which reflects his statement in "Fate" that evil may be "good in the making," is to learn from history "the good of evil. Good is a good doctor but Bad is sometimes a better" (W 6:253; cf. JMN 13:458–59).[14] His advice is essentially to make the best of whatever comes our way, be it good or evil, following the example of nature herself by converting it "into new creations" (W 6:262).

As for practical rules, the first is "that every man shall maintain himself." He should "get health" and avoid sickness, cultivating a cheerful disposition and genial manners while practicing "accommodation to any circumstances." But "the high prize of life . . . is to be born with a bias to some pursuit which finds him in employment and happiness," whatever his work may be, and "the best property" we can acquire in life is the friends we make (W 6:267, 273). "The secret of culture," in short, lies in "a few great points" that reappear wherever we find ourselves and "are alone to be regarded;—the escape from all false ties; courage to be what we are, and love of what is simple and beautiful; independence and cheerful relation, these are the essentials,—these, and the wish to serve, to add somewhat to the well-being of men" (W 6:278).

"Beauty," the new eighth chapter, grew out of the lecture of that title that Emerson had first given independently in 1855 and 1856, but the subject itself had attracted him since the time of *Nature*. There he had discussed in turn "the simple perception of natural beauty," the presence in nature of "the spiritual element," and the beauty of the world "as it becomes an object of the intellect"; here, again emphasizing intellect, he terms Beauty "the form under which the intellect prefers to study the world" (*CW* 1:13–16; *W* 6:287). From both nature and art he has learned "that all beauty must be organic; that outside embellishment is deformity" (*W* 6:290). And in accordance with the concepts of growth and development that he had begun to emphasize in "Circles" and "The Method of Nature," he also writes, in familiar Emersonian phrasing: "Nothing interests us which is stark or bounded, but only what *streams with life*, what is in act or endeavor to reach somewhat beyond. . . . Beauty is *the moment of transition*, as if the form were just ready *to flow into other forms*. Any fixedness, heaping or concentration on one feature, . . . is the reverse of the flowing, and therefore deformed" (*W* 6:292; emphasis added).

If any created form is to attain true beauty, Emerson goes on to say, its "sovereign attribute" will necessarily be its power to speak not merely to the senses but to the imagination and intellect. This is in accordance with the scholar's thinking in *Nature* and "The Poet." Imagination suggests the relations of individual parts to the unified whole, and by showing "the convertibility of every thing into every other thing," it turns common objects into symbols. Now Emerson adds that beauty will possess a moral as well as an intellectual quality: "All high beauty has a moral element in it," and the beauty of art—for its beholder as well as for its creator—will ever be "in proportion to the depth of thought" that it engenders. In conclusion, where he returns to the motif of ascension, he writes of that "climbing scale of culture" that leads us up from mere "agreeable sensation" to "the ineffable mysteries of the intellect"—ultimately to "the perception of Plato that globe and universe are rude and early expressions of an all-dissolving Unity" (*W* 6:302–3, 304, 306).

The Conduct of Life could well have concluded with "Beauty," since this ultimate perception of "an all-dissolving Unity" presumably refers to that same "Blessed Unity" of Fate with Power that is envisioned at the close of "Fate." Instead of ending at this point, however, Emerson chose to round out the book still further with a ninth chapter, "Illusions," written from an angle of vision that differs strikingly from that of "Beauty." Their juxtaposition resembles that of "Experience" with "The Poet" in *Essays: Second Series,* and indeed the very title of "Illusions" recalls the opening paragraphs of "Experience." But in this new volume the final chapter is like "Behavior" and "Considerations by the Way" in the scholar's renewed emphasis on the values of self-possession and self-reliance in addressing the question "How shall I live?"

"Illusions" begins with recollections of a visit to Kentucky's Mammoth Cave that Emerson had made in June of 1850. Given his reference to "the perception of Plato" at the close of the preceding chapter, he may well have been thinking of Plato's allegory of the cave in the *Republic,* offering this introductory episode as what Richard Lee Francis has termed "an earthly parable of Plato's cave."[15] In Kentucky he had enjoyed "the mysteries and scenery of the cave," we are told, but what he chiefly remembered was that "the best thing" it had to offer was "an illusion": namely, a "theatrical trick" that yielded a vision of what *seemed* to be "the night heaven thick with stars." Recalling this occasion reminded him of "many experiences like it, before and since" (*W* 6:310–11; cf. *JMN* 14:162–63), thus raising once again the scholar's old problem of perception—the questions of sight and insight, being and seeming, nominalism and realism, that had engaged him repeatedly since the 1830s and 1840s.

Because we live by our imaginations, our admirations, our sentiments, Emerson continues, we are "victims of illusions in all parts of life," though we "rightly accuse the critics" who destroy too many of them (*W* 6:312–13). We come to learn the true nature of these phantasms only through a series of lessons, resisting each lesson in its turn. And as we gradually accept "the mental laws" that govern this process, we must face the prospect that the scholar himself was confronting when he wrote "Circles": the likelihood that "even our thoughts are not finalities, but the incessant flowing and ascension reach these also, and each thought which yesterday was a finality, to-day is yielding to a larger generalization" (*W* 6:320).

In exploring the consequences of "our shifting moods and susceptibility," Emerson writes now that though "the capital facts of human life are hidden from our eyes," we do have occasional moments of insight—when "for an instant" (in the words of the final paragraph of the chapter), "the air clears and the cloud lifts a little" (*W* 6:325). The treatment of insight here differs markedly from that of the passage on Thought that he added to "Fate" in 1859. Here he observes regretfully that such experiences of true vision are rare indeed, and in "this kingdom of illusions," we are left to "grope eagerly for stays and foundations." These will turn out to be domestic and personal: "There is none but a strict and faithful dealing at home and a severe barring out of all duplicity or illusion there. Whatever games are played with us, we must play no games with ourselves, but deal in our privacy with the last honesty and truth" (*W* 6:322).

The scholar is restating here, though in a new sense, what he had written in "Self-Reliance": "Nothing is at last sacred but the integrity of your own mind" (*CW* 2:30). In the reality of private honesty and truth lies "the foundation of friendship, religion, poetry and art," and "it is what we really are that avails with friends, with strangers, and with fate or fortune. . . . The permanent interest of every man is never to be in a false position, but to have the weight of nature to back him in all that he does." Seeming differences, such as one's riches or poverty, are illusory—merely "a thick or thin costume," for the lives of all of us share a common identity (*W* 6:323; cf. *JMN* 14:160, 11:99–100).

In view of all this, Emerson concludes, every individual needs to accept the "mental and moral philosophy" epitomized in a Persian sentence: "'Fooled thou must be, though wisest of the wise: / Then be the fool of virtue, not of vice.'" If he himself thought of "Illusions" as a Platônic parable, then his implication here is that we mortals cannot hope to emerge from the cave of sense in this our life. Nevertheless, the individual may come to realize, in those rare moments when the "snow-storms of illusions" suddenly give way to insight, that "There is no chance and no anarchy in the universe. All is system and gradation" (*W* 6:325).

v. Evaluations

The final paragraph of "Illusions" especially pleased Carlyle, who in a letter to Emerson praised *The Conduct of Life* as "the best of all your books. . . . You have grown older, more pungent, piercing:—I never read from you before such lightning-gleams of meaning" (*CEC* 533–34). Among Emerson's New England circle, Charles Eliot Norton hailed the appearance of such a dispassionate work at a time of national crisis, but the book disappointed Alcott and Thoreau. Published reviews both at home and abroad were mixed. Some critics thought Emerson's style less idiosyncratic, though others still found him obscure; some charged that in content he was merely repeating himself; others predictably objected to what he said—or failed to say—about religion. A few English reviewers complained that the title was misleading; they had expected a more practical manual of conduct.

Emerson himself remarked that he had read both friendly and hostile paragraphs about the book, "but seldom or never a just criticism. . . . I often think that I could write a criticism on Emerson, that would hit the white" (*JMN* 15:11). None of the reviewers had made him "wince," he said, by touching "the fault"—whatever he may have supposed "the fault" to be. He perhaps realized that *The Conduct of Life* is not a wholly unified book. Although the initial chapter on "Fate" envisions a balance of Fate and Power, there is no single chapter of the eight which follow—not even that entitled "Power"—to match "Fate" in its impact on the reader. Even in the original lecture series the intended balancing of Fate with Power was compromised structurally (one lecture on Fate versus five on Power). The four added chapters of the book do strengthen it thematically, since they all deal with an individual's conduct of life, but they fail to maintain the original upward progression from Power and Wealth to Culture and Worship; indeed, there is some inconsistency between the last two chapters, "Beauty" and "Illusions," and also between "Illusions" and the late additions to "Fate."

Among twentieth-century commentators, "Fate" has received disproportionate attention while the rest of the book has been largely neglected. But as Francis has pointed out in his challenging essay of 1980, this almost exclusive emphasis on a single component distorts both our reading of "Fate" itself and our understanding of the entire book. "Fate" is "the foundation and not the crowning achievement of the volume," Francis reminds us, and its very placement at the beginning of the book "should affect how we read the essay in relation to the whole."[16] The entire work deserves comparison with *Nature*, not only in its organization but as epitomizing Emerson's thought at a significant time in his career as a scholar. Although the two books have something in common, they also differ significantly: there is no "transparent eye-ball" in *The Conduct of Life,* and where *Nature* advances upward to its climax in "Spirit" and "Prospects," the later book concludes with a "young mortal" alone amid a snowstorm of illusions. Only when "the air clears and the clouds lift a little" do the gods appear "for an instant" around him.

16. TERMINUS, 1860–1882

❖

As the bird trims her to the gale,
I trim myself to the storm of time,
I man the rudder, reef the sail,
Obey the voice at eve obeyed at prime.
—"Terminus," lines 33–36 (*W* 9:252)

Late in 1866, when young Edward Emerson joined his father in a New York hotel, he was given a reading of several "poems for the new May-Day volume" of 1867, among them "Terminus." "It is time to be old," the poem begins, "To take in sail. . . . " The young man was "almost startled" to hear these lines, for he had never before thought of his father as aging:

> There he sat, with no apparent abatement of bodily vigor, and young in spirit, recognizing with serene acquiescence his failing forces; I think he smiled as he read. He recognized, as none of us did, that his working days were nearly done. They lasted about five years longer, although he lived, in comfortable health, yet ten years beyond those of his activity. (*W* 9:489–90)

Although the younger Emerson "strongly hinted" both here and elsewhere that "Terminus" was newly written at this time, the editors of the *Poetry Notebooks* conclude that the first draft of the poem was composed much earlier—at some undetermined period "between April 1846 and the end of 1851"—and that the draft of its ending that is entered in Poetry Notebook NP "is probably much later" (*PN* 932). This is to say that Waldo Emerson may have been conscious of his failing powers even before his second visit to England.

As we know, the ensuing decade of the 1850s was a difficult time for Emerson, given the nation's drift toward war, his own engagement in the Anti-Slavery cause, and his efforts to complete *English Traits* and *The Conduct of Life* while maintaining a rigorous schedule as a traveling lecturer. By the spring of 1859, when he had temporarily given up his "almost daily" journal entries, he "sometimes" believed "that I have no new thoughts, and that my life is quite at an end" (*JMN* 14:248). But during the war years he enjoyed a renewed vitality: as he wrote in 1864, "Within, I do not find wrinkles & used heart, but unspent youth" (*JMN* 15:416). And in the course of his remaining period of activity, as his son called the years from 1860 to about 1872, he outlived many of his close associates: Henry Thoreau died in 1862, Mary Moody Emerson in 1863, Nathaniel Hawthorne in 1864, Sarah Alden Ripley and Abel Adams, his financial advisor, in 1867, and his brother William in 1868. Emerson spoke at Thoreau's funeral and later expanded his remarks for publication in the *Atlantic Monthly*; he summed up his impressions of Hawthorne in a long journal entry (*JMN* 15:59–60) that he did not choose to publish. Both "Thoreau" and the sketch of his Aunt Mary appear in *Lectures and Biographical Sketches*, edited by Cabot after Emerson's death (*W* 10:449–85, 397–433).

In the decade of the 1860s Emerson resumed a demanding schedule of lecturing as soon as wartime conditions permitted, being in need of money at a time when neither his books nor his investments were yielding much income. By the early months of 1863 he was again speaking in cities as far removed from Concord as Toronto and Montreal and as far west as Chicago and Milwaukee; the winter lecture tours continued as late as 1871–1872. Besides *May-Day and Other Pieces* (1867) he published *Society and Solitude* in 1870, collecting and polishing earlier lectures not included in *The Conduct of Life*.[1] It is ironic that his greatest fame—and, incidentally, his highest fees as a lecturer—came in these later years, when his most original thinking and writing were behind him and his physical and mental powers were gradually failing.

During this period, in common with other lecturers, Emerson was facing another problem: even before the Civil War, as Carl Bode has demonstrated in *The American Lyceum*, a gradual shift in emphasis from adult education to popular entertainment was transforming the lyceum movement. These changes, both personal and social, had their effect on the kind of lectures Emerson was able to offer as he toured beyond New England. When he was able to resume lecturing in the West, he customarily elected to speak on less abstruse subjects than "Fate," "Power," and "Wealth." In 1864 he introduced and later took to Chicago and Milwaukee a series on "American Life" that included "Education," "Social Aims," "Resources," "Table Talk," "Books," and "Character."[2] At home in New England he enjoyed his contacts with academic audiences; "all through life," as his son remarked, "he had been writing to and for scholars" (*W* 10:563).

i. The Scholar's "white lot in life"

Ever since his college days Emerson had wished to be a "professor of rhetoric and elocution"—a "teacher of the art of writing well to young men," and he would gladly have accepted a faculty appointment. "Why has never the poorest country college offered me a professorship of rhetoric?" he asked. "I think I could have taught an orator, though I am none."[3] Invitations to speak on New England college campuses were especially welcome during the war years, when travel to distant states was difficult. In 1861 he addressed the students of Tufts College on "The Celebration of Intellect," pursuing a familiar Emersonian theme beyond what he had recently written in *The Conduct of Life*. As early as 1834 he had held that the scholar represents—however imperfectly—"the intellectual man" (*JMN* 4:370); in his late years he returned again and again to what in the 1830s he had called the scholar's "duty and discipline." The address at Tufts was the first of several related discourses to young scholars on intellectual matters that he delivered during the 1860s. Although complete texts of these addresses have not been published, the available extracts and summaries clearly set forth once again, under the shadow of war, Emerson's ideal conception of the scholar.

The seminal discourse at Tufts College took place on 10 July 1861, "before the forces of North and South had met in the disastrous battle of Bull Run," as Edward Emerson noted, adding that the published text (*W* 12:111–32) "is incomplete, as many passages were taken from it" for later addresses on "The Man of Letters" and "The Scholar" (*W* 12:447).[4] It was Emerson's decision when he spoke at Tufts to praise "the heroism of scholars"—Archimedes, Michelangelo, Milton—rather than that of soldiers, and to exalt "the intellectual interest" as "the only reality." What so deeply troubled him at this time of crisis was his fear that the American college and American scholars of his day had manifestly failed in their duty to the nation. Here is his indictment:

> 'T is because the college was false to its trust, because the scholars did not learn and teach, because they were traders and left their altars and libraries and worship of truth and played the sycophant to presidents and generals and members of Congress, and gave degrees and literary and social honors to those whom they ought to have rebuked and exposed, incurring the contempt of those whom they ought to have put in fear; then the college is suicidal; ceases to be a school; power oozes out of it just as fast as truth does; and instead of overawing the strong, and upholding the good, it is a hospital for decayed tutors. (*W* 12:116–17)

Ideally, as Emerson declared at Tufts, those "capable of the high privilege of thought" constitute a much-needed "band of priests of intellect and knowledge; and great is the office." But in actuality, men of "the class called intellectual" pervert their wit and learning to evil ends. "There are bad books and false teachers and corrupt judges; and in the institutions of education a want of faith in their own cause." Colleges, like the Church, should be counterbalancing forces to "bad politics and selfish trade," but instead, both higher education and religion "take their tone from the City, and do not dictate their own." Indeed, thought is rare in colleges, mere drill replaces inspired teaching, and all too often "the best scholar, he for whom colleges exist," will find himself "a stranger and an orphan therein." A college *ought* to be an assembly of true scholar-teachers, in whom the young student can find sympathy and "an order that corresponds to that in his own mind, and in all sound minds." Emerson's ideal "theory of Education" envisions

> the happy meeting of the young soul, filled with the desire, with the living teacher who has already made the passage from the centre forth, step by step, along the intellectual roads to the theory and practice of special science. Now if there be genius in the scholar, . . . he is made to find his own way. He will greet joyfully the wise

teacher, but colleges and teachers are in no wise essential to him; he will find teachers everywhere. (*W* 12:128)

Two years later, on 22 July 1863, shortly after the Union victory at Gettysburg, Emerson spoke by invitation at Dartmouth College, delivering a new address on "The Scholar" that incorporated parts of the manuscript he had read at Tufts. On 11 August he repeated the address, evidently with some additions, at Waterville College in Maine (see *JMN* 15:5, 22–32); a shortened version, retitled "The Man of Letters," appears in *Lectures and Biographical Sketches* (*W* 10:239–58).[5] "The times," as Emerson said at Waterville, "are dark, but heroic." The college, he knew, had "sent its full quota to the field," and some young men had "returned wounded and maimed." The cost of war had been great. But "Slavery is broken, and, if we use our advantage, irretrievably. For such a gain," Emerson was moved to declare, "one generation might well be sacrificed."

The listeners on both campuses were "Gentlemen of the Literary Societies," and as "an old scholar" Emerson counseled them "in regard to the career of letters,—the power and joy that belong to it, and its high office in evil times. I offer perpetual congratulation to the scholar; he has drawn the white lot in life" (*W* 10:241). But the ideal and the actual, as he had acknowledged at Tufts two years before, are poles apart. In theory, the scholar is sent by Heaven "as a leader to lead"; so he had said even longer ago in "The American Scholar." "He is a learner of the laws of Nature and the experiences of history," Emerson now declares once again; and he is also "a prophet surrendering with self-abandoning sincerity to the Heaven which pours through him its will to mankind." But his listeners know how far this theory is from the fact, for "nothing has been able to resist the tide with which the material prosperity of America in years past has beat down the hope of youth, the piety of learning."

Here Emerson is resuming the attack on nineteenth-century materialism he had begun in the mid–1840s and continued in both *English Traits* and *The Conduct of Life.* As in "The Celebration of Intellect," he charges that even "men of intellectual culture"—"the spiritual class"—have turned their energies to the pursuit of wealth, neglecting to balance their labor by "mental activity, and especially by the imagination—the cardinal human power." American society is neither imaginative nor religious; instead, it has become utilitarian and frivolous, aimless and wanting in thought. "Our profoundest philosophy (if it were not contradiction in terms) is skepticism. . . . Our industrial skill, arts ministering to convenience and luxury, have made life expensive, and therefore greedy, careful, anxious; have turned the eyes downward to the earth, not upward to thought." Such charges echo Emerson's criticism of nineteenth-century England in *English Traits,* notably in the chapters on "Religion" and "Literature"; once again he is thinking of America as inheriting modern England's strengths and weaknesses. Nations "die of suicide," and "the sign of it is the decay of thought."

"Where there is no vision, the people perish." As at Providence in 1837, so

Emerson at Waterville again quotes the scriptural admonition; as he had at Williams College in 1854, he particularly blames "the educated class, the men of study and thought," for their deference to "the men of this world" and their own failure of leadership. Being idealists, they "should stand for freedom, justice, and public good," but "the clerisy, the spiritual guides, the scholars, the seers have been false to their trust." In consequence, "Our people have this levity and complaisance—they fear to offend, do not wish to be misunderstood; do not wish, of all things, to be in the minority." Though the scholar may well grant that these are "evil times," Emerson continues, he must nevertheless abjure the temptation of "homeless despondency," remembering always that he "represents intellectual or spiritual force." The scholar is to "rely on the spiritual arm" and "live by his strength, not his weakness. A scholar defending the cause of slavery, of arbitrary government, of monopoly, of the oppressor, is a traitor to his profession. He has ceased to be a scholar. . . . The worst times only show him how independent he is of times; only relieve and bring out the splendor of his privilege" (W 10:247; cf. JMN 15:31).

As the scholar beholds the ravages of war he must not forget nature's restorative power: "There is no unemployed force in Nature," Emerson declares. "All decomposition is recomposition. War disorganizes, but it is to reorganize." His young listeners, being scholars, are therefore "carriers of the power of Nature"—and for him, "Every man is a scholar potentially." Here Emerson is restating the democratic faith he had proclaimed in 1837 in "The American Scholar": each individual "believes himself inspired by the Divine Soul which also inspires all men" (CW 1:70); on that faith he had grounded his insistence in the 1840s that education should be designed for the many, not just for the privileged few. In this lecture he holds that scholars as spiritual men represent "the subtle force which creates Nature and men and states;—consoler, upholder, imparting pulses of light and shocks of electricity, guidance and courage" (W 10:250).

Citing the self-reliant cadets he had recently talked with at West Point, Emerson also told the students at Waterville that "a primary duty of the man of letters" is "to secure his independence," adding that in "your art and profession as thinkers" is "the secret of power." For it is thought that "makes us men"; thought is "the prolific source of all arts, of all wealth, of all delight, of all grandeur" (W 10:252). A year later, on 9 August 1864, Emerson developed a similar line of thought when he again addressed "the Literary Societies of Dartmouth College"; his subject was "Greatness of the Scholar" (partially printed in "Greatness," W 8:301–20).[6] Scholars, he declared at Dartmouth, "represent the intellect, by which man is man; the intellect and the moral sentiment,—which in the last analysis can never be separated."

> Let the scholar measure his valor by his power to cope with intellectual giants. Leave others to count votes and calculate stocks. His courage is to weigh Plato, judge Laplace, know Newton, Faraday, judge of Darwin, criticise Kant and Swedenborg, and on all these arouse the central courage of insight. The scholar's courage should be as terrible as the Cid's, though it grow out of spiritual nature, not out of brawn. Nature, when she adds difficulty, adds brain. (W 8:211–312; cf. JMN 10:28, 42; 12:607)

"The secret of the true scholar" is that "every man I meet is my master in some point, and in that I learn of him" (cf. *JMN* 10:79).

ii. "The Natural History of Intellect"

With the ending of the war in 1865 Emerson was once again in demand as a lecturer; during that busy year alone he appeared seventy-seven times, on platforms throughout the Northern states. Following the assassination of Abraham Lincoln in April he spoke at the memorial service in Concord for the late President, and in the following June he read an existing lecture on "Resources" at Ripley Female College in Poultney, Vermont. On 31 July he gave a new address at the Williams College Adelphi Union, "Conduct of the Intellect," all or parts of which he adapted for later use: first in May of 1866 as the fifth of a six-part lecture series on "Philosophy of the People," delivered privately at Chickering's Hall in Boston,[7] and again in his Harvard lectures of 1870 and 1871 on "The Natural History of Intellect" (*W* 12:43–46). In his preliminary notes for the original form of this address (*JMN* 15:66–68) Emerson had settled on "the eternal topic the praise of intellect," writing at the outset that "I gain my point, gain all points, whenever I can reach the young man with any statement which teaches him his own worth." To do so, he continued, he must first "touch his imagination" and thereby "open for him for a moment the superiority of knowledge to wealth or physical power."[8] This statement admirably sums up Emerson's aim in all his college addresses.

Emerson frequently repeated all or parts of his new "American Life" series of six lectures, not only to general audiences but also on a return visit in November 1865 to Williams College, where the "Literary Societies" had invited him for one lecture but persuaded him to remain for an entire week and deliver all six. In October his daughter Edith had married Colonel William H. Forbes, a son of Emerson's friend John Murray Forbes, a railroad magnate; both father and son were to be great benefactors in his later years. Meanwhile, the old dispute over Emerson's Divinity School Address at Harvard had finally been forgotten. He was appointed to a committee charged with planning the new Memorial Hall, and on 21 July 1865 he read his "Harvard Commemoration Speech" (*W* 11:339–45) as a tribute to those Harvard "scholars and idealists who went to the war in their own despite."

At Cambridge in 1867, thirty years after "The American Scholar," Emerson delivered another Phi Beta Kappa address, "Progress of Culture" (*W* 8:205–34). In 1866 Harvard made him an honorary Doctor of Laws, and in the following year he became an elected Overseer of the College. In "The Celebration of Intellect" he had deplored what he saw as the domination of Harvard by Boston's State Street financiers (*W* 12:126); during his long service as an Overseer (1867–1879) he gladly supported the plans of Charles William Eliot, who became president in 1870, to inaugurate various educational reforms, including the enhancement of undergraduate education in Harvard College, the establishment of separate graduate and professional schools, and the organization of all of these components into Harvard University.[9]

In 1870 Emerson was invited to become one of several lecturers on philosophy in a new Harvard course for advanced students, but though he had long wished for a professorship, his rightful subject was rhetoric rather than philosophy. Moreover, in the words of Edward Emerson, it was then "too late for the satisfactory performance of the duty. . . . His strength was now failing, and the task of arrangement—always for him the most difficult part of his work—sorely burdened him. . . . He used his old notes, with changes, and much that was later printed in the essays on Poetry and Imagination, Inspiration, and Memory" (W 12:422–23).[10]

This is to say that these lectures, like so much of his work of the late 1840s and after—including *Representative Men, English Traits, The Conduct of Life,* and the later *Society and Solitude* (1870)—were to a large degree retrospective rather than newly conceived. As early as 1835, in Journal RO Mind, Emerson had attempted to formulate "the original laws of the mind" (*JMN* 5:270); at London in 1848 he first lectured on "Natural History of the Intellect," discussing "Powers and Laws of Thought," "Relation of Intellect to Natural Science," and "Tendencies and Duties of Men of Thought." The "old notes" specifically used for the Harvard course came from a variety of sources: the London lectures of 1848 and also his more recent courses at Boston on "The Natural Method of Mental Philosophy" in 1858 and "Philosophy of the People" in 1866, which were themselves derivative.

As Edward Emerson also remembered, his father was "disappointed and mortified as to his Cambridge courses, which proved too much for his strength" (W 12:424). Emerson himself wrote to Carlyle in June of 1870 of the "oppressive" and "formidable" task of "writing & reading 18 lectures on Philosophy . . . in six successive weeks." Having agreed to repeat the engagement in the following year, he planned to revise the lectures, partly out of the materials now collected "& partly by large rejection of these, & by large addition to them" (*CEC* 570), but the second course proved to be only a "doleful ordeal," as he confessed to Carlyle in the following April. "I have abundance of good readings & some honest writing on the leading topics,—but in haste & confusion they are misplaced & spoiled" (*CEC* 578). The surviving manuscripts, which reflect his difficulties, present a challenging problem for an editor; the texts so far published in *Natural History of Intellect* do not reproduce the individual lectures as they were actually delivered in either 1870 (16 lectures) or 1871 (17 lectures).[11] The present discussion concentrates on the writings Cabot assembled under a title borrowed from the London lectures, "Powers and Laws of Thought" (W 12:3–64), a compilation that includes passages from various component lectures which in sum represent the core of Emerson's mature thinking about "the intellectual nature" (W 12:10)—a subject closely bound to his basic conception of the scholar as the intellectual man.

As we know, Emerson's interest in what was then called "Natural History" had begun in the early 1830s, well before the writing of *Nature;* it continued through the 1840s and after when as a layman he sought to keep abreast of current scientific theory. At Harvard as earlier in London, having stated his belief that "the laws and powers of the intellect" can be formulated like the laws of nature, he reaffirmed his old preference for poetry rather than "the analytic process" employed by naturalists, which he termed "cold and bereaving" (*W* 12:14). In *Nature*, we remember, he had referred in a similar way to the limited vision of those "patient naturalists" who "freeze their subject under the wintry light of the understanding," for in his view, nature demands affection as well as perception (*CW* 1:44). In the lectures, he said, he would attempt only "some sketches or studies" toward the formulation of possible laws of the mind, beginning with praise of the "excellence" of Intellect itself (14–15)—the first numbered topic in "Powers and Laws of Thought" as assembled by Cabot. "I believe the mind is the creator of the world, and is ever creating;—that at last Matter is dead Mind; that mind makes the senses it sees with; that the genius of man is a continuation of the power that made him and that has not done making him" (17). This statement of belief sums up Emerson's many years of thinking about the relations of man and nature to the One Universal Mind—his "old thrum," as he called it in 1837 (*JMN* 5:376).

The next numbered topic, "identity of the thought with Nature," recalls the title of the second London lecture, "Relation of Intellect to Natural Science." As Emerson had said in the 1830s, the mind is able to arrange and classify natural phenomena because of the "parallel unity" between intellect and external nature (20). And as he had come to think during the 1840s, the human mind itself is the product of "development from less to more, from lower to superior function, steadily ascending to man" (21), a concept of melioration leading to "a whole system of ethics" (27). Here as in *The Conduct of Life* Emerson emphasizes once more his doctrine of self-reliance and self-trust; that intellectual persons should "believe in the ideas of others" is for him simply unforgivable (31).

What Emerson might have called "the scholar's ethics" is the concern of an ensuing passage of "Powers and Laws of Thought" (38–45) that opens by noting the intellect's power to detach itself from the individual and particular so as to see facts "under a universal light" (39). Thus "the true scholar" is "one who has the power to stand beside his thoughts or to hold off his thoughts at arm's length and give them perspective" (44). Moreover, thought demands utterance: it "exists to be expressed. That which cannot externize itself is not thought" (41). Although these ideas go back to Emerson's early lectures on "The Philosophy of History," their more immediate source is his Boston lectures of 1866 on "Philosophy of the People," which incorporates the Williams College address of 1865 on "Conduct of the Intellect" in company with "Laws of Mind" and "Relation of the Intellect to Morals."[12] "Our thoughts at first possess us," he declares. "Later, if we have good heads, we come to possess them" (43); indeed, "The primary rule for the conduct of Intellect is to have control of the thoughts without losing their natural attitudes and action" (45). True wisdom, moreover, requires a blending of "the intellectual perception of truth and the moral sentiment of right" (46)—long a cardinal tenet of Emerson's thinking.

"Instinct and Inspiration," the third numbered topic in "Powers and Laws of Thought," deals with a fundamental source of all mental power. This section appears to touch on materials that Emerson had covered in a number of his Harvard lectures, several of which are amplified in essays published separately: one of these essays bears the same title, "Instinct and Inspiration" (W 12:65–89); the others are "Memory" (W 12:90–110), "Poetry and Imagination" (W 8:1–75), and "Inspiration" (W 8:267–97). At Harvard he had evidently drawn once again upon his recent addresses to other college audiences and from his "Philosophy of the People" series; there are close correspondences in thought and sometimes in actual phrasing between "Powers and Laws of Thought" and these addresses and lectures as published or as summarized in Cabot's Memoir.

In "Instinct and Inspiration," for example, Emerson holds that Instinct "ascends, step by step, to suggestions, which are, when expressed, the intellectual and moral laws," and that Inspiration is "this instinct, whose normal state is passive, at last put in action" (W 12:68). In "Powers and Laws of Thought" he speaks of Inspiration as Instinct "excited" (35), regarding it as "the continuation of the divine effort that built the man. The same course continues itself in the mind which we have witnessed in Nature, namely the carrying-on and completion of the metamorphosis from grub to worm, from worm to fly." But human history is "the history of arrested growth," and for most of us the development of "high powers" and "access to rare truths" cease in childhood, while "all the pagan faculties" continue ripening (59–60). To counteract "this premature stop" in himself and others, and so to foster "the carrying-on and completion" of human development, was Emerson's lifelong aim as a scholar.

As early as "Self-Reliance" Emerson had written of "Spontaneity or Instinct" in religious terms, relating Instinct to "that source, at once the essence of genius, of virtue, and of life," that he called "the aboriginal Self" (W 2:37); at Harvard he declared in more secular language that Instinct is "Nature when it first becomes intelligent" (36). Then, in phrasing that recalls his amplification of "Fate" for The Conduct of Life, he treats Perception as differing from Instinct "by adding the Will"— subsequently defining Will as "the presence of God to men" (37, 46). When Will appears, "the mind's eye opens and we become aware of spiritual facts, of rights, of duties, of thoughts,—a thousand faces of one essence. We call the essence Truth; the particular aspects of it we call thoughts" (37–38). [13]

Ever since the 1830s Emerson had been stressing the moral implications of the relation between nature and man. "The moral law lies at the centre of nature and radiates to the circumference," he wrote in Nature, and "The laws of moral nature answer to those of matter as face to face in a glass" (CW 1:26, 21). During the 1860s, in The Conduct of Life and the addresses and lectures that followed it, he again emphasized "the unity of thought and of morals running through all animated Nature," as he put it in "The Sovereignty of Ethics": "The high intellect is absolutely at one with moral nature" (W 10:184, 185). Scholars, he said in "Greatness," "represent the intellect, by which man is man; the intellect and the moral sentiment,—which in the last analysis can never be separated" (*W* 8:302). In "Powers and Laws of Thought" as earlier in "Fate" he holds that "The revelation of thought takes us out of servitude into freedom. So does the sense of right" (45–46; cf. *W* 6:25, 28). In Emerson's mature view, "the spiritual power of man" is· in fact "twofold, mind and heart, Intellect and morals; one respecting truth, the other the will" (60),[14] and to both aspects of that power he remained dedicated throughout his life as a scholar.

iii. The Last Years

As Edward Emerson recognized, his father's strength had begun to fail in the late 1860s, even before he experienced difficulties in preparing his Harvard lectures. During this same period there had been other pressing demands as well: not only numerous speaking engagements but also several new publications. After *May-Day and Other Pieces* in 1867 came a two-volume collection of his *Prose Works* in 1869. Emerson contributed an introduction to an edition of Plutarch's *Morals* (*W* 10:291–322) that appeared in 1870; so too did a volume of his own, *Society and Solitude,* that he had begun to plan as early as 1860. Though "all or nearly all the essays" in the book "existed in some form as lectures in 1858 or 1859," as his son recognized, "they underwent much change during the long period of rehearsal, and sheets from them often did duty in other lectures, before the final crystallization" (*W* 7:345).[15] *Society and Solitude* appeared in both Boston and London during March of 1870 and was soon translated into German; its favorable reception justified frequent reprintings in both America and England. Carlyle, who read it "with great attention" and "clear assent for most part," praised Emerson's "calm insight," "beautiful sympathy," "*epic* humour," and inimitable style, but wished that he had taken more heed of "the frightful quantities of *friction* and perverse *impediment*" in "this Life of ours" (*CEC* 566–67).

In April and May 1871, after a winter of speaking in various cities and laboring to complete his second course at Harvard, a weary Emerson traveled west by train with his daughter Edith Forbes and her husband as guests of John Murray Forbes. While in California he lectured in both San Francisco and Oakland; during the following November he made another lecture tour to Illinois and Iowa. By this time some of his listeners had begun to complain of a lack of unity in his discourses, particularly when they observed him passing over several pages of his manuscript for every one that he read; as one Ohio reviewer of 1867 had put it, "he turned his pile of paper first one way and then the other, with an air which seemed to say, 'I don't know where to find my thought.'"[16] A San Francisco paper made a similar comment in 1871, remarking that Emerson began to read "as if at a loss whether to commence in the first page or the middle," and when he spoke in Chicago later in the year his daughter Ellen "implored him 'to write his lecture large and to give up turning over & skipping.'"[17] But in spite of his obvious problems, Emerson continued his public lecturing, though he was clearly more at ease in a series of private "Conversations" on literature, arranged by his son-in-law, William Forbes, that took place in Boston during April and May 1872.

At Amherst College on 10 July 1872 Emerson repeated an existing lecture on "Greatness of the Scholar"; later in the month came a devastating blow: fire on 24 July seriously damaged the Emerson house in Concord. Neighbors were able to save the scholar's books and papers along with most of the household furnishings, but Emerson himself never completely recovered from the shock. Generous friends not only arranged to have the house rebuilt but also provided for recuperative travel abroad while repairs were being made. The trip, which took Emerson and his daughter Ellen as far as Egypt, lasted from October 1872 until May 1873. It included Emerson's last visit with Carlyle and other old friends in England, a heavy schedule of social engagements there, and a brief talk at the Working-Men's College in London. Nearly the entire town of Concord turned out to welcome the travelers on their return home.

Before leaving for Europe in 1872 Emerson had reluctantly begun work on a volume of his uncollected writings in order to forestall an unauthorized publication that had been projected in London. Back in Concord but clearly unable to proceed, he at last "admitted the necessity of some assistance." The family, knowing that he intended to make Cabot his literary executor, persuaded him to let them ask for Cabot's help in preparing the book, *Letters and Social Aims*.[18] "Before long," as Cabot wrote afterwards in a revealing comment, Emerson

> had committed the business of selection and preparation for the press, almost entirely to me. Of course he was constantly consulted, and he would sometimes, upon urging, supply a needed word or sentence, but he was quite content to do as little as possible, and desired to leave everything in my hands. . . . What he desired was simply to bring together under the particular heading whatever could be found that seemed in place there, without regard to the connection in which it was found. This had been his own practice, and all his suggestions to me were to this effect. (*W* 8:xi, xii)

The book, dated "1876" on the title page, appeared during late December 1875 in Boston and shortly afterward in London; numerous printings followed. As of 1 September 1876, its American publisher, James R. Osgood, had contracted to pay a flat annual fee of $1,500, in lieu of further royalties, for all of Emerson's books.

Progressively failing mental powers made new composition impossible for Emerson during these years. With the aid of both Ellen Emerson and Cabot, who arranged existing manuscripts for his occasional lectures and addresses, the scholar continued to accept a limited number of speaking engagements after his return from abroad, though his public performances were a matter of great anxiety to his daughter if not to Emerson himself. On 12 May 1874, for example, he addressed the graduating class at Harvard Divinity School, and on 28 June 1876 he spoke under difficult conditions at the University of Virginia on "The Scholar" (*W* 10:259–

89). This last address was drawn principally from the "Discourse at Middlebury College" of 1845, omitting passages used in his lectures and essays on Montaigne and Goethe. He was able to appear occasionally in public as late as 1881, when, shortly after the death of Carlyle, he read briefly from a letter and journal entries about his old friend in an invited appearance before the Massachusetts Historical Society (*W* 10:487–98).

On 27 April 1882 Emerson died peacefully at his home, four weeks before his seventy-ninth birthday. Newspapers and magazines were filled with panegyrics. At his funeral, besides his family and fellow townsmen, trainloads of mourners came from beyond Concord to pay their respects to their late friend and teacher.

iv. Emerson: The Man and the Scholar

The renewed interest in Emerson that has come about during the second half of the twentieth century is attested by a steadily increasing flood of books and articles concerning him. This revival of interest, though remarkable in itself, is directly traceable to the rediscovery of the man behind the formal writings—a living man, now seen at close range as he appears in new scholarly editions: of his correspondence (1939, 1964, 1990–), of the full texts of his journals and notebooks (1960–1982), of his sermons (1938, 1989–) and early lectures (1959–1972), as well as of his published works (1971–).

Earlier editors and biographers had presented a genteel and decorous figure: "Mr. Emerson," a carefully crafted image that must seem singularly bloodless to anyone who has worked with Emerson manuscripts or with the printed materials now readily available. Especially in his lectures, as we can now see for ourselves, Emerson included more personal anecdotes and even more humor than he permitted himself in his formal essays, where he maintained a greater distance between author and reader than there had been between speaker and lecture-goer. The journals, the "Savings Bank" from which he drew the basic material of his sermons, lectures, and essays, bring the man even closer, for they record his day-to-day thinking. "Men are as they think," as he liked to say; indeed, "Life consists in what a man is thinking of all day" (*W* 12:121, 252, 10; cf. *JMN* 10:146). And as we know, Emerson patterned his own life upon the ideal image of the American Scholar as "*Man Thinking.*"

Throughout his career Emerson used the term *scholar* to include a variety of intellectual activities: those of clerics, orators, poets, philosophers, and writers generally—even traveling lecturers. "The true scholar," he held, will be perpetually a student, always learning, always thinking—not only for himself but as the cause of thinking in others; he will be a say-er as well as a see-er and thus a teacher as well as a student. The late Henry Nash Smith concluded in 1939, before most of the new editions had appeared, that Emerson's conception of the scholar "seems not to have undergone any significant evolution" during the 1840s and after, and in one sense Smith was surely correct: as late as the 1870s Emerson still thought of scholars as representing, more or less faithfully, the intellectual ideal. But by that period, in response to events of the day and to his low estimate of professional scholars among his contemporaries, his understanding of the scholar's ethics, or his "duty and discipline," and particularly of what he himself *ought* to be saying and doing as an American and a scholar, had undergone significant change.

It was during the 1840s, when the former clergyman's thinking became more secular-minded, more critical and even skeptical, that Emerson began to pay greater attention to public affairs and to reappraise his early conviction that the scholar's position with respect to current issues should be solely that of "an observer, a dispassionate reporter, no partisan." Though continually pressed to join actively in organized reform movements, especially the Anti-Slavery Society, to which his wife and many of his Concord friends belonged, he had remained disengaged, committing himself only to reform in general, as a member of what he called the Movement party, rather than to particular causes, and trusting for eventual reform to what he saw as a universal tendency in nature toward "melioration." But beginning in 1844, when he called publicly for America to follow the example of Great Britain and emancipate its slaves, he began gradually to shift his position. Passage in 1850 of the Fugitive Slave Law and its subsequent enforcement in Massachusetts presented him with a scholar's dilemma: should he simply continue his efforts to free those "quite other slaves"—imprisoned spirits and imprisoned thoughts—that he was addressing through his lectures and essays, or should he work actively for abolition?

Emerson's decision was that as a scholar, he had a moral obligation to do both, though he was scrupulous about separating his public addresses calling for action against slavery from his scheduled lectures and from his published writings. It was the imperatives of what he had long called "the moral sentiment" that finally caused him to abandon the scholar's "armed neutrality," to attack those who condoned the evil of slavery, and to castigate those individuals and educational institutions that had betrayed the scholarly ideal in an age of increasing materialism. True scholars, he said repeatedly, "represent the intellect, by which man is man"—and in that sense he regarded *every* individual as a potential scholar.

During his later and less creative years, while remaining active as a speaker and writer, Emerson drew heavily on the rich literary capital he had stored up in the 1830s and 1840s, but with some modifications. One pertinent example is a change of emphasis in his treatment of intellect and intellectuals: in 1844 he remarked, with reference to Napoleon, that "there is no crime to the intellect," which is "antinomian or hypernomian" (CW 3:45), but in the 1850s and 1860s, particularly in addressing college audiences on "the eternal topic the praise of intellect," he came more and more to emphasize his belief in "the unity of thought and morals," the oneness of intellect and the moral sentiment.

The early development of Emerson's conception of the intellectual man, epitomized in his guiding image of the Scholar, and the subsequent testing of that image in later years of crisis, for himself and for his country, have been the primary concerns of this book. "As a good chimney burns its smoke," he wrote in *Representative Men,* so a thinker like Plato "converts the value of all his fortunes into his intellectual performances" (*CW* 4:25). This conversion of experience into thought and thought into creative expression is manifest in Emerson's own thinking and writing as an American scholar.

EPILOGUE

The greatest gift of God is a Teacher and teaching is the perpetual end and office of all things.

   —Sermon 165, "Religion and Society," 27 October 1833 (*YES* 192)

THE SCHOLAR AS TEACHER

Truly speaking, it is not instruction, but provocation, that I can receive from another soul. What he announces, I must find true in me, or wholly reject.
—The Divinity School Address, 1838 (*CW* 1:80)

"To every serious mind," Emerson liked to say, "Providence sends from time to time five or six or seven teachers" (*W* 10:101; cf. *JMN* 10:300–301 and *W* 6:147). He was a graduate of Harvard College, in the class of 1821, but there was not a single Harvard professor on the private list of personal benefactors he drew up in 1836, when he was thirty-three (*JMN* 5:160). Emerson was no academic himself, though he occasionally spoke on college campuses and in the 1870s gave a course at Harvard, but many other men and women, in all walks of life and with varying amounts of schooling, looked on him as their teacher and benefactor, known to them either through his published writings or by his appearance on local lecture platforms.

When Matthew Arnold came to lecture in America, not long after Emerson's death in 1882, he recalled Emerson as one of the great "voices" heard in England during his youth and affirmed that "snatches of Emerson's strain" had continued to haunt his memory ever since. In his *Discourses in America* (1885) Arnold warmly praised this "friend and aider of those who would live in the spirit" and singled out his *Essays* as "the most important work" written in English prose during the nineteenth century.[1] As Arnold recognized, the essays aren't exactly *philosophy*; indeed, few professional philosophers later than William James and George Santayana have looked in a kindly way on Emerson, any more than professional historians of recent years have been hospitable to Henry Adams. Like Teufelsdröckh in his friend Carlyle's *Sartor Resartus,* Emerson was a "Professor of Things in General"—*Allerley Wissenschaft*—and was rightly suspicious of all compartmentalizing and departmentalizing.

As a practicing scholar, Emerson looked on specialization as necessary enough, but as a kind of necessary evil, or evil necessity. In an age of increasing specialization his American Scholar should ideally be "Man Thinking," speaking for Man to men—as a generalist rather than a specialist or narrow advocate; we might well say that the substance of the Scholar's discourse would be the substance of a liberal education. The Scholar as Teacher, having access to what Emerson calls "this original unit, this fountain of power," is one who can help others to "possess" themselves—the phrase turns up again in Emerson and also in Arnold—by returning to the same fountain, the common source accessible to every one of us (*CW* 1:53).

Here is a clue not only to Arnold's response to Emerson but to Emerson's own admiration for Milton. "Better than any other," he said in an early lecture of 1835, Milton "discharged the office of every great man, namely, to raise the idea of Man"— capital M—"in the minds of his contemporaries and of posterity." Milton was thus a master teacher of true humanism, "foremost of all men . . . in the power *to inspire*" (*EL* 1:148–49), and for Emerson the great business of books and teachers alike was "to inspire" rather than merely to instruct (*CW* 1:56). "Truly speaking," he said at Harvard in 1838, "it is not instruction, but provocation, that I can receive from another soul" (*CW* 1:80). The teacher may inspire or provoke; in the last analysis the student, responding actively and not passively, must finally *learn* for himself.

The occasion for Emerson's remark about "provocation" was his Divinity School Address of 1838. What he said then was provocative enough to shock old-guard Unitarians who looked on his liberal ideas about preaching and teaching as "the latest form of infidelity"; it would be thirty years before he was again invited to speak at Harvard. Having in effect left the ministry, Emerson would in fact have welcomed a professorship, as he freely admitted in his journal—if not at Harvard then perhaps in one of the "country colleges" like Dartmouth where he sometimes spoke; it would serve as a base of operations, he thought, and he needed the challenge of "a stated task" (*JMN* 10:28). But no such post was offered him, and in the absence of other opportunities he continued lecturing and writing, not to enrolled students in college classrooms but to a whole generation of general listeners and readers at home and abroad, inspiring and provoking an ever-widening audience as his reputation steadily grew. Like all teachers of power, moreover, he attracted a broad spectrum of students, not all of whom liked what they read and heard or stayed to finish the course.

In Cambridge and Concord, Emerson the scholar was able to teach directly— face-to-face. "What are you doing now?" he asked young Henry Thoreau of Concord in 1837. "Do you keep a journal?" Thoreau's response was prompt: "So I make my first entry to-day." A Brooklyn newspaper editor, Walt Whitman, first knew Emerson indirectly, through his books: "I was simmering, simmering, simmering," Whitman is said to have told John Townsend Trowbridge in 1860, speaking of the years before *Leaves of Grass;* "Emerson brought me to a boil." But though Emerson heated up some students like Thoreau and Whitman, others who sampled his offerings were cooled off or turned off. Nathaniel Hawthorne, his neighbor in Concord, was never sympathetic to Emerson's teachings; he wrote with amusement of how the village was "infested" by the "variety of queer, strangely dressed, oddly behaved mortals" who pursued Emerson to his home. Herman Melville, whose New York friends had warned him against Emerson's supposed obscurity, was pleasantly surprised on hearing Emerson lecture in Boston in 1849; "they told me that that night he was unusually plain," he reported.[2] For years to come, both in private jottings and in published works, Melville alternately praised and damned "this Plato who talks thro' his nose." Had Emerson "not been there both to stimulate and exasperate Herman Melville," the late Perry Miller once remarked, "*Moby-Dick* would have emerged as only another sea-story."[3] Miller no doubt exaggerated, but his basic point was well taken: Emerson could indeed both inspire and provoke—in every sense of both words. "*Emerson was their cow, but not all liked the milk.*" So ran a caption in *Time* magazine some years ago under a panel of photographs: Hawthorne, Thoreau, Whitman, and Melville, in that order, with Emerson gazing benignantly from one side.[4]

It was not only literary figures of the day who responded to Emerson. "His works, other men found, were in many respects diaries of their own which they had not kept," as Professor Lyon Richardson finely said. A good example is Rutherford B. Hayes, lawyer, soldier, congressman, thrice-elected Governor of Ohio, and later President of the United States. As a young attorney in Cincinnati, Hayes helped to arrange for Emerson's first lectures there in 1850. Emerson remained his favorite author; in Hayes' judgment he had "the best mind of our time and race."[5] As Emerson continued distilling his lectures into published essays and his readers in distant places grew increasingly eager to see and hear him, like Hayes in Ohio, his field of operations as itinerant teacher inevitably expanded. By the 1850s he was in steady demand as a lecturer, not only along the eastern seaboard as far south as Baltimore but across the Atlantic to England and Scotland in 1847–1848 and also beyond the Hudson into what was then "the West."[6] The vogue of the popular lecturer and the growth of the lyceum movement in the United States during the second quarter of the nineteenth century reflected the prevalent desire for self-improvement and the widespread interest in adult education that accompanied westward expansion and growing national prosperity. By the 1860s Emerson was making annual western tours: to Ohio, Indiana, and Illinois; to Michigan and Wisconsin; and eventually across the Mississippi to Missouri, Iowa, and Minnesota. In 1868 James Russell Lowell called him "the most steadily attractive lecturer in America."[7]

Emerson traveled west by train, stage, carriage, and boat, often under the most trying conditions; during one bitterly cold winter he crossed the frozen Mississippi four times on foot. When he made his first trip to Ohio in 1850 for his engagement in Cincinnati, he was en route by Lake Erie steamer to Sandusky when the vessel caught fire off Cleveland, where it made port safely in time for local Emersonians to assemble for an unscheduled lecture he was persuaded to give.[8] The lecture in Cleveland was free; by the 1860s the going rate for a one-night stand in the larger western cities had risen to fifty dollars. Thus Emerson's contemporary T. Starr King, when asked what he lectured for, answered: "FAME—Fifty and My Expenses."[9] Emerson himself wrote of lecturing in the West as an annual wager: "'I'll bet you fifty dollars a day for three weeks, that you will not leave your library & wade & freeze & ride & run, & suffer all manner of indignities, & stand up for an hour each night reading in a hall:' and I answered, 'I'll bet I will,' I do it, & win the $900" (*JMN* 15:457).[10]

Early in January of 1856, after a week of temperatures "varying from 20 to 30 degrees below zero," Emerson observed that the climate and people of the West

are a new test for the wares of a man of letters. . . . At the lyceum, the stout Illinoian, after a short trial, walks out of the hall. The Committee tell you that the people want a hearty laugh, and [those] who give them that, are heard with joy. . . . [T]hese are the new conditions to which I must conform. . . . And Shakspeare or Franklin or Aesop coming to Illinois, would say, I must give my wisdom a comic form, instead of tragics or elegiacs. (*JMN* 14:27–28)

Emerson's words seem prophetic of Mark Twain, who in the late 1850s, as Samuel L. Clemens of Missouri, was learning to be a riverboat pilot on the Mississippi, his other vocation as lecturer and writer being still some years before him.

In the course of a long career Emerson filled nearly 1,500 lecture engagements in twenty-two states and Canada plus his lectures in England and Scotland. Some cities and towns brought him back repeatedly. He spoke on many subjects, from popular science, biography, and literature in the early 1830s to an address on Carlyle in 1881, the year before his death. During the 1850s, when he appeared most often, he was giving more than fifty lectures every winter; in the 1860s both his platform reputation and his fees reached their highest peak.

Apart from local newspaper reviews, which varied widely in tone, some of the best testimony about what it was like to hear Emerson speak comes from younger contemporaries who attended his lectures repeatedly from their student days into middle age—men of letters such as Lowell, George William Curtis, and E. P. Whipple. With younger listeners in the early years, if not with their elders or the authorities of Harvard, Emerson was immediately popular; for Lowell and his generation he became "our favorite teacher." An older man once told Curtis that though *he* couldn't understand "Mr. Emerson," "my daughters do."[11] Emerson himself quickly recognized the difference in generations. He remembered a question his uncle Samuel Ripley had asked him years before, when as a boy of thirteen he had done his first actual teaching in his uncle's school: "How is it, Ralph, that all the boys dislike you & quarrel with you, whilst the grown people are fond of you?" "Now am I thirty six," Emerson reflected in the year after the Divinity School affair, "and the fact is reversed,—the old people suspect & dislike me, & the young love me" (*JMN* 7:253).

What the young people liked and understood in their teacher was less the explicit message than the spirit of the man who spoke it; as Lowell explained, "We do not go to hear what Emerson says so much as to hear Emerson." Certainly they did not go for cheap popularization or sidewinding oratory, though both were common enough at a time when public speakers customarily performed with all stops out. Emerson seldom spoke extemporaneously or even from notes; he preferred to read from a prepared manuscript, though in his later years, as I have noted above, he had a disconcerting habit of shuffling his pages about while he was talking. His delivery was simple and even conversational; in speaking he was "apt to hesitate in the course of a sentence," according to the senior Oliver Wendell Holmes, as though "picking his way through his vocabulary, to get at the best expression of his thought." "There was no rhetoric, no gesture, . . . no dramatic familiarity and action," said Curtis, "but the manner was self-respectful and courteous to the audience, and the tone supremely just and sincere."[12]

Moncure Conway agreed: Emerson depended not on "tricks of any kind" but rather on "clearness of thought and simplicity of statement." The elder Henry James emphasized his modesty and grace on the platform, recalling

> his deferential entrance upon the scene, his look of inquiry at the desk and the chair, his resolute rummaging among his embarrassed papers, the air of sudden recollection with which he would plunge into his pockets for what he must have known had never been put there, for his uncertainty and irresolution as he rose to speak, his deep, relieved inspiration as he got well from under the burning glass of his auditors' eyes, and addressed himself at length to their docile ears instead. . . . And then when he looked over the heads of his audience into the dim mysterious distance, and his weird monotone began to reverberate in your bosom's depths, and his words flowed on, now with a river's volume, grand, majestic, free, and anon diminished themselves to the fitful cadence of a brook . . . and you saw the clear eye eloquent with nature's purity, and beheld the musing countenance turned within, as it were, and hearkening to the rumour of a far-off but on-coming world:

it was all "intensely personal," James continued, and also "exquisitely characteristic" of Emerson the man.[13]

Audiences everywhere were particularly struck with Emerson's voice. It had "a strange power," said E. P. Whipple, "which affected me more than any other voice I ever heard on the stage or on the platform." Holmes described it as "never loud, never shrill, but singularly penetrating," observing that "the music of his speech pleased those who found his thought too subtle for their dull wits to follow." However entranced by Emerson's way of speaking, few of his auditors grasped everything they had listened to or even agreed with what they thought he had said. Hawthorne's son Julian recalled leaving the lecture room in Concord one evening when he overheard "Prescott, the grocer, say to Jonas Hastings, the shoemaker, 'Did you get that about the Oversoul?' . . . Jonas . . . shook his head: 'No use wondering what he means; we know he's giving us the best there is.'"[14]

At the other end of the spectrum there was downright hostility, particularly when Emerson ventured outside New England. In Wisconsin, for example, the Kenosha *Democrat* stigmatized him in 1860 as "an infidel—an abolitionist—a monarchist—all these, though he talk as musically as any dying swan."[15] Some unenthusiastic listeners, like the "stout Illinoian" Emerson himself mentioned, simply walked out of the hall. Those who stayed enjoyed Emerson's quiet humor, more characteristic of his lectures than of his published essays.[16] They especially liked the illustrative anecdotes "that sparkled for a moment upon the surface of his talk," as

Curtis remarked, "and some sat inspired with unknown resolves, soaring upon lofty hopes."[17]

By the 1860s, when Emerson had become something of an institution, Lowell felt that younger members of the audience were taking him for granted, failing to realize what they owed to him; their elders, Lowell said, better recognized "how much the country's intellectual emancipation was due to the stimulus of his teaching and example." Curtis, who was a successful lecturer himself, put the same idea somewhat differently. Emerson, he said,

> was never exactly popular, but always gave a tone and flavor to the whole lyceum course. . . . "We can have him once in three or four seasons," said the committees. But really they had him all the time without knowing it. He was the philosopher Proteus, and he spoke through all the more popular mouths. . . . They were . . . the middlemen between him and the public. They watered the nectar, and made it easy to drink.[18]

Like all teachers, especially those who teach other teachers, the scholar thus reached students even at second or third hand. "A teacher affects eternity," said Henry Adams in *The Education;* "he can never tell where his influence stops" (chapter 20). The thought is disturbing, since "when?" and "how?" and "by what channels?" and "to what effect?" are questions difficult to answer on any chart or evaluation, however well intentioned. Doubtless Emerson himself, who thought a discourse should have some edge to it, wasn't too troubled when the response of listeners and readers was not unanimously favorable, though the outburst occasioned by the Divinity School Address proved more than he had quite bargained for. Religious conservatives then and now have protested against his liberal theology. When he lectured in Scotland in 1848 he was accused of being a pantheist.[19] At Columbus, Ohio, in 1867, a local Presbyterian minister preached against his appearance there, saying that "he had not expected to live to see the time when a Presbyterian pulpit would be disgraced by Ralph Waldo Emerson lecturing from it."[20] Among twentieth-century critics, Yvor Winters called Emerson and the Transcendentalists "moral parasites upon a Christian doctrine which they were endeavoring to destroy," and Randall Stewart stigmatized him as "the arch-heretic of American literature." On the other extreme, the obvious vestiges of clericalism in Emerson have always offended the secular-minded. D. H. Lawrence, for example, admired "Emerson's real courage," but disliked the limitations of his idealism. In Lawrence's words, "all those gorgeous inrushes of exaltation and spiritual energy which made Emerson a great man, now make us sick," and some contemporary readers agree.[21]

There has been a similar difference of opinion about scholar's political and social views, which have also offended the extreme left and the extreme right of two centuries. In the 1840s, as we have seen, Emerson inclined toward the principles of what he called "the Movement party" (CW 1:172) rather than toward the conservatism of "the establishment" (*CW* 1:190, 195), but he was never a partisan in the conventional sense. His increasing antipathy to slavery led him to support Free-Soil candidates and later to gravitate toward the new Republican party, though for a long time he resisted identification with the abolitionist movement. But believing as he did that slavery was flatly wrong, and seeing its evil increasingly compounded by abridgement of the right of free speech and coercion of Northern freemen as well as of Southern slaves, he ultimately found himself endorsing even John Brown's use of violence in retaliation. And so during the 1850s the peace-loving teacher became a militant activist, remaining so for the duration of the Civil War.

If Emerson's moral activism seems inconsistent with his vocational role, it was not altogether out of character for a man who had insisted in his first published book that "The moral law lies at the centre of nature and radiates to the circumference" (*CW* 1:26). To condone slavery was unnatural and immoral, a denial of human worth and dignity and freedom; he *must* stand up and be counted with the opposition. "I divide men as aspirants & desperants," he wrote to Holmes in 1856, adding that

> A scholar need not be cynical to feel that the vast multitude are almost on all fours; that the rich always vote after their fears[;] that cities churches colleges all go for the quadruped interest, and it is against this coalition that the pathetically small minority of disengaged or thinking men stand for the ideal right, for man as he should be, & . . . for the right of every other as for his own. (*L* 5:17)

And in 1863 he told a college audience that "A scholar defending the cause of slavery, of arbitrary government, of monopoly, of the oppressor, is a traitor to his profession. He has ceased to be a scholar" (*W* 10:247).

However one may judge Emerson's reluctant foray into public affairs, his prolonged engagement with moral issues at considerable cost to his own peace and prosperity illustrates what he liked to call "the Scholar's courage"—courage that "should grow out of his conversation with spiritual nature" (*JMN* 10:28; 12:607). Here is the basis of his cardinal principle of self-reliance. To borrow a phrase from David Riesman's *The Lonely Crowd*, he was an *inner-directed* man, living from within. What he regarded as "the moral law of human nature" he had enunciated as early as 1833, when he was thirty:

> A man contains all that is needful to his government within himself. He is made a law unto himself. All real good or evil that can befal him must be from himself. He only can do himself any good or any harm. . . . The purpose of life seems to be to acquaint a man with himself. . . . The highest revelation is that God is in every man. (*JMN* 4:84)

On this moral and religious basis Emerson deplored imitation of any model however fine and refused conformity to all wholly external patterns, rituals, creeds, sects, parties, precedents, curricula, or institutions of any kind, including churches, colleges, and governments. The law he followed, though wholly internal, was rigorous: "If any one imagines that this law is lax," as he said in "Self-Reliance," "let him keep its commandment one day" (CW 2:42). When a man can look within and "read God directly," as "The American Scholar" has it, the hour is too precious for secondhand readings (CW 1:57). On this same basis, looking back with a measure of detachment on the Divinity School controversy—that "storm in our wash-bowl," as he called it (CEC 196), he could write in 1840 that "In all my lectures I have taught one doctrine, namely, the infinitude of the private man" (JMN 7:342).

This "one doctrine" lay at the vital center of the scholar's teaching over a lifetime, whether the subject addressed was religion, morality, or teaching itself. Emerson's conception of "the private man" was essentially religious, idealistic, and optimistic. Where "desperants" such as his Puritan forebears and his less sanguine contemporaries stressed the finite limitations of humanity, as in the fiction of Hawthorne and Melville, his own abiding impulse, like that of Thoreau and Whitman, was to emphasize mankind's infinite potential, though the experience of his middle years brought him to an increasing realization of the limiting power of circumstance. By temperament Emerson was an idealist, an "aspirant." But as his journals reveal, he was forever being reminded of that "yawning gulf" that stretches "between the ambition of man and his power of performance," and it is this disparity between desire and capacity that for him "makes the tragedy of all souls" (CW 4:103), a tragedy all too frequently compounded by distorted aims and wasted forces.

If the purpose of life, as Emerson thought, is "to acquaint a man with himself," the purpose of a teacher should be to foster one's full realization, in every sense, of his or her own worth and potential. This is the burden of the lectures and addresses in which Emerson touches in some way on learning and teaching: the Address on Education and "The American Scholar" of 1837, the Divinity School Address and "Literary Ethics" of 1838, the lecture on "Education" of 1840, and the addresses to college audiences of the 1850s and 1860s, notably "The Celebration of Intellect." Relevant too are such essays of 1841 and 1844 as "Self-Reliance," "Spiritual Laws," "The Over-Soul," "Intellect," and "The Poet," this last with its Emersonian emphasis on the human need for self-expression—"It is in me, and shall out" (CW 3:23)—that not only brought Walt Whitman to a boil but also anticipated the teachings of John Dewey.

Emerson's thinking about education, being of a piece with his general ideas, was essentially religious in character, though it has obvious secular implications and applications. To educate means to draw out; Emerson complained that "We do not believe in a power of Education. We do not think we can call out God in man and we do not try" (EL 3:290; cf. CW 2:158). His own basic objective, to "call out God in man," was not inherently different from that of the builders of medieval universities or nineteenth- century church-related colleges. Like them, he believed that religion and learning spring from a common source. He delighted to celebrate that source, that "original unit" and "fountain of power," as he called it in "The American Scholar," common to all individuals and linking them both with Man—again, capital *M*—and also with Nature.

Every human being, Emerson believed, stands "in need of expression," students and teachers included: "In love, in art, in avarice, in politics, in labor, in games, we study to utter our painful secret" (*CW* 3:4). It is no different in teaching, though what a teacher expresses, he felt, is less what he *knows* than what he *is*. For him there were two kinds of teachers, whether "sacred or literary": those who "speak *from within*, or from experience," and therefore teach with firsthand knowledge and authority; and those who speak only "*from without*, as spectators merely," on the basis of secondhand evidence (*CW* 2:170). For him, only the former—Emerson's "true scholars"—deserve the name of teacher. Like Alfred North Whitehead in our own century, Emerson protested against dead knowledge—what Whitehead in *The Aims of Education* (1929) would call "inert ideas."[22]

"Life, authentic life, you must have," Emerson insisted, "or you can teach nothing" (*JMN* 7:27). If life and power are present within, they will manifest themselves outwardly, whether by our conscious intention or otherwise. "That which we are, we shall teach," he wrote, "not voluntarily but involuntarily. . . . Character teaches over our head" (*CW* 2:169). "If a teacher have any opinion which he wishes to conceal, his pupils will become as fully indoctrinated into that as into any which he publishes" (*CW* 2:85). Again: "The man may teach by doing, and not otherwise. If he can communicate himself, he can teach, but not by words. He teaches who gives, and he learns who receives" (*CW* 2:88).

Since for Emerson a student's self-realization meant self-reliance, he reminded himself of "the cardinal virtue of a teacher" exemplified by Socrates: "to protect the pupil from his own influence" (*JMN* 10:471). Neither teachers nor parents should try to make duplicates of themselves, he cautioned in his lecture of 1840 on "Education" (*EL* 3:294–95). "Get off that child! You are trying to make that man another you. One is enough"—so his friend Moncure Conway remembered Emerson's words. Writing of Emerson's powerful stimulation of a variety of writers differing in both their aim and their style, Conway rightly observed that "they who came to his fontless baptism were never made Emersonians."[23] His words would have pleased Emerson himself, who in his later years remarked in his journal that

I have been writing & speaking what were once called novelties, for twenty five or thirty years, & have not now one disciple. Why? Not that what I said was not true; not that it has not found intelligent receivers but because it did not go from any wish in me to bring men to me, but to themselves. I delight in driving them from me. . . . This is my boast that I have no school & no follower. I should account it a measure of the impurity of insight, if it did not create independence. (*JMN* 14:258)

Independence, self-reliance, self-knowledge, self-expression, self-fulfillment—

these were the "novelties" that Emerson taught as writer and lecturer, whatever his subjects and courses, and the lesson was heard and repeated. By recurrent challenge and by cumulative example, Emerson the scholar provoked and inspired and *educated* his students—and in turn his students' students—to walk on their own feet, to work with their own hands, to speak their own minds (cf. *JMN* 1:70), just as every great teacher invariably does. Indeed he is no teacher unless, like Emerson, he truly creates independence.

NOTES

Let [the scholar] open his breast to all honest inquiry. . . . [To the scholar:]
Show frankly . . . all your experience, your methods, tools, and means. Welcome all comers to the freest use of the same.

—"Literary Ethics" (*CW* 1:114)

Notes to Introduction

1. Robert E. Spiller, "From Lecture into Essay: Emerson's Method of Composition,"
28.
2. Henry James (1843–1916), "Emerson," 20.
3. Henry Nash Smith, "Emerson's Problem of Vocation: A Note on 'The American
Scholar,'" 58, 59.
4. See Smith, "Emerson's Problem of Vocation," 62.
5. Such studies were characteristic of the 1950s and early 1960s; see, respectively,
Sherman Paul on "correspondence" in *Emerson's Angle of Vision: Man and Nature in American
Experience* (1952); Stephen E. Whicher, *Freedom and Fate: An Inner Life of Ralph Waldo Emerson*
(1953); Paul Lauter, "Truth and Nature: Emerson's Use of Two Complex Words" (1960);
Philip L. Nicoloff, *Emerson on Race and History: An Examination of English Traits* (1961); James
Emanuel, "Emersonian Virtue: A Definition" (1961); Henry F. Pommer, "The Contents
and Basis of Emerson's Belief in Compensation" (1962); Jonathan Bishop, *Emerson on the Soul*
(1964).
6. Smith, "Emerson's Problem of Vocation," 66.

Notes to Chapter 1

1. Ralph L. Rusk, *The Life of Ralph Waldo Emerson*, 167.
2. Rusk, *Life*, 26.
3. Arthur Cushman McGiffert, Introduction to *YES*, xxxiv.
4. Rusk, *Life*, 89.
5. Rusk, *Life*, 108.
6. Rusk, *Life*, 112; Gay Wilson Allen, *Waldo Emerson: A Biography*, 84; John McAleer,
Ralph Waldo Emerson: Days of Encounter, 82–83; Evelyn Barish, "The Moonless Night," 10,
14.
7. Moncure Daniel Conway, *Emerson at Home and Abroad*, 42, 43.
8. Rusk, *Life*, 149; Henry F. Pommer, *Emerson's First Marriage*, 67.
9. In his ground-breaking article of 1931, "Emerson and Science," Harry Hayden
Clark inferred from Emerson's journal of 1832 that "the immediate influence" encouraging his resignation from the Second Church "was that of writers on astronomy such as

Mary Somerville, author of the *Mechanisms of the Heavens,* and especially J. F. W. Herschel" (234).

10. "That Emerson as a young preacher did not abandon belief in miracles arises in part from the transitional character of his thinking," according to McGiffert. His mind "was the stage on which struggled for supremacy two theories of the universe"—i.e., static mechanism and dynamic organicism (note to Sermon 103, *YES* 239–40). Elsewhere McGiffert remarks that once Emerson came to think of an organic universe and an immanent God he lost touch with his congregation, "brought up as he himself had been brought up. . . . He and his people belonged to two different worlds of thought" (*YES* 221).

11. In the third chapter of *"The Strains of Eloquence": Emerson and His Sermons* (especially 68–78), Mott traces the gradual development of this theme. As early as 1839 Emerson had ended his Sermon 43 with what Mott terms his "willful, telling revision of the Gospel definition of Emmanuel: Matthew's 'God with us' (Mt 1:23) becomes 'this literal Emmanuel *God within us*'" (68).

12. Rusk, *Life,* 153.

Notes to Chapter 2

1. The journal entry of 6 January 1832 (*JMN* 3:315–16), a kind of bench mark for surveying the development of Emerson's maturing thought, begins:

> Shall I not write a book on topics such as follow
> Chap. 1 That the mind is its own place
> Chap. 2. That exact justice is done
> Chap. 3. That good motives are at the bottom of ⟦many⟧ bad
>   actions.   ↑e.g. 'Business before friends'↓
> Chap. 4. That the Soul is immortal
> Chap. 5. On prayers
> Chap. 6 That the best is the true.
> Chap. 7 That the Mind discerns all things.
> Chap 8. That the Mind seeks itself in all things.
> Chap. 9 That truth is its own warrant.

The topic for the projected first chapter is an allusion to the opening book of *Paradise Lost,* where Satan, newly arrived in Hell, boasts that his mind will never "be chang'd by Place or time": "The mind is its own place, and in itself / Can make a Heav'n of Hell, a Hell of Heav'n" (1.253–55). An avowed Miltonist, Emerson surely remembered also that the poet wrote later of the fallen archangel:

> within him Hell
> He brings, and round about him, nor from Hell
> One step no more than from himself can fly
> By change of place.
>
>   (4.20–24)

The second chapter would have been that "discourse on Compensation" that Emerson had wanted to write ever since he was a boy, as he remarked in 1841 (*CW* 2:55); here, in the following day's journal entry, he affirms his belief in "a perfect system of compensations, that exact justice is done" (*JMN* 3:317).

2. "Which way I fly is Hell," cries Milton's Satan; "myself am Hell" (*Paradise Lost* 4.75). Emerson's subjective assertion of "the indifference of places," an essentially Stoic idea

evidently fostered by his reading of Milton, is repeated in *Nature,* which rings changes on the early observation that "Nature always wears the colors of the spirit" (*CW* 1:10).

3. During his homeward voyage Emerson had been asked by a fellow passenger to define the term *Morals.* "I cannot define & care not to define," he declared in a journal entry of 17 September 1833. "It is man's business to observe & the definition of Moral Nature must be the slow result of years, of lives, of states perhaps of being. Yet in the morning watch on my berth I thought that Morals is the science of the laws of human action as respects right & wrong." Granting that his conceptions of "Right" were "dim & vague," he asserted that nothing hindered his "constant conviction of the eternal con-cord of those laws. . . . Milton describes himself in his letter to Diodati as enamoured of moral perfection. He did not love it more than I. That which I cannot yet declare has been my angel from childhood until now. . . . It is the soul of religion" (*JMN* 4:86–87).

4. "The two conditions of Teaching," Emerson was to write in December of 1834, "are, 1. That none can teach more than he knows. 2. That none can teach ⟨more⟩ ↑faster↓ than the scholar can learn. Two conditions more: 1. He must say that they can under-stand. 2. But he must say that which is given to *him*" (*JMN* 4:348).

5. "If science was always of secondary interest to Emerson," Clark also remarked in "Emerson and Science," "this fact should not prevent us from recognizing the important function of science in suggesting novel *reinforcement* for views which were primarily, I think, native, Christian, classical, Oriental, romantic, or transcendental" (229). For a reaffirmation of Clark's findings in the light of more recent scholarship, see Gay Wilson Allen, "A New Look at Emerson and Science."

6. For further discussion of Emerson's response to the scientific exhibits he saw in Paris, see David M. Robinson, "Emerson's Natural Theology and the Paris Naturalists: Toward a Theory of Animated Nature."

7. Emerson and his mother rented rooms from Mr. and Mrs. Bethuel Allen; Mrs. Allen, it now appears, was the mother of Herman Melvill's half-sister. See Henry A. Murray, Harvey Myerson, and Eugene Taylor, "Allan Melvill's By-Blow," which repro-duces a nineteenth-century drawing of the Allen house, and Philip Young, "Small World: Emerson, Longfellow, and Melville's Secret Sister."

8. Carl F. Strauch, "The Year of Emerson's Poetic Maturity: 1834," 353.

9. Clark, "Emerson and Science," points out that the "technical botanizing" antedates Emerson's acquaintance with Thoreau (248–49). Clark's article assesses not only the influence of Emerson's reading but also that of friends and acquaintances who shared his interest in natural history and science.

10. See Carl F. Strauch, "Emerson's Phi Beta Kappa Poem."

Notes to Chapter 3

1. The manuscript of the introductory lecture having disappeared, the discussion here is based on surviving notes printed in *EL* 1:424–25.

2. In a letter to Charles Godfrey Leland, 23 December 1861, acknowledging that Goethe's influence was operative "twenty years ago." See Kenneth Walter Cameron, "A Sheaf of Emerson Letters," 477.

3. Stephen E. Whicher, *Freedom and Fate: An Inner Life of Ralph Waldo Emerson,* 66.

4. "The division of Philosopher and Poet is only apparent, and to the disadvantage of both," Thomas Carlyle had written in his "Novalis," *Foreign Review* 4 (1829): 129. "It is a sign of disease, and of a sickly constitution." Emerson in turn had cited Carlyle in 1834 as

"an exemplification of Novalis's maxim concerning the union of Poetry & Philosophy. He has married them, & both are the gainers. . . . Sartor Resartus is a philosophical Poem" (*JMN* 4:302).

5. In this same journal entry, dated 14 May 1835, Emerson asks himself:

> Can you not express your one conviction that moral laws hold? Have you not thoughts & illustrations that are your own; the parable of geometry & matter; the reason why the atmosphere is transparent; the power of Composition in nature & in man's thoughts; the Uses & uselessness of travelling; the law of Compensation; the transcendant excellence of truth in character, in rhetoric, in things; the sublimity of Self-reliance; and the rewards of perseverance in the best opinion? Have you not a testimony to give for Shakspear, for Milton? one ⟨penny weight⟩ ↑sentence↓ of real praise of Jesus, is worth a century of legendary Christianity. Can you not write as though you wrote to yourself & drop the ⟨seed⟩ token assured that a wise hand will pick it up? (*JMN* 5:40)

Emerson's survey of his key ideas in this passage testifies to the continuity of his thought between the early 1830s and the *Essays* of 1841.

6. For an analysis of Journal RO Mind in the light of Emerson's problem of vocation, see Richard Lee Francis, "Morn at Mid Noon: The Emerging Emersonian Method." Francis regards this brief journal as "a pivotal exploration by the Preacher turning Poet." Here, he writes, Emerson was "moving toward the realization of the Transparent Eyeball" in *Nature* (see *CW* 1:10), "which would give him the perspective of double vision, of inner and outer consciousness, that would permit him to see and to meditate on the dual existence of Man as thinking and acting being" (8).

7. Journal B; see *JMN* 5:79–80: the continuation of an entry begun on 2 August 1835. There are two citations under "Scholar" to Journal A (1833–1834), pp. 119 and 137; see *JMN* 4:353–54 and 369–70.

8. The entry illustrates Emerson's method of assembling congruent manuscript materials for use in his lectures and essays. In 1834 he had written that the scholar stands as the imperfect representative of "the intellectual man"—that "real object in Nature to which the grocer's reverence instinctively turns" (*JMN* 4:370); in this entry the grocer reappears, but it is now the *writer* who represents "the intellectual man." As he had said in his August address to the American Institute of Instruction, scholars and poets, like soldiers and sailors, are born and not made; in the lecture he declares once more that the *writer's* character is "founded on natural gifts as specific & rare as military genius." In the previous February, using an Italian phrase he had picked up from Coleridge, he had described Michelangelo's view of beauty as "*il piu nell' uno,* i.e. the many in one or Multitude in Unity, intimating . . . that what is truly beautiful seems related to all nature" (*EL* 1:101); he now affirms that the man of letters too has power "to form *il piu nell' uno.*"

Emerson also draws repeatedly on personal experience in characterizing the man of letters. In July of 1835 he had written introspectively, "I study the art of solitude. I yield me as gracefully as I can to my destiny" (*JMN* 5:58); now it is *the man of letters* who "studies the art of solitude." (In that same earlier journal entry it is "the man of genius" who "shows the world of thought to be infinite again which you had supposed exhausted"; now it is once more "the man of letters.") In December of 1834 Emerson had confessed that he "could not go into conversation with any person of good understanding without being presently gravelled," explaining that to be faced with even the slightest question from another individual disconcerted him "beyond recovery" (*JMN* 4:354); now the literary man is similarly "gravelled in every discourse with common people."

Such revisions illustrate Emerson's characteristic practice of moving from the particular and personal to the universal, converting his private experience into general truths.

9. Concerning the first lecture on Shakespeare, originally read on 10 December 1835, the editors of *EL* remark: "The entire passage on language and the nature of the imagination [*EL* 1:289–91] . . . is a revision, presumably for a later reading, with an insertion [the passage quoted above] from Lecture 1 of this series and from 'The Uses of Natural History.' Most of this material in turn went into *Nature*, chiefly the chapter 'Language,' which thus has a complicated manuscript history, now partly lost" (1:287: headnote).

10. Emerson is adapting a favorite remark of Bacon from *The Advancement of Learning*: poesy "doth raise and erect the mind, by submitting the shows of things to the desires of the mind; whereas reason doth buckle and bow the mind unto the nature of things"; see *JMN* 3:247; 5:190; *EL* 1:162.

11. Emerson reverts to the more conventional implications of the term *scholar* in the ninth lecture of the series, "Ethical Writers": "Many of the English writers of most reputation in their day have been prodigious scholars, readers of all unchosen learning, and have claimed and received fame from the number of the books they have read. Such is . . . a merit which only scholars can understand and very subordinate when unaccompanied by other accomplishments. These are the clerks and librarians of the Muses. It is a merit that excites a species of admiration among superficial readers, because their own impatience of a book raises their reverence for a thorough scholar." Then he adds that this is "not a merit which a philosopher will highly prize" (*EL* 1:357).

12. Early in 1832 Emerson had first discovered Carlyle's articles and books on German literature; by October of that year he was proposing "to read Schiller of whom I hear much" (*JMN* 4:54–55). He shared these new enthusiasms with his brother Charles, introducing him to the "Specimens of German Genius" that had appeared serially in the *New Monthly Magazine* for 1830. Charles particularly liked "a story from Goethe" and "a character of the true scholar, the man of genius, by Schiller" (Ralph L. Rusk, *The Life of Ralph Waldo Emerson,* 165); Waldo himself copied extracts from the "Specimens" (*JMN* 6:107–9), including part of a lecture by Schiller that contrasts the plans for study proposed by "the philosopher" on the one hand and "the trader in science & literature" on the other (*JMN* 6:107). Presumably Emerson was thinking of this same passage when he wrote in 1834 of Schiller as "prescribing the ethics of the Scholar" (*JMN* 4:367).

Notes to Chapter 4

1. "We are among the sepulchres of our fathers," Webster had declared in *An Address Delivered at the Laying of the Corner Stone of the Bunker Hill Monument* (Boston, 1825); the address is among works listed in Emerson's Journal 1826 (*JMN* 3:38).

2. Sherman Paul, *Emerson's Angle of Vision: Man and Nature in American Experience,* offers a comprehensive treatment of Emerson's patterns of visual imagery.

3. The quoted sentence comes from Coleridge's "Preliminary Treatise on Method"; see *JMN* 5:114, and "Spiritual Laws," *CW* 2:84, and compare *Nature, CW* 1:24 ("progressive arrangement"). In "The Growth of the Soul: Coleridge's Dialectical Method and the Strategy of Emerson's *Nature,*" Barry Wood provides an admirable discussion of the book's specific indebtedness to Coleridge.

4. For Bishop's discussion, quoted here and below, see his *Emerson on the Soul,* 10–15.

5. Cranch's several illustrations of *Nature* are reproduced and discussed in F. DeWolfe Miller, *Christopher Pearse Cranch and His Caricatures of New England Transcendentalism,* 38–44.

6. As Bishop remarks in *Emerson on the Soul* (223 n. 14), there is a "source" for the eye image—or at least an analogue—in Plotinus, who held that in the intelligible world

"everybody is pure, and each inhabitant is, as it were, an eye." See John S. Harrison, *The Teachers of Emerson*, 105. On the *tone* of Emerson's passage on "the transparent eye-ball," see Barbara Packer's comments in "Uriel's Cloud: Emerson's Rhetoric."

7. In an 1856 printing Emerson substituted "parcel" for "particle"; *CW* restores the "particle" of the 1836 and 1849 printings.

8. "Have you not thoughts & illustrations that are your own?" Emerson had asked himself in 1835, citing—among other motifs he was to use in *Nature*—"the reason why the atmosphere is transparent" (*JMN* 5:40; the passage is quoted above in chapter 3 n. 5). On "the notion of the 'transparent'" as signifying *transcendence*, see Kenneth Burke, "I, Eye, Ay—Emerson's Early Essay 'Nature': Thoughts on the Machinery of Transcendence," 13–14. For another discussion of Emerson's terminology, which appears to derive in part from his reading of David Brewster, *The Life of Sir Isaac Newton* (1831), see B[arbara]. L. Packer, *Emerson's Fall: A New Interpretation of the Major Essays*, 72–78.

9. "One and all"—that is, a single event or fact that epitomizes the universe (*JMN* 5:128 and n. 393), "an Epiphany of God" (*JMN* 7:29). The scholar, Emerson had recently written, "knows all by one" (*JMN* 5:117); like Michelangelo, he sees—or forms—"*il piu nell' uno*," or "Multitude in Unity" (*EL* 1:101). Emerson quoted the Italian phrase in chapter 3, "Beauty," echoing his own poem "Each and All" in adding that "Nothing is quite beautiful alone: nothing but is beautiful in the whole" (*CW* 1:17); in chapter 5, "Discipline," alluding to Xenophanes, he recurs to the idea of nature's "Unity in Variety" (*CW* 1:27).

10. "The Imagination is Vision," Emerson wrote in a journal entry of 1 August 1835; it "regards the world as symbolical & pierces the emblem for the real sense, ↑sees all external objects as types↓" (*JMN* 5:76). Cyrus Bartol fittingly wrote of Emerson following his friend's death as "a perceiver" who used "his imagination for an eye" ("Emerson's Religion" 145).

11. The common misconception that Emerson wrote all or most of *Nature* before 1836, the year of its publication, is traceable in part to "The Old Manse," Nathaniel Hawthorne's prefatory sketch opening his *Mosses from an Old Manse* (1846), in which "The Author Makes the Reader Acquainted with His Abode." There Hawthorne recalled the small writing room at the rear of the old house at Concord to which he had brought his wife in 1842. It was "the most delightful little nook of a study that ever afforded its snug seclusion to a scholar," he declared, adding that in the very same room "Emerson wrote 'Nature'" while he was an earlier inhabitant of the house (5). The implication is that *Nature* was composed during that period of roughly eleven months when Emerson and his mother were living with Dr. Ripley in Concord, from October of 1834 until Emerson's second marriage on 14 September 1835. But in 1887, after Emerson's death, James Elliot Cabot in his *Memoir of Ralph Waldo Emerson* "conjectured" that the first five chapters of *Nature* had "been for some time in hand" even before the removal to Concord, where the seventh and eighth chapters "seem to have been written" next and "the sixth, Idealism, last of all, as the connection of the two" (1:259).

Cabot's conjectures about the composition of *Nature*, tentative as they were, have been widely accepted as fact even in recent years, when the editing of new scholarly texts of Emerson's writings has uncovered information unavailable to earlier commentators. For example, the editors of an anthology widely used in colleges and universities have gone well beyond Cabot, stating without qualification that Emerson had "already written five chapters" of *Nature* by the time he settled in the Manse, so that what he did "in the very room in which Hawthorne later wrote his *Mosses from an Old Manse*" was to complete "the first draft"; see Sculley Bradley, Richmond Croom Beatty, E. Hudson Long, and George Perkins, eds., *The American Tradition in Literature*, 4th ed. (1974), 1:1040 n. 1.

12. Journal and lecture passages used in the successive chapters of *Nature* are listed and dated in Merton M. Sealts, Jr., and Alfred R. Ferguson, eds., *Emerson's 'Nature': Origin, Growth, Meaning* (1979 ed.), 46–65, and tabulated more briefly in *CW* 1:269–73. Sealts and Ferguson quote in full the earlier formulations of material used in the key chapter on "Language" in order "to bring out their central importance in Emerson's emerging conception of the book he wanted to write" (46). As Robert E. Spiller and Alfred R. Ferguson explain in *CW* with respect to Emerson's methodology, "a given passage or reference could appear several times" after its initial entry in his journal or other manuscript. "Sometimes the used passage would appear in the new context almost verbatim, but more frequently it would be edited in varying degrees. . . . A prose work by Emerson must therefore be regarded as *a composition*—in the sense that one speaks of a musical composition or the composition of a painting—rather than as a piece of exposition or argument developed logically at a single sitting" (*CW* 1:331; emphasis added).

13. From Friedrich Schleiermacher, by way of his friend Hedge, Emerson had picked up the term *Ascetic*, defined as "the discipline of life produced by the opinions" (*JMN* 4:360), and he had used it in his journal as recently as 5 March 1836 (*JMN* 5:135). "I think the Scholar's Ascetic ought to be systematically and gen[era]ally taught," he told Hedge on 14 March (*L* 2:7).

14. Whether in kitchens and cottages or in parlors and fashionable society, Emerson had written on 22 May 1836, the talk "is exclusively occupied with . . . the sickness, crimes, disasters, airs, fortunes of persons; never is the character of the action or the object abstracted." Among "the cultivated class," however, "in proportion to their cultivation," there is "a studious separation of personal history from their analysis of character & their study of things. Natural History is elegant, astronomy sublime for this reason, their impersonality. And yet when cultivated men speak of God they demand a biography of him as steadily as the kitchen & the bar room demand personalities of men" (*JMN* 5:162).

15. When the two concluding paragraphs of "Discipline" are read in connection with their immediate sources in the journal it becomes clear that Emerson was acknowledging his indebtedness not only to his brother but to other men and women as well. On 19 May 1836 he named eight of that "scattered company" who had "ministered to my highest wants": "Theirs is the true light of all our day. They are the argument for the spiritual world for their spirit is it" (*JMN* 5:160–61). But in "Discipline" he says only that from such "forms, male and female," does "the spirit" draw "joy and knowledge." These forms show us "the power and order that lie at the heart of things," he affirms, but he does not "follow into detail their ministry to our education." Instead, he draws on the journal entry of 14 June 1836 quoted above, writing that when a particular friend has "become an object of thought, and, whilst his character retains all of its unconscious effect, is converted in the mind into solid and sweet wisdom,—it is a sign *to us* [not "to you" as in the journal entry] that his office is closing, and he is commonly withdrawn from *our* sight in a short time" (*CW* 1:28–29; emphasis added).

16. See Odell Shepard's editorial comment in *The Journals of Bronson Alcott*, 78 n. 3, and the counterargument of Kenneth Walter Cameron in "Emerson's Daemon and the Orphic Poet."

17. See Cabot as quoted in n. 11 above and Rusk in *L* 2:26 n. 76: "'Spirit' became the seventh chapter of *Nature*."

Notes to Chapter 5

1. *The Journals of Bronson Alcott,* 77–78. The remarks on *Nature* by Carlyle and Alcott and by the reviewers cited below are quoted in their entirety in the section of "Contemporary Comments, 1836–1841," in Merton M. Sealts, Jr., and Alfred R. Ferguson, eds., *Emerson's 'Nature': Origin, Growth, Meaning* (1979 ed.), 74–110.

2. In an undated letter to James Elliot Cabot, in Cabot, *A Memoir of Ralph Waldo Emerson* 1:244–45. For the circumstances, see Joel Myerson, "A History of the Transcendental Club."

3. Emerson's brother Charles once spoke of "the nimbleness & buoyancy which the conversation of a spiritualist awakens; the world begins to dislimn" (*JMN* 5:99; cf. 5:124); Alcott in his journal called *Nature* "the production of a spiritualist, subordinating the visible and outward to the inward and invisible" (*The Journals of Bronson Alcott,* 78).

4. The manuscript of "Literature" survives in virtually its original form, but since that of "Art" is no longer extant, the editors of *EL* reprint Emerson's "Thoughts on Art" from *The Dial* 1 (January 1841): 367–78, on the likely assumption that it constitutes "at least the greater part of the lecture" (*EL* 2:41). Both "Thoughts on Art" and "Literature" draw heavily on journal and notebook entries and outlines (printed in *JMN* 5 and 12) that Emerson made between May of 1836 and the dates when he delivered the two lectures: 29 December 1836 ("Art") and 5 January 1837 ("Literature").

5. The editors of *EL* incorporate Emerson's revisions and rearrangement of his original journal entry: compare *JMN* 5:221–22. His third proposition reappears virtually word-for-word in the second paragraph of "Art" (*EL* 2:42).

6. When Emerson composed "The Problem" he had evidently been rereading either his lecture on "Art" or some of the antecedent journal passages he had drawn upon in composing it. Near the end of the lecture, for example, is a statement that all high art arises from such "enthusiasms" as "love, patriotism, or religion"; Gothic cathedrals are an illustration, for they were built only "when the builder and the priest and the people were overpowered by their faith. Love and fear laid every stone" (*EL* 2:54; cf. *JMN* 5:211, 196). Lines 31–32 of the poem echo this last sentence: "Such and so grew these holy piles, / Whilst love and terror laid the tiles."

7. Many of the references to architecture and architectural theory in "Art" are based on entries in Emerson's Journal B (1835–1836) which he derived from his recent reading in Goethe.

8. The connection is clearly visible in notes for the lecture that incorporate phrasing from the journal entry: see, in sequence, *JMN* 5:117; *JMN* 12:620–21; *EL* 2:55–56, 59. Additional notes for "Literature" that make specific reference to other journal passages are printed in *JMN* 12:96–98.

9. See also Alcott, *The Journals of Bronson Alcott,* 89–90.

10. F. B. Sanborn and William T. Harris, *A. Bronson Alcott: His Life and Philosophy* 1:221.

11. See Conrad Wright, "Emerson, Barzillai Frost, and the Divinity School Address."

12. "Emerson could not help but feel that Frost was imprisoned in an immature phase of belief that he himself had outgrown," according to Wright, who observes also that "in religion it sometimes happens that the intensest reaction occurs when the convert is confronted by those whom he has left behind" (27).

13. Quoted by Wright (26–27) from the sermon preached by Henry A. Miles at Frost's burial, 10 December 1858. On the opposing tendencies within contemporary Unitarianism represented by Frost and Emerson, see Lawrence I. Buell, "Unitarian Aesthetics and Emerson's Poet-priest."

Notes to Chapter 6

1. Named an honorary member of the Harvard chapter in 1828, seven years after his graduation, Emerson had twice been invited to deliver original poems at the annual exercises. He declined in 1831, when he was seeking to overcome the effects of Ellen's recent death, but accepted in 1834. His late brothers Edward and Charles, by contrast, had both been elected to the society as undergraduates on the basis of their superior academic records.

2. John C. Broderick, "Emerson: Not Yet Clarified," suggests that Emerson may have intended "not yet" in the extremely rare or even obsolete sense of "no longer," a meaning authorized by the *New English Dictionary.* If so, he is saying, according to Broderick, "that the clinkered present is likely to fix its attention upon some past utterance of once flaming genius."

3. Odell Shepard, *Pedlar's Progress: The Life of Bronson Alcott,* 206.

4. Emerson's "old fable" has been variously identified. Edward Emerson, in *W* 1:417, suggested possible sources in Plato's *Symposium* and Plutarch's essay "On Brotherly Love"; more recently, Sacvan Bercovitch, "The Philosophical Background to the Fable of Emerson's 'American Scholar,'" has argued that its "whole tenor, as well as several specific references, indicate that perhaps its most important source is the Vth-century Greek philosopher, Empedocles of Acragas" (123).

5. Emerson's argument in the sixth paragraph of "The American Scholar" has frequently been misread, even in published commentary. An excellent analysis is that of Stephen E. Whicher in *The Explicator* (1962):

> Man in the ideal is one and contains in himself *in potentia* all functions; man 'in the social state' is divided into delegated functions, and is farmer, soldier, sailor, priest, etc. This second is not a fallen state, but describes all social states, including the most perfect. (As long as men are plural, after all, there must be *some* social state.) The distinction between man in the right state and man in the degenerate state is the distinction between the man who can *both* perform his delegated function *and* at need 'return from his own labor' to recover his ideal manhood, and the man who has become *only* his function, 'suffered amputation' and become 'metamorphosed into a thing.' On the one hand there is the man who can obey both the 'law for man' and the 'law for thing'; on the other the one who can obey only the 'law for thing.'"

In Whicher's summary, "the whole meaning" of the paragraph is this: "In the *social* state the scholar is the delegated intellect; in the *right* state he is Man Thinking; in the *degenerate* state he is a mere thinker. Or to put it in logical form, the whole class 'scholar' is termed 'delegated intellect'; the subclass 'scholar-in-the-right-state' is termed 'Man Thinking'; the subclass 'scholar-in-the-degenerate-state' is termed 'mere thinker.'"

6. More than a third of "The American Scholar" is directly traceable to journal and lecture passages taken over with relatively little rewriting or rearrangement. Some of them date from as early as 1834; others were drafted during the six weeks immediately preceding Emerson's delivery of the oration on 31 August 1837. Expansion of existing passages and provision for necessary transitional phrasing accounts for a considerable part of the additional writing evidently done late in August when he organized his materials and literally *composed* his final manuscript. As we know, he had brought together some of his existing ideas concerning the scholar in January of 1836 (*JMN* 5:116–17) before turning to *Nature;* other items could always be readily located through his systematic indexing of every manuscript journal, though it is worth noting that he made no specific use in "The American Scholar" of his projected sermon to scholars (*JMN* 5:167). Most but not all of the journal passages that Emerson incorporated into the oration are

listed in *CW* 1:273–74; unmentioned in this tabulation are the several lectures from which he also drew both general ideas for the address and specific phrasing.

7. As noted in the Introduction above, Emerson's terminology has troubled even so astute a reader as Henry Nash Smith. In "Emerson's Problem of Vocation: A Note on 'The American Scholar,'" Smith called this part of the address "a long and confused discussion of the issue of Action *versus* Contemplation" and objected that within it Emerson used the word *action* "in a new sense" (62). Clarification of Emerson's intended meaning here has come with the publication in *EL* of his lectures on "Art" and "Literature" and his later Address on Education at Providence, where he had previously explored the relation of thought and art to the actions and events of prior experience.

8. In the words of Robert E. Spiller and Alfred R. Ferguson, the late Bliss Perry, after studying records of the Harvard Chapter of Phi Beta Kappa, "wrote an essay on 'Emerson's Most Famous Speech' in which he gave a word picture of the events of that summer afternoon which makes all other comment superfluous" (*CW* 1:50). The foregoing paragraph draws on Perry's essay.

9. Ralph L. Rusk, *The Life of Ralph Waldo Emerson*, 266.

10. Rusk, *Life*, 265.

Notes to Chapter 7

1. In 1833, after being asked to define the term *Morals*, Emerson had remarked that the concept "which I cannot yet declare has been my angel from childhood until now. . . . It is the soul of religion" (*JMN* 4:86–87; see chapter 2 above, n. 3). Sources and implications of his idea of the moral sense are explored in Merrell R. Davis, "Emerson's 'Reason' and the Scottish Philosophers"; Stephen E. Whicher, *Freedom and Fate: An Inner Life of Ralph Waldo Emerson*, 175–76; Wallace E. Williams, "Emerson and the Moral Law"; Jonathan Bishop, *Emerson on the Soul*, 66–72; Joel Porte, *Emerson and Thoreau: Transcendentalists in Conflict*, 68–92; and David M. Robinson, *Apostle of Culture: Emerson as Preacher and Lecturer*, 50–55, and "The Sermons of Ralph Waldo Emerson: An Introductory Historical Essay," 24–29.

2. Brownson wished Emerson to join him in the ranks of social activists; among more recent critics, Sherman Paul, *Emerson's Angle of Vision: Man and Nature in American Experience* (1952), has offered a reading of this aspect of "Literary Ethics" that is somewhat akin to Brownson's (186). O. W. Firkins in his *Ralph Waldo Emerson* (1915) found Emerson's effort at balance to be generally successful (167), but Joel Porte in *Emerson and Thoreau* (1966) saw only "a characteristic equivocation" (21). In *Representative Man: Ralph Waldo Emerson in His Time* (1979) Porte offered a far more penetrating and sympathetic reading of the oration, rightly emphasizing its close relation to the Divinity School Address (91–113, 137–58).

3. As Mary Kupiec Cayton has observed in *Emerson's Emergence: Self and Society in the Transformation of New England, 1800–1845*, the Divinity School Address "followed hot on the heels of a celebrated trial for 'infidelity' that explicitly linked heretical religious doctrines to radical calls for economic and political change. It is entirely probable that many perceived some connection to the celebrated case of Abner Kneeland" (172–73). See also Robert E. Burkholder's discussion in "Emerson, Kneeland, and the Divinity School Address."

Notes to Chapter 8

1. The present discussion of *Essays* (1841) draws upon two exemplary studies: Linda Allardt's Foreword to *JMN* 12, "The Lecture Notebooks from 1835 to 1862" (especially

xxv–xxviii) and Joseph Slater's Historical Introduction to *CW* 2 (especially xvi–xxxiii). The notebooks comprise "a complex mixture of index-like surveys of his journals and more narrowly focused collections of journal references, lists of topics and titles, salvaged journal passages and revisions, notes and translations from his reading, working notes, fragmentary drafts, and near outlines." Taken alone, they "seem a 'cold mechanical preparation,' as Emerson fretted; but used as Emerson used them, . . . they reveal Emerson at work" (*JMN* 12:xi).

2. In 1832, when outlining a projected book, Emerson had included among its topics "a perfect system of compensations," or the idea "that exact justice is done" (*JMN* 3:315, 317; see chapter 2 above, n. 1); in 1833 "compensation" appeared in a statement of his "First Philosophy" (*JMN* 4:84); in 1835 he referred to "the law of Compensation" (*JMN* 5:40; see chapter 3 above, n. 5). See also Henry F. Pommer, "The Contents and Basis of Emerson's Belief in Compensation."

3. Stephen E. Whicher, *Freedom and Fate: An Inner Life of Ralph Waldo Emerson*, 36.

4. The idea appears repeatedly in Emerson's earlier lectures and orations, most recently "The American Scholar," the Divinity School Address, and "Literary Ethics." In various contexts he had used interchangeably such terms as "the God Within," "the Universal Mind," "the infinite Reason" (or "Soul"); his equivalent term in "Self-Reliance" is "the aboriginal Self," and the same concept also emerges elsewhere in the volume. The opening sentence of the first essay, "History," repeats Emerson's "old thrum" of 1837, the corollary idea that "There is one mind common to all individual men" (*CW* 2:3; cf. *JMN* 5:376). In the ninth essay, entitled "The Over-Soul," God is "this better and universal self" (*CW* 2:173); in "Circles" He is "the eternal generator," "superior to creation, superior to knowledge and thought" (*CW* 2:188). As Edward Emerson observed, "When it is remembered that the Self-Reliance which Mr. Emerson taught is on the sublimated self, the individual giving passage to the universal Soul, it is seen that both positions, the haughty courage of the hero, and the renunciation of all choice by the saint, are one. Each loses himself to save himself" (note to "Greatness," *W* 8:432).

5. One example will illustrate the point. A twentieth-century classroom anthology, Cleanth Brooks, R. W. B. Lewis, and Robert Penn Warren's *American Literature: The Makers and the Making* (1973), prints "Self-Reliance" only in part, dropping altogether both the central passage on "the aboriginal Self" and the concluding paragraphs with their correlative final sentences: "Nothing can bring you peace but yourself. Nothing can bring you peace but the triumph of principles" (see *CW* 2:51). The editors, while acknowledging that the omitted passages are "eminently worth reading," nevertheless characterize them as being, "perhaps, of chiefly historical interest" (1:711).

6. "Pantheism," Emerson's friend C. A. Bartol remarked in 1872, "is said to sink man and nature in God; Materialism to sink God and man in nature, and Transcendentalism to sink God and nature in man" (quoted in Octavius Brooks Frothingham, *Transcendentalism in New England: A History*, 342). In 1902 William James, who knew Emerson's writings intimately, identified "the object of the transcendentalist cult" as "Not a deity *in concreto*, not a superhuman person, but the immanent divinity in things, the essentially spiritual structure of the universe" (*The Varieties of Religious Experience: A Study in Human Nature*, 32). In 1988, when David M. Robinson lectured at Harvard Divinity School in commemoration of the 150th anniversary of Emerson's Divinity School Address, he focused on Emerson's conception of the Deity as impersonal ("Poetry, Personality, and the Divinity School Address").

7. David M. Robinson, "Grace and Works: Emerson's Essays in Theological Perspective," 124.

8. Herman Melville, *Moby-Dick*, chapter 132.

9. Whicher, *Freedom and Fate*, 31.

10. See, for example, entries of 16 August and 17 September 1840 in *JMN* 7:509–10, 400, and Carl F. Strauch's conjecture in his "Hatred's Swift Repulsions: Emerson, Margaret Fuller, and Others" that the latter passage, as the editors of *JMN* 7 put it, "reflects on a recent declaration of love for Emerson by Margaret Fuller." John McAleer in chapters 39 and 45 of his *Ralph Waldo Emerson: Days of Encounter* has concisely reviewed the Emerson-Fuller relationship.

11. Whicher, *Freedom and Fate*, 72.

12. The classic discussion is Daniel B. Shea's "Emerson and the American Metamorphosis" (1975).

13. Emerson's considerable gift for portraiture in words is well illustrated during this period of his career by his sketch of Dr. Ripley, begun in his journal on the day of Ripley's death, 21 September 1841, and later elaborated in "Ezra Ripley, D. D." (*JMN* 8:53–57; *W* 10:379–95) and his graphic account for *The Dial* 3 (July 1842) of the "Chardon Street and Bible Conventions" (see *W* 10:371–77).

14. Henry Nash Smith, "Emerson's Problem of Vocation: A Note on 'The American Scholar,'" 59.

15. Emerson was evidently thinking of "the Garrisons & fanatics,—forgive me, if when I come near to them & sit in the same stage coach, I seem to see nothing but management, tactics, boys' play & *philisterei*. . . . I told [William Lloyd] Garrison that I thought he must be a very young man or his time hang very heavy on his hands who can afford to think much & talk much about the foibles of his neighbors, or *'denounce'* and play 'the son of thunder' as he called it" (*JMN* 8:116).

16. Henry Fairlie, "Onward and Upward with the Arts: Evolution of a Term," credits Emerson with originating "the term 'the Establishment' as it is now popularly used" (187).

17. When Emerson lectured in New York in March 1842 he wrote to his wife that his "new friends" Horace Greeley and Albert Brisbane "fasten me in their thought to 'Transcendentalism,' whereof you know I am wholly guiltless"; he later asked Mary Moody Emerson to "observe that in the Transcendental Lecture I only write biographically,—describing a class of young persons whom I have seen—I hope it is not confession and that, past all hope, I am confounded with my compassionated heroes & heroines" (*L* 3:18, 65).

Notes to Chapter 9

1. Letters and journal entries of 1841 reveal both Emerson's weariness from the labor of reading and correcting proof and his continuing dissatisfaction with "those poor cramp arid 'Essays'" (*L* 2:444). "Lately it is a sort of general winter with me," he wrote in February 1841, though "I am not sick that I know. . . . A puny limitary creature am I, with only a small annuity of vital force to expend" (*JMN* 7:419). To Carlyle he wrote in the following July that "when I see how much work is to be done, what room for a poet—for any spiritualist—in this great, intelligent, sensual, and avaricious America, I lament my fumbling fingers and stammering tongue" (*CEC* 304).

2. David M. Robinson, "The Sermons of Ralph Waldo Emerson: An Introductory Historical Essay," 27; cf. *JMN* 7:521 and "Circles," *CW* 2:188.

3. Stephen E. Whicher, *Freedom and Fate: An Inner Life of Ralph Waldo Emerson*, 94.

4. David M. Robinson, "*The Method of Nature* and Emerson's Period of Crisis," 88–89, 77. Were the skeptical implications of "The Method of Nature" apparent to Emerson's Waterville audience? According to E. P. Whipple, Emerson himself recalled that the

address "was heard with cold, silent, unresponsive attention, in which there seemed to be a continuous unuttered rebuke and protest" (*Recollections of Eminent Men, with Other Papers,* 146). But contemporary reports suggest that his listeners may simply have had difficulty in following his argument, elaborated as it was by levies on his recent reading in history, philosophy, and astronomy that possibly obscured rather than enhanced his message. Even Carlyle, who praised the published oration "as a piece of composition," nevertheless wished it were less abstract (*CEC* 312).

5. For further examination of the skeptical strain in Emerson's thought, see Carl F. Strauch, "The Importance of Emerson's Skeptical Mood" (1957), and John Michael, *Emerson and Skepticism: The Cipher of the World* (1988).

6. Most of the material for *Essays: Second Series* was drafted and composed between 1842 and the early summer of 1844, although Emerson drew as well on still earlier journal and lecture passages. By August of 1844 he was reading proof for the book, but its publication was delayed until mid-October. (On his surviving notes and drafts, see *JMN* 8:412, *JMN* 12:576–77, and Linda Allardt's concise discussion in *JMN* 12:xxx–xxxi.)

On 31 March 1842 Emerson had told Carlyle of his intention to rework two of his recent lectures on "The Times," "The Poet" and "Character," and in preparation he soon began reading "to the subject of poetry." But the new version of "The Poet" grew "very slowly," and on 1 July it was only "in rudest beginnings" (*CEC* 321; *L* 3:47, 59; *CEC* 323). Passages used in both "The Poet" and "Experience" (originally titled "Life") soon began to appear in the journal, but not until 16 February 1844 could Emerson report to his brother William, who had inquired about his new book, that "'The Poet' is only one of its chapters though much the longest[.] The others that are ended or nearly so are 'Life' and 'Character.'" All three were "ready or nearly so for the printer" by 1 April (*L* 3:242, 245). "Character" and its complement "Manners" probably absorbed the paired lectures of 1841 with the same titles; manuscripts of the two lectures have not survived.

The fifth essay, "Gifts," is a revised version of a brief contribution to *The Dial* 4 (July 1843): 93–95. The sixth essay, "Nature," presumably began as the unfinished draft with the same title that Emerson had hoped to include in the *Essays* of 1841, evolving later with reference to "The Relation of Man to Nature" in lectures on "The Times" and his address on "The Method of Nature"; Emerson's "Tantalus," printed in *The Dial* 4 (January 1844): 357–63, "formed about one-third" of the final text (see Richard Lee Francis, "The Evolution of Emerson's Second 'Nature'" and *CW* 3:xlviii). In "Politics," the seventh essay, Emerson drew on two of his previous lectures with the same title: one of 1837 in "The Philosophy of History" series and another of 1840 in "The Present Age"; he also added much new material. The eighth essay, "Nominalist and Realist," was altogether new. When asked by his printer to fill out the volume with additional material, Emerson chose as a ninth essay his recent "sermon" at Amory Hall in Boston, calling it "New England Reformers"; it served as "an application of 'Nominalist and Realist'" (*CW* 3:xxix).

7. On scholars, see also *CW* 3:84, 137.

8. Here I must reluctantly take issue with Richard Lee Francis, who in his fine discussion of "The Poet" and "its complement," "Experience," holds that the figure of the poet "represents the final realization of Emerson's vocational quest, the fullest embodiment of all the previous roles of naturalist, moralist, and scholar." In support of this contention Francis quotes Emerson's letter of 1 March 1842 to Lidian (*L* 3:18), where Emerson declares himself "in all my theory, ethics, & politics a poet"—but then goes on to distinguish himself from such New Yorkers as Greeley and Brisbane, who had tried to pigeonhole him as "a Transcendentalist." See Francis, "The Poet and Experience: *Essays: Second Series,*" 94, 95.

9. The contemporary author who responded most fully to Emerson's vision of the nation as "a poem in our eyes" was of course Walt Whitman, beginning with the first edition of *Leaves of Grass* in 1855. In 1842 Whitman had reported for the New York *Aurora* what Emerson said of the poet in the lecture of that year that became a draft of his 1844 essay; for Whitman the lecture was "One of the richest and most beautiful compositions, both for its matter and style, we have ever heard anywhere, at any time." In 1860 he is said to have told his friend Trowbridge that he was "simmering, simmering, simmering; Emerson brought me to a boil" (quoted in Jerome Loving, *Emerson, Whitman, and the American Muse*, 10–11, 195 n. 5).

Herman Melville, however, was more reserved with respect to Emerson's conception of the poet. In his copy of *Essays: Second Series*, acquired in 1870, he marked and annotated as "noble" a number of passages in "The Poet" but objected to other assertions that he regarded as either puritanical or naively idealistic, as when Emerson declared that the poet reattaches "even artificial things, and violations of nature, to nature, by a deeper insight," and so "disposes very easily of the most disagreeable facts" (*CW* 3:11). See William Braswell, "Melville as a Critic of Emerson," 321–24.

10. Leo Marx, "The Railroad-in-the-Landscape: An Iconological Reading of a Theme in American Art," 188.

11. David W. Hill, "Emerson's Eumenides: Textual Evidence and the Interpretation of 'Experience,'" 110.

12. In "Montaigne" Emerson was to write of "a bead of dew of vital *power . . .* one drop of *the water of life*" (*CW* 4:404; emphasis added). In "Experience," noting that men lack "power of expansion," he describes persons who "appear to us as representatives of certain ideas, which they never pass or exceed. They stand on the brink of *the ocean of thought and power,* but they never take the single step that would bring them there" (*CW* 3:33; emphasis added).

Notes to Chapter 10

1. The "Discourse" itself was to be published from the manuscript (Houghton ₆MS Am 1280.199.9) in *The Later Lectures of Ralph Waldo Emerson,* edited by the late Wallace E. Williams; Professor Williams generously shared information concerning the address, its sources, and its sequels. Most of the passages that are quoted below employ either the wording Emerson himself published in 1850 in his *Representative Men* (vol. 4 of *CW;* the manuscripts of the lectures of 1844–1845 on "Representative Men" have apparently not survived) or that of the remaining paragraphs as they were used in 1876 for "The Scholar" (*W* 10:259–89); pagination is indicated accordingly.

2. Emerson made several rough outlines for segments of the "Discourse" in both Index Minor (*JMN* 12:548–49) and Journal W (*JMN* 9:210, 223–24, 228, 231–32, 254–55)—presumably while he was assembling materials and composing the manuscript.

3. Determination of every man's character is "to a peculiar end . . . called his Idea," Emerson had written in 1834. "It is that which rules his most advised actions, those especially that are most his, & is most distinctly discerned by him in those days or moments when he derives the sincerest satisfaction from his life" (*JMN* 4:378).

4. "Mr. Emerson as a boy read Plutarch, and never tired of this early friend," according to his son Edward. "When I was fourteen years old, he put *Plutarch's Lives* into my hand and bade me read two pages every week-day and ten every holiday" (*W* 12:569, in a note to Emerson's "Plutarch," *W* 12:291–322). See also "Emerson's Acquaintance with Plutarch" in Edmund G. Berry, *Emerson's Plutarch,* 35–54.

5. Oliver Wendell Holmes, *Ralph Waldo Emerson,* 197.

6. Williams's detailed notes to the individual lectures (*CW* 4:169–255) provide valuable information concerning antecedent journal entries that derive from Emerson's prior reading. With "Plato, or the Philosopher," for example, the notes survey Emerson's previous knowledge of Plato and Socrates and specify the several editions of Plato that he used, notably the Sydenham-Taylor translation (5 vols., London, 1804)—a work in which Plato "is thoroughly neoplatonized" (xxviii). (Volumes of *JMN* meticulously identify the works and editions that Emerson was using as he wrote.)

7. Clarence P. Hotson's pioneering study of Emerson and Swedenborg (1929) has been published only in part—in various scholarly articles too numerous for individual citation here.

8. Patrick F. Quinn, "Emerson and Mysticism," 414, 405. For differing views, see the more recent discussions by Dieter Schulz, "Emerson's Visionary Moments: The Disintegration of the Sublime," and Herwig Friedl, "Mysticism and Thinking in Ralph Waldo Emerson."

9. Was Emerson's judgment of Swedenborg in 1845 influenced by his dealings with Jones Very in the late 1830s? A Harvard graduate, tutor in Greek, and student at the Divinity School, Very by 1838 was in "a state that his friends hoped was mystical and his foes were certain was lunacy" (John McAleer, *Ralph Waldo Emerson: Days of Encounter,* 282; see Emerson's allusion to an unnamed acquaintance—evidently Very—in "Friendship," *CW* 2:119–20). Very's frank criticisms of Emerson during these years may be echoed in the latter's journal entry of 28 April 1842 (made not long after the death of Waldo) that bears on the subject of mystical union:

[Q.]   Why not great and good?
Ans.   Because I am not what I ought to be[.]
Q.   But why not what you ought[?]
Ans.   ⟨Always⟩ The Deity still solicits me, but this self, this individuality, this will resists.
Q.   Well for you that it does; if it did yield, you would die, as it is called. But why does it resist?
Ans.   I can only reply, God is great: It is the will of God. When he wills, he enters: when he does not, he enters not. (*JMN* 8:172)

10. Charles Lowell Young, *Emerson's Montaigne* (1941), is the most extended study of Emerson's indebtedness to the French essayist.

11. Robert Falk, "Emerson and Shakespeare" (1941), surveys Emerson's comments on the poet; Sanford E. Marovitz, "Emerson's Shakespeare: From Scorn to Apotheosis," traces his changing views. Marovitz correctly emphasizes the fact that "Shakspeare, or the Poet," is not "a piece complete in itself" but part of the overall design of *Representative Men:* "Emerson wishes to expose the ineffable flaw inherent in every member of the human race, regardless of the genius that makes of some men the great figures they are" (146).

12. Frederic Ives Carpenter, *Emerson Handbook,* 85.

13. Frederick B. Wahr, *Emerson and Goethe* (1915; reprinted 1971), is still useful. That Emerson developed his sense of modernity primarily in response to Goethe is the contention of Gustaaf Van Cromphout in *Emerson's Modernity and the Example of Goethe* (1990).

Notes to Chapter 11

1. Len Gougeon, "Aboliton, the Emersons, and 1837," 345. Although the manuscript of Emerson's address has apparently not survived, his preliminary notes are printed in *JMN*

12:152–55, and excerpts from the address itself are given in James Elliot Cabot, *A Memoir of Ralph Waldo Emerson* 2:425–30. Gougeon's article, which I have drawn upon here, gives an account of the occasion and its background that has since been elaborated in his *Virtue's Hero: Emerson, Antislavery, and Reform*, the definitive treatment of its subject. The book is based on "the evaluation of over a thousand primary documents relating in one way or another to Emerson's abolition activities" (19)—documents that his biographers have slighted.

2. Cabot, *Memoir* 2:426.

3. Emerson printed "The Young American" in *The Dial* 4 (April 1844): 484–507, but when he edited it for publication in *Nature, Addresses, and Lectures* in 1849 he deleted much of the more topical material. *CW* follows the magazine text.

4. As Nathaniel Hawthorne noted in "The Old Manse," many odd "young visionaries" and "gray-headed theorists" had been coming to Concord during these years in order to speak "face to face" with Emerson (30). When Emerson himself referred to "Sabbath and Bible Conventions" he obviously had in mind "The Chardon Street Convention," a "public discussion of the institutions of the Sabbath, the Church, and the Ministry" held in Boston during 1840 and 1842, that he had described in a humorous but kindly way in *The Dial* for July 1842 (*W* 10:371–77). As for "socialists," whose experiments he had touched on in "The Young American," he was probably thinking of such communities as George Ripley's Brook Farm, Bronson Alcott's abortive Fruitlands, and the Shaker farm at Harvard, Massachusetts, that he had visited with Hawthorne. He also knew of the Fouieristic ideas of Horace Greeley and Albert Brisbane, whom he had met in New York.

5. I am indebted to Linck C. Johnson for calling my attention to Emerson's reservations concerning Mann's address.

6. Len Gougeon, "Emerson and Abolition: The Silent Years, 1837–1844" 567; see also his *Virtue's Hero*, 46–47.

7. As Slater has shown in "Two Sources for Emerson's First Address on West Indian Emancipation," Emerson was particularly indebted to Thomas Clarkson, *The History of the Rise, Progress, and Accomplishment of the Abolition of the African Slave Trade by the British Parliament* (1808, 1839), and James A. Thome and J. Horace Kimball, *Emancipation in the West Indies: a Six Months' Tour in Antigua, Barbadoes, and Jamaica, in the Year 1837* (1838). "Both books, though quite unread today, were the common property of educated men in 1844" (97). What Emerson took from them "he made his own. The verbatim borrowings fit perfectly his rhythms and his tone" (100).

8. Gougeon, *Virtue's Hero*, 85.

9. Gougeon, "Emerson and Abolition," 575; *Virtue's Hero*, 84.

Notes to Chapter 12

1. The book has fared much better with the more recent twentieth-century critics, who have come to value its innovative modes of expression as well as its substance. "The Poet" has been widely anthologized along with "Experience," which Stephen Whicher in 1957 called "probably" Emerson's "strongest essay" (*Selections from Ralph Waldo Emerson: An Organic Anthology*, 253); "Politics," "Nominalist and Realist," and "New England Reformers" are seen as foreshadowings of Emerson's later thought.

2. Len Gougeon treats the episode more fully in "Emerson and the New Bedford Affair" and also in *Virtue's Hero: Emerson, Antislavery, and Reform*, 101–7.

3. In November of 1970, as editor of *JMN* 10 (1973), I was working in the Houghton

Library with Emerson's manuscript journals of 1847 and 1848. When I came upon his bitter remarks about the Mexican War, I was inevitably reminded of more recent protests on American campuses against the war in Vietnam. Back in Madison, I addressed the Round Table of the University of Wisconsin-Madison on the implications for present-day scholars of Emerson's response to the Mexican War, to the associated problem of slavery in America, and ultimately to the Civil War. My paper was later published by invitation in *Ariel* as "The American Scholar and Public Issues: The Case of Emerson"; it is drawn upon here and in the following chapter by special permission of The Board of Governors, The University of Calgary.

4. Lewis Simpson and Carl Bode, in their respective reviews of *JMN* 9, were quick to note the tensions in Emerson's mind that are reflected in the journals of 1843–1847, when he had to face this question. Simpson, aware of the disparity between Emerson's self-reliant individualism and his persistent sense of the scholar's obligations to society, saw the link between his personal problems of the 1840s and "the growing crisis in American life—political, social, and literary" that he experienced "with an increasing apprehension as he became inescapably a well-known public figure" (491). During this period, according to Bode, Emerson yearned to deny that he was a public man, but could not honestly do so (313).

5. First in his journal and again in *English Traits* (1856), Emerson tallied the many distinguished persons he encountered while abroad (*JMN* 10:361–62; *W* 5:292–93).

6. Sacvan Bercovitch has argued in "Emerson, Individualism, and the Ambiguities of Dissent" that in Emerson's "antipathy to socialism" lies the key to the shift he detects "between the radical early essays and the conservative 'later Emerson'" (636). Bercovitch traces the development of Emerson's thinking during the 1840s concerning individualism, or individuality, versus socialism, socialism being "a catchall neologism of the time for any collectivist scheme for radical change" (626).

7. "Ironically, Emerson, who viewed the French revolution of 1848 with skepticism, had, unbeknownst to himself, contributed to its outbreak," as Larry J. Reynolds has remarked. "Three famous professors at the Collège de France—Jules Michelet, Edgar Quinet, and Adam Mickiewicz—became during the early forties great admirers of Emerson, and they in turn through their lectures cultivated revolutionary impulses in their students" ("Emerson and the Movement," in his *European Revolutions and the American Literary Renaissance*, 4). Their influence upon French students, Reynolds notes, is stressed in Daniel Stern's *Histoire de la Révolution de 1848*.

8. Never completely satisfied with these three lectures in particular, Emerson introduced revisions when he gave a somewhat different version of the "Mind and Manners" series during 1849 and 1850, after his return to the United States (see *JMN* 12:233). In 1858 and 1866 and later in 1870 and 1871, when he was invited to lecture on philosophy at Harvard, he made further revisions and additions. The several papers brought together in *W* 12:1–132 under the heading "Natural History of Intellect" are drawn from Emerson's much-revised manuscripts; they differ considerably from the original versions read in London.

9. "Eloquence" (*W* 7:109–33) is apparently a version of "Poetry and Eloquence"; "Aristocracy" in *W* 10:29–66 is "Natural Aristocracy" as later revised and rearranged by Cabot; "Politics and Socialism" has remained unpublished. Good accounts of the "Mind and Manners" series as it was first given in London and of its reception there can be found in Scudder's "Emerson in London and the London Lectures" and in Reynolds' *European Revolutions and the American Literary Renaissance*, 36–42; Reynolds quotes from the lecture manuscripts, now in the Houghton Library at Harvard. A contemporary London

report in *Jerrold's Newspaper* of "Mr. Emerson's Lectures" is reproduced from *The Daguerreotype* 2 (12 August 1848): 467–73 in Kenneth Walter Cameron, *Emerson Among His Contemporaries,* 20–24.

10. Reynolds, *European Revolutions and the American Literary Renaissance,* 42.

11. "Napoleon" and "Shakspeare" are of course from the series on "Representative Men"; later revisions of "Domestic Life" and "The Superlative" appear in *W* 7:101–33 and *W* 10:161–79, respectively.

12. As documented in my "Melville and Emerson's Rainbow." Like Emerson, Melville had been reading Plato in the Taylor-Sydenham translation; could his later acquisition of the new Bohn edition have been suggested by Emerson's mention of it in "Plato: New Readings" when Melville read *Representative Men* in 1850?

13. Wallace Williams, Historical Introduction, *CW* 4:lix.

14. Ann Douglas Wood, "Reconsiderations: Ralph Waldo Emerson," 29.

Notes to Chapter 13

1. Len Gougeon, *Virtue's Hero: Emerson, Antislavery, and Reform,* 23.

2. What Ralph L. Rusk in a note to the text termed the "lone indication" of a projected lecture in the far South is Emerson's canceled draft of a letter of 15 November 1853 concerning a possible engagement in New Orleans (*L* 4:397). He did not lecture there, or elsewhere in the deep South.

3. Quoted in Ralph L. Rusk, *The Life of Ralph Waldo Emerson,* 367.

4. James Elliot Cabot, *A Memoir of Ralph Waldo Emerson* 2:586.

5. After *Representative Men* was in page proof Emerson recorded several "after thoughts" which "as usual, with my printing, come just a little too late" to be included. He should have emphasized "the unexpressed greatness of the common farmer & labourer," he believed, and stated "the most important defect" of Swedenborg: "that he does not awaken the sentiment of piety" (*JMN* 11:192, 193).

6. As for France, another failed attempt at revolution during June of 1848, which was sensationalized in American newspapers, apparently served to renew Emerson's doubts about the French character; he never developed a still-unpublished lecture on "France, or Urbanity," that he read occasionally during the mid–1850s. See Larry J. Reynolds, *European Revolutions and the American Literary Renaissance,* 43.

7. A reference in Emerson's journal (*JMN* 11:313) and William Charvat's *Emerson's American Lecture Engagements: A Chronological List* (25) show that by January 1851 Emerson had already written and delivered at least two of the new lectures in the series: "Wealth" ("Property"[?]) and "Power"; in addition, material that he would be using in "Fate" was accumulating in his journal. In 1851 and after he offered various numbers and groupings of old and new lectures under the title "The Conduct of Life"; the book published in 1860 (which will be discussed in the following chapter) includes a total of nine components.

8. Quoted from the New York *Weekly Tribune* in Reynolds, *European Revolutions,* 161. Emerson, as Reynolds notes, also gave a reception for Kossuth and later "referred to him as one of the great men of the age," but Henry Thoreau was "disappointed by Emerson and the proceedings."

9. Emerson used Notebook WO Liberty from 1854 to 1857 to collect "material about abolition, slavery, and human liberty" (*JMN* 14:373: headnote); it includes drafts or records of several Anti-Slavery speeches.

10. Leonard Neufeldt, "Emerson and the Civil War," 506–7.

11. These words first appear in the draft of a private letter from Emerson to Governor Henry A. Wise of Virginia (*JMN* 14:334). Wise, said Emerson in his Boston address, was "forced to hang a man whom he declares to be a man of the most integrity, truthfulness and courage he has ever met" (*W* 11:269–70).

12. In his lecture on "Courage," given in Boston on 8 November 1859; he was recalling a remark made by "a brilliant young lady," Mattie Griffith (*JMN* 14:333 and n. 100). In 1870, when "Courage" was published in *Society and Solitude* (*W* 7:251–80), these words were omitted: "distance of time" had by then "brought the case into a juster perspective" (Cabot, *Memoir* 2:596–97).

13. Moncure Daniel Conway, *Emerson at Home and Abroad*, 251.

14. Cabot, *Memoir* 2:600–601.

15. Gougeon, *Virtue's Hero*, 271, 272; Marjory M. Moody, "The Evolution of Emerson as an Abolitionist," 19.

16. Cabot, *Memoir* 2:605.

17. Cf. Cabot, *Memoir* 2:783.

18. Cabot, *Memoir* 2:607.

19. Neufeldt, "Emerson and the Civil War," 512.

20. "For Emerson," Gougeon has written, "the major cause of America's moral malaise was its gross materialism—the general tendency to place the value of things above people—and slavery was the epitome of this corrupt philosophy" (*Virtue's Hero*, 337).

Notes to Chapter 14

1. The journals of the 1850s include many striking observations on Emerson's friends and neighbors. Of Bronson Alcott and Henry Thoreau, for example, he wrote in 1852 that he might have learned to treat the Platonic world "as cloud-land, had I not known Alcott, who is a native of that country," adding in the same entry that Thoreau gave him "in flesh & blood & pertinacious ⟨living⟩ Saxon belief, my own ethics," being "far more real" in obeying them "than I" (*JMN* 13:66). Even so, Emerson felt that Thoreau "wants a little ambition in his mixture," and so, "instead of being the head of American Engineers, he is captain of a huckleberry party" (*JMN* 11:400; cf. "Thoreau," *W* 10:480). The two friends had drifted somewhat apart following Emerson's return from England, and Ellery Channing—a better conversationalist than a poet, in Emerson's view—had replaced Thoreau as the usual companion of his Concord walks. If Emerson was aware of Thoreau's intensive work on *Walden* during these years there is no sign of it in the journal, where the book is unmentioned, but following its appearance in August 1854, Emerson did take note of it in a letter to George Bradford as "cheerful, sparkling, readable, with all kinds of merits, & rising sometimes to very great heights" (*L* 4:460).

2. See Jerome Loving, *Emerson, Whitman, and the American Muse*, for an admirable account of their personal and professional relationship.

3. James Elliot Cabot, *A Memoir of Ralph Waldo Emerson* 2:757–59.

4. Robert E. Burkholder, "The Contemporary Reception of *English Traits*," 158.

5. Philip L. Nicoloff, *Emerson on Race and History: An Examination of English Traits*, 36–37.

6. "The most conspicuous result" of this abundant talent was that national institution the London *Times*, discussed in chapter 15 (*W* 5:261–72): "No power in England is more felt, more feared, or more obeyed." Emerson well remembered how that paper had affected public opinion during his stay in England, when it continually "denounced and

discredited the French Republic of 1848, and checked every sympathy with it." Though he admired the *Times* and its able writers, he was very much aware of the paper's arrogant tone and its capacity for political trimming. The editors, he wrote, "give a voice to the class who at the moment take the lead; and they have an instinct for finding where the power now lies, which is eternally shifting its banks"; in later years he would observe that the *Times*, a supporter of the South during the early years of the American Civil War, suddenly discovered in 1864, when the tide of events had turned, "what 'temper, valor, constancy, the Union has shown'" and "what a noble 'career of honor & prosperity lies before her'" (*JMN* 15:451).

7. In this chapter Emerson may have drawn from Julius Charles Hare's "Sketch of the Author's Life" in John Sterling, *Essays and Tales*, edited by Hare (London, 1848), a two-volume work sent to Emerson during his stay in Manchester, England. In Journal LM is an entry of 1848 reading "Religion in England. Sterling, Vol. I, cx lii ccxxx" (*JMN* 10:337); in the pages cited, Hare quotes Sterling's comments on the low state of religion in England and also offers an analysis of his own.

8. Hallam had asked Emerson at a dinner in London "'whether Swedenborg were all mad, or partly knave?' He knew nothing of Thomas Taylor, nor did [the poet Henry Hart] Milman, nor any Englishman"; when transcribing this passage in Notebook ED, Emerson added that "Plato is only read as a Greek book," and in *English Traits* he subsequently remarked: "The logical English train a scholar as they train an engineer. Oxford is a Greek factory, as Wilton mills weave carpet and Sheffield grinds steel" (*JMN* 10:260, 512; cf. 304; *W* 5:204). He reported telling Wordsworth, as he "usually did all English scholars, that it was not creditable that no one in all the country knew anything of Thomas Taylor, the Platonist," and he and Wordsworth agreed that if Plato's *Republic* were newly published, it would find no readers in England. "And yet," Wordsworth was moved to add, "we have embodied it all" (*JMN* 10:559; *W* 5:295). Emerson's awareness of the prevailing British attitude toward Greek philosophy was the probable reason for the omission of the lecture on Plato from his series on "Representative Men" while he was in England; he read it only once during his stay abroad: in January 1848, at a farewell dinner in Manchester.

9. Emerson's examples are "Jared Sparks, [Rufus] Griswold, [Horace] Greeley, [Francis] Bowen here; and [J. D.] Morell, [John Henry] Newman, [Sir Charles] Lyell, there, down to the [John] Oxenfords & [William] Howitts" (*JMN* 11:81).

10. *Critic*, 15 July 1853, 379 (quoted by Burkholder, "The Contemporary Reception of *English Traits*," 159); the printing information can be found in Joel Myerson, *Ralph Waldo Emerson: A Descriptive Bibliography*, 247–49.

11. Nathaniel Hawthorne, *The Letters, 1853–1856*, 540. As Benjamin Goluboff contends in "Emerson's *English Traits*: 'The Mechanics of Conversation,'" Hawthorne recognized "the interplay of concession and denial" that runs throughout the book. Where some critics have claimed to see contradictions and reversals in the argument, Goluboff accounts for this dynamic interplay in terms of an idea that Emerson had expressed in "Circles": during a conversational exchange, the "first speaker" sets forth a tentative position and the second speaker then draws a larger circle around it. Goluboff holds that *English Traits* "so successfully records Emerson's complex vision of England because it presents affirmation and criticism—pro and con—through a method of conversation." And Emerson, he concludes, offers his alternations of concession and denial "as a model of creative exchange to a divided audience historically incapable of friendly dialogue" (155–56, 166). I would add that a similar methodology is discernible elsewhere in Emerson—notably in the successively larger circles he draws in "Experience" and "Fate."

12. The loose organization of the book has especially troubled reviewers and critics. Neither the opening chapter, "First Visit to England," nor the last, which prints the "Speech at Manchester" that Emerson gave in November 1847, shortly after arriving on his second visit, seems integrated with the core chapters, where variations in perspective and tone are frequent: at times their author speaks out of his experience as an individual traveler and at other times he renders judgments both pro and con as a detached scholar.

13. Nicoloff, *Emerson on Race and History*, 128–31; Howard Mumford Jones, in the Introduction to his edition of *English Traits*, thus takes exception to Nicoloff's view (xxi, note).

14. Henry Steele Commager, "Speaking of Books: *English Traits*," 2, 28.

15. Compare Emerson's comments in "Powers and Laws of Thought" on the experience of a man "who has been in Spain [read *England*]. The facts and thoughts which the traveller has found in that country gradually settle themselves into a determinate heap of one size and form and not another. That is what he knows and has to say of Spain; he cannot say it truly until a sufficient time for the arrangement of the particles has elapsed" (*W* 12:27).

16. For a radically different interpretation of *English Traits* and of Emerson's idealism, see Julie Ellison, "The Edge of Urbanity: Emerson's *English Traits*." "The impulse to confront and overturn superiors is one of the structuring principles of Emerson's work from his first visit to England . . . to his second," she argues (100), and "the major plot of his prose" is "the simultaneous demonstration of the liberating power and reductive violence of idealistic thought" (104). In her view, the tone of *English Traits* in particular is "predicated on the savagery of the British and the more attenuated spirituality of Americans" (102).

Notes to Chapter 15

1. Emerson collected material for the series in Notebook BO Conduct (*JMN* 12:581–614), which he dated "October 1851"; as Linda Allardt writes in her headnote, most of the components had been given earlier, as single lectures. The concentrations of material in this notebook include notes for the probable revision of "Wealth," "Economy," "Culture," and "Worship," and for the new lecture on "Fate." Emerson mentioned in a letter of 10 April 1853 to Carlyle that "within a year or eighteen months" he had drafted a "chapter on Fate" (*CEC* 485); additional material for that lecture, which he continued to revise (*L* 4:330), appears in Notebook EO (*TN* 1:57–92). "Power," added to the series in December 1851, had first been given in the previous January and February.

2. In 1848, the year of his return from England, the phrase "conduct of life" began to appear as a topic for entries in Emerson's journal (*JMN* 10:290–91, 352, 361, 433; 11:142, 166, 218, 246, 320); it also turned up in two passages of *Representative Men* (*CW* 4:96, 160).

3. The journals of the 1840s and the editorial apparatus of *JMN* document both the nature and the chronology of Emerson's reading during those years. An earlier study by Carl F. Strauch, "Emerson's Sacred Science" (1958), examines the philosophical, scientific, and mythological background of "Fate" and the related poem "Song of Nature." David W. Hill has recently emphasized Emerson's use of mythology in both "Experience" and "Fate": see his "Emerson's Eumenides: Textual Evidence and the Interpretation of 'Experience'" (1982) and "God, Will, and Law: Emerson's Indeterminate 'Fate'" (1988). I am indebted to all of this material, primary and secondary.

4. Phyllis Cole, "Emerson, England, and Fate," 92, 84; on England as "a terrible machine," see the related passages from *English Traits* assembled by Julie Ellison in "The Edge of Urbanity: Emerson's *English Traits*," 106–7.

5. In August 1856, the month in which *English Traits* was published, Emerson began his Notebook EA, "England and America" (*TN* 1:186–217). As Susan Sutton Smith has conjectured, he "may have been meditating a comparison of the two countries," but whatever he intended to do with the material collected in EA, "he ultimately used very little of it" (*TN* 1:11).

6. Given Emerson's continuing alteration of his lectures in "The Conduct of Life" series, I have chosen for illustrative quotation only passages that seem to have been part of the six lecture manuscripts well before 1859–1860, when he made his final revisions for *The Conduct of Life*. Although these extracts are taken from the published text as given in *W* 6, the phrasing in most cases is quite close to that of their original sources, those journal passages that I have also cited. The forthcoming edition of *The Conduct of Life* in *CW* will provide further data on the interrelation of Emerson's journals, notebooks, lecture manuscripts, and published text.

7. The underlying principle here, as in the essay on "Politics" of 1844, is that of laissez faire: "The basis of political economy is non-interference. The only safe rule is found in the self-adjusting meter of demand and supply. Do not legislate" (*W* 6:105; cf. a journal entry of 1848 in which he wrote that "Laissez faire" is "the only way" [*JMN* 11:45]).

8. James Elliot Cabot, *A Memoir of Ralph Waldo Emerson* 2:498.

9. David Mead, *Yankee Eloquence in the Middle West: The Ohio Lyceum, 1850–1870*, 33–52.

10. Mary Kupiec Cayton, "The Making of an American Prophet: Emerson, His Audiences, and the Rise of the Popular Culture Movement in Nineteenth-Century America," 613. As an example of possible misapprehension, she notes that when Emerson said that "Life is a search after power" (*W* 6:53), "the audience who heard common sense but no organizing idea may have interpreted this comment as sanction for an aggressive economic expansionism they could readily recognize as part of their current practice." But what they were not prepared to grasp was "Emerson's advocacy of a power that derives from a moral understanding of the laws of nature and a 'sympathy with the course of things' [*W* 6:56]. His larger message has little to do with economics." What these listeners did respond to, Cayton declares, was Emerson's frequent analogies, which he took "from the realm of affairs with which his audience was familiar—business" (613).

11. Even so astute a reader as the late A. Bartlett Giamatti—a Renaissance scholar rather than an Americanist—castigated Emerson on the basis of a single passage in "Power" (1860) that deals sharply with nineteenth-century American political practice (*W* 6:61–65). In a baccalaureate address of 1981, given while he was President of Yale University, Giamatti characterized Emerson as a worshiper of sheer naked energy and force. Through his teaching in this single essay, according to Giamatti, he "freed our politics and our politicians from any sense of restraint by extolling self-generated, unaffiliated power as the best foot to place in the small of the back in front of you. . . . Emerson's views are those of a brazen adolescent, and we ought to be rid of them" ("Power, Politics, and a Sense of History," 101, 103).

12. Cabot, *Memoir* 2:769; cf. *JMN* 14:346.

13. All or parts of "Considerations by the Way" are from the single lecture called "Conduct of Life" that Emerson presented on several occasions in 1857 and again in February 1860 (Mead, *Yankee Eloquence*, 39 n. 23); another lecture, "Conversation," read on 25 December 1859, probably contributed to discussion of that topic in later pages of the chapter (*W* 6:269–272).

14. This assertion had provoked "a newspaper quarrel" at Columbus, Ohio, in 1857 over Emerson's religious views: see Mead, *Yankee Eloquence*, 41–42.

15. Richard Lee Francis, "Necessitated Freedom: Emerson's *The Conduct of Life,*" 87.

16. Francis, "Necessitated Freedom," 75.

Notes to Chapter 16

1. In an undated journal entry of 1860 that refers to lectures he had previously delivered, Emerson set down tentative titles and tables of contents for both *The Conduct of Life* and a still untitled *"Vol. II"* that he thought of calling either "Home" or "Solitude & Society" (*JMN* 14:346). But not until ten years later, with *Society and Solitude,* did he publish the projected second volume, the twelve chapters of which include somewhat revised versions of three of the six lectures he had specified for it in 1860.

2. As early as 1856, in the course of his lecture tour in Illinois and Wisconsin, Emerson realized that "This climate & people are a new test for the wares of a man of letters"; "I must conform" to the expectations of lyceum-goers who, as he was told, "want a hearty laugh" (*JMN* 14:27–28). Thereafter he attempted to tailor his offerings to suit his listeners. In February 1857, when he could count on a more select audience at Moncure Conway's Unitarian church in Cincinnati, he did not hesitate to speak on "The Scholar" (originally "A Plea for the Scholar"), a lecture he had given on college campuses in 1854 and 1856 and read again in 1856 before a private group in Boston; as he told Conway, it "did very well at Boston" (*L* 5:54).

Entries in Journal DL suggest that he may have tentatively planned "American Life" and other more popular lecture series as early as October 1860, before the outbreak of war; however, a reference to "'Waterville oration' 1863" indicates at least one later addition (*JMN* 15:4–5).

3. Moncure Daniel Conway, *Emerson at Home and Abroad,* 43; *JMN* 11:133; 10:28; 15:246.

4. James Elliot Cabot summarizes the entire address in his *Memoir of Ralph Waldo Emerson* 2:780–82. Edward Emerson's notes to the published text identify some of the passages that his father used in later writings (*W* 12:447–49).

5. Emerson's own manuscript has apparently not survived; Cabot's transcript of part of the address as it was given at Waterville, evidently used as printer's copy for "The Man of Letters," is in the Houghton Library: ᵇMS Am 1280.235 (118) folder 1 of 2.

6. Cabot, *Memoir* 2:788. According to Edward Emerson, whose notes (*W* 8:429–34) include additional passages from the manuscript, the printed text is "drawn largely from the concluding lecture of a course given . . . in Boston in the autumn of 1868" (429).

7. Summarized in Cabot, *Memoir* 2:793.

8. Emerson described the address itself as "compiled from my lectures on Art and Criticism; Books; Some Good Books; Success"; see Cabot, *Memoir* 2:791.

9. In 1868, as a member of the Overseers' Committee to Visit the Library, Emerson prepared the Committee's annual report, which was included in the minutes of the Committee for that year. See Kenneth E. Carpenter, ed., "Ralph Waldo Emerson's Report on the Harvard College Library."

10. According to Edward Emerson, his father had first read "Memory" at the Concord Lyceum in 1857, repeated it in 1858 at Boston in his course on "The Natural History of Mental Philosophy," and included "essentially the same lecture, no doubt with additions," in his courses at Harvard (*W* 12:445). The published text of "Poetry and Imagination" is from two lectures that Emerson gave at Boston in 1872; his son thought it "probable" that these lectures included "many sheets" from the Harvard courses, where Emerson presumably drew upon his earlier discussions of poetry in lectures of 1841, 1847

and 1848, 1854, and 1861 (*W* 8:357–58). "Inspiration" is, "with the omission of a few sheets," the lecture as Emerson delivered it at Baltimore in 1872; Edward Emerson believed that it was based upon a lecture on that same subject that was included in the first Harvard course (*W* 8:422).

11. A glance at Emerson's sequence of topics will suggest the scope and continuity of the Harvard lectures. In 1870 he began with "Praise of Mind" and touched in turn on "Transcendency of Physics," "Perception," "Memory," "Imagination," "Inspiration," "Genius," "Common Sense," "Identity," "Metres of Mind," "Platonists," "Conduct of Intellect," and "Relation of Intellect to Morals"; in 1871 he combined several of these topics and added "Wit and Humor," "Demonology," "Poetry," and "Will and Conduct of the Intellect." After Emerson's death, Cabot as his literary executor did "what was possible" to arrange the manuscripts for publication in the Riverside Edition of Emerson's works (1883–1893); for the Centenary Edition (1903–1904) Edward Emerson supplemented Cabot's work with additional material (*W* 12:423).

12. Summarized in Cabot, *Memoir* 2:793–96.

13. See also Cabot, *Memoir* 2:792; cf. *JMN* 14:305–7 and *W* 6:25–30.

14. Cf. Cabot, *Memoir* 2:795–96.

15. Emerson sent the first four chapters of *Society and Solitude* to his publisher in October 1869 and was soon reading proof, but in January 1870 he told Carlyle that though the new book had been "going on passably," it was "found better to divide the matter, & separate & postpone the purely literary portion . . . & therefore to modify & swell the elected part" (*CEC* 559). The volume as published contained twelve chapters; Edward Emerson later suggested that the omitted "literary portion" consisted of the essays on "Poetry and Criticism" and "Persian Poetry" that were subsequently included in the volume of 1875 entitled *Letters and Social Aims* (*W* 7:344).

16. David Mead, *Yankee Eloquence in the Middle West: The Ohio Lyceum, 1850–1870*, 58–59.

17. Ralph L. Rusk, *The Life of Ralph Waldo Emerson*, 447, 449.

18. See Nancy Craig Simmons, "Arranging the Sibylline Leaves: James Elliot Cabot's Work as Emerson's Literary Executor." Cabot collaborated with Emerson's daughter Ellen in the preparation of *Letters and Social Aims*; Cabot's procedure in assembling materials was to continue after Emerson's death when he prepared four posthumous volumes for the collected Riverside Edition of 1882–1893: *Poems, Lectures and Biographical Sketches, Miscellanies,* and *Natural History of Intellect.* Emerson's verse as edited by Cabot and later by Edward Emerson is more inclusive than the *Selected Poems* of 1876, in which Emerson himself had added six new pieces but omitted many others (*W* 9:v).

In 1874, with the aid of his daughter Edith, Emerson had published *Parnassus,* an anthology of poetry that originated in his old habit of copying any poem or lines of verse that happened to interest him. The book was marred by errors and curious omissions—there was nothing from Shelley, from Poe or Whitman or Melville, or from Emerson himself. Even so, sales were brisk, with earnings of $1,000 within some nine months of its publication (Rusk, *Life,* 486). For a study of the origin and significance of this long-neglected volume in relation to Emerson's essay "Poetry and Imagination," see Ronald A. Bosco, "'Poetry for the World of Readers' and 'Poetry for Bards Proper': Poetic Theory and Textual Integrity in Emerson's *Parnassus.*" According to Bosco, the book is "Emerson's unacknowledged conclusion to 'Poetry and Imagination'" (283), which he had once envisioned as "the 'connecting narrative' for *Parnassus*" that he promised his publisher in 1871 (273). The shock of the fire of 1872 left Emerson unable to carry out this earlier intention; instead, Bosco holds, he wrote a brief "Preface" to *Parnassus* that was based on

"Poetry and Imagination." Cabot then used "Poetry and Imagination" as the opening essay of *Letters and Social Aims.*

Notes to Epilogue

1. Matthew Arnold, "Emerson," 146, 179, 196, 178.

2. Henry David Thoreau, *Journal* 1:5; John Townsend Trowbridge, *My Own Story*, 367 (cf. Jerome Loving, *Emerson, Whitman, and the American Muse*, 195 n. 5); Nathaniel Hawthorne, "The Old Manse," 31; Herman Melville, *The Letters of Herman Melville*, 79.

3. Perry Miller, Introduction to *The Golden Age of American Literature*, 12.

4. *Time*, 2 June 1941: 84.

5. Lyon N. Richardson, "What Rutherford B. Hayes Liked in Emerson," 28, 23.

6. "Lecturing was his business," Emerson's daughter Ellen said of her late father in 1902; "he had to work at it as other men do at their business. He said he wished he could give it up, that Mrs. [Caroline Sturgis] Tappan was ashamed to have him travel peddling lectures all over the country. But we told him we weren't ashamed, we felt he was trying to benefit and to teach his country, as well as to make his living" (Edith Emerson Webster Gregg, "Emerson and His Children: Their Childhood Memories," 413).

7. James Russell Lowell, "Emerson the Lecturer," 375.

8. David Mead, *Yankee Eloquence in the Middle West: The Ohio Lyceum, 1850–1870*, 24–27.

9. Carl Bode, *The American Lyceum: Town Meeting of the Mind*, 201.

10. See Eleanor Bryce Scott, "Emerson Wins the Nine Hundred Dollars," which illustrates Emerson's western experiences with an account of his reception in Rock Island, Illinois, on New Year's Day 1856.

11. Lowell, "Emerson the Lecturer," 375; George William Curtis, "Emerson Lecturing," 22.

12. Lowell, "Emerson the Lecturer," 378; Oliver Wendell Holmes, *Ralph Waldo Emerson*, 363–64; Curtis, "Emerson Lecturing," 26.

13. Moncure Daniel Conway, *Emerson at Home and Abroad*, 43; Henry James (1811–1882), "Emerson," 741.

14. Edwin Percy Whipple, "Some Recollections of Ralph Waldo Emerson," 131; Holmes, *Ralph Waldo Emerson*, 363, 376; Julian Hawthorne, *The Memoirs of Julian Hawthorne*, 99.

15. C. E. Schorer, "Emerson and the Wisconsin Lyceum," 468.

16. "Often there were very funny stories and remarks in his lectures," according to Emerson's daughter Ellen, "and he would read them over and over at home—sometimes, he said, twenty times—to get through laughing at them himself, that he might be sure not to laugh at the lecture" (Gregg, "Emerson and His Children," 413).

17. Curtis, "Emerson Lecturing," 22.

18. Lowell, "Emerson the Lecturer," 382; Curtis, "Emerson Lecturing," 23–24.

19. His lectures in Edinburgh occasioned a pamphlet entitled *Emerson's Orations to the Modern Athenians; or, Pantheism* (Ralph L. Rusk, *The Life of Ralph Waldo Emerson*, 338).

20. Mead, *Yankee Eloquence in the Middle West*, 60.

21. Yvor Winters, *In Defense of Reason*, 587; Randall Stewart, *American Literature and Christian Doctrine*, 55; D. H. Lawrence, "Model Americans," 507.

22. As early as 1830 Emerson remarked in a sermon on the "wide difference between the power of two teachers," one of whom speaks "*living* truth" while the other presents "dead truth, . . . passively taken . . . like a lump of indigestible matter in his animal

system, separate and of no nourishment or use. It is, compared with the same truth quickened in another mind, like a fact in a child's lesson in geography, as it lies unconnected and useless in his memory, compared with the same fact as it enters into the knowledge of the surveyor or the shipmaster" (*YES* 92–93). The parallel with Whitehead's "inert ideas" is striking.

23. Conway, *Emerson at Home and Abroad*, 241.

WORKS CITED

... much is to say on both sides, and, while the fight waxes hot, thou,
dearest scholar, ... add a line every hour, and between whiles add a line.
—"Experience" (*CW* 3:38)

Alcott, Bronson. *The Journals of Bronson Alcott.* Selected and edited by Odell Shepard. Boston: Little, Brown and Company, 1938.

Allen, Gay Wilson. "A New Look at Emerson and Science." In *Literature and Ideas in America,* edited by Robert Falk, 58–78. Athens: Ohio University Press, 1975.

————. *Waldo Emerson: A Biography.* New York: The Viking Press, 1981.

Arnold, Matthew. "Emerson." In *Discourses in America,* 138–207. London: Macmillan, 1885.

Barish, Evelyn. "The Moonless Night." In *Emerson Centenary Essays,* edited by Joel Myerson, 1–16. Carbondale and Edwardsville: Southern Illinois University Press, 1982.

Bartol, Cyrus Augustus. "Emerson's Religion." In *The Genius and Character of Emerson: Lectures at the Concord School of Philosophy* (1885), edited by F. B. Sanborn, 109–45. Port Washington, N.Y.: Kennikat Press, 1971.

Bercovitch, Sacvan. "Emerson, Individualism, and the Ambiguities of Dissent." *South Atlantic Quarterly* 89 (Summer 1990): 623–62.

————. "The Philosophical Background to the Fable of Emerson's 'American Scholar.'" *Journal of the History of Ideas* 28 (January–March 1967): 123–28.

Berry, Edmund G. *Emerson's Plutarch.* Cambridge: Harvard University Press, 1961.

Bishop, Jonathan. *Emerson on the Soul.* Cambridge: Harvard University Press, 1964.

Bode, Carl. *The American Lyceum: Town Meeting of the Mind.* New York: Oxford University Press, 1956.

————. Review of *JMN,* vol. 9. In *Yearbook of English Studies, 1975, and Modern Language Review,* 313. Warwick/Birmingham, England, 1975.

Bosco, Ronald A. "'Poetry for the World of Readers' and 'Poetry for Bards Proper': Poetic Theory and Textual Integrity in Emerson's *Parnassus.*" In *Studies in the American Renaissance, 1989,* edited by Joel Myerson, 257–312. Charlottesville: University Press of Virginia, 1989.

Bradley, Sculley, Richmond Croom Beatty, E. Hudson Long, and George Perkins, eds. *The American Tradition in Literature.* 4th ed. 2 vols. New York: Grosset and Dunlap, 1974.

Braswell, William. "Melville as a Critic of Emerson." *American Literature* 9 (November 1937): 317–34.

Broderick, John C. "Emerson: Not Yet Clarified." *Emerson Society Quarterly* 27 (2d Quarter 1962): 24.

Brooks, Cleanth, R. W. B. Lewis, and Robert Penn Warren, eds. *American Literature: The Makers and the Making.* Vol. 1 of 2. New York: St. Martin's Press, 1973.

Brownson, Orestes. Review of "Literary Ethics." *Boston Quarterly Review* 2 (January 1839).

Reprinted in *The Transcendentalists: An Anthology,* edited by Perry Miller, 431–34. Cambridge: Harvard University Press, 1950.

Buell, Lawrence I. "Unitarian Aesthetics and Emerson's Poet-priest." *American Quarterly* 20 (Spring 1968): 3–20.

Burke, Kenneth. "I, Eye, Ay—Emerson's Early Essay 'Nature': Thoughts on the Machinery of Transcendence." In *Transcendentalism and Its Legacy,* edited by Myron Simon and Thornton H. Parsons, 3–24. Ann Arbor: University of Michigan Press, 1966. Also in *Emerson's 'Nature': Origin, Growth, Meaning,* edited by Merton M. Sealts, Jr., and Alfred R. Ferguson, 150–63. Carbondale and Edwardsville: Southern Illinois University Press, 1979.

Burkholder, Robert E. "The Contemporary Reception of *English Traits.*" In *Emerson Centenary Essays,* edited by Joel Myerson, 156–72. Carbondale and Edwardsville: Southern Illinois University Press, 1982.

———."Emerson, Kneeland, and the Divinity School Address." *American Literature* 58 (March 1986): 1–14.

Cabot, James Elliot. *A Memoir of Ralph Waldo Emerson.* 2 vols. Boston: Houghton Mifflin Company, 1887.

Cameron, Kenneth Walter. *Emerson Among His Contemporaries.* Hartford, Conn.: Transcendental Books, 1967.

———. "Emerson's Daemon and the Orphic Poet." In his *Emerson the Essayist,* 1:361–99. 2 vols. Raleigh, N.C.: The Thistle Press, 1945.

———. "A Sheaf of Emerson Letters." *American Literature* 24 (January 1953): 476–80.

Carpenter, Frederic Ives. *Emerson Handbook.* New York: Hendricks House, 1953.

Carpenter, Kenneth E., ed. "Ralph Waldo Emerson's Report on the Harvard College Library." *Harvard Library Bulletin,* n.s., 1 (Spring 1990): 6–12.

Cayton, Mary Kupiec. *Emerson's Emergence: Self and Society in the Transformation of New England, 1800–1845.* Chapel Hill and London: University of North Carolina Press, 1989.

———. "The Making of an American Prophet: Emerson, His Audiences, and the Rise of the Popular Culture Movement in Nineteenth-Century America." *American Historical Review* 92 (1987): 597–620.

Charvat, William. *Emerson's American Lecture Engagements: A Chronological List.* New York: The New York Public Library, 1961.

Clark, Harry Hayden. "Emerson and Science." *Philological Quarterly* 10 (July 1931): 225–60.

Cole, Phyllis. "Emerson, England, and Fate." In *Emerson: Prophecy, Metamorphosis, and Influence,* edited by David Levin, 83–105. New York and London: Columbia University Press, 1975.

Commager, Henry Steele. "Speaking of Books: *English Traits.*" *New York Times Book Review,* 18 June 1967.

Conway, Moncure Daniel. *Emerson at Home and Abroad* (1882). London: Trübner and Company, 1883.

Curtis, George William. "Emerson Lecturing." In *From the Easy Chair,* 21–26. New York: Harper and Brothers, 1892.

Danly, Susan, and Leo Marx, eds. *The Railroad in American Art: Representations of Technological Change.* Cambridge: MIT Press, 1988.

Davis, Merrell R. "Emerson's 'Reason' and the Scottish Philosophers." *New England Quarterly* 17 (June 1944): 209–28.

Ellison, Julie. "The Edge of Urbanity: Emerson's *English Traits.*" *ESQ: A Journal of the American Renaissance* 32 (2d Quarter 1986): 96–109.

Emanuel, James. "Emersonian Virtue: A Definition." *American Speech* 36 (May 1961): 117–22.

Emerson, Ralph Waldo. *The Complete Sermons of Ralph Waldo Emerson*. Edited by Albert J. von Frank et al. 4 vols. Columbia and London: University of Missouri Press, 1989–.

Fairlie, Henry. "Onward and Upward with the Arts: Evolution of a Term." *New Yorker* 19 October 1968.

Falk, Robert. "Emerson and Shakespeare." *PMLA* 56 (June 1941): 523–43.

———, ed. *Literature and Ideas in America: Essays in Memory of Harry Hayden Clark*. Athens: Ohio University Press, 1975.

Firkins, O. W. *Ralph Waldo Emerson* (1915). New York: Russell and Russell, 1965.

Francis, Richard Lee. "The Evolution of Emerson's Second 'Nature.'" *American Transcendental Quarterly* 21 (Winter 1974): 33–35.

———. "Morn at Mid Noon: The Emerging Emersonian Method." *Pacific Coast Philology* 15 (December 1980): 1–8.

———. "Necessitated Freedom: Emerson's *The Conduct of Life*." In *Studies in the American Renaissance, 1980*, edited by Joel Myerson, 73–89. Boston: Twayne Publishers, 1980.

———. "The Poet and Experience: *Essays: Second Series*." In *Emerson Centenary Essays*, edited by Joel Myerson, 93–106. Carbondale and Edwardsville: Southern Illinois University Press, 1982.

Friedl, Herwig. "Mysticism and Thinking in Ralph Waldo Emerson." *Amerikastudien* 28 (1983): 33–46.

Frothingham, Octavius Brooks. *Transcendentalism in New England: A History* (1876). Reprint. New York: Harper and Brothers, 1959.

Giamatti, A. Bartlett. "Power, Politics, and a Sense of History" (1981). In *A Free and Ordered Space: The Real World of the University*, 94–105. New York and London: W. W. Norton and Company, 1988.

Goluboff, Benjamin. "Emerson's *English Traits*: 'The Mechanics of Conversation.'" *American Transcendental Quarterly*, n.s., 3.2 (June 1989): 153–67.

Gougeon, Len. "Abolition, the Emersons, and 1837." *New England Quarterly* 54 (September 1981): 345–64.

———. "Emerson and Abolition: The Silent Years, 1837–1844." *American Literature* 54 (December 1982): 560–75.

———. "Emerson and the New Bedford Affair." In *Studies in the American Renaissance, 1981*, edited by Joel Myerson, 257–64. Boston: Twayne Publishers, 1981.

———. *Virtue's Hero: Emerson, Antislavery, and Reform*. Athens and London: University of Georgia Press, 1990.

Gregg, Edith Emerson Webster. "Emerson and His Children: Their Childhood Memories." *Harvard Library Bulletin*, 28 (October 1980): 407–30.

Gura, Philip F., and Joel Myerson, eds. *Critical Essays on American Transcendentalists*. Boston: G. K. Hall and Company, 1982.

Harrison, John S. *The Teachers of Emerson*. New York: Sturgis and Walton Company, 1910.

Hawthorne, Julian. *The Memoirs of Julian Hawthorne*. Edited by Edith Garrigues Hawthorne. New York: Macmillan, 1938.

Hawthorne, Nathaniel. *The Letters, 1853–1856*. Edited by Thomas Woodson, James A. Rubino, L. Neal Smith, Norman Holmes Pearsen. Vol. 17 of the Centenary Edition. Columbus: Ohio State University Press, 1987.

———. "The Old Manse." In *Mosses from an Old Manse* (1846), edited by J. Donald Crawley, 3–35. Vol. 10 of the Centenary Edition. Columbus: Ohio State University Press, 1974.

Hill, David W. "Emerson's Eumenides: Textual Evidence and the Interpretation of 'Experience.'" In *Emerson Centenary Essays*, edited by Joel Myerson, 107–21. Carbondale and Edwardsville: Southern Illinois University Press, 1982.

————. "God, Will, and Law: Emerson's Indeterminate 'Fate.'" *ESQ: A Journal of the American Renaissance* 34 (4th Quarter 1988): 229–55.

Holmes, Oliver Wendell. *Ralph Waldo Emerson*. Boston: Houghton Mifflin Company, 1884.

James, Henry (1811–1882). "Emerson" (ca. 1868). *Atlantic Monthly* 94 (December 1904): 740–45.

James, Henry (1843–1916). "Emerson" (1887). In *Partial Portraits*, 1–33. London and New York: Macmillan, 1888.

James, William. *The Varieties of Religious Experience: A Study in Human Nature*. New York and London: Longmans, Green and Company, 1901.

Jones, Howard Mumford. Introduction to *English Traits*, by Ralph Waldo Emerson, ix–xxvi. Cambridge: The Belknap Press, 1966.

Lauter, Paul. "Truth and Nature: Emerson's Use of Two Complex Words." *ELH: A Journal of English Literary History* 27 (March 1960): 66–85.

Lawrence, D. H. "Model Americans." Review of *Americans*, by Stuart P. Sherman. *The Dial* 74 (May 1923): 503–10.

Levin, David, ed. *Emerson: Prophecy, Metamorphosis, and Influence*. New York and London: Columbia University Press, 1975.

Loving, Jerome. *Emerson, Whitman, and the American Muse*. Chapel Hill: University of North Carolina Press, 1982.

Lowell, James Russell. "Emerson the Lecturer." In *My Study Windows*, 373–84. Boston: Houghton, Mifflin, and Company, 1885.

McAleer, John. *Ralph Waldo Emerson: Days of Encounter*. Boston: Little, Brown and Company, 1984.

Marovitz, Sanford E. "Emerson's Shakespeare: From Scorn to Apotheosis." In *Emerson Centenary Essays*, edited by Joel Myerson, 122–55. Carbondale and Edwardsville: Southern Illinois University Press, 1982.

Marx, Leo. "The Railroad-in-the-Landscape: An Iconological Reading of a Theme in American Art." In *The Railroad in American Art: Representations of Technological Change*, edited by Susan Danly and Leo Marx, 183–208. Cambridge: MIT Press, 1988.

Mead, David. *Yankee Eloquence in the Middle West: The Ohio Lyceum, 1850–1870*. East Lansing: Michigan State College Press, 1951.

Melville, Herman. *The Letters of Herman Melville*. Edited by Merrell R. Davis and William H. Gilman. New Haven: Yale University Press, 1960.

Michael, John. *Emerson and Skepticism: The Cipher of the World*. Baltimore: Johns Hopkins University Press, 1988.

Miller, F. DeWolfe. *Christopher Pearse Cranch and His Caricatures of New England Transcendentalism*. Cambridge: Harvard University Press, 1951.

Miller, Perry. Introduction to *The Golden Age of American Literature*. New York: George Braziller, 1959.

————, ed. *The Transcendentalists: An Anthology*. Cambridge: Harvard University Press, 1950.

Moody, Marjory M. "The Evolution of Emerson as an Abolitionist." *American Literature* 17 (March 1945): 1–21.

Mott, Wesley T. *"The Strains of Eloquence": Emerson and His Sermons*. University Park and London: Pennsylvania State University Press, 1989.

Murray, Henry A., Harvey Myerson, and Eugene Taylor. "Allan Melvill's By-Blow." *Melville Society Extracts* 61 (February 1985): 1–6.

Myerson, Joel. "A History of the Transcendental Club" (1977). In *Critical Essays on Ameri-*

can Transcendentalism, edited by Philip Gura and Joel Myerson, 596–608. Boston: G. K. Hall and Company, 1982.

———. *Ralph Waldo Emerson: A Descriptive Bibliography.* Pittsburgh: University of Pittsburgh Press, 1982.

———, ed. *Emerson Centenary Essays.* Carbondale and Edwardsville: Southern Illinois University Press, 1982.

———, ed. *Studies in the American Renaissance, 1980, 1981, 1983,* and *1989.* Boston: Twayne Publishers, 1980, 1981; Charlottesville: University Press of Virginia, 1983, 1989.

Neufeldt, Leonard. "Emerson and the Civil War." *Journal of English and Germanic Philology* 71 (October 1972): 502–13.

———. *The House of Emerson.* Lincoln: University of Nebraska Press, 1982.

Nicoloff, Philip L. *Emerson on Race and History: An Examination of English Traits.* New York: Columbia University Press, 1961.

Packer, B[arbara]. L. *Emerson's Fall: A New Interpretation of the Major Essays.* New York: The Continuum Publishing Company, 1982.

———. "Uriel's Cloud: Emerson's Rhetoric." *Georgia Review* 31 (Summer 1971): 322–42.

Paul, Sherman. *Emerson's Angle of Vision: Man and Nature in American Experience.* Cambridge: Harvard University Press, 1952.

Perry, Bliss. "Emerson's Most Famous Speech." In *The Praise of Folly and Other Papers,* 81–113. Boston and New York: Houghton Mifflin Company, 1923.

Perry, Ralph Barton. *The Thought and Character of William James.* 2 vols. Boston: Little, Brown and Company, 1935.

Pommer, Henry F. "The Contents and Basis of Emerson's Belief in Compensation." *PMLA* 77 (June 1962): 248–53.

———. *Emerson's First Marriage.* Carbondale and Edwardsville: Southern Illinois University Press, 1967.

Porte, Joel. *Emerson and Thoreau: Transcendentalists in Conflict.* Middletown, Conn.: Wesleyan University Press, 1966.

———. *Representative Man: Ralph Waldo Emerson in His Time.* New York: Oxford University Press, 1979.

Quinn, Patrick F. "Emerson and Mysticism." *American Literature* 21 (January 1950): 397–414.

Reynolds, Larry J. *European Revolutions and the American Literary Renaissance.* New Haven and London: Yale University Press, 1988.

Richardson, Lyon N. "What Rutherford B. Hayes Liked in Emerson." *American Literature* 17 (March 1945): 22–42.

Robinson, David M. *Apostle of Culture: Emerson as Preacher and Lecturer.* Philadelphia: University of Pennsylvania Press, 1982.

———. "Emerson's Natural Theology and the Paris Naturalists: Toward a Theory of Animated Nature." *Journal of the History of Ideas* 41 (January–March 1980): 69–88.

———. "Grace and Works: Emerson's Essays in Theological Perspective." In *American Unitarianism, 1805–1865,* edited by Conrad Edick Wright, 121–41. Boston: Massachusetts Historical Society and Northeastern University Press, 1989.

———. "*The Method of Nature* and Emerson's Period of Crisis." In *Emerson Centenary Essays,* edited by Joel Myerson, 74–92. Carbondale and Edwardsville: Southern Illinois University Press, 1982.

———. "Poetry, Personality, and the Divinity School Address." *Harvard Theological Review* 82 (1989): 185–99.

———. "The Sermons of Ralph Waldo Emerson: An Introductory Historical Essay." In

The Complete Sermons of Ralph Waldo Emerson, Volume 1, edited by Albert J. von Frank et al. 1–32. 4 vols. Columbia and London: University of Missouri Press, 1989–.

Rusk, Ralph L. *The Life of Ralph Waldo Emerson.* New York: Charles Scribner's Sons, 1949.

Sanborn, F. B., ed. *The Genius and Character of Emerson: Lectures at the Concord School of Philosophy* (1885). Port Washington, N.Y.: Kennikat Press, 1971.

Sanborn, F. B., and William T. Harris. *A. Bronson Alcott: His Life and Philosophy* (1893). 2 vols. Reprint. New York: Biblo and Tannen, 1965.

Schorer, C. E. "Emerson and the Wisconsin Lyceum." *American Literature* 24 (January 1953): 462–75.

Schulz, Dieter. "Emerson's Visionary Moments: The Disintegration of the Sublime." *Amerikastudien* 28 (1983): 23–32.

Scott, Eleanor Bryce. "Emerson Wins the Nine Hundred Dollars." *American Literature* 17 (March 1945): 78–85.

Scudder, Townsend III. "Emerson in London and the London Lectures." *American Literature* 8 (March 1936): 22–36.

Sealts, Merton M., Jr. "The American Scholar and Public Issues: The Case of Emerson." *Ariel: A Review of International English Literature* 7 (July 1976): 109–21.

———. "Melville and Emerson's Rainbow." *ESQ: A Journal of the American Renaissance* 26 (2d Quarter 1980): 53–78.

Sealts, Merton M., Jr., and Alfred R. Ferguson, eds. *Emerson's 'Nature': Origin, Growth, Meaning* (1969). Revised and enlarged edition. Carbondale and Edwardsville: Southern Illinois University Press, 1979.

Shea, Daniel B. "Emerson and the American Metamorphosis." In *Emerson: Prophecy, Metamorphosis, and Influence,* edited by David Levin, 29–56. New York and London: Columbia University Press, 1975.

Shepard, Odell. *Pedlar's Progress: The Life of Bronson Alcott.* Boston: Little, Brown and Company, 1937.

Simmons, Nancy Craig. "Arranging the Sibylline Leaves: James Elliot Cabot's Work as Emerson's Literary Executor." In *Studies in the American Renaissance, 1983,* edited by Joel Myerson, 335–89. Charlottesville: University Press of Virginia, 1983.

Simon, Myron, and Thornton H. Parsons, eds. *Transcendentalism and Its Legacy.* Ann Arbor: University of Michigan Press, 1966.

Simpson, Lewis P. Review of *JMN,* vol. 9. *American Literature* 44 (November 1972): 491.

Slater, Joseph. "Two Sources for Emerson's First Address on West Indian Emancipation." *Emerson Society Quarterly* 44 (3d Quarter 1966): 97–100.

Smith, Henry Nash. "Emerson's Problem of Vocation: A Note on 'The American Scholar.'" *New England Quarterly* 12 (March 1939): 52–67.

Spiller, Robert E. "From Lecture into Essay: Emerson's Method of Composition." *Literary Criterion* 5 (Winter 1962): 28–38.

Stewart, Randall. *American Literature and Christian Doctrine.* Baton Rouge: Louisiana State University Press, 1958.

Strauch, Carl F. "Emerson's Phi Beta Kappa Poem." *New England Quarterly* 23 (March 1950): 65–90.

———. "Emerson's Sacred Science." *PMLA* 73 (June 1958): 237–50.

———. "Hatred's Swift Repulsions: Emerson, Margaret Fuller, and Others." *Studies in Romanticism* 7 (1968): 65–103.

———. "The Importance of Emerson's Skeptical Mood." *Harvard Library Bulletin,* o.s., 11 (Winter 1957): 117–39.

————. "The Year of Emerson's Poetic Maturity: 1834." *Philological Quarterly* 34 (October 1955): 343–77.

Thoreau, Henry David. *Journal.* Vol. 1, *1837–1844.* John C. Broderick, General Editor. Princeton: Princeton University Press, 1981.

Trowbridge, John Townsend. *My Own Story.* Boston: Houghton Mifflin Company, 1903.

Van Cromphout, Gustaaf. *Emerson's Modernity and the Example of Goethe.* Columbia and London: University of Missouri Press, 1990.

Wahr, Frederick B. *Emerson and Goethe* (1915). Reprint. Hartford, Conn.: Transcendental Books, 1971.

Whicher, Stephen E. *Freedom and Fate: An Inner Life of Ralph Waldo Emerson.* Philadelphia: University of Pennsylvania Press, 1953; 2d ed., 1971.

————. [On "The American Scholar."] *The Explicator* 20.8 (April 1962): item 68.

————, ed. *Selections from Ralph Waldo Emerson: An Organic Anthology.* Boston: Houghton Mifflin Company, 1957.

Whipple, Edwin Percy. "Some Recollections of Ralph Waldo Emerson" (1882). In *Recollections of Eminent Men, with Other Papers,* 119–54. Boston: Ticknor and Company, 1887.

Williams, Wallace E. "Emerson and the Moral Law." Ph.D. diss., University of California, Berkeley, 1963.

Winters, Yvor. *In Defense of Reason.* New York: The Swallow Press and William Morrow and Company, 1947.

Wood, Ann Douglas. "Reconsiderations: Ralph Waldo Emerson." *The New Republic,* 1 and 8 January 1972: 27–29.

Wood, Barry. "The Growth of the Soul: Coleridge's Dialectical Method and the Strategy of Emerson's *Nature.*" *PMLA* 91 (May 1976): 385–97. Also in *Emerson's 'Nature': Origin, Growth, Meaning,* edited by Merton M. Sealts, Jr., and Alfred R. Ferguson, 194–208. Carbondale and Edwardsville: Southern Illinois University Press, 1979.

Wright, Conrad. "Emerson, Barzillai Frost, and the Divinity School Address." *Harvard Theological Review* 49 (January 1956): 19–43.

Wright, Conrad Edick, ed. *American Unitarianism, 1805–1865.* Boston: Massachusetts Historical Society and Northeastern University Press, 1989.

Young, Charles Lowell. *Emerson's Montaigne.* New York: Macmillan, 1941.

Young, Philip. "Small World: Emerson, Longfellow, and Melville's Secret Sister." *New England Quarterly* 60 (September 1987): 382–402.

INDEX

Among the seven ages of human life the period of indexes should not be forgotten.
—Undated entry of early July 1847 in Emerson's Journal CD (*JMN* 10:105)